COLLAPSE OF THE GLOBAL ORDER ON DRUGS

COLLAPSE OF THE GLOBAL ORDER ON DRUGS: FROM UNGASS 2016 TO REVIEW 2019

EDITED BY

AXEL KLEIN
Global Drug Policy Observatory, UK

BLAINE STOTHARD
Independent Consultant, UK

emerald
PUBLISHING

United Kingdom – North America – Japan – India – Malaysia – China

Emerald Publishing Limited
Howard House, Wagon Lane, Bingley BD16 1WA, UK

First edition 2018

Reprints and permissions service
Contact: permissions@emeraldinsight.com

British Library Cataloguing in Publication Data
A catalogue record for this book is available from the British Library

ISBN: 978-1-78756-488-6 (Print)
ISBN: 978-1-78756-487-9 (Online)
ISBN: 978-1-78756-489-3 (Epub)

Printed and bound by CPI Group (UK) Ltd, Croydon, CR0 4YY

ISOQAR
REGISTERED
Certificate Number 1985
ISO 14001

ISOQAR certified Management System, awarded to Emerald for adherence to Environmental standard ISO 14001:2004.

INVESTOR IN PEOPLE

Contents

Abbreviations

AMMD	ASEAN Ministerial Meeting on Drug Matters
AP	Associated Press
ARQ	Annual Report Questionnaire
ASEAN	Association of Southeast Asian Nations
ATS	Amphetamine-type stimulants
BBC	British Broadcasting Corporation
BRICs	Brazil Russia India China
CBD	Cannabidiol
CDT	Commission for the Dissuasion of Drug Use (Portugal)
CELAC	Community of Latin America and Caribbean States
CICAD	Inter-American Drug Abuse Control Commission
CIS	Commonwealth of Independent States
CND	Commission on Narcotic Drugs
CNN	Cable News Network
COW	Committee of the Whole
CSO	Civil Society Organisation
CSTF	Civil Society Task Force
DAINAP	Drug Abuse Information Network for Asia and the Pacific
DEA	Drug Enforcement Administration (USA)
DPA	Drug Policy Alliance (USA)
DSG	Deputy Secretary General
ECDD	Expert Committee on Drug Dependence
ECOSOC	Economic and Social Council of the United Nations
ECOWAS	Economic Community of West African States
EECA	Eastern European and Central Asian countries
ELDD	European Legal Database on Drugs
EMCDDA	European Monitoring Centre for Drugs and Drug Addiction
EKDF	Eidgenössische Kommission für Drogenfrage (Switzerland)
ENCOD	European Commission for Just and Effective Drug Policies
EU	European Union
FBN	Federal Bureau of Narcotics (USA)
FDCS	Federal Drug Control Service
GCDP	Global Commission on Drug Policy
HDG	Horizontal Drugs Group
HONLEA	Heads of National Law Enforcement Agencies

HRC	Human Rights Council
HRC	Harm Reduction Coalition
iERG	Independent Expert Review Group
IAHPC	International Association for Hospice and Palliative Care
IDPC	International Drug Policy Consortium
IISC	Informal Interactive Stakeholder Consultation
INCB	International Narcotic Control Board
IRCCA	Instituto de Regulación y Control del Cannabis (Uruguay)
ISSDP	International Society for the Study of Drug Policy
MAS	Movimiento al Socialismo (Bolivia)
MENA	Middle East and North Africa
NEP	Needle Exchange Programme
NGO	Non-governmental organisation
NPS	New (or Novel) Psychoactive Substances
NYNGOC	New York NGO Committee on Drugs
OAS	Organisation of American States
OFDT	Observatoire Français des Drogues et des Toxicomanies (France)
OHCHR	Office of the High Commissioner on Human Rights
ONDCP	Office of National Drug Control Policy (USA)
OST	Opiate Substitution Therapy
PGA	President of the General Assembly
PWID	People who inject drugs
PWUD	People who use drugs
SCOPE	Strategy for Coca and Opium Poppy Elimination
SDGs	Sustainable Development Goals
StatComm	Statistical Commission
THC	Tetrahydro-cannabinols
TNI	Transnational Institute
TRP	Transnational Radical Party
UN	United Nations
UNAIDS	United Nations Programme on HIV/AIDS
UNDP	United Nations Development Programme
UNGASS	United Nations General Assembly Special Session
UNODC	United Nations Office on Drugs and Crime
VNGOC	Vienna NGO Committee on Drugs
WACD	West Africa Commission on Drugs
WACSI	West African Civil Society Institute
WADPN	West Africa Drug Policy Network
WCO	World Customs Organization
WHA	World Health Assembly
WHO	World Health Organisation

About the Editors

Axel Klein is a Researcher and Project Consultant with a long-standing commitment to drug policy reform. Axel has headed the research and international units at DrugScope and been a trustee for Transform, two UK NGOs. His publications include *The Khat Controversy: Stimulating the Debate on Drugs* (2007), *Caribbean Drugs: From Criminalization to Harm Reduction* (2004), and Drugs and the World (2009). More recently, Axel has published on cannabis cultivation and the anthropology of drugs. He has been the editor of journal *Drugs and Alcohol Today* since 2007.

Blaine Stothard is an Educationalist and Prevention Specialist who came to drug policy through an advisory role in a London LEA at the time of the UK's first national drug policy. He was active in the Healthy Schools programmes from 1998 to 2010 as an independent consultant, has worked on related policy development and implementation in the UK and Eastern Europe and was the external consultant for the Moscow-based schools drug education programme run by Project HOPE from 1998 to 2006. He has been the co-editor of *Drugs and Alcohol Today* since 2014.

About the Authors

Maria-Goretti Ane is a private Legal Practitioner based in Ghana and a renowned expert on drug policy, having been involved in high-level engagements and advocacy on drug use and the law both locally and internationally. She is also an author of a number of articles on drug use and drug policy reform in Africa.

Danilo Ballotta (MSc) has been working for the last 20 years in the field of international drug policy. He joined the European Monitoring Centre for Drugs and Drug Addiction (EMCDDA) in 1997 where he has worked on national and European legislation, policy and anti-drug coordination systems and has contributed to the agency's work on international drug policy. Since 2005, he has been the EMCDDA's Principal Policy Analyst coordinating relations with the European Institutions. In this capacity, he represents the agency at the horizontal working group on drugs. Prior to joining the EMCDDA, he worked at the United Nations Office on Drugs and Crime and at the European Commission's Task Force 'Justice and Home Affairs'. Most recent publications include articles on European observations on cannabis legalisation with Brendan Hughes; on the United Nations General Assembly Special Session 2016 'The Turning Point in International Drug Policy?' with Tim Pfeiffer-Gerschel and Alexis Goosdeel (*SUCHT* (2016), *62*, 59–60); and a review of regional drug strategies across the world: 'How is prevention perceived and addressed?' with Marica Ferri and Giuseppe Carrà (*Drugs: Education Prevention and Policy* (2015), *22*(5)).

Leandre Banon is the Capacity Development Programme Officer for the West Africa Civil Society Institute. Prior to that he was the lead person at the West Africa Drug Policy Reform Project from 2015 to 2017 and led regional consultations that gave birth to the West Africa Common Position towards the United Nations General Assembly Special Session 2016.

Isabela Barbosa joined the Office of the UN Special Envoy on HIV/AIDS in Eastern Europe and Central Asia in 2014. Her work is mainly focussed on migration in Central Asia. Previously, she worked in the private sector and non-governmental organisations in her native Brazil, and most recently for the Global Commission on Drug Policy and the Global Health Centre at the Graduate Institute of International and Development Studies in Geneva. Her research interests focus on the connection between migration, development and public health. She studied Law (Pontifical University of Rio de Janeiro) and International Relations (University of Geneva) and is currently pursuing Migration studies (Georgetown University) and a Master's of Science in Global Health (London School of Hygiene and Tropical Medicine).

David R. Bewley-Taylor is a Professor of International Relations and Public Policy and founding Director of the Global Drug Policy Observatory (GDPO) at Swansea University. He has been researching aspects of drug policy for over 20 years, his main areas of interest being US drug policy and the United Nations and international drug control. David is the author of two major research monographs – *The United States and International Drug Control, 1909–1997* (Continuum, 2001) and *International Drug Control: Consensus Fractured* (Cambridge University Press, 2012) – several book chapters and has published in a wide range of academic journals. He has collaborated with and produced policy reports for a number of drug policy organisations beyond academia. He is currently an Associate of the International Drug Policy Consortium and an Associate Fellow of the Transnational Institute's Drugs and Democracy Programme. He is on the editorial board of the *International Journal of Drug Policy* and Editor-in-Chief of GDPO Policy Reports, Policy Briefs and Situation Analyses.

Tom Blickman is a Senior Policy Analyst with the Transnational Institute, based in Amsterdam, the Netherlands. He has been working in the drug policy field for the last 20 years, specializing in international drug control policy and the UN conventions, drug markets, alternative development, money laundering and organised crime. He is a regular Speaker at international policy conferences and advises on developments in the drugs field. Mayor recent publication include *The Rise and Decline of Cannabis Prohibition* (2014), *Cannabis Policy Reform in Europe: Bottom Up Rather Than Top Down* (2014) and *Morocco and Cannabis: Reduction, Containment or Acceptance* (2016).

Caroline Chatwin is a Reader in Criminology at the University of Kent, where she runs Masters and Undergraduate courses on drugs, culture and control. Her research focusses on European drug policy, drug policy reform and new psychoactive substances. She is the author of *Drug Policy Harmonization in the European Union* (Palgrave Macmillan, 2011) and has recently published articles on the lessons Europe can provide for an increasingly harmonised global drug policy, the European approach to new psychoactive substances and the added value of European-level interventions in national drug policy.

Ann Fordham directs the work of IDPC, leading on the coordination and development of the network. Ann was appointed as Executive Director in 2011. She joined IDPC in 2008 as the first coordinator of the network and in that time has grown the network from 32 to more than 170 organisations. Ann leads on international advocacy efforts on drug policy and human rights, specifically calling for reform of laws and policies that have proven ineffective in reducing the scale of the drug market and have negatively impacted vulnerable population groups such as people who use drugs and growers of illicit crops. Ann is the Chair of the Strategic Advisory Group to the UN on HIV and Drug Use and is regularly invited to comment on global drug policy issues in the media. She has a Masters Degree in Human Rights from Sussex University where she specialised in human rights and harm reduction.

Maziyar Ghiabi is a Lecturer at the University of Oxford and Titular Fellow at Wadham College. Prior to this position, he was a a Postdoctoral Fellow at the Paris School of Advanced Studies in Social Sciences (EHESS) and a member of the Institut de Recherche Interdisciplinaire des Enjeux Sociaux (IRIS). Maziyar obtained his Doctorate in Politics at the University of Oxford (St Antony's College) where he was a Wellcome Trust Scholar in Society and Ethics (2013–2017). He edited a Special Issue on 'Drugs, Politics and Society in the Global South' published by Third World Quarterly. His first monograph book is under contract by Cambridge University Press and will be in press in Spring 2019. Beside working on drug policy, Maziyar has published on urban ethnography and history.

Mikhail Golichenko is a Senior Policy Analyst at the Canadian HIV/AIDS Legal Network, leading research and advocacy work in Russian-speaking countries, with a particular focus on drug policy issues. Previously, Mikhail was a Legal Officer with the United Nations Office on Drugs and Crime Country Office for the Russian Federation in Moscow. He has also worked for the UN Peacekeeping in West Africa and the Russian police service in different positions, including as an Instructor. Mikhail holds a Candidate of Sciences degree (PhD equivalent) in Russian Civil Law from Saratov State Academy of Law and an LLM in Canadian Common Law from Osgoode Hall Law School of York University. He has been a Member of the Russian Bar Association since 2007.

Ricky Gunawan is a Human Rights Lawyer and the Director of Community Legal Aid Institute (LBH Masyarakat), based in Jakarta. LBH Masyarakat provides free legal services for marginalised groups and victims of human rights abuses, including people who use drugs. Ricky earned his Law degree from the University of Indonesia and MA degree in Theory and Practice of Human Rights from University of Essex (UK).

Heather Haase has served as the IDPC members' link to UN Headquarters on drug policy issues since 2013, most notably during the 2016 UN General Assembly Special Session (UNGASS) and its aftermath. Her work includes interfacing with key missions and UN agencies on drug policy issues, following UN activities and processes around drugs, and disseminating information to IDPC membership, with the goal of maximizing the involvement of civil society in UN processes around drugs. Heather also chairs the New York NGO Committee on Drugs, a Substantive Committee organized under the Conference of NGOs in Consultative Status with the UN (CoNGO), which promotes global NGO participation in UN processes around drugs. Through the NYNGOC she helped lead efforts to form the Civil Society Task Force for UNGASS 2016, which gave a voice in the UNGASS process to drug policy NGOs from all over the world.

Heather holds a law degree from the Wake Forest University School of Law in North Carolina, and is currently earning an LL.M degree at Columbia Law School, concentrating on international law & diplomacy, human rights, and drug policy.

Jonas von Hoffmann is a DPhil Candidate at the University of Oxford, UK. His chapter is part of a larger project that examines the variation of recent cannabis policy reforms in Latin America. Jonas holds a BA degree in Politics, Psychology and Sociology from the University of Cambridge (2013) and an MPhil in Latin American Studies from the University of Oxford (2015). He has been an Amelia Jackson Scholar at Exeter College and won the Crowley Price for his Master's dissertation on Cannabis Legalisation in Uruguay. Currently, his research is funded by the ESRC.

Brendan Hughes has been working at European Monitoring Centre for Drugs and Drug Addiction since 2001 in the field of national drug legislation, after gaining a Master's degree in International Criminal Law (LLM) specialising in narcotics law. He manages the European Legal Database on Drugs, which holds various comparative overviews and analyses on different topics relevant to drug laws; not only use, possession and trafficking laws but also issues such as drug classifications, threshold quantities, alternatives to punishment, drug driving and control systems for new psychoactive substances. He published the first European quantitative comparison of drug law sentencing and outcome statistics in 2009, followed by a qualitative comparison of trafficking scenarios in 2016. He has advised ministers and parliamentary committees on issues such as decriminalisation and legalisation and has authored several articles published in peer-reviewed journals. Brendan Hughes is a British national.

Michel Kazatchkine has over 30 years of experience in the fight against AIDS as a leading physician, researcher, administrator, advocate, policy-maker, and diplomat. He attended medical school in Paris and has completed postdoctoral fellowships at St. Mary's hospital in London and Harvard Medical School. He is Professor of Immunology at Université René Descartes in Paris and has authored or co-authored over 500 publications. Professor Kazatchkine has played key roles in various organizations, serving as director of the national Agency for Research on AIDS in France (1998-2005), and as French ambassador on HIV/AIDS and communicable diseases (2005-2007). In 2007, Professor Kazatchkine was elected Executive Director of the Global Fund to fight AIDS, Tuberculosis and Malaria, a position in which he served until March 2012. Between 2012 and 2017, Professor Kazatchkine served as the UN Secretary General's Special Envoy on HIV/AIDS in Eastern Europe and Central Asia. Since 2018, he is the Special Advisor to the Joint UN Programme on HIV/AIDS (UNAIDS) for Eastern Europe and Central Asia. He is also Senior Fellow with the Global Health Centre of the Graduate Institute for International and Development Studies, and a member of the Global Commission on Drug Policy.

Gloria Lai is the Regional Director for Asia for the International Drug Policy Consortium, based in Bangkok, Thailand. She previously worked as a Senior Policy Advisor on Law Enforcement and Drugs, and as a Lawyer, for the Australian Government. Gloria holds a double Master's degree in Public Policy (Central European University) and International Development (Institute of Social Studies, Erasmus University) and Undergraduate degrees in Law and Asian Studies (Chinese) from the Australian National University.

Rick Lines is Associate Professor of Criminology and Human Rights at the Hillary Rodham Clinton School of Law, Swansea University, Wales. He has been called 'a key figure in the emerging field of human rights and drug policy', and is known for his leading research and teaching on subjects including international drug control law, prisoners' rights, capital punishment and harm reduction. Rick is the author of '*Drug Control and Human Rights in International Law*' (Cambridge University Press, 2017).

Larissa Maier is a psychologist and postdoctoral addiction researcher at the University of California, San Francisco (UCSF). Prior to this, she was appointed as a consultant in Drug Use Epidemiology at the United Nations Office on Drugs and Crime (UNODC) in Vienna. In March 2015, she completed her PhD in Psychology at the University of Zurich in 2015, while working at the Swiss Research Institute for Public Health and Addiction (ISGF). Larissa is part of the Core Research Team of Global Drug Survey (GDS) aiming to make drug use safer, regardless of the legal status of the drug. She is also a member of the European Society of Prevention Research (EUSPR) and the related Early Career Forum as well as a member of the International Society for the Study of Drug Policy (ISSDP) and the College on Problems of Drug Dependence (CPDD).

Marie Nougier has been responsible for the communications and publications work stream of International Drug Policy Consortium (IDPC) since 2008 and also engages in networking, civil society capacity building activities and policy advocacy engagement, in particular at the United Nations. Marie supports IDPC's activities in Latin America, where she helps coordinate a project to reduce the incarceration rate of women for drug offences. Marie is also a Member of the Core Group of the EU Civil Society Forum on Drugs. Marie has a Masters' degree in International Law, Human Rights and the Law of Armed Conflicts. Before working at IDPC, she worked on issues related to compulsory drug detention in South East Asia at the World Health Organisation, as well as immigration, racism and police brutality in Western Europe at Amnesty International.

Katherine Irene Pettus is Advocacy Officer at the International Association for Hospice and Palliative Care, a global charitable organisation based in the United States. She holds a PhD in Political Theory from Columbia University and a Master's degree in Health Policy and Law from the University of California, San Diego. She is a trained hospice Volunteer and a Graduate of the Metta Institute for End of Life Care. As IAHPC Advocacy Officer, Katherine advocates at the UN organisations, and at regional and national palliative care meetings, for improved access to internationally controlled essential medicines such as oral morphine as a component of the internationally recognised rights to health for children, adults and persons with disabilities, and to the right to be free from cruel, inhuman or degrading treatment. Palliative care and controlled medicines are essential components of Universal Health Coverage under Target 3.8 of the Sustainable Development Goals, or Agenda 2030.

Gen Sander is a Human Rights Analyst at Harm Reduction International (HRI) in London, UK, where she leads on human rights and prison-related research.

Prior to working at HRI, she was a Senior Researcher at the Essex Human Rights Centre, where she worked with Prof. Paul Hunt, former UN Special Rapporteur on the Right to Health, on issues relating to health and human rights and taught a module on international human rights law. She has worked with various human rights non-governmental organisations in Canada, Europe and the Middle East and has also been a Consultant for the World Health Organisation and the Independent Expert Review Group on right to health issues.

Anya Sarang is the President of Andrey Rylkov Foundation for Health and Social Justice (ARF) – the main activist group fighting for the rights and health of people who use drugs in Russia. While focussing on human rights activism, she has carried out a number of research projects focussing on qualitative studies on health and rights of people who use drugs and gender issues. Anya received an MSc in Alcohol and Drugs: Policy and Interventions from the University of London in 2009 and MSc in Medical Anthropology and Sociology from the University of Amsterdam in 2016. She has been recognised as a courageous human rights and public health advocate and awarded with the International Rolleston Award for outstanding contributions to Harm Reduction by Harm Reduction International; the Crystal of Hope Award for ARF's HIV advocacy and the Human Rights Watch-Canadian HIV/AIDS Legal Network Award for Action in HIV and Human Rights.

Zara Snapp is the Co-Founder of Instituto RIA, a member of the Drugs, Politics and Culture Collective, board member of ReverdeSer Colectivo (all in Mexico) and the International Advisor for Acción Técnica Social (Colombia). From 2014−2017, Zara formed part of the Secretariat of the Global Commission on Drug Policy, where she focused on the Latin American strategy and UNGASS 2016. She often writes and gives presentations on innovative public policies related to the regulation of psychoactive substances, from a human rights and social justice based framework. Zara is the author of *Drugs Dictionary*, published in 2015 by Ediciones B. She has a bachelor's degree in Political Science from the University of Colorado at Denver, where she was awarded a National Truman Scholarship and a master's in Public Policy from the Kennedy School of Government at Harvard where she was a Public Service Fellow.

Khalid Tinasti, is an Honorary Research Associate at Swansea University, a guest researcher at the University of Geneva, and the Executive Secretary of the Global Commission on Drug Policy. Before joining the Global Commission's Secretariat as a Policy Analyst in 2013, he worked as an Independent Consultant for United Nations Program on AIDS, World Health Organisation, the Graduate Institute and others. Prior to that, Khalid worked as a Press and Communications Officer in the Office of the Minister of Urban Cohesion in France and as an Administrative Officer in Gabon. Khalid holds a PhD in Political Science and held Research Fellowships at the Graduate Institute of International and Development Studies (Switzerland). He is the author of scientific papers and policy research reports with a focus on public policies, democracy and the role of elections and international drug control mechanisms.

Mike Trace is a former UK Drug Czar, who has held senior drug policy responsibilities at the European Union and the United Nations. He founded and, until 2016, chaired the Board of the International Drug Policy Consortium. Through all of these roles, he has promoted drug policies that are rational, effective and based on principles of human rights and the promotion of positive public and mental health. His reflections in the Epilogue are based on 20 years of close involvement in international diplomacy around drug control and are the author's own views.

Jorge Herrera Valderrábano is a Policy Analyst and Co-Founder within the RIA Institute, based in Mexico City, Mexico. During the last five years, he has been working on human rights issues, specializing in drug policy reform, and sexual and reproductive rights. He is a founding member of the Ágora México civic movement, aiming to promote citizen engagement in political affairs among young people, and is currently co-presiding Dilo Escuelas Incluyentes, a Mexican organization fostering inclusive policies in educational environments.

Frank Zobel is a Sociologist and Public Health Researcher. He is Deputy Director at Addiction Switzerland, the largest centre for substance use epidemiology in the country. His former positions were with the European Monitoring Centre for Drugs and Drug Addiction (EMCDDA) in Lisbon, as Policy Analyst and Coordinator of the European Drug Report, and with the University Institute of Social and Preventive Medicine (ISPM) in Lausanne, as external evaluator of the Swiss drug strategy. Frank is a member of the national advisory board for addiction issues of Switzerland and of the scientific board of the French Monitoring Centre for Drugs and Drug Addiction (OFDT).

Foreword

Drug policy is about good and bad governance and government at global, national and local levels. It is about striking the right balance in policies that would ensure both the equality and safety of all and the autonomy/freedom of every citizen, a debate that has been ongoing in our societies from the times of Plato's *Republic* to contemporary politics. Few specific policy areas, however, have been as controversial in this respect as that of drug policy, since the endorsement of the International Drug Control Conventions by United Nations member states over 30 years ago and the subsequent implementation of prohibition-based law enforcement policies across the world.

I warmly welcome Axel Klein and Blaine Stothard's initiative, together with a broad circle of experts, to review the current tensions in the field, ahead of the 2019 UN summit aimed at assessing the 10-year achievements of the 2009 political declaration and action plan on drugs.

The tensions are many, exemplified throughout this volume through the analysis of country contexts, issues relating to specific substances, access to controlled medicines, metrics and human rights.

The first and obvious tension resides in the contraposition between the steady increase in illicit drug availability and consumption documented in the last 10 years; and the original aim set up by the Political declaration to 'eliminate or significantly reduce illicit drug supply and demand and the diversion and trafficking of precursors'. One may wonder for how long a number of governments will refuse to admit the simple reality that demand for psychoactive substances will always be there; that as long as prohibition will remain, supply will come from parallel criminal sources; and that prohibition-based policies have not only failed in their own objectives of decreasing illicit drug production and use but have actually proven harmful for the health and rights of people and fuelled a criminal economy.

Another tension of the current debate resides between governments and theorists who wish to stick to the outdated/unrealistic political orientation of 2009 and those who will promote a fresh and modernised look at drug policies based on evidence, building on the progressive language adopted at the 2016 UNGASS on drugs, the follow up of which is a mandate of the Commission on Narcotic Drugs in the 2016–2019 interval.

The major tension – it seems to me – is more fundamental: whether the debate should be about the governance of substances or about the welfare of people. Clearly, there remains a huge gap between the original objective of the

Conventions to ensure 'the health and welfare of mankind' and the reality that prohibition-based policies have generated for people on the ground: a 'war on drugs' that turned into a war against people who use drugs; an international black market that fuels corruption, spreads violence and insecurity for citizens; mass incarceration of people who use drugs; the spread of HIV/AIDS and Hepatitis C; epidemics of overdose; stigmatisation and marginalisation of people who use drugs across the world, who continue to live under the threat of arrest and face often unsurmountable obstacles to access services and treatment.

The latter tension pertains to the interference of government and policies with human life and to ways by which political power, here based on enforcement of prohibition of certain substances, has regulated/prohibited conducts and behaviours, something that Michel Foucault referred to as 'biopower' and 'biopolitics'.

The 2019 debate on drug policy should, however, go beyond the question of regulating behaviours based on the pretext of regulating a substance. It should start from restoring the value of the lives of people who use drugs and their dignity. People who use drugs are criminalised and discriminated against on a daily basis in almost every country of the world, and repressive prohibition policies impact on their health, life expectancy and quality of life. The issue here is about how governments and policies at all levels address human lives and put different price tags on different lives; it is about policies that target certain groups of the population whose lives have less value to governments; it is about the fundamental tension between global ethics that promote the universal value of human life and the reality of political management of lives in the frame of repressive drug policies.

Mike Trace's analysis in this volume rightly states that the lack of international consensus at the 2016 UNGASS should be seen as a positive development and the end of an era during which member states have worked hard to maintain unity behind a single global strategy of widespread punishment of consumers and suppliers. A consensus that was based on considering illicit drugs as 'evil' rather than focussing on people.

It is now time to shift the debate from substances to people; start the discussion on policies with a people's perspective, people's fundamental liberties and rights and people's health. This will be the main challenge for debating the future of drug policy in Vienna next year and the next 10 years' plan of action.

Michel Kazatchkine
Special Advisor to the Joint United Nations Program on AIDS (UNAIDS) in Eastern Europe and Central Asia

Acknowledgements

Putting together a book like this is a collective undertaking that could never have been realised without the support of many friends and colleagues. We would like to thank all the people with whom we have been talking about drug policy for longer than we care to remember. It is to the credit of all who continue to engage in this field in spite of setbacks, frustration and tedium. We are particularly indebted to David Bewley-Taylor, Khalid Tinasti and Chris Hallam for their generous support from the outset of this project, helping to give it shape and suggesting authors. The input from Vicky Hanson, Marcus Day, Isidor Obot, Bia Labate and Esbjörn Hörnberg was invaluable in moving the process forward. We also want to mention Mike Ashton, John Collins, Maik Dunnbier, Chris Ford, Willem Scholten, Alexander Soderholm and John Witton for taking a critical interest and sharing their ideas throughout the process. We were greatly encouraged by the support and inspiring leadership of Ruth Dreifuss and Michel Kazatchine from the Global Commission on Drug Policy, to whose work this volume will, we hope, contribute. Most of all, of course, we want to thank our authors, who in these straitened times have contributed their energy and genius in writing a remarkable collection of papers. Although we will get the printed credit as editors, we hope that this collection will also serve as a testament to professionalism, collegiality and co-operation.

Introduction

Axel Klein and Blaine Stothard

Abstract

The landscape for international drug policy is shifting rapidly as the tensions between the objectives, assumptions and activities that are being introduced at local level are tearing apart the assumptions on which the system was founded. Countries are divided into camps that pursue different aims with drug policy. In addition to an established distinction between those that seek to reduce drug harms and those pursuing a vision of a drug-free world, some UN member states have established licit markets for products that the conventions hold are available for medical and scientific purposes. This incongruence is matched by states in the other camp who apply capital and corporal punishment ostensibly in pursuit of a public health objective. These differences over underlying values, but also in the use of evidence, and interpreting the purpose of the drug control system are no longer reconcilable. While there is pressure on maintaining the system, it no longer serves an organic function and continues mainly for the benefit of constituent members. With the dissolution of US leadership, drug policy is no longer operating within an effective international framework.

Keywords: International drug policy; UN conventions; drugs and human rights; evidence-based policy; policy reform

> He who seeks to regulate everything by law is more likely to arouse vices than to reform them. It is best to grant what cannot be abolished, even though it be in itself harmful. How many evils spring from luxury, envy, avarice, drunkenness and the like, yet these are tolerated because they cannot be prevented by legal enactments.
>
> (Baruch Spinoza)

Collapse of the Global Order on Drugs: From UNGASS 2016 to Review 2019, 1–19

doi:10.1108/978-1-78756-487-920181001

The premise behind collecting this series of papers on the international drug policy process in the interval between the 2016 United Nations General Assembly Special Session on Drugs and the 2019 High Level Meeting is that the global order is on the brink of collapse. The multiple incongruities between open drug markets in some states and severe penalisation in others, the pursuit of public health and the exercise of authoritarian control, have reached a tipping point where the system cannot survive in its current form.

Dissatisfaction with the regime has been growing over decades in the light of mounting evidence of its patent failure to fulfil its objectives – a drug-free world – and the high cost of enforcement in human, financial, environmental and social terms. The run-up to the 2016 United Nations General Assembly Special Session (UNGASS) was therefore accompanied by great anticipation within the reform community that led to an equally great sense of disappointment at the end of the United Nations General Assembly Special Session on Drugs (Godfrey, 2016; Jelsma, 2016). After the build-up to what some commentators thought of as a paradigm shifting event (Fordham & Haase, Chapter 1), what transpired was more akin to re-affirmation of the established system, where the drug control conventions remain the central international drug policy reference point, with the role of the 'Vienna Institutions' (Commission on Narcotic Drugs, CND; United Nations Office on Drugs and Crime, UNODC; and International Narcotics Control Board, INCB) shored up and their mandates extended. There is no explicit reflection on impact, no concern over unintended consequences, no acknowledgment that the policies themselves have been the cause of any harm. Instead the Outcome Document attributes the high price paid by societies to the postulated 'world drug problem' and in an explicit endorsement of the prevailing repressive approach pays the first tribute to 'law enforcement and judicial personnel' (United Nations Office on Drugs and Crime (UNODC), 2016, p. 4).

Resolving the problem is primarily presented as a question of resources, which the international community is then invited to invest across a range of thematic areas. The list that follows covers an extraordinarily wide band of technical areas. This very breadth of activities, reminiscent in scope of the Sustainable Development Goals, is a striking, yet plausible, consequence of the very vagueness defining an underlying 'world drug problem'. The Operational Recommendations that make up the bulk of the documents therefore require member states inter alia to:

- Put in place effective drug use prevention strategies (Outcome Document, p. 5).
- Ensure the prevention of blood-borne diseases (Outcome Document, p. 7).
- Establish comprehensive drug treatment systems (Outcome Document, p. 6).
- Set up health and social welfare measures (Outcome Document, p. 7).
- Ensure access to controlled medicines (Outcome Document, p. 8).
- Monitor trafficking trends and promote intelligence exchange (Outcome Document, p. 11).
- Enhance anti-money laundering capacity (Outcome Document, p. 12).
- Gather data on trafficking flows (Outcome Document, p. 11 and 13) and crop cultivation (Outcome Document, p. 15).

- Raise awareness of the drug problem at governmental (Outcome Document, p. 14) and societal (Outcome Document, p. 5) levels.
- Improve law enforcement information exchange (Outcome Document, p. 16).
- Gather information on New Psychoactive Substances and join early warning networks of the global Synthetics Monitoring: Analysis, Reporting and Trends (Outcome Document, p. 17).
- Raise national laboratory capacity (Outcome Document, p. 19).
- Provide information exchange on non-medical use of prescription medicines (Outcome Document, p. 20).
- Update states drug policies in line with new developments such as internet-based drug distribution (Outcome Document, p. 20).
- Elicit alternative development programmes and research on illicit crop cultivation (Outcome Document, p. 23).

In each of those 15 thematic areas member states are furthermore called upon to work closely with UN agencies, particularly UNODC (2016), 'the leading entity in the United Nations system for addressing and countering the world drug problem' (p. 3). As global problems require global solutions, a premise of the international system, while financial resources and technical capacities are unevenly distributed the document exhorts donor states to enhance 'North-South' cooperation along the principle of 'common and shared responsibility' (UNODC, 2016, p. 2). For operational purposes, then, the UNGASS Outcome Document puts pressure on donor states to invest in the UNODC regional programmes that shape up alongside the Operational Recommendations. In a previous paper, we argued that the 'Outcome Document' can also be seen as 'fundraiser for the perpetuation and expansion of the existing system' (Klein & Stothard, 2016). In the immediate aftermath of the event, it appeared to most observers that the key institutions and the countries supporting the status quo had succeeded in averting change and consolidating the existing mechanisms.

And yet, reform advocates have since drawn comfort from the document, in particular the creation of seven pillars that include: access to controlled medicines; human rights and gender; and development, to replace the three-pillar structure of demand reduction, supply reduction and money laundering. These developments can be seen as an historic break with the prevailing discourse on punitive controls (Fordham & Haase, Chapter 1). The call, led by member states, to broaden the system out to specifically include and involve other UN agencies (UNAIDS, UNDP, WHO and United Nations High Commissioner for Refugees (UNHCR)), can also be seen as an implicit questioning of and dissociation from the status quo and the increasingly meretricious claims of the system advocates. The shift away from calls for the elimination or significant reduction of drug supply and demand, and the tussles between different member states at subsequent CND meetings over the status of the document vis à vis other UN documents, is indicative of the discomfort of some countries with the document's provisions (Bewley-Taylor & Nougier, Chapter 3).

More trenchant still are the reforms taking place within a growing number of UN member states where the bundle of interventions known as 'harm reduction' is increasingly, but not yet universally, replacing heavy-handed enforcement of zero tolerance. In most European countries but also in Oceania and South America, drug possession itself is being widely decriminalised, de facto and de jure. Indeed, as we will explore further below, the entire panoply of 'drugs' as a particular and peculiar category of substances is put into questions and is now under review.

This process is most evident in the comprehensive changes that are sweeping across countries such as Uruguay and parts of North America, where legal markets are being created for the non-medical use of cannabis products (von Hoffmann, Chapter 9; Snapp & Herrera, Chapter 12). For the first time, countries that are signatories to the same set of international treaties have policies in place concerning the way a particular psychoactive substance is managed that are diametrically opposed. There are precedents for a dramatic divergence in the regulatory arrangements for consumption items. The commercial market for alcohol is flourishing in many countries, yet distribution and even possession are punished severely in a number of Islamic states and some other jurisdictions. But alcohol is not covered by any international treaty obliging signatories to adopt strict controls. Going further, the emerging marijuana economy, from Colorado to Montevideo, is merely the most conspicuous manifestation of divergence.

The contents of the Outcome Document, with their recurrent referencing of human rights, and the tone of many of the national statements, mark a distancing between signatory states across a range of issues that is no longer reconcilable within the framework of an international system (Gunawan & Lai, Chapter 7; Zobel & Maier, Chapter 14). The very 'success' of drug policy in encroaching upon so many areas of contemporary public life, from health to wealth management, and the protean character of drug control as pretext and alibi for authoritarianism, is bringing the conflict between prohibition and human rights to a head. In the process, fault lines are appearing between and within states in their approach and response to particular issues. Differences boil down to conflicting sets of values, to different notions of evidence and respect for scientific investigation, and to fundamentally differing ideas about the purpose of the system – as a way of promoting public health or as a tool for the security state.

The Clash of Values: 'Drug-free World' versus Human Rights

The countries coming together to restructure the international drug control system in the period after the Second World War staked out a common terrain between the 'evil of drug addiction' and 'the health and welfare of mankind'. In the Spanish language version, the preamble of the Single Convention on Narcotic Drugs has a slight but important difference in that the contracting parties are concerned with '*la salud física y moral de la humanidad*' – the physical *and moral* welfare of humanity (UN, 1961). At its core, the international drug control system is built on a set of values as part of an early twentieth century project to 'roll back those parts of the market whose social costs had proved too high' (Rodgers, 1998). To contain the damage caused by the nonmedical use of drugs they mobilised the state, and, at its apex, intergovernmental cooperation through the newly created global institutions (McAllister, 2000).

Today, however, the anxiety of the most vociferous drug policy activists no longer revolves around the damage inflicted by drugs, but the measures that have been put into place to combat them. With traffickers matching the efforts by governments to stop drug production and distributions, with ever more sophisticated concealment and deception, violence has escalated, leading in many countries to the militarisation of law enforcement and the rise of organised crime. Reform campaigners are concerned about the impact on third parties, such as women and children in drug crop cultivation areas; the excessive severity of penalties for drug offences; the criminalisation of people struggling with substance use disorders.

Yet, no other issue raises such heated debate as the application of the death penalty for drug-related offences. Perversely, at a time when the number of countries retaining the death penalty is declining, there has been a rise in those applying capital punishment for drug offences. Currently, 33 countries use the death penalty for drug offences (Sander, 2018). At the opening segment of the UNGASS, the EU representative, in a statement to which 56 countries aligned themselves, expressed deep regret that the Outcome Document did not include language mentioning the death penalty. Other countries, including Brazil, Costa Rica, Norway, Switzerland and Uruguay, expressed their disappointment in separate statements. In response, Indonesia, speaking on behalf of 15 'retentionist' states, noted that there was no international consensus on the prohibition of the death penalty and that every state had the sovereign right to choose what was in its own best interest. China warned that drug control should be no pretext for interfering in another country's affairs. Countries, it is clear, are digging in their heels on the issue.

But such criticism cannot mask a degree of complicity, since these killings take place in the context of the international drug control regime and are premised on a putatively shared understanding of the 'world drug problem'. Critics go further, to argue that the very focus on capital punishment should not distract from the incarceration of people for drug consumption, mandatory sentencing, felony disenfranchisement, warrantless stop and search policies, mandatory drug testing at school, in the workplace or as a condition for welfare payments and the application of corporal punishment (Sander & Lines). The impact of these practices is predominantly borne by domestic minority groups and by foreigners, eternal scapegoats whose role is to divert governmental and public attention from reflective consideration of the origins of social ill health. This accumulation of abusive practices has reached a tipping point, where the harms committed by governments can no longer be justified by pursuing the ever-more elusive goal of a drug-free world.

Quibbling over Indicators: Producing the Evidence Base

Assessing the number of people executed globally for drug offences is not possible because China withholds information on the grounds of 'national security'. In fact, accurate data collection across the entire range of indicators relevant for measuring 'the world drug problem' is hampered by inadequate data provision, according to Bewley-Taylor and Nougier (Chapter 3), with many countries lacking the capacity for the comprehensive monitoring or collection of data (see too

Golichenko et al., Chapter 6). Technical shortcomings are further exacerbated by the political sensitivities of governments worried about being 'shown up' when reporting increases in supply or consumption. The information Member States supply to UNODC via the Annual Review Questionnaire goes into the World Drug Report, an authoritative document and point of reference within CND discussions. Data provision is less than perfect, because reporting against the 219 plus questions, many with extensive sets of sub questions, is a cumbersome exercise even for countries with well-resourced administrations and established data collection systems. Moreover, some respondents are wary of having 'information used against us'[1] and refuse to participate. Others are selective, prioritising those sections advertising national achievements, particularly around arrests and seizures. In an effort to enrich the analysis, the drafters tap into other information sources but can only publish extraneous data with the agreement of the member states who, after all, 'own' the report.

Dissatisfaction with the current preoccupation over measuring 'scale and flow' fed into the review, with the addition of new thematic areas for data collection mandated by the Outcome Document. What these thematic areas are and how they will be reported constitute a bone of contention at CND, with reformers looking for better reporting on the impact of policy measures on individuals and communities; indicators to track the seven pillars; and voluntary reporting on human rights. These demands met resistance at the Expert meeting in January 2018, and future reporting is likely to remain subsumed to national concerns over image. Though the Outcome Document pays lip service to the need for evidence-based policy making, the system struggles with generating even the most basic data.

Drugs as Medicine or Menace: Palliative Care and Cannabis

Disagreements are running not merely over what to count and how to count it, but even over the underlying concepts on which the system to combat the 'world drug problem' is based. When the international drug control order was constructed at the beginning of the twentieth century, the dual use of the two substances and their derivatives that were brought under control, opium and cocaine, was recognised, and reporting and recording systems established to facilitate importation of controlled medicines.[2] Yet, for many health systems, anticipating the demand for palliative medication is challenging, due to what Pettus (Chapter 4) refers to as an 'epistemic abyss', and the administrative process for submitting requests and then managing such medicines is difficult. Over the past 100 years, the assumptions of the system have changed as well, and repressive measures enforced by the criminal justice system have become a standard response to perceived problems with substances.

---

[1]The phrase was used by a national focal point in South America interviewed by AK in 2015.

[2]Reporting and recording systems were foreseen in the 1911 The Hague Conference.

The real conflict arises, however, with the objective of governments to control a substance and the behaviours in particular population groups that are associated therewith, and the needs of patients relying on their medication, particularly for pain management. National delegations at CND meetings usually comprise officials from interior ministries and law enforcement, with little awareness of or concern for medical needs and systems; and a reified notion of 'drugs' as an embodiment of evil – a position emphatically underlined by the representative of the Holy See, who pronounced that 'drugs are an evil and with evil there can be neither surrender nor compromise' (UN.ORG, 2016a). The instruments available through the systems are therefore used for tackling security problems, and, perversely, security instruments are pressed into service for dealing with reported medical issues.

A case in point is the recent request by the government of Egypt that the WHO Expert Committee on Drug Dependence review the medicine Tramadol with a view to bringing it under international control. Tramadol is a synthetic opioid that is widely used for pain relief and is particularly important in developing countries where morphine is often unavailable. Though placing the substance on an international schedule may help to reduce non-medical tramadol use in Egypt, it will have severe consequences in countries where no alternative analgesics are available. Similarly, with China and ketamine in 2015, when the Chinese government attempted to use the international drug control system to solve the problem of extensive illicit production and use of ketamine within its own borders, and in doing so presented a real risk of denying ketamine for medical and anaesthetic purposes in nations with under-developed health infrastructures.

The systematic 'demonisation' (Pettus, Chapter 4) of certain psychoactive substances was an ideological accomplishment of the war on drugs, manifest in the underdetermined category of 'drugs' itself. It managed to displace the understanding of the dual nature that substances had as medicine or poison, depending on circumstances of use and dosage (Porter, 1996). While advocates are extending the controls to a wider list of medications, one substance, condemned for many years as the quintessential 'drug of abuse', has had a re-birth in medical practice: cannabis.

Beginning with the 1996 ballot decision in California, cannabis has been officially re-established as a medical substance in spite of its international scheduling as a 'drug of abuse' without medical value. Though it was removed from the official US pharmacopeia in 1942, cannabis is now available for medical use in 30 US States (Snapp & Herrera, Chapter 12). In Europe, medical cannabis is available in Austria, Czech Republic, Denmark, Finland, Germany, Italy, Portugal, Poland and Spain. According to a report for the UK All Party Parliamentary Committee on Drugs (Barnes & Barnes, 2016), there is now good evidence for therapeutic benefits for, inter alia, Movement disorders, Spasticity, Epilepsy, Fibromyalgia and pain relief. The two processes of the revival in medical applications and the normalisation of recreational use make the inclusion of cannabis in the conventions appear increasingly anomalous. As Blickman (Chapter 5) demonstrates this is even understood within UNODC itself, with successive calls for a revision of this anomaly, but at the same time cannabis is the central pillar of the control system because of its use by 183 million of the total 255 million users of illegal drugs globally (UNODC, 2017). Were it to be removed the system would lose much of its urgency and scope.

The prominence of cannabis in drug control debates raises further questions over the purpose and need for the conventions. International collaboration was needed at a time when drugs were traded commodities, produced, like opium, in India and sold to China. The different trading and imperial powers had to come to an accord so as not to simply hand the trade over to a competitor, like Iran or Turkey. But two developments have changed this. First, cannabis is now cultivated globally, particularly in North America and Europe, once 'importing' countries. Secondly, the advances in underground chemistry have rolled out the production of amphetamine type substances, MDMA and the so-called new psychoactive substances. Only the production of the classic two plant-based substances, cocaine and opiates, is concentrated in specific geographical areas, though even these are increasingly being displaced by synthetic analogues such as fentanyl or methamphetamine.

Defending the Status Quo: Cost and Benefits

None of these arguments cut any ice with the staunchest defenders of the status quo. Chinese attitudes towards drug control have been formed through the experience of the so-called 'opium wars' of the nineteenth century, when national efforts at controlling domestic production and imports triggered invasion and defeat by British military forces. China has imposed a rigorous zero tolerance policy and has emerged as a strong champion of the international drug control system even while rolling out key harm reduction measures such as opiate substitution therapy (OST) at home. At UNGASS, China confirmed its commitment to the international control system and vehemently opposed steps towards legalisation (UN.Org, 2016b).

In Russia, the massive inflow of heroin in the 1990s is associated with the collapse of the Soviet Union and temporary loss of control and authority by state agencies. Though the origins of the severe repression of drug offences go back to the early decades of the Soviet era, as Golichenko et al. (Chapter 6) demonstrate, when many consumers were sent to gulags during the 1930s, a new punitive regime has been built up over the past 10 years. Tough penalties are accompanied by broad surveillance measures, including drug testing in schools and workplaces, the illegality of OSTs and little respect for civil liberties or individual privacy.

The negative impact of these measures is plain to see, as Russia suffers from an HIV epidemic with more than 1 million people infected, the highest number of people who inject drugs globally (estimated between 1.5 and 3 million), and the rapid spread of blood-borne viruses and TB associated with injecting drug use and mass incarceration. But public health never was the driving concern, for the 'drug issue' has been treated as a law enforcement prerogative and 'a threat to national security and the social order' (Golichenko et al., Chapter 6). At UNGASS and at CND, Russia is countering efforts aimed at refocussing drug policy towards health-based outcomes; is contesting the authority of the

Outcome Declaration vis à vis that of the 2009 Political Declaration and Plan of Action and continues to invoke the objective of a 'drug-free world'.

Countries in Southeast Asia share that vision and continue to strive, in spite of setbacks, for a 'drug-free ASEAN' (Gunawan & Lai, Chapter 7). With a long-standing commitment to zero tolerance, the region includes countries with the most notoriously repressive drug control regimes, including the application of capital and corporal punishments. Yet, there are signs that Thailand and Vietnam are now conceding the inevitability of recreational drug use, with a move towards health-based interventions, the introduction of alternative forms of sentencing for drug offences and proportionate sentencing. These measures are designed to ease the high levels of prison congestion and to provide an alternative approach to managing the high levels of methamphetamine consumption that continue to characterise the region.

Countries in the Middle East, Ghiabi (Chapter 8) reminds us, are known for their social conservatism across a range of issues, such as pre- and extra-marital sex, homosexuality, clothing, alcohol and freedom of expression, as well as drugs. But here too there are significant differences between, and a much more nuanced range of policy measures within, countries. Lebanon and Iran both implement a range of harm reduction measures, such as needle exchanges and OST, with Iran even pioneering new (old) substitution medicines such as opium tinctures, and extending services to vulnerable populations, for example, in prisons. At the same time, Iran executes more drug offenders than any other country, with the possible exception of China. Saudi Arabia[3] takes the most austere approach in the region and yet has also high, though poorly researched, patterns of recreational use, owing to a large extent to the general lack of entertainment opportunities for young people. Across the region policies are driven by codes of morality that are derived from Islam and are strongly censorious of public displays of intoxication. At international level, this translates into solid support by MENA countries for the aims of the international control system, including the provision of funding for UNODC-coordinated activities.[4] Yet, there is no coordination of positions at regional level, because of rivalries, particularly between Saudi Arabia and Iran.

It seems increasingly evident that the stances of, in particular, Russia and China have less to do with a response to the use of illegal drugs, more to do with establishing or maintaining a position of political strength. The objective health and welfare of their domestic populations is of less importance than the maintenance of a powerful image on the international stage. This is in the face of increasing opposition and evidence from CSOs, nations, regional associations and international bodies, and the abandonment of any claims to approaches, which are realistic and evidence-based. This exercise of power is more and more deployed through coercion, as our chapter (6) on the role of the Russian Federation shows.

[3]Saudi Arabia could be considered as being indifferent to the Conventions, basing its objections to illegal drug use and other behaviours on Islamic interpretations of haram, not adherence to the international Conventions.

[4]In 2016, for example, Qatar gave UNODC US $50 million for the 'Implementation of the Doha Declaration: Towards the Promotion of a Culture of Lawfulness'.

It is important to underline that hard line polices retain the support of some CSOs such as International Organisation of Good Templars (IOGT) International[5] with its 151 Member Organisations from 60 countries.

These civil society advocates of control regime extension argue that the public health problems caused by psychoactive substance use have reached alarming proportions and constitute a significant, but to a large extent preventable, health and social burden. Rapid globalisation, technological and communication developments, growing availability and diversity of synthetic compounds with psychoactive and dependence-producing properties all require adequate and proportionate policy and programmatic responses. They maintain that regulation, as in the case of alcohol, has not been a success story and should be a warning against legalising other harmful substances. They are also concerned about the current discourse with its emphasis on the 'war on drugs', the polarisation of debate between legalisation and incarceration, and the lack of attention paid to 'harm to others' caused by drugs. They advocate a shift in focus from the individual drug user to the community and the rights of the child, arguing that children have the right to grow up in a drug-free environment (IOGT, 2016).

Radical Reformers: Latin America

At the other end of the spectrum are Latin American countries that have a very different experience of both patterns of drug use and the impact of drug policies, above all those targeted at supply reduction. As the 'forwarding strategy' in the US war on drugs gathered momentum in the 1980s, it was Latin America that experienced the most traumatic economic and political dislocations. The very call for UNGASS 2016, as discussed above, was prompted by South American governments concerned about the impact of internationally sanctioned drug policies on human security and political and social stability. In Colombia and Peru, eradication efforts pushed drug producers into the arms of rural guerrilla groups such as the FARC, ELN and Sendero Luminoso. In Mexico and Central America, drug trafficking gangs are threatening the authority of the state. The vulnerability of state institutions to violence and corruption, *plumo y plata* (lead or silver) is nowhere more evident.

While Colombia has been driving the international policy dialogue and has used its credentials as a leading drug control champion with a close relationship to the United States to good effect in driving the UNGASS process, the most radical drug policy reforms have been implemented by Bolivia and Uruguay. Both countries have taken the unprecedented step of legalising, respectively, coca leaf and cannabis, substances that are controlled under the international conventions. The motives that inspired these changes, and the methods that were employed, were substantially different, according to von Hoffmann (Chapter 9). Bolivia had tried for years to 'legalise' the coca leaf and proactively challenged

[5]IOGT International aims for a world where all human beings are able to live 'free from the harm caused by alcohol and other drugs'. See: http://iogt.org/about-iogt/.

the Conventions, whereas Uruguay reactively devised a defence to shield its cannabis reform. Uruguay sought to make policy changes within the global drug control regime, while Bolivia stepped outside, temporarily leaving the conventions before rejoining with a reservation on the status of the coca leaf. Moreover, the legalisation of the coca leaf was a long overdue alignment of legal status with cultural practice and the first and most logical step in a broader attempt to rehabilitate the coca leaf. In Uruguay, by contrast, cannabis legalisation was part of a broader justice campaign intended to extend legal protection to discriminated minorities, comparable to the legalisation of homosexual marriage in Uruguay. Additionally, it was a crime reduction strategy, designed to remove opportunity for trafficking gangs that were importing cannabis from neighbouring Paraguay.

Both countries risked international isolation, with potentially damaging consequences, for example, when a number of states, led by the US, tried unsuccessfully to block Bolivia's application to rejoin the UN Conventions with a reservation over the status of the coca leaf. One way of overcoming this has been participation in regional association, and, more potently still, in inter-regional dialogues such as the EU-CELAC dialogue on drug issues.[6] Over a series of meetings representatives from both blocks were able to coordinate their positions on a number of issues, particularly the role of human rights.

Moderate Reformers: Europe

According to the European Union, UNGASS was a success, as well as an excellent platform for demonstrating the added benefit of the European Union External Action Service in getting EU member states to speak with one voice. Often seen as a soft reformer, the EU is a dynamic proponent of public health approaches, evidence-based policies and compliance with human rights, and backs these calls with extensive international cooperation projects in third countries. This has not been an easy feat because positions within Europe, as in other blocs, are diverse. Many Eastern European countries and, until recently, Sweden adhere to repressive policies, while others are among the forefront of the reform movement.

Three EU countries, as Ballotta & Hughes (Chapter 10) describe, are in the vanguard of reform: the Netherlands, with its well-established cannabis decriminalisation strategy via the coffee shop system; Portugal, for having decriminalised all drug possession offences in response to an alarming increase in the HIV infection rate; and the Czech Republic, for advancing medical cannabis and other decriminalisation measures. In these different cases, it is the methods and principles that are of interest. In the Netherlands, the objective of separating 'soft' from 'hard' drug markets was achieved by legal pragmatism, where the public interest was understood as best being served by not pursuing low level offences. The underlying ethos was made explicit in Portugal, with the principle of humanity and the 'absence of paternalism and moral judgment between the judging State

[6]The European Union and the Community of Latin American and Caribbean States (CELAC) hold regular meetings on a number of thematic areas, one of which is drugs.

and the drug consumer' (Ballotta & Hughes, Chapter 10). These clearly articulated beliefs that drugs are better dealt with in the health realm than as a criminal justice issue are broadly shared by most member states, which have extensive, publicly funded drug treatment systems and, increasingly, decriminalisation of drug possession. Switzerland has gained a reputation as a country developing its drug policy and practice on the basis of health outcomes while remaining within the terms of the Conventions (Zobel & Maier, Chapter 14).

A significant reflection of the acceptance of a human rights approach to people who use drugs is harm reduction, a concept whose practice and even mention remain contested. For many, harm reduction is seen as being for the benefit of people who use drugs and takes as its focus and aim to support and assist people who use drugs to ameliorate, but not necessarily stop, their use and adopt behaviours which are less likely to present risks to their own health and well-being. This involves some recognition of reality −that some people who use drugs will continue to do so. For others, harm reduction is interpreted as being to keep people who use drugs away from, and so 'protect', the 'mainstream' population, and adopting punitive responses, an approach more accurately described as reducing the harms associated with drug use. While the outcome of the arguments about harm reduction at the March 2005 CND seemed to have confirmed the acceptance of the principle of harm reduction by the Vienna Institutions, more recent documents (UNODC, 2016; United Nations Office on Drugs and Crime, World Health Organisation, 2017) have made no mention of harm reduction.

But as Chatwin (Chapter 11) reminds us, public health, evidence-based policy and human rights do not equate with radical reform. 'The EU has, however, also played a significant role in defending the status quo by confirming their ongoing and unwavering support of the current system of international drug control encapsulated by the international drug and psychotropic substance conventions' – not least for reasons extraneous to the 'drug issue' itself, that is that the EU strongly believes in a rule based international order determined by agreements such as those on drug control.

The United States: Giant without Compass

The United States was one of the architects of the international drug control system, as co-sponsor of the 1908 Shanghai conference, by pushing for the inclusion of drug control in the treaty of Versailles, and the reconstruction of international system under the auspices of the United Nations in the 1950s. As Snapp & Herrera (Chapter 12) demonstrate, in effect, drug control became a foreign policy tool, through which the US was able to influence and shape policies in other countries. At home, they argue, the increasingly aggressive measures that from the 1970s onwards came to be known as 'the war on drugs', had a decidedly domestic agenda. Successive presidents, it has been argued, were able to use drug control as a pretext for targeting political opponents, and the egregious racial disparity in arrest and conviction rates are strongly suggestive of drug control being a method for systemic discrimination rather than the promotion of public health.

In a country where the market is widely regarded as a positive force and the restriction of state functions is seen as a national virtue, drug control is a palpable policy anomaly. Ironically, the very expansion of control bureaucracies that has occurred not only at Federal but also at State and local level, with rising budgets and a de-coupling of inputs from outcomes, the vociferous lobbying efforts by vested professional interests, from prison guard unions to attorneys general, and the feedback loops of problem exacerbating policy outcomes, only go to confirm those libertarian anxieties. Reform efforts have been systematically and vehemently opposed by professional groups (control bureaucracies, law enforcement and medical professionals), whose interests in maintaining and investing in the control apparatus have converged with those of policy makers at different levels. Yet, precisely because the interests of core professional groups (control bureaucracies, law enforcement and medical professionals) have converged with political benefits for multi-level political beneficiaries, internal reform has been impossible. The push for change has therefore come from below, with popular initiatives establishing medical marijuana dispensaries and the legally controlled production and distribution for recreational use.

This has left US diplomacy in an odd position. For decades, US representatives have played a prominent role at the UN as well as at regional meetings (e.g., Organisation of American States) in enforcing controls. The US State Department even runs an annual exercise, assessing so-called drug producer and transit countries for their efforts in adhering to international counter narcotics agreements. Countries that fail do to so are potentially subject to sanctions, including the loss of US development assistance and access to funding from international financing institutions (e.g., the IMF and the World Bank) (see Snapp & Herrera, Chapter 12.)

In part as a response to this real and present threat, countries with well-established and culturally embedded traditions of cannabis use, for example Jamaica, Lebanon and Morocco, have, over the years, been making great efforts to eradicate production and use, at considerable social, political and human cost, only to see US companies based in legalising States emerge as global leaders in the development of cannabis products.

In the run up to UNGASS, US representatives took advantage of the lack of transparency in the preparatory sessions (Fordham & Haase, Chapter 1; Snapp & Herrera, Chapter 12; Trace: Chapter 15) in maintaining their national influence. Notwithstanding such adept use of the processes and attempts at claiming 'flexibility' in interpreting the conventions, there has been a loss of moral authority, notably in the rise of Russia and China as the most strident champions of the system.

It is likely that the drift towards a health and human focussed approach that became apparent under the Obama administration is being reversed, with, for instance, declarations by the US Attorney General to allow Federal agencies to go after cannabis producers in 'legalising' States; and the US president calling for the extension of the death penalty to drug traffickers. As Snapp & Herrera argue, further encroachments are likely to be challenged by States on both constitutional and economic grounds. Cannabis – marijuana – is already a growth industry and a major contributor to the tax base in Colorado, Oregon and Washington. These developments will be difficult to reverse, leaving the Federal government claiming to be in compliance with the conventions that strictly rule out the distribution of controlled substances for non-medical/scientific purpose.

Caught in the Process: West Africa

Countries that formed part of colonial empires until the second half of the twentieth century had drug policy imposed upon them and have since been struggling to adopt an appropriate response. West Africa, a region with low incidence of illicit drug use, has borne the full brunt of drug war perversity, as criminal organisations have used it for shipping cocaine to buoyant European markets. The region has suffered from what is casually known as 'spill-over' – the spread of cocaine use as international traffickers pay their local associates in kind, a sharp increase in law enforcement arrests, searches and incarceration, and, most seriously, massive corruption of security agencies, judiciary and all levels of governance. Governments, under pressure from the international control agencies and development partners, had adopted a tough 'war on drugs' approach with lamentable results according to Banon & Loglo (Chapter 13). Subsequently, regional civil society organisations and governmental activity have recognised this, and national and regional actors are now working together to introduce evidence-based, health-centred responses, including expanding treatment capacity adopting harm-reduction approaches. Regional opinion and practice have become more sceptical of a reliance on prohibition and law-enforcement approaches. If fully implemented and sustained, this could be an exemplary regional model for policy review and reform, with CSO, national, governmental and regional agencies collaborating on regional practice and in adopting a joint reformist approach in their relationship with the Vienna Institutions.

The Evaporation of the Moral Authority of the Drug Control System

In the deepest recesses of European collective subconscious is a memory of wretched victims tied to stakes on a moonlit night. Close up is a cloaked figure bearing a torch to light the pyre. As the flames consume so-called heretics and witches, the priest looks pitifully into their eyes and commends their souls to heaven. The flesh must suffer so that man or woman's better part can gain eternal life. Thomas Szasz, 1970s champion of anti-psychiatry, invoked the precedent of religious persecutions to draw a parallel with the contemporary treatment of drug users (Szasz, 1970).

The contempt that is commonly expressed for the figure of the addict, coupled with the vilification of drug traders, has prepared the ground for a similar suspension of the most fundamental human rights, above all the right to life. Addicted life is a lesser life, a sentiment aptly articulated by the head of the Armenian Drug Squad when interviewed in the context of a European Commission funded evaluation project: 'Parents would prefer to see their children killed rather than on drugs because it is an insult to the family' (Klein & Bremmers, 2006).

It is this kind of moral judgement – of drug users not having lives worth saving – that informs policy decisions on the provision of life saving and cost-effective OSTs, needle exchanges and other harm-reduction activity. Policy is being made on the basis of moral value judgements where the lives of people who use drugs are deemed disposable. One function of the stigmatising language used in reference to junkies, crack heads, stoners or addicts, facilitates the routine application of force and dehumanising practices. Whether it is the extra-judicial killing by security forces of alleged drug sellers in the Philippines, the denial of life saving medication in Russia, the mass incarceration of nonviolent repeat offenders in the United States, or, at a different place on the continuum of devaluing human life, the indifference of the UK government to the startling recent increases in drug-related deaths, human life is being sacrificed in pursuit of the vision of an illusory ideal, the drug-free world. Law enforcement officers and international bureaucrats have effectively been turned into the guardians of global morality and the enforcers of an ideological conformity.

As with the spectacular *auto da fé*, the means that are being employed in pursuit of a drug-free vision – the killing, rhetorical or actual, of children to prevent the shame – has perverted the original cause. Cleverly deployed metaphors of surgical interventions (cutting out the cancer) or epidemiological precautions (quarantining the vectors) cannot permanently obscure the underlying perversity in presenting capital punishment, floggings and mass prison camps as public health measures. The reforming states, driven by a clamorous civil society campaign and widespread dissatisfaction with the results, have clearly distanced themselves from these distorted interpretations of the drug control conventions. Their reservations have found expression in the UNGASS Outcome Document, with its references to human rights, proportionality and scientific evidence. It is the first time that the warnings to the 'custodians of the convention' that the consequences of their actions are under scrutiny have been so assertively expressed and recorded, a further and significant stage in a series of challenges which began at the 1998 UNGASS (Fordham & Haase, Chapter 1).

The Collapse of the Global Order

With the rising awareness that the drug control system serves fundamentally different objectives, the various state groupings have begun drifting apart. The landscape has shifted so dramatically with regard to concern over policy costs and the status of drugs per se that the consensus over an underlying threat or evil that prevailed in 1961 and, arguably, up to the 1990s, has now fractured. Alternative World Drug Reports appeared from 2012 (Transform, 2012, 2016) Ruth Dreifuss of the Global Commission on Drug Policy (GCDP, 2014) has stated: 'Today, the consensus on which the international drug control regime was established more than fifty years ago is broken'. According to Mike Trace (Chapter 15), UNGASS 2016 marked the 'breaking of a 50-year orthodoxy' (see too Trace, 2017), acknowledged de facto by the shift in focus of UN bodies other than UNODC. And Tom Blickman (Chapter 5) from the Transnational Institute writes:

> The question facing the international community today is no longer whether or not there is a need to reassess and modernize the UN drug control system, but rather when and how to do it.

It is the member states, however, that are leading the charge, with the avant-garde of states such as Uruguay that have effectively departed from the conventions even while remaining officially members. Given the tenacity with which institutions cling to any vestige of functionality long after the original rationale for their existence has vanished, and the sheer force of habit that propels the circus of international diplomacy, the façade will stay in place for many years to come. CND will continue to convene, and the INCB will publish annual reports, but the process will become increasingly meaningless. This said, other member states, in particular Russia and China, continue to resist and oppose the change, both of these states having as recently as the 2011 CND opposed the inclusion of NGOs and CSOs in the events and discussions of the Vienna Institutions (Fordham & Haase, Chapter 1, p. 2).

The transformation of cannabis, from the most widely used illegal drug globally to medicine and recreational pleasure, is the battering ram tearing down the gates of the drug control citadel. Cannabis is offering unanticipated profit opportunities and tax income sources that are generating an unprecedented momentum for reform. The growing acceptance of the plant's medical benefits is further removing the rationale for prohibition regimes, particularly as regulatory systems are beginning to prove more effective in reducing access by vulnerable populations; and harms. The blatant commercialisation witnessed in legalising US States is simply incompatible with the vicious punishment for simple consumption in other countries. These are not mere differences in interpretation; they are irreconcilable differences that cannot be accommodated under a single system if that notion is to maintain any meaning.

So we argue that the conventions are unlikely to be rescinded but are destined to become increasingly devoid of meaningful content in the face of growing differences between the methods chosen by countries in managing drugs. Consequently, there will no longer be a 'global drug problem' around which the nations can be rallied.

Moving Forward

Scenarios for the collapse that have been explored in previous publications (Bewley-Taylor, 2012) include a process of 'soft defections' by countries simply moving away from the spirit of the conventions without committing an actual breach. It is equally conceivable that groupings of like-minded states will create substantively different control regimes within the context of the drug-control conventions. Three regional blocks where harmonisation is already under way are the ASEAN countries, West Africa and the European Union.

Given the increasingly decentralised character of drug production, the need for global controls is no longer as compelling as it once appeared. Advances in the understanding of different substances and shifts in attitude towards plant-based substances, such as the coca leaf and cannabis, make it likely that legal controls are going to be more aligned with the emerging scientific evidence, evolving cultural contexts and prevailing social mores. At the same time, authoritarian regimes will continue to misuse drug control as a repressive tool for intimidating citizens and keeping dissidents in check, while elsewhere corporations will increasingly realise the profit potential in marketing new commodities.

Even within reform-minded states, a powerful domestic drug control lobby and a legacy of policy decisions will make for a difficult and negotiated process. A critical question for managing the transition is the role of the INCB and UNODC, organisations that have evolved on the back of the conventions and whose significance goes well beyond playing a supportive and secretarial function to the CND. Employing thousands of staff and contractors, and with a budget topping US$ 1 billion, UNODC has become one of the most important implementers of global drug control. For both organisations, the prospect of Colorado-style legalisation represents a mortal threat that will be sharply resisted.

A current example of such resistance can be seen in the preparation by UNODC, jointly with the WHO, of draft standards for the treatment of drug-use disorders (United Nations Office on Drugs and Crime, World Health Organisation, 2017). These proposals are being opposed by civil society organisations on the grounds that the document uses stigmatising and pathologising language; makes unsubstantiated claims and assumptions; makes no mention of harm reduction or other health interventions; emphasises abstinence; and did not involve user organisations in its preparation. Later 'consultation' with user organisations was tokenistic in that those invited to look at the text were told it was already agreed and finalised in preparation for CND 2018, a scenario familiar to many CSOs in the 2016 run-up to UNGASS. Old habits die hard.

Here, it would seem, is an indication of the Vienna Institutions cleaving to their familiar orthodoxy, in spite of the arguments and apparent development in thinking in the past 15 years or so. This document and its reversion to older patterns of thinking would appear to disregard and dismiss the inputs from other UN agencies and CSOs, and even the language and tone of the 2016 Outcome Document. This latest flurry is a clear warning that opinions on the purpose and focus of drug control are deeply divided, and that the organisations at the heart of the system remain deeply sceptical of reform, possibly because of the existential threat these pose.

One pressing task for the reform movement will therefore be in working out a roadmap for the future of these powerful organisations. It will be interesting to explore the potential of devoting the expertise stored up in Vienna to fight other aspects of transnational organised crime, for instance in tackling such intricate international issues as the trade in arms, trafficking in human beings, wildlife or toxic and hazardous waste. There are already nascent initiatives within UNODC that can be built on, as well as the wide spectrum of activities from prison reform to youth prevention work that is compatible with a different global regime.

Most importantly, however, both UNODC and INCB could leverage their drug-specific expertise to remodel themselves as regulatory agencies in the emerging international drug markets. Deliberating on the future of the control agencies might be a fitting topic for side events at the 2019 High Level Meeting. They have failed to serve their purpose but have passed their time. The machinery, alliances and expertise they have developed could be put to better use in examining more pressing social issues and challenges for which there is, or might be, a more realistic international consensus and prospect of success, and to support progress towards the sustainable development goals.

References

Barnes, M., & Barnes, J. (2016). Cannabis: The evidence for medical use. *Report for the All Party Parliamentary Group on Drugs*. Retrieved from https://drive.google.com/file/d/0B0c_8hkDJu0DUDZMUzhoY1RqMG8/view

Bewley-Taylor, D. (2012). *International drug control: Consensus fractured*. Cambridge: Cambridge University Press.

Global Commission on Drug Policy. (2014). *Pathways to drug policies that work: Addressing the real needs of people and societies*. Geneva, Switzerland: Global Commission on Drug Policy.

Godfrey, W. (2016). *Global Commission Slams UNGASS 2016 outcome that strains the credibility of international law*. Geneva, Switzerland: Global Drug Policy Commission on Drugs.

IOGT. (2016). *Towards a drug free society*. Stockholm: IOGT. Retrieved from http://iogt.org/wp-content/uploads/2015/04/Swedish-drug-policy-web.pdf. Accessed on March 01, 2018.

Jelsma, M. (2016). *UNGASS 2016: Watershed event or wasted opportunity*? Amsterdam, The Netherlands: Transnational Institute.

Klein, A., & Bremmers, G. (2006). *South Caucasus anti drug programme midterm evaluation report*.

Klein, A., & Stothard, B. (2016). All well with world drug control system – Just give us more money. *Drugs and Alcohol Today*, *16*(2). Retrieved from https://doi.org/10.1108/DAT-04-2016-0013

McAllister, W. B. (2000). *Drug diplomacy in the twentieth century*. London: Routledge.

Porter, R. (1996). The history of the drugs problem. *Criminal Justice Matters*, *24*, 3–5.

Rodgers, D. T. (1998). *Atlantic crossings: Social politics in a progressive age*. Cambridge, MA: Harvard University Press.

Rolles, S. (2017). Reflections on the UN General Assembly special session on drugs – One year on. *Drugs and Alcohol Today 17* (2), 74–80. Retrieved from https://doi.org/10.1108/DAT-03-2017-0009

Sander, G. (2018). *The death penalty for drug offences: Global overview 2017*. London: Harm Reduction International. Retrieved from https://www.hri.global/the-death-penalty-for-drug-offences

Szasz, T. S. (1970). *The manufacture of madness. A comparative study of the inquisition and the mental health movements*. New York, NY: Harper and Row.

Tinasti, K. (2018). HIV and AIDS among adolescents who use drugs: Opportunities for drug policy reform within the sustainable development agenda. *Journal of the International AIDS Society, 21*(S1). doi: org/10.1002/jias.25045

Trace, M. (2017). After UNGASS – Where do governments go from here? *Drugs and Alcohol Today, 17*(2). Retrieved from https://doi.org/10.1108/DAT-12-2016-0030

Transform. (2012). *Alternative World Drug report: Counting the costs – 50 years of the war on drugs*. Bristol: Transform Drug Policy Foundation.

Transform. (2016). *Alternative World Drug report: Count the costs* (2nd ed.). Bristol: Transform Drug Policy Foundation.

United Nations Office on Drugs and Crime (UNODC). (2016). Outcome document of the 2016 United Nations General Assembly special session on the world drug problem, our joint commitment to effectively addressing and countering the world drug problem. *Thirtieth Special Session, General Assembly*, New York, NY, 19–21 April. Retrieved from www.unodc.org/documents/postungass2016// outcome/V1603301-E.pdf

United Nations Office on Drugs and Crime (UNODC). (2017). *Fact sheet on substances and trends in illicit drugs*. Vienna, Austria: UNODC. Retrieved from http://www.unodc.org/wdr2017

United Nations Office on Drugs and Crime, World Health Organisation. (2017). *International Standards for the treatment of drug use disorders*. Vienna, Austria: UNODC.

UN.ORG. (2016a). *Statement by the Holy See*. Retrieved from http://statements.unmeetings.org/media2/7657598/holy-see.pdf. Accessed on March 01, 2018.

UN.ORG. (2016b). Statement by China. Retrieved from http://statements.unmeetings.org/media2/7657324/china-eng-.pdf. Accessed on March 01, 2018.

WHO, UNODC, UNAIDS. (2012). *Technical guide for countries to set targets for universal access to HIV prevention, treatment and care for injecting drug users*. Geneva, Switzerland: WHO. Retrieved from http://www.who.int/hiv/pub/idu/targets_universal_access/en/

Chapter 1

The 2016 UNGASS on Drugs: A Catalyst for the Drug Policy Reform Movement

Ann Fordham and Heather Haase

Abstract

This chapter reviews the history of civil society engagement on drug policy at the UN. Despite the challenging beginnings characterised by small numbers of civil society attendees at the Commission on Narcotic Drugs, coupled with government mistrust, in the last two decades, civil society representatives have made visible progress in advocating for policy reform and changing the terms of the debate.

Efforts by non-governmental organisations (NGOs) in the lead up to, as well as during the 2016 United Nations General Assembly Special Session on Drugs (UNGASS), best illustrate this increase in impact and engagement. Reform-orientated civil society strategised heavily on how to bring 'comprehensive, diverse, balanced, and inclusive' representation to the UNGASS and achieved this through the Civil Society Task Force, which was carefully balanced in terms of geographic, gender and ideological diversity, and included nine representatives from affected populations, including people who use drugs, people in recovery from drug use disorders, families, youth, farmers of crops deemed illicit, harm reduction, prevention, access to controlled medicines and criminal justice.

The 2016 UNGASS saw the fruition of greater civil society engagement. Eleven speakers were chosen to speak in the forum showcasing the calibre and diversity of civil society representatives. They made powerful, at times poignant statements and pleas for better, more compassionate treatment of people who use drugs, farmers of crops deemed illicit, as well as respect for human rights, sustainable livelihoods and the need to approach the issue through a public health and human rights lens.

The chapter concludes with the finding that reform-orientated civil society had a significant impact on the UNGASS – both on the gains in the Outcome

Collapse of the Global Order on Drugs: From UNGASS 2016 to Review 2019, 21–47

doi:10.1108/978-1-78756-487-920181016

Document and at the actual event, while noting that the most impactful ways to influence has nonetheless been through reform advocacy efforts outside of the official civil society mechanisms. Civil society engagement remains a serious challenge. International solidarity and global networking remain a central part of the drug policy reform movement's strategy to advocate for change at the national, regional and global levels.

Keywords: Civil society participation; drug policy reform; UN General Assembly Special Session on Drugs 2016; harm reduction; networking; decriminalisation

The History of Civil Society Engagement on Drug Policy at the UN Leading up to UNGASS 2016

Historic Resistance to Civil Society Engagement in Drug Policy

Globally, drug control is highly centralised, and the international regime exerts a great deal of normative pressure on national and regional drug policies. Narrow interpretations of the UN drug control treaties are often presented by the UN drug control bodies and national governments opposed to reform to justify continuing repressive responses and to stifle reform attempts (e.g., harm reduction, decriminalisation or cannabis regulation).

Civil society has played a role in international drug control since it was debated under the League of Nations and has been critical in shaping the trajectory of policy developments (Bruun, Pan, & Rexed, 1975).[1] Despite the limited space for engagement, civil society representatives have been attending Commission on Narcotic Drugs (CND) meetings almost since the meetings began in 1947, albeit initially in quite small numbers. At the 9th session of the CND in 1954, six non-governmental organisations (NGOs) attended,[2] in 1964 only two, in 1976 there were eight and in 1981 six attended (Economic and Social Council of the United Nations (ECOSOC), 1964, 1976, 1981). Regular participants were the International Criminal Police Organisation and the International Federation of Women Lawyers – in some of the early years they were the only two NGOS represented.

[1]At the time of the League of Nations, 'civil society' was generally understood to include corporate interest groups. Today, the terms 'civil society' is commonly used, with the term 'stakeholder' gaining more prominence.

[2]During the session, the International Confederation of Free Trade Unions (A) was represented by Miss Toni Sender, the World Federation of Trade Unions (A) by Miss Elinor Kahn, the International Conference of Catholic Charities (B) by Dr Louis C. Longarzo, PaxRomana (B) by Mr J. H. Price, The International Federation of Women Lawyers (Register) by Miss Viola Smith, the World's Alliance of Young Men's Christian Associations (B) by Mr Owen E. Pence and the World Union for Progressive Judaism (B) by Mr Ronalds.

Governments have not always welcomed civil society engagement on this issue at the national level or the United Nations, because drug control is seen as a sensitive area of policy making strongly linked to other agendas such as national security, terrorism or insurgency.

The International Drug Policy Consortium (IDPC, 2008) noted that many member states still spoke out against civil society participation at the CND and that 'NGOs are still largely assumed to have suspicious intentions, and are simplistically viewed through the prism of whether they are "liberal" or "prohibitionist"'.

In the very early days, civil society groups that were active at the UN comprised NGOs calling for greater controls (from the temperance or anti-opium movements) and representatives from industry and commerce that sought to limit controls (Bruun et al., 1975). The composition of NGOs attending the CND has changed dramatically in the last two decades, with the emergence of advocacy groups calling for policy reform, upholding human rights, ensuring the centrality of public health, promoting just and proportionate criminal justice responses and highlighting structural elements such as socio-economic pre-determinants of low-level engagement in the drug trade. Much of this progress is visible in the debates and Outcome Document of the 2016 UNGASS and as such, it is critical to take account of the important role played by civil society organisations in changing the terms of the debate.

Civil Society Engagement in Vienna from the Early 1990s

The main seat of drug policy at the UN is in Vienna, where the UN bodies with the lead responsibilities for drugs are housed – the CND, the United Nations Office of Drugs and Crime (UNODC) and the International Narcotics Control Board (INCB), collectively known as 'the Vienna Institutions'. The CND, as a Functional Commission of the ECOSOC, has to engage NGOs in its work, however the space provided for participation has previously been severely limited (Cook, 2009), although this situation has improved in recent years. At regular sessions of the CND meetings, NGOs have to wait until the end of each agenda item after all the government statements and interventions before being given the floor. NGO representatives have sometimes been ejected from the Committee of the Whole (COW) and there have been instances of security confiscating NGO publications. The provision of formal spaces for NGOs to interact with UN and government officials was also previously very limited.

To improve civil society participation at the CND, the Vienna NGO Committee on Drugs (VNGOC) was founded in 1983, and the New York NGO Committee (NYNGOC) the following year. In 1984, 28 NGOs attended the CND (ECOSOC, 1984).[3] Numbers remained at this level for several years with 27 NGOs in 1988 and 28 in 1996 (ECOSOC, 1988, 1996a). In the PrepCom of the 1998 UNGASS at the 39th CND session, 25 NGOs attended (ECOSOC, 1996b).

[3]Another factor to consider that may have contributed to the heightened civil society engagement in processes around drugs was the drug war 'panic' building in the United States in the early 1980s (Goode & Ben-Yehuda, 1994).

Regular NGO attendees during the 1980s and 1990s included the International Council of Women, International Council on Alcohol and Addictions, General Arab Women Federation, the International Association of Lions Clubs –Lions Club International, International Federation of University Women and the World Organisation of the Scout Movement. While participation remained steady for the next decade, there was a clear shift in the composition of civil society groups in attendance in the early 2000s. In 2003, Open Society Foundations appeared on the participants list and in 2005 (ECOSOC, 2003, 2005), Human Rights Watch attended the CND for the first time – both organisations and other civil society representatives had attended previously under different ECOSOC badges.

The first resolution on civil society participation, adopted in 2011 at the 54th session of the CND, was arguably the most contentious that year. Though China and Russia in particular succeeded in watering down the final text, it was still a critical milestone. The first informal Civil Society Hearing took place at the CND the following year. Since 2008 there have also been informal 'dialogues' between senior officials and civil society, kicking off with a meeting with the previous Executive Director of the UNODC, Antonio Maria Costa – although he made derogatory remarks about reform-orientated NGOs (IDPC, 2008), whom he would often refer to as the 'pro-drug lobby' (Easton, 2009). A different tone was taken by his successor, Yury Fedotov, who although not exactly friendly towards civil society, particularly reform NGOs, was professional and courteous. There has been a marked improvement in how civil society is received in Vienna under Mr Fedotov's tenure. For example, to make the debates at thematic sessions and intersessionals[4] more interactive, NGOs interventions are now interspersed between the statements from the member states, and many of the sessions are also now webcast.

The 1998 UNGASS: A Crucial Starting Point for Broader Civil Society Mobilisation

The policy positions of civil society organisations attending the CND meetings today range from those advocating for a drug-free world, proponents of harm reduction and decriminalisation and those calling for the full legal regulation of all drugs. There is much nuance in between these positions and a diverse range of organisations, including those working on human rights, criminal justice reform and palliative care or HIV/AIDS.

This is a relatively recent development, because until the mid-1990s, most NGOs were focussed on 'demand reduction' efforts,[5] such as drug prevention,

---

[4]These are CND meetings that take place outside of the regular sessions in March or the reconvened session in December.

[5]A list taken from TNI's blog (https://www.tni.org/en/archives/act/1596#3a) of early VNGOC members – Centro Italiano di Solidarietà (CeIS-Italy), International Council of Women, World Organisation of the Scout Movement (WOSM), Christian Drug Prevention (The Netherlands), Consumers International, Drug Abuse Prevention Centre (DAPC-Japan), SOS Drogue International, World Federation of Mental Health and Human Resource Development Institute (United States).

treatment and rehabilitation, towards the goal of achieving a drug-free world. Then in 1996, two years before the UNGASS on drugs in June that had been initiated by Mexico, the Transnational Institute (TNI, 1998) joined the only other 'reform-orientated' group at the VNGOC – the Transnational Radical Party (Jelsma, 2005). Forming the International Coalition of NGOs led by the European Coalition of NGOs, they submitted a 'draft manifesto' calling on member states to revise punitive and damaging drug policies at the 1998 UNGASS (European Coalition for Just and Effective Drug Policies (ENCOD), 2007).

With the tentative support of some member states (TNI, 1998), ECOSOC-accredited NGOs were able to observe all the preparatory meetings in Vienna, and the UNGASS itself in New York. Space was given for six civil society interventions from the floor during the formal proceedings in the COW, including a representative from the 'producers' and one from the 'consumers'. These two powerful and critical interventions made by representatives from these affected 'communities' from the two opposite ends of the drug market were considered to be an important achievement for the reform groups in 1998. Their statements brought the realities of failing and disastrous policies momentarily to the fore. It was 'a clear moment when the hypocrisy of the event became briefly apparent and perceptible, even to the ones who were running the show' (ENCOD, 1998).

Civil society representatives were able to attend the member state and UN agency led side events and participate in the open discussions following the presentations from the panels. However, with only one NGO side event[6] held inside the UN building owing to VNGOC concerns that controversial topics would antagonise UNDCP[7] and member states, an 'NGO Village' was set up in the Church Centre opposite the UN building where all the NGO activities took place. The NGO Village proved to be useful for networking amongst the civil society groups, but predictably hardly any of the UN and government delegates crossed the street to attend the side events. Nonetheless, the 1998 UNGASS was crucial for mobilising civil society towards drug policy reform through creating alliances between people who use drugs, farmers, human rights activists, women's rights campaigners, cannabis activists and others including a good spread from both the global south and north sharing space and ideas in the NGO Village.

The other important success by civil society groups in 1998 was the effort to ensure that the SCOPE plan (the 'Strategy for Coca and Opium Poppy Elimination' by 2008) proposed by UNDCP was not taken forward. It was originally meant to be the main outcome of the UNGASS (supported by the USA). Preventing its adoption was one of the main priorities for groups such as TNI, the Washington Office on Latin America, Accion Andina and others. The civil society effort managed to kill it off and it was not mentioned in the 1998 UNGASS outcomes and has never been referred to since. What remained of it, however,

[6]Side event on the war on drugs in the Andes – TNI, Accion Andina, WOLA and Consejo Andino.

[7]The United Nations Drug Control Programme was renamed United Nations Office on Drugs and Crime in 2002.

was the inclusion in the 1998 Political Declaration of its most controversial paragraph 19:

> Welcome the global approach by the United Nations International Drug Control Programme to the elimination of illicit crops, and commit ourselves to working closely with the Programme to develop strategies with a view to eliminating or reducing significantly the illicit cultivation of the coca bush, the cannabis plant and the opium poppy by the year 2008.

So in a way, the SCOPE plan gave birth to the targets to eliminate the global drug market that continue to plague the global debate to date (TNI, 1998).

The 'Dear Bobby' Letter and Ever-increasing Civil Society Engagement

Another watershed moment for the reform community was the collective advocacy around harm reduction in 2005 that was precipitated by the UNODC succumbing to US pressure and reversing its position on harm reduction. Prior to this, UNODC had begun to endorse harm reduction measures[8] for people who inject drugs in response to the HIV/AIDS epidemic, falling into line with the general UN position. In response, the United States, then a staunch opponent of harm reduction, prevailed upon the Executive Director, Antonio Maria Costa, to cease supporting such interventions and to withdraw mention of harm reduction from all communications. Fearing the loss of funding Mr Costa yielded to these demands and wrote an apologetic letter to Robert Charles, the US Assistant Secretary of State for International Narcotics and Law Enforcement Affairs in late 2004.

Made public because of an administrative blunder the 'Dear Bobby' letter (United Nations Office of Drugs and Crime (UNODC), 2004) gained notoriety amongst member states that were implementing HIV-related harm reduction measures, as well as civil society organisations from the HIV/AIDS and human rights sectors. The story was picked up by mainstream media (New York Times, 2005) ahead of the following session of the CND in March 2005 and, in an unprecedented mobilisation effort, over 200 NGOs from 56 countries, sent a joint letter to the CND calling on them to stand firm on harm reduction, noting that 'No less than the future of the HIV epidemic is at stake' (UNODC, 2005). The mobilisation effort did keep UNODC in check on this issue (Bewley-Taylor & Woodiwiss, 2005), and the agency, while sometimes less than forthcoming on harm reduction, did not fully adhere to the demands from the United States at the time (TNI). In more recent years, the current Executive Director, Yury Fedotov, has referred explicitly to the need for harm reduction measures (UNODC, 2014) in responding to HIV.

[8]E/CN.7/2004/3 – Strengthening strategies regarding the prevention of HIV/AIDS in the context of drug abuse. Report of the UNODC Executive Director for the 47th session of the CND, 12 January 2004.

The Beyond 2008 Initiative

Following the 2005 push back on harm reduction, the number of more reform-oriented civil society representatives attending the annual sessions of the CND steadily increased, and the IDPC was formed in 2006 as a vehicle for collective drug policy reform advocacy, for providing comment and analysis on the UN debates as well as encouraging NGO participation (IDPC, 2007).

This increased engagement of groups from the harm reduction and human rights sectors helped to set the stage for the most visible civil society moment up to that point with the establishing of the 'Beyond 2008' initiative. The VNGOC and the NYNGOC, with support from UNODC, set up this mechanism to facilitate civil society input into the 10-year review of progress against the targets set in 1998. The process took over two years and involved several regional consultations and an online questionnaire. It culminated in a Global Civil Society Forum in July 2008 attended by three hundred civil society representatives, who worked together to agree a consensus declaration that was formally presented to the CND in 2009 (UNODC, 2008).

The 'Beyond 2008' declaration was a major achievement in bringing NGOs from across the ideological spectrum behind a consensus statement. Reform groups welcomed the commitment to harm reduction, to human rights issues, the need for a culturally appropriate response, the inclusion of the most affected communities, as well as improved access to controlled medicines and alternatives to incarceration. It was lauded as a:

> remarkable accomplishment that will impress many officials now involved in the UNGASS review process as this can be presented as a consensus outcome of NGOs from all around the world and from all different ideological perspectives. (Jelsma, 2008)

There were however concerns over the failure to meaningfully engage groups representing farmers growing crops for the illicit market for subsistence purposes (Jelsma, 2008), an issue that was taken up more seriously by civil society representatives in the lead up to the 2016 UNGASS.[9]

Preparations for the 2016 UNGASS

"Where Things Stood" in 2012–2013

In 2012, the Presidents of Colombia, Mexico and Guatemala issued a joint declaration calling for an UNGASS to be held urgently on the drugs issue. The proposal was incorporated into a resolution (United Nations (UN), 2013a), which was supported by all of the members of the General Assembly and led to the organisation of a Special Session in New York in April 2016. At the General Assembly when the call was made, Colombia stated that 'revising the approach

[9]The membership of the civil society task force specifically included a representative for the affected population: farmers of crops deemed illicit.

on drugs maintained so far by the international community can no longer be postponed' and that the UN needed to exercise leadership to 'conduct an in depth review, analysing all available options, including regulatory or market measures, in order to establish a new paradigm'.[10] This urgency echoed the increasing calls from reform-oriented NGOs that the dominant approach to drug control, grounded in repression and zero-tolerance ideology, was disastrous, counterproductive and fuelling immense harm.

Although the reform community had made significant progress at the CND since the 1998 UNGASS, the situation remained challenging. Conservative organisations advocating a 'drug-free world' dominated the membership and executive board of VNGOC (which had been the case since its inception), and the VNGOC chairman was the sole civil society representative at almost all formal UN events. Access by the harm reduction community to these 'official' channels was tightly controlled.

In New York, the picture was even more tenuous – NYNGOC had become dormant after Beyond 2008, leaving no formal platform for NGO engagement at the UN headquarters. The oft repeated refrain was 'everything happens in Vienna', where UNODC maintained its 'monopoly' over drug policy, sidelining other agencies.

Meanwhile, the reform community was extending its network to new regions and forging relationships with supportive governments such as Norway, the Netherlands, Costa Rica, Colombia and even a growing, if somewhat tentative, relationship with the United States. As a result, when preparations for the UNGASS began in 2013, reformers were well positioned to land in New York.

Early UNGASS Preparations in Spring 2013

When in the fall of 2012, the UN Generally Assembly set the date for UNGASS policy reformers were awed by the sheer possibilities such a meeting presented. A core group comprising TNI, the Harm Reduction Coalition and IDPC came together at the CND in 2013 to map out a plan of action. The main objectives were decided early on as (1) to raise awareness about drug policy and the reform community's goals with key New York missions and agencies; (2) to encourage the participation of UN agencies in the lead-up to UNGASS, and, most importantly, (3) to maximise the participation of civil society.

---

[10]*/'revising the approach on drugs maintained so far by the international community can no longer be postponed'/, and the UN needed to exercise leadership to /'conduct an in depth review, analysing all available options, including regulatory or market measures, in order to establish a new paradigm that would impede the flow of resources to organized crime groups'/. An international meeting had to be convened /'capable of taking the decisions necessary to//increase the effectiveness of the strategies and instruments with which the global community addresses the challenges of drugs and their consequences'/.* (See http://mision.sre.gob.mx/onu/images/dec_con_drogas_esp.pdf.)

UN Mission and Agency Engagement at New York Headquarters

In early 2013, IDPC recruited a New York-based representative and led the engagement with Harm Reduction Coalition, reaching out to the more friendly member states in the New York missions. A key area of work in New York was to follow negotiations around the drugs 'omnibus' resolution. Led by Mexico, this annual resolution is the General Assembly's opportunity to highlight the drugs issue by supporting existing processes and resolutions on drugs, and also calls on member states or UN agencies to take additional actions (UN, 2013b).

In parallel, IDPC and Harm Reduction Coalition began meeting with UN agencies including the United Nations Development Programme (UNDP), the Department of Political Affairs and UNAIDS, who while supportive of the drugs agenda lacked a strong mandate to fully engage in UNGASS preparations.

Against this backdrop IDPC, Harm Reduction Coalition and partners started holding events to raise awareness of drug policy in the UN community in New York on topics such as the Organisation of American States' (OAS, 2013) Report on the Drug Problem in the Americas, women and incarceration and the modernisation of drug law enforcement.[11] Despite the fact that the UNGASS wouldn't take place for another three years, these events were usually well attended by a wide range of member states, and their content provoked lively discussions.

The Creation of the UN System Task Force on Transnational Organised Crime and Drug Trafficking

In an effort to foster 'more meaningful coordination within the system' (UN, 2011) on drug policies, in 2011, the UN Secretary General formed the 'UN System Task Force on Transnational Organised Crime and Drug Trafficking', known as the 'TOC Task Force'. Co-chaired by the Department of Political Affairs and UNODC, it struggled from the start with internal politicking. Though few missions in either Vienna or New York were even aware of its existence, the Deputy Secretary General called on the TOC Task Force to be active in the UNGASS preparations. This resulted in a 'talking points' document for the UN agency members and a mandate directing the agencies to submit working papers on how each of their mandates related to the UNGASS and the drugs issue (UNODC, 2016). This seemingly simple directive proved to be nothing short of a game changer as it stimulated the many progressive written submissions from the agencies to the UNGASS preparations.[12]

Civil Society Engagement in New York and Vienna: A Tale of Two Cities

The Vienna and the New York NGO Committee on Drugs are the two '"substantive committees" on the topic of drugs with formal UN affiliation under

---

[11]See http://idpc.net/theme/modernising-drug-law-enforcement.

[12]See official website of the UNGASS 2016 where all contributions from UN entities have been posted. Retrieved from http://www.unodc.org/ungass2016/en/contribution_UN_Entities.html.

the Conference of NGOs in Consultative Status with the UN'[13] (Committee on NGOs, CoNGO). Although owing to the centrality of Vienna in drug deliberations, the VNGOC has enjoyed more visibility, both committees have a record of engagement, including at the June 1987 International Conference on Drug Abuse and Illicit Trafficking; at the 1994 NGO World Forum on Drug Demand Reduction that resulted in the Bangkok Declaration (NGO Committee on Narcotics and Substance Abuse, 1994); and when coordinating the 'NGO Village' at the 1998 UNGASS on drugs. The NYNGOC also played a role in the 'Beyond 2008' Global NGO Forum and the nine regional consultations leading up to it.[14] Yet, by 2011, the NYNGOC had become dormant, while VNGOC took advantage of the 'Vienna monopoly' to develop a close relationship with UNODC and INCB, as the only functioning substantive committee around drugs until the NYNGOC was re-established in 2013 (Jelsma, 2015).

The call for a Special Session to be held in 2016 presented a key opportunity to revive and continue the work of the NYNGOC, then the NY NGO Committee on Narcotic Substances. Rosalind Harris, one-time chair of NYNGOC and a member since the 1980s, was instrumental in transitioning the leadership of the committee and guiding the NGOs through the CoNGO rules and procedures.[15] After a year and a half of preparations, the NYNGOC held its first meeting at the UN Church Centre – the site of the 1998 UNGASS 'NGO Village'. In attendance were 21 NGOs mostly from New York and nearby states, including Drug Policy Alliance (DPA), StoptheDrugWar.org, Virginians Against Drug Violence, the NYC Bar Association, Center for Court Innovation, NY Academy of Medicine, VOCAL NY and of course IDPC and Harm Reduction Coalition. One year later, under the procedures in the committee's existing Bylaws, an Executive Committee was elected comprised of organisations from Canada, the US, Brazil, Argentina and Mexico, and the committee was renamed the 'New York NGO Committee on Drugs'.

Early Roadblocks, Challenges and Successes

While reformers were encouraged by the interest in a progressive drug policy agenda shown by some member states, particularly certain Latin American countries, challenges and roadblocks appeared early and with surprising intensity. Longstanding tensions within the UN systems erupted when choosing between New York and Vienna as the venue for the preparatory meetings. While civil society lobbied hard for New York, the omnibus resolution of December 2014 decided that almost the entire process would take place in Vienna,

[13]Retrieved from https://www.ngocongo.org/. Other substantive committees include Migration, Mental Health, HIV/AIDS, Human Rights, Rights of Indigenous Peoples, Status of Women and several others.

[14]'Beyond 2008' was governed by a Steering Group which was led by a Chair from VNGOC and a co-vice chairs from VNGOC and NYNGOC.

[15]It should be noted that the then Chair of VNGOC was also involved in early efforts to revitalise the New York committee.

with the President of the General Assembly invited to 'support, guide and stay involved in the process' (UN, 2015). As a compromise measure, it was later agreed that a high-level thematic debate would be held in New York in May 2015, to be chaired by the President of the General Assembly and organised under his office in coordination with the CND. This would be only the second occasion since the 1998 UNGASS that a debate on drug policy had been held in the General Assembly.[16]

Progress with UN agencies was also difficult, as without a specific mandate, they were loath to infringe on UNODC's 'turf'. With inter-agency tensions growing the once promising TOC Task Force began to wither. Finally, the tensions between New York and Vienna were also playing out in the NGO committees. The NYNGOC leadership found that despite its status as a substantive committee under CoNGO, it had to continually fight for recognition. VNGOC leadership, once collaborative around the reorganisation of NYNGOC, now denied ever having been involved. In New York, UNODC refused to recognise NYNGOC, did not communicate or issue invitations to UNGASS briefings and held out VNGOC as the only CSO committee.

In response, reform-minded CSOs, such as IDPC and Harm Reduction Coalition, looked to civil society structures in other thematic areas of the UN, such as migration, HIV/AIDS, non-communicable diseases and the rights of indigenous peoples, to find instances of best practice around high-level meetings. Through this process, they formulated the proposal to form a 'civil society task force', which would combine the leadership of the two committees with regional and thematic representatives, thereby ensuring diverse and inclusive representation. They also expended considerable effort building support for the proposal at UN Headquarters. They could only hope that all of their work would not now be blocked by the suddenly resistant VNGOC.

The week before the March 2014 high-level meeting, through a series of behind-the-scenes efforts, the reform community learnt that the Deputy Secretary-General, Jan Eliasson, had agreed to meet with a small group of civil society representatives at the CND in Vienna. By the time delegations were arriving in Vienna (and after a weekend of tense committee negotiations), a small group with members from across the ideological spectrum of drug policy had been assembled. Agreeing on the benefits of a coherent approach, the representatives decided to present the idea of a civil society task force to the Deputy Secretary-General together as a unified group. Once the meeting commenced, however, the approach changed and it was clear that some still held reservations about the task force, preferring to see VNGOC as the sole vehicle for civil society participation for the UNGASS. Regardless of this last-minute resistance, the proposal was officially and publicly tabled with the Deputy Secretary-General.

[16]The only other drug policy debate held by the General Assembly since the 1998 UNGASS was the thematic debate on drugs and crime as a threat to development which was held on 26 June 2012 in New York.

The Civil Society Task Force

Formation

With input from broader civil society, the path to the formation of the civil society task force (CSTF) finally cleared, and following significant changes in VNGOC leadership, true collaboration began.

It was agreed from the beginning that the CSTF was to bring 'comprehensive, diverse, balanced and inclusive' representation to the UNGASS, and that its members would need to set aside ideological differences to achieve the common goal of civil society participation. A steering committee was formed with two representatives from each committee, chaired by the Chair of VNGOC with the NYNGOC and VNGOC representatives serving as co-Vice-Chairs. Further, it was agreed for two representatives from each global region to lead regional consultations. The one unique characteristic of the CSTF for UNGASS 2016 was the addition of nine representatives from affected populations/global voices, including people who use drugs, people in recovery from drug use disorders, families, youth, farmers of crops deemed illicit,[17] harm reduction, prevention, access to controlled medicines and criminal justice. In the end, the CSTF consisted of 31 members of civil society and was carefully balanced in terms of geographic, gender and ideological diversity.

In December 2014, just eight months after the contentious civil society meeting with the Deputy Secretary-General, the CSTF was launched at the reconvened CND in Vienna with UNODC declaring it the 'official' civil society platform for UNGASS 2016. After over two decades of marginalisation by dominant 'status quo' forces, the harm reduction/reform community had finally achieved equal footing.

The Work of the CSTF: Challenges and Opportunities

Once formed, the CSTF sought to ensure the physical presence of civil society members in the debates. An early opportunity presented itself when the CSTF was called on to select speakers for the roundtable discussions in the pre-UNGASS segment held during the 57th session of the CND. One speaker was chosen per roundtable in the five topics of UNGASS: drugs and health; drugs and crime; human rights, women, children and communities; new challenges, threats and realities in addressing the world drug problem and alternative development.

Notably, for the first time, civil society speakers' interventions from the floor were interspersed with member states', instead of at the end. These early discussions were a favourable sign for civil society participation in the UNGASS processes to follow.

The first major opportunity for the CSTF came a few months later in New York during preparations for the May 2015 High Level Thematic Debate on drugs.

[17]Farmers of crops deemed illicit started to organise themselves and held a Global Farmers Forum in January 2016. The report can be accessed here https://www.tni.org/en/publication/the-global-forum-of-producers-of-prohibited-plants-gfppp.

The UN machinery (presumably under the recommendation of the CND) had reached out to the new VNGOC Chair, and now also the Chair of the Civil Society Task Force, Esbjörn Hörnberg, to represent civil society in the first debate. The CSTF Steering Committee pushed back immediately, and Mr Hörnberg stepped aside to allow for the CSTF to select speakers who would be geographically diverse and representative of civil society working on the ground on drug issues – in line with the CSTF mission. Working with the President of the General Assembly (PGA)'s office, the CSTF selected two speakers through a collaborative and transparent process – one from a treatment facility in Lebanon and the other from a harm reduction services centre in upper Manhattan.

The CSTF had shown that they could work towards the common goal of civil society inclusion. Both sides decided to forego opportunities for gaining unfair advantages in the spirit of fairness and balance. These early compromises built trust and a strong foundation for the UNGASS preparations ahead.

Probably the biggest success – as well as one of the biggest challenges – in the lead up to UNGASS was the Informal Interactive Stakeholder Consultation (IISC), also held by PGA 'with the support' of CND, in February 2016. Not only was civil society able to persuade the PGA to hold this controversial hearing (itself not authorised by CND resolution) but it was also enthusiastically supported by his office despite the objection of certain member states who would rather have kept all of the proceedings in Vienna.

Further drama followed when the PGA's office and the CND Secretariat ignored the closely negotiated list of CSTF speakers and moved to select a number of more conservative speakers. After a stressful night of back channelling to protect the CSTF's mandate and push back on political interference on speaker selection, the CSTF list was formally accepted.

The first of its kind in drug policy, the full-day IISC was opened by the PGA himself and featured civil speakers from all over the world from people who use drugs and farmers of crops deemed illicit to those working in prevention, treatment, harm reduction and as well human rights advocates. Over 300 civil society representatives attended the meeting and made over 50 interventions, the vast majority of which were distinctly reform oriented.

The IISC itself was like a bright light finally being switched on in a very dark room. With the exception of the keynote speaker who did utter the words 'drug-free world', voice after voice from the podium and the floor called for reform – decriminalisation, harm reduction, a health-based approach, human rights and proportionality in sentencing and regulation – all were part of the discussion that day, in the company of a moderately sized group of member state delegates. Best of all, every one of these concepts appeared in the meeting summary (despite direct efforts by certain UN officials to exclude reform-oriented statements), which was to become an official document of UNGASS.[18]

[18]Summary of the Informal Interactive Stakeholder Consultation. Retrieved from http://www.unodc.org/documents/ungass2016//Contributions/Civil/CSTF/UNGASS-Summary-of-Informal-Interactive-Stakeholder-consultations-9-March-2016.pdf.

With all of its challenges, the IISC had marked a turning point in drug policy – when the messages of reform overtook the balance in terms of civil society voices in the UN debates.

Momentum for Reform

For the drug policy reform community, the UNGASS was seen as a critical opportunity to shift the paradigm. Criticism of the system had been building up with the strong call for reforms by the Global Commission on Drug Policy, formed in 2011,[19] that included global heavyweights such as former UN Secretary-General Kofi Annan and ex-Presidents of Brazil, Colombia, Mexico and Switzerland. At CND, the number of countries voicing their displeasure with the international drug control system had also been increasing (IDPC, 2012). Meanwhile, genuine policy reforms were taking place on the ground particularly around cannabis, most dramatically in Uruguay but also at the state-level in the United States as well as in smaller jurisdictions in Western Europe (Blickman, 2013). The Obama Administration had also toned down the language of repression (Roberts, 2013) and moved to address disproportionate sentences for drug offences at the Federal level (Urban Institute, 2016).[20] This shift in rhetoric from the United States was significant, given their role as a long-time enforcer of the global prohibition regime.

The actual catalyst of change was a private meeting on drugs convened by Colombia in October 2012 on the margins of the 2012 Summit of the Americas in Cartagena (IDPC, 2013) – where the Presidents of Mexico, Colombia and Guatemala had first called for an UNGASS to take place. Afterwards, Colombian President Santos announced that the OAS had been tasked with reviewing existing drug policies as well as exploring new, more effective approaches. The resulting report was groundbreaking, in outlining future possible scenarios for shifting course on drug control, including the option of legal regulation. The Scenarios Team included leaders from civil society, government, business, academia, indigenous peoples, police, the military, young people, politicians, activists and others (OAS, 2012).

With this backdrop to the UNGASS, reform NGOs understood that this moment had to be fully leveraged. The IDPC (2015) (as the global network of reform minded civil society organisations) led this charge and began mobilising its membership around key advocacy messages, policy analysis and advice to government and UN officials. Open Society Foundations, the most prominent funder of drug policy reform, rallied their grantees and used the

---

[19]Global Commission on Drug Policy. See http://www.globalcommissionondrugs.org/.

[20]In 2016, the Colston Task Force recommended the removal of mandatory minimum sentences for all but the most serious drug offences. Retrieved from https://www.urban.org/research/publication/transforming-prisons-restoring-lives/view/full_report.

UNGASS lead-up to bring new civil society and academic actors into the movement.[21]

The work of the reform movement developed around the following four distinct strands:

(1) Bringing in more diverse civil society perspectives from other sectors that had not traditionally been engaged on drug policy reform (e.g., criminal justice, development, palliative care, peace building, women's rights and religious groups).

(2) Engaging other parts of the UN system in the UNGASS process to consider the human rights, health and wider development impacts of repressive drug policies that were not duly considered by the Vienna bodies. As the written submission of United Nations Development Programme (UNDP, 2015) noted:

> UNGASS 2016, and preparations thereto… provide an important opportunity to widen the discussion to include UN organisations that approach issues of drugs and crime from health, sustainable development, human rights and peace building perspectives, and ultimately, to promote system-wide coherence with respect to global drug control strategies.[22]

Written submissions by UNAIDS, WHO, UNDP, the Office of the High Commissioner on Human Rights (OHCHR) and UN Women further amplified the message that punitive drug policies are undermining other UN commitments to health, human rights and development.[23]

(3) Supporting progressive member states achieve a reorientation of international drug control and rebalance the narrative towards health and human rights considerations. This work included providing suggested language inputs into the negotiations and highlighting previously agreed UN language on key issues (the Book of Authorities[24] was repackaged online and managed by IDPC). Furthermore, meetings for groups of like-minded states were convened outside of the UN setting and the pressure of consensus, to find common ground and find ways for moving the discussions

[21]The many civil society organisations that played a role but a few of the leading ones include CELS, the Drug Policy Alliance, Harm Reduction Coalition, Harm Reduction International, Human Rights Watch, the International Network of People who Use Drugs, Mexico UnidoContra la Delincuencia, Transform Drug Policy Foundation, the TNI and the Washington Office on Latin America.

[22]All UN written contributions for the UNGASS are available here http://www.unodc.org/ungass2016/en/contribution_UN_Entities.html.

[23]UNODC, Contributions. Retrieved from http://www.unodc.org/ungass2016/en/contributions.html.

[24]Originally developed by TNI, HRI and Human Rights Watch but now hosted by IDPC. Retrieved from http://bookofauthorities.info/.

forward.[25] NGOs were also connecting the debates across the UN settings – between Vienna, Geneva and New York and then also back to capitals. The collaborative nature of the reform-minded NGOs, facilitated by the IDPC, engendered this kind of information sharing and encouraged member states to be consistent in their messaging in different UN forums.

(4) Media work and communications to build public support for drug policy reform. The idea was to translate the more detailed policy 'asks' being into punchy and engaging messages for the public and the media. Open Society Foundations funded the Museum of Drug Policy in New York, which was a pop-up cultural hub that held a full programme of talks and events that ran for the same three days as the UNGASS. There was also a public rally outside the UN building, which marked the end of the journey for the 'Caravan for Peace, Life and Justice' (Krasovitzky & Lewis, 2017), which had travelled through El Salvador, Guatemala, Mexico and the United States, highlighting the human costs of the 'war on drugs' on its route. A joint coordinating umbrella campaign called 'Stop The Harm' (Canadian Drug Policy Coalition, 2016) was set up to bring together the many diverse drug policy campaigns and initiatives, and the Drug Policy Alliance (DPA, 2016) coordinated a letter to UN Secretary General Ban Ki-moon urging him to set the stage 'for real reform of global drug control policy', which was signed by over a thousand prominent individuals from all over the world, echoing a similar effort for the 1998 UNGASS.

The 2016 UNGASS – Highlights, Challenges, Impact of Civil Society and Lessons Learned

Highlights and Challenges

For many of the Civil Society participants, UNGASS was a once-in-a-lifetime event. The main highlight was the caliber and diversity of representatives who had been chosen to speak. Eleven speakers in total from all around the world were selected to speak – two in each of the five roundtables (one on the panel and one from the floor) – and five more in the plenary. The negotiations to select these speakers went through several layers of CSTF scrutiny and were carefully selected and hard fought. This time, there were no sweeping changes to the CSTF's recommended list but the changes came more slowly, trickling in, as the regional representatives for member states were chosen by the PGA's office – if there was a need for geographical diversity, it was invariably the civil society representative

[25]This model of 'dialogues' had been used by TNI since 2004 in Europe, Latin America and South East Asia bringing together government officials, UN representatives and civil society for an 'open-minded exchange of views on current dilemmas in international drug policy making and discuss strategies on how contradictions might be resolve'. Retrieved from https://www.tni.org/en/collection/informal-drug-policy-dialogues.

who was called on to be 'flexible' (i.e., taken off the panel). A prolonged moment of tension surrounded the selection and last minute de-selection of the star civil society representative on the human rights panel: Ricky Gunawan, an Indonesian human rights lawyer representing defendants facing the death penalty for their involvement in the drug trade. His work represented everything the reform community was fighting for. In his stead, an Indonesian governmental representative was to appear.

Ricky was still slated to make an intervention from the floor, and when he was called on to speak, a hush fell over the room as all of civil society rose to their feet in silent solidarity. As Ricky spoke about his work with people who had been arrested on drug offenses and had spent years on death row, some suffering from mental illness, some who had died at the hands of his government, member state delegates also began to silently stand. When he finished the crowd delivered a solid, prolonged applause and it was clear that many had been moved. It was truly a triumph for civil society – the voices of the community had been heard.

Other speakers were also outstanding – from Kenya, India, Norway, New Zealand, UAE, Brazil, Senegal, Costa Rica, Ghana, Indonesia, Slovenia, Myanmar, Peru and Puerto Rico – made powerful, poignant statements and pleas for better, more compassionate treatment of people who use drugs, farmers of crops deemed illicit as well as respect for human rights, sustainable livelihoods and the need to approach the issue through a public health lens.

Of course, there were other challenges at UNGASS, the most obvious being the logistical issues NGOs faced from the moment they arrived at UN Headquarters. There were not enough passes the day preceding the UNGASS and hundreds were shut out of the civil society forum and left out on the street. The first day was no better as issue after issue ensued on account of an extremely haphazard pass system. Countless NGO delegates were unable to attend the opening of the UNGASS, including half of the CSTF Steering Committee. NGO representatives were sent to the overflow room but then denied access to that room and ending up stuck in the hall, during this historic event they had travelled from all over the world to attend. Later, civil society representatives could not attend the side events they had been asked to speak at as experts. Member states who had sponsored the events had not been informed that they were to provide passes for each event, and directions issued by the UN days before the meeting were in direct conflict with what transpired during the event. Further, despite repeated requests, no table space for literature had been provided as is customary at UN events (and had been provided in 1998). Finally, several NGOs reported having their materials confiscated by security – including a t-shirt that said 'cannabis is safer than alcohol' and a pamphlet on marijuana regulation. When confronted, UN officials – from the PGA's office to UN-DESA (the civil society coordination arm) to security – shirked responsibility and blamed communications issues. It was a shame that, after months of planning and coordinating by the NGO committees and the CSTF to ensure access for civil society, such an opposite chain of events unfolded.

The Impact of 'Reform' Messages in the Debate and the Tense Disagreement Between Member States on Key Issues

It was clear to reform-orientated civil society groups that the preparatory process had been neither inclusive nor transparent (IDPC, 2016). All the negotiations had taken place in Vienna with little effort to ensure participation of member states without a Vienna presence, particularly from Africa and the Caribbean. Furthermore, there appeared to be rather heavy use of closed-setting 'informal' meetings rather than official 'intersessionals', which excluded civil society observers and contributed to the lack of transparency.

A civil society sign-on letter was circulated at the 59th session of the CND in March 2016 (IDPC, 2016a) to express the concern that the UNGASS process had failed to be the 'wide-ranging and open debate that considers all options' called for by UN Secretary-General Ban Ki Moon in 2013 (UN, 2013b) given the 'non-inclusive and non-transparent nature' of the preparatory process. The letter also heavily criticised the inability of member states to recognise the 'lack of progress achieved by international drug control over the past 50 years', alongside the failure 'to acknowledge the damage caused by current approaches'.

At the UNGASS itself, however, the many procedural frustrations that had marked the preparations, and the final access issues for civil society, could not mute the clear impact of the reform messages that came through in the debates (IDPC, 2016c). The outcome document was essentially agreed in advance of the UNGASS (another point of frustration for civil society) and was adopted by consensus at the start of the session before the debate began, but that was largely the point at which the so-called 'spirit of consensus' ended.

Immediately following the adoption of the document, there were nine statements from governments and regional groups to express dissatisfaction with the outcome document noting issues that had not survived the negotiations such as the abolition of the death penalty for drug offences, decriminalisation and references to allowing traditional use (IDPC, 2016).

In the following three days, one could observe government representatives constantly contradicting one another on the basic premises of drug control (Lai, 2013). Russia, Singapore, Pakistan, Iran and South Africa vehemently opposed the 'defeatist' idea that the fight against drugs had been lost. But these views, although perhaps more entrenched than ever, were no longer the dominant voices. President Santos of Colombia, who had in fact led the call for this debate in the first place stated:

> The question we have to ask, looking at the efforts made over years, over decades, over a century is this: After so many lives that have been destroyed, after so much corruption and so much violence and after so many young people being marched off to jail – can we say that we have won the war? Or could we at least say we are winning it? Unfortunately, the answer is no. We have not won the war and we are not winning it now. (IDPC, 2016b)

Other countries as diverse as Tanzania, Jamaica, Costa Rica, Canada, Argentina, Bolivia, Lichtenstein, New Zealand amongst others echoed this sentiment. St Vincent and the Grenadines gave one of the most damning statements of the session:

> 'The road out of this cul de sac of trite, ineffective rhetoric requires an approach that is focused not on drugs but on the people and populations affected by addiction, abuse, violence and fear. It demands the courage of new thinking and innovative approaches. Ten years from today, let it not be said that the international community continued to delude itself about the efficacy of its war on drugs.[26]

On many issues there were prominent divisions in the positions put forward by member states, but the tables were tipped in favour of more progressive views. On the long-fought issue of harm reduction, an unprecedented forty-seven member states spoke out explicitly in favour of the approach while only two registered their direct opposition to it.[27] On the issue of the death penalty, 66 states called for an end to its use for drug offences, while 16 dug their heels in. Nine countries spoke out in favour of legal regulation, including some that called for an examination of the current drug control treaty framework, while 14 spoke out against it.

Further reinforcing the message that reform was crucial, most UN officials who addressed the UNGASS highlighted both the human damage and the failure of punitive drug policies.[28] Their statements repeated the same messages made in their written contributions (Hallam, 2016) submitted during the preparations. Compared with the last UNGASS in 1998, no UN officials openly supported the 'harmful concept of a "drug-free world"' (Office of the High Commissioner on Human Rights (OHCHR), 2016).

---

[26]Gonsalves, C. M., Statement by Camillo M. Gonsalves, Minister of Economic Planning, Sustainable Development, Industry, Information and Labour, St. Vincent and the Grenadines, Special Session of the UN General Assembly on the World Drug Problem, New York, 21 April 2016.

[27]In favour of harm reduction: Belgium, Brazil, Canada, Colombia, Cyprus, Czech Republic, Denmark, Ecuador, European Union, Finland, Georgia, Germany, Ghana, Iran, Israel, Latvia, Luxembourg, Macedonia, Maldives, Malta, Netherlands, New Zealand, Norway, Romania, Slovenia, Sweden, Tunisia, United States, Uruguay, Vietnam, Austria, Bulgaria, Croatia, Estonia, France, Greece, Hungary, Ireland, Italy, Lithuania, Luxembourg, Poland, Portugal, Slovakia, Spain and United Kingdom. Against: Singapore and China.

[28]The High Commissioner for Human Rights statement was particularly sharp in this regard. See 'Remarks Mr. ZeidRa'ad Al Hussein, United Nations High Commissioner for Human Rights at United Nations Special Session on the world drug problem'. Retrieved from http://www.druglawreform.info/en/un-drug-control/ungass/item/7080-remarks-mr-zeid-raad-al-hussein-united-nations-high-commissioner-for-human-rights.

In recognition that the UNGASS had been overwhelming marked by calls for reform, the President of the General Assembly, Mogens Lykketoft, highlighted civil society contributions in his closing remarks (UN, 2016):

> With your experience and expertise, you have brought home to us the immense human cost of this problem and indeed, at times, of the approaches we take to address it.

He also acknowledged that affected populations 'need interventions that have proven to work and perhaps as importantly: they need honesty about those that have failed'. It was an unprecedented admission of the failure of drug control policies in the highest possible UN setting.

Gains and Lessons Learned

The immediate aftermath of the UNGASS was marked by disappointment. The Global Commission on Drug Policy led the charge, holding a press conference on the day after and calling the UNGASS a failure and a missed opportunity (Godfrey, 2016). Some actors who had built expectations of 2016 as the end of the 'war on drugs' felt disappointed. In a more nuanced way, many civil society reformers also felt that once again member states had failed to leverage a key opportunity to fundamentally shift course on drug policy. However, some groups that have closely followed the UN debates for over decade or more, recognised that a significant shift had taken place (Fordham, 2016). It seemed that while the Outcome Document had not met expectations, opportunities had been created for continuing the momentum towards reform (Bewley-Taylor & Jelsma, 2016).

In fact, the broader view of the UNGASS Outcome Document has shifted over the past two years, and it is now viewed much more favourably. In the context of the UN drug control debates, it is seen as a forward-looking document with clear progress on human rights, health, harm reduction, access to controlled medicines, proportionate sentencing and appropriate criminal justice responses, gender and development. The structure of the document represents an important shift away from the traditional three pillars enshrined in the 2009 Political Declaration and Action Plan (demand reduction, supply reduction and money laundering) towards a new seven-theme structure that includes specific themes on access to controlled medicines, human rights and gender and development. The actual UNGASS debates marked an irrevocable break in the long revered global consensus on punitive drug control, with member states in open disagreement with each other in New York despite adopting the Outcome Document under the guise of consensus.

Reform-orientated civil society had a significant impact on the UNGASS – both on the gains in the Outcome Document and at the actual event. The UNGASS demonstrated that civil society actors can have a real impact on the tone of the debate. Strategic advocacy efforts that chime with the objectives of progressive member states can bear fruit. It is clear, however, that the most impactful ways to influence have been through reform advocacy efforts outside of the official civil society mechanisms.[29] The products of the official civil society structures such as the PGA's report of the Informal Interactive Stakeholder Consultation or the report of the CSTF (both hard-fought-for and intensive products) were never formally considered or discussed in the preparations. This is still a serious challenge for broader civil society efforts to influence the debates through the official channels.

As reform groups have had time to reflect back on the UNGASS process and outcomes, other lessons have emerged. The widespread disappointment from many civil society actors after the UNGASS now seems misplaced given the shift in how the Outcome Document is perceived. It could be said that civil society might have managed their own expectations better, which may have resulted in a more muted response in the aftermath; however, it is only with the passing of time that such perspectives emerge. The ambition of reform groups towards the UNGASS had a significant and positive impact, and the flipside of that ambition is naturally some initial disappointment with falling somewhat short of the mark. Would it have been better not to have been so ambitious? Undoubtedly not, given the current state of the debate. The UNGASS Outcome Document is under serious attack at the time of writing,[30] with the core of the 'status quo'-oriented member states fighting to roll back on the gains that it represents by seeking to ensure that the 2009 Political Declaration and Action Plan has primacy over the Outcome Document as they look towards the next decade of international drug control beyond 2019.

The Way Forward to 2019 and Beyond

Reform-orientated civil society organisations have made great strides in the last decade. Much of this success has been built on the increasing international solidarity, shared objectives, collaboration and networking. The IDPC has galvanised and mobilised civil society organisations from all over the world in a clear example of a successful transnational advocacy network with 'shared values, a common discourse and dense exchanges of information' (Keck & Sikkink, 1998, p. 2). The drug policy reform movement, while still relatively young, has gained in strength, diversity, visibility and credibility – and the recent momentum of the UNGASS has been a major catalyst for this. There is now solid and fertile ground on which to continue to grow the movement. Drug policy reform is increasingly being seen as one of the key social justice issues of the times and new actors from different disciplines and sectors are increasingly joining the calls for change. The 'Support. Don't Punish'[31] campaign has brought together diverse voices from all

---

[29]For example, IDPC advocacy notes or informal inter-governmental 'dialogues' or direct personal communications to government official from civil society advocates.

[30]Just ahead of the 61st session of the CND in March 2018 where the CND will likely negotiate a resolution that points the way forward for beyond 2019.

[31]'Support. Don't Punish' is a global campaign, established in 2013, that was initially grounded in the need to promote harm reduction and decriminalisation. Over the years, diverse groups have joined the campaign from the farmers of crops deemed illicit to cannabis reform organisations. Retrieved from http://supportdontpunish.org/.

over the world under one key message of reform and continues to grow in visibility. The key moment each year being a 'Global Day of Action' taking place on the 26th June to reclaim the message of the International Day Against Drug Abuse and Illicit Trafficking.[32]

Reform-orientated civil society groups must capitalise on the gains made in the UNGASS and continue to use the moral leverage of the human rights arguments to highlight why repressive drug policies must end. A successful element of the strategy has been to link domestic advocacy to global advocacy and there is definitely a scope to improve on this in the coming period. National-level reforms will move faster than the pace of the global debate and will naturally have implications at the UN level.

The important progress made on the balance and structure of civil society organisation around the 2016 UNGASS – from the reorganisation of the NYNGOC to the formation and functioning of the Civil Society Task Force – must also be retained and built upon. Immediately after UNGASS, there was a certain amount of backlash against the new more collaborative relationship amongst the two NGO committees and civil society as a whole and a desire by some to return to the 'Vienna monopoly'. However, the forward momentum after the UNGASS was stronger, and the reform community has continued to push for balance and inclusivity. These efforts have paid off as a new civil society task force for the high level ministerial segment was convened (again after more than a year of negotiations), and the balance on the NGO committees themselves has finally significantly shifted.[33]

In light of the move towards integration of drug policy with the 2030 Agenda, human rights and other UN processes, the 'Vienna monopoly', is simply no longer sustainable. The trend amongst civil society groups organised around global issues is a move away from leadership centred in the north towards decentralisation and regional leadership. The CoNGO itself is now encouraging the formation of regional groups; the Committee on the Status of Women now has four different regional groups in addition to its New York, Geneva and Vienna committees. The most prominent example of course is the NGO Major Group[34] organised around the 2030 Agenda, which is led by two global organising partners from the north and south, supported by five regional organising partners in Africa, Asia, the Caribbean, Europe and North America. These structures will provide useful models for the civil society community around drugs as it looks to a future beyond 2019.

[32]By resolution 42/112 of 7 December 1987, the General Assembly decided to observe 26 June as the International Day against Drug Abuse and Illicit Trafficking as an expression of its determination to strengthen action and cooperation to achieve the goal of an international society free of drug abuse. Retrieved from http://www.un.org/en/events/drugabuseday/.

[33]In March 2018, for the first time in its 35-year history, a representative from the reform community was elected as the Chair of the VNGOC.

[34]See http://www.ngomg.org.

The UNGASS has proved that ambition is important in order to affect a lasting change, and like all great social movements, advocates must push far beyond what they think is immediately possible. The increasing polarisation between more progressive and human rights friendly member states and more repressive, 'status-quo' ones, creates the opportunity to keep trying to force a real, honest debate about the future of drug policies and make adherence to the status quo of repressive and damaging policies untenable. Resistance to the UNGASS from more repressive states is very likely to be because the Outcome Document has opened the door, more firmly than ever before, to ensuring more human rights accountability and oversight. The OHCHR has stepped up its engagement on this issue and the High Commissioner himself has become increasingly more outspoken regarding the abuses relating to the 'war on drugs'.[35] This shift in norms has changed the terms of the debate in Vienna and although the pace of change at the UN is always slow, the direction of travel is clear (IDPC, 2017).

Looking forward to the next moment in global drug policy in 2019, the battle lines have already been drawn. The 2009 Political Declaration and Plan of Action was agreed for 10 years and outlined targets focussed on significantly 'reducing or eliminating' the global drug market by 2019.[36] As member states begin to negotiate both the review process of evaluating progress against these targets and what comes next, progressive countries want to move away from the targets set out in the 2009 Political Declaration and Action Plan while less forward-looking governments are pushing to reaffirm these targets. These 'drug-free' targets are not only unachievable and unrealistic but also underpin damaging and repressive measures.[37] In these coming years, reform-orientated civil society effort must be to continue to 'beat the drum', speak truth to power and leverage the growing international solidarity on this critical social justice and human rights issue of our times.

[35]UN High Commissioner for Human Rights (2018), '"High Commissioner's global update of human rights concerns" 37th session of the Human Rights Council. Item 2: Annual Report and Oral Update by the High Commissioner for Human Rights on the activities of his Office and recent human rights developments. Statement by the UN High Commissioner for Human Rights, Zeid Ra'ad Al Hussein' (7 March 2018). Retrieved from http://www.ohchr.org/EN/NewsEvents/Pages/DisplayNews.aspx?NewsID=22772&LangID=E.

[36]2009 Political Declaration and Plan of Action on International Cooperation towards an Integrated and Balanced Strategy to Counter the World Drug Problem. The targets are outlined in operational paragraph 36 of the Political Declaration. Retrieved from https://www.unodc.org/documents/commissions/CND/CND_Sessions/CND_52/Political-Declaration2009_V0984963_E.pdf.

[37]See http://www.scmp.com/news/asia/southeast-asia/article/2091724/duterte-opens-manila-summit-call-drug-free-asia for how Philippines President Duterte has called for a drug-free ASEAN while simultaneously sanctioning extra-judicial killings of suspected drug offenders in the Philippines. In January 2018, Human Rights Watch reported that there had been over 12,000 extra-judicial killings in the Philippines since Duterte began his 'drug war' in June 2016 (https://www.hrw.org/world-report/2018).

References

Bewley-Taylor, D., & Jelsma, M. (2016). *UNGASS 2016: A broken or B-r-o-a-d consensus?* Retrieved from https://www.swansea.ac.uk/media/Broken%20or%20broad_FINAL.pdf

Bewley-Taylor, D., & Woodiwiss, M. (2005). *The global fix: The construction of a global enforcement regime*. Policy Briefing 13. Amsterdam, The Netherlands: Transnational Institute.

Blickman, T. (2014). *Cannabis policy reform in Europe – Bottom up rather than top down*. Retrieved from https://www.tni.org/files/download/dlr28.pdf

Bruun, K., Pan, L., & Rexed, I. (1975). *The Gentlemen's Club: International control of drugs and alcohol*. In Studies in Crime and Justice Series. Chicago, IL: The University of Chicago Press.

Canadian Drug Policy Coalition. (2016). *Join the global initiative stop the harm*. Retrieved from http://drugpolicy.ca/take-action/campaigns/join-the-stop-the-harm-global-initiative/

Cook, C. (2009). *Civil society: The silenced partners?* London: International Harm Reduction Association.

Drug Policy Alliance (DPA). (2016). *A public letter to UN Secretary General Ban Ki-moon*. New York, NY: DPA. Retrieved from http://www.drugpolicy.org/publications-resources/sign-letters/public-letter-kofi-annan/ungass-world-drug-problem

Easton, M. (2009). Give drug users a break. *BBC News*. Retrieved from http://www.bbc.co.uk/blogs/thereporters/markeaston/2009/06

Economic and Social Council of the United Nations (ECOSOC). (1964). *CND report of the 19th session*, E/CN.7/466. New York, NY: ECOSOC.

Economic and Social Council of the United Nations (ECOSOC). (1976). *CND report of the fourth special session*, E/CN.7/587. New York, NY: ECOSOC.

Economic and Social Council of the United Nations (ECOSOC). (1981). *CND report of the 29th session*, E/CN.7/668. New York, NY: ECOSOC.

Economic and Social Council of the United Nations (ECOSOC). (1984). *CND report of the eighth special session*, E/CN.7/1984/13. New York, NY: ECOSOC.

Economic and Social Council of the United Nations (ECOSOC). (1988). *CND report of the tenth special session*, E/CN.7/1988/14. New York, NY: ECOSOC.

Economic and Social Council of the United Nations (ECOSOC). (1996a). *CND report on the 39th session*, E/CN.7/1996/19. New York, NY: ECOSOC.

Economic and Social Council of the United Nations (ECOSOC). (1996b). *List of participants, second session of the special session of the General Assembly devoted to the fight against the illicit production, sale, demand, traffic and distribution of narcotic drugs and psychotropic substances and related activities*, E/CN.7/1998/PC/INF.1. New York, NY: ECOSOC.

Economic and Social Council of the United Nations (ECOSOC). (2003). *CND report of the 46th session*, E/CN.7/2003/19. New York, NY: ECOSOC.

Economic and Social Council of the United Nations (ECOSOC). (2005). *CND report of the 48th session*, E/CN.7/2005/11. New York, NY: ECOSOC.

European Coalition for Just and Effective Drug Policies (ENCOD). (1998). *UNGASS report: Some observations for ENCOD and ICN*. Antwerp, Belgium: ENCOD.

European Coalition for Just and Effective Drug Policies (ENCOD). (2007). *Manifesto for just and effective drug policy*. Antwerp, Belgium: ENCOD. Retrieved from http://www.encod.org/info/MANIFESTO-FOR-JUST-AND-EFFECTIVE.html

Fordham, A. (2016). The drugs consensus is not pretty – It's been ripped apart at the seams. *Huffington Post*. Retrieved from http://www.huffingtonpost.co.uk/ann-fordham/drug-policy_b_9819900.html

Godfrey, W. (2016). *Global Commission slams UNGASS 2016 outcome that strains the credibility of international law*. Retrieved from http://www.globalcommissionondrugs.org/21-april-2016-global-commission-slams-ungass-2016-outcome-that-strains-the-credibility-of-international-law/

Gonsalves, C. M. (2016). Statement by Camillo M. Gonsalves, Minister of Economic Planning, Sustainable Development, Industry, Information and Labour, St. Vincent and the Grenadines, Special Session of the UN General Assembly on the World Drug Problem, New York, 21 April 2016.

Goode, E., & Ben-Yehuda, N. (1994). The American drug panic of the 1980s. In *Moral Panics: The Social Construction of Deviance* (p. 12). Oxford, UK: Blackwell Publishing.

Hallam, C. (March, 2016). *IDPC briefing paper – Striving for system-wide coherence: An analysis of the official contributions of United Nations entities for the UNGASS on drugs*. London: International Drug Policy Consortium. Retrieved from http://idpc.net/publications/2016/03/striving-for-system-wide-coherence-an-analysis-of-the-official-contributions-of-united-nations-entities-for-the-ungass-on-drugs

International Drug Policy Consortium (IDPC). (2007). *The United Nations review of global policy on illegal drugs – An advocacy guide for civil society*. London: IDPC. Retrieved from http://fileserver.idpc.net/library/IDPC_Advocacy_v2_Dec2007.pdf

International Drug Policy Consortium (IDPC). (2008). *The 2008 Commission on Narcotic Drugs – Report of the proceedings*. London: IDPC. Retrieved from http://fileserver.idpc.net/library/IDPC_BP_08_RptProcedings2008CND_EN.pdf

International Drug Policy Consortium (IDPC). (2012). *Statement by the Argentina Minister of Health at CND on 16th March 2012 (English), CND Blog*. London: IDPC. Retrieved from http://cndblog.org/2012/03/statement-by-the-argentina-minister-of-health-at-cnd-on-16th-march-2012-english/

International Drug Policy Consortium (IDPC). (2013). *Launching the debate: The OAS reports on hemispheric drug policy*. London: IDPC. Retrieved from http://fileserver.idpc.net/library/IDPC_advocacy-note_Launching-the-debate-OAS-reports.pdf

International Drug Policy Consortium (IDPC). (2015). *The road to UNGASS 2016: Process and policy asks from the IDPC*. Retrieved from http://idpc.net/publications/2014/10/the-road-to-ungass-2016-process-and-policy-asks-from-idpc

International Drug Policy Consortium (IDPC). (2016). *UNGASS: Thirtieth special session of the General Assembly on the world drug problem (5th plenary meeting)*. London: IDPC. Retrieved from http://cndblog.org/2016/04/ungass-thirtieth-special-session-of-the-general-assembly-on-the-world-drug-problem-5th-plenary-meeting/

International Drug Policy Consortium (IDPC). (2016a). *Civil society statement the UNGASS outcome document: Diplomacy ordenialism?* London: IDPC. Retrieved from http://idpc.net/alerts/2016/03/civil-society-statement-on-the-ungass

International Drug Policy Consortium (IDPC). (2016b). *Negotiating the UNGASS outcome document: Challenges and the way forward*. London: IDPC. Retrieved from http://fileserver.idpc.net/library/IDPC_Advocacy_Note_UNGASS-process_February_2016.pdf

International Drug Policy Consortium (IDPC). (2016c). *The United Nations General Assembly Special Session (UNGASS) on the world drug problem – Report of proceedings*. London: IDPC. Retrieved from http://fileserver.idpc.net/library/UNGASS-proceedings-document_ENGLISH.pdf

Jelsma, M. (2005). *Background on the United Nations General Assembly Special Session on drug control*. Amsterdam, The Netherlands: Transnational Institute. Retrieved from https://www.tni.org/en/archives/act/1596#3a

International Drug Policy Consortium (IDPC). (2017). *Edging forward: How the UN's language on drugs has advanced since 1990*. London: IDPC. Retrieved from http://idpc.net/publications/2017/09/edging-forward-how-the-un-s-language-on-drugs-has-advanced-since-1990

Jelsma, M. (2008). *Beyond 2008 – A truly remarkable event*. Amsterdam, The Netherlands: Transnational Institute. Retrieved from https://www.tni.org/en/article/beyond-2008-a-truly-remarkable-event

Jelsma, M. (2015). *UNGASS 2016: Prospects for treaty reform and UN system-wide coherence on drug policy*'. Brookings Institute, Center for 21st Century Security and Intelligence Latin American Initiative. Retrieved from https://www.tni.org/files/download/treaty_reform_drug_policy_ungass2016.pdf

Jelsma, M., & Kramer, T. (2005). *Downward spiral: Banning opium in Afghanistan and Burma*. Policy Briefing 12. Amsterdam, The Netherlands: Transnational Institute.

Keck, M. E., & Sikkink, K. (1998). *Activists beyond borders: Advocacy Networks in International Politics*. Ithaca, NY: Cornell University Press.

Krasovitzky, L., & Lewis, T. (2017). *'No more drug war' Caravan to visit five impacted countries on way to UN session in NY. Huffpost*. Retrieved from https://www.huffingtonpost.com/laura-krasovitzky/no-more-drug-war-caravan-_b_9548024.html

Lai, G. (2016). *Delusion and disillusion at the global UN meeting on drugs*. Retrieved from http://idpc.net/blog/2016/04/delusion-and-disillusion-at-the-global-un-meeting-on-drugs

New York Times. (2005). *Ideology and AIDs*. Retrieved from http://www.nytimes.com/2005/02/26/opinion/ideology-and-aids.html

NGO Committee on Narcotics and Substance Abuse. (1994). *Bangkok declaration. New York, 1994*. Retrieved from http://www.uitti.net/unngonsa/1994NGOBangkok.htm

Organisation of American States (OAS). (2012). *Scenario for the drug problem in the Americas 2013–2025*. New York, NY: OAS. Retrieved from http://www.oas.org/documents/eng/press/Scenarios_Report.PDF

Organisation of American States (OAS). (2013). *The drug problem in the Americas*. New York, NY: OAS. Retrieved from http://www.oas.org/documents/eng/press/Introduction_and_Analytical_Report.pdf

Office of the High Commissioner on Human Rights (OHCHR). (2016). *Joint open letter by the UN Working Group on arbitrary detention*. United Nations, OHCHR. Retrieved from http://www.ohchr.org/EN/NewsEvents/Pages/DisplayNews.aspx?NewsID=19828&LangID=E

Roberts, D. (2013). Eric Holder calls for criminal justice reforms aimed at easing drug sentences. *The Guardian*. Retrieved from https://www.theguardian.com/world/2013/aug/12/eric-holder-prison-reform-mandatory-minimums

Transnational Institute (TNI). (March, 1998). *Background briefing on UNGASS*. Amsterdam, The Netherlands: TNI.

Transnational Institute (TNI). (1998). *Caught in the crossfire*. Retrieved from https://www.tni.org/en/publication/caught-in-the-crossfire

United Nations (UN). (2011). *Coordinated United Nations-led action needed to tackle transnational criminal networks, world body's anti-drugs chief tells Security Council*. New York, NY: UN. Retrieved from http://www.un.org/press/en/2011/sc10295.doc.htm

United Nations (UN). (2013a). *Resolution adopted by the General Assembly on 23 April 2013*. Retrieved from https://www.unodc.org/documents/commissions/CND/Drug_Resolutions/2010-2019/2012/GA_Res-67-193.pdf

United Nations (UN). (2013b). *Secretary-General's remarks at special event on the International day against drug abuse and illicit trafficking*. New York, NY: UN. Retrieved from https://www.un.org/sg/en/content/sg/statement/2013-06-26/secretary-generals-remarks-special-event-international-day-against

United Nations (UN). (2015). *Resolution adopted by the General Assembly on 23 April 2013*. New York, NY: UN. Retrieved from http://www.un.org/en/ga/search/view_doc.asp?symbol=A/RES/69/200

United Nations (UN). (2016). *Concluding remarks UN General Assembly Special Session on world drug problem*. Retrieved from https://www.un.org/pga/70/2016/04/22/concluding-remarks-un-general-assembly-special-session-on-world-drug-problem/

United Nations Development Programme (UNDP). (2015). *Perspectives on the development dimensions of drug control policy*. New York, NY: UNDP. Retrieved from http://www.unodc.org/documents/ungass2016//Contributions/UN/UNDP/UNDP_paper_for_CND_March_2015.pdf

United Nations Office of Drugs and Crime (UNODC). (2004). *Letter on harm reduction*. Vienna, Austria: UNODC. Retrieved from http://idpc.net/publications/2004/08/dear-bobby-unodc-letter-on-harm-reduction

United Nations Office of Drugs and Crime (UNODC). (2005). *An open letter to the delegates of the forty-eighth session of the CND*. Vienna, Austria: UNODC. Retrieved from http://www.undrugcontrol.info/images/stories/cnd010305_open_letter.pdf

United Nations Office of Drugs and Crime (UNODC). (2008). *Beyond 2008 declaration*. Vienna, Austria: UNODC. Retrieved from https://www.unodc.org/documents/NGO/B2008_Declaration_and_Resolutions_English.pdf

United Nations Office of Drugs and Crime (UNODC). (2014). *Statement of the UNODC Executive Director, Yury Fedotov, on World AIDS Day*. Vienna, Austria: UNODC. Retrieved from https://www.unodc.org/unodc/en/press/releases/2014/November/statement-of-the-unodc-executive-director--yury-fedotov--on-world-aids-day.html

United Nations Office of Drugs and Crime (UNODC). (2016). *UN System Task Force on Transnational Organised Crime and Drug Trafficking*. Vienna, Austria: UNODC. Retrieved from http://www.unodc.org/ungass2016/en/contributions/UN/un-system-task-force.html

Urban Institute. (2016). *Transforming prisons, restoring lives*. Retrieved from https://www.urban.org/research/publication/transforming-prisons-restoring-lives/view/full_report

Chapter 2

The Death Penalty for Drug Offences: Pulling Back the Curtain to Expose a Flawed Regime

Gen Sander and Rick Lines

Abstract

The intersection between drug control and the death penalty represents a key nexus for human rights and drug reform advocacy and constitutes one of the most visible examples of the link between abusive law enforcement and drug control in the current period. The issue has emerged as a flashpoint of international debates on drugs and is one that raises important questions and challenges for both 'abolitionist' countries that oppose the death penalty and 'retentionist' States that continue to execute people. The death penalty for drug offences cannot be dismissed as simply an internal matter for States. Not only do executions for drug offences violate significant international human rights legal protections, domestic capital punishment laws in many cases cannot be separated from the influence of the international drug control treaty regime. This chapter will explore the question of the death penalty for drug offences and the challenges it presents for the international drug control regime more broadly.[1]

Keywords: Death penalty; drug offences; human rights; drug enforcement; International drug control regime; corporal punishment

The death penalty for drug offences is one of the most significant and politically charged issues within the current global drug reform debate. As described by one leading scholar, 'the death penalty, today as in the past, symbolises the ultimate

[1]Parts of this chapter have been published in the Global Overview https://www.hri.global/files/2018/03/06/HRI-Death-Penalty-Report-2018.pdf.

Collapse of the Global Order on Drugs: From UNGASS 2016 to Review 2019, 49–63

doi:10.1108/978-1-78756-487-920181002

power of the state, and of the government of society, over the individual citizen' (Bedau, 1987). At the same time, drug control – as both a policy objective and body of law – serves to legitimise and centralise the authority of the State. Indeed, the shared international mission to suppress drug use and drug markets provides not only an operational framework through which the State can exercise coercive social control – including capital punishment – but also an ideological and moral justification for those control measures. The intersection between drug control and capital punishment therefore represents a key nexus for human rights and drug reform advocacy and constitutes one of the most visible examples of the link between abusive law enforcement and drug control in the current period. The issue has emerged as a flashpoint of international debates on drugs, such as the 2016 United Nations General Assembly Special Session (UNGASS) on the world drug problem, and is one that raises important questions and challenges for both 'abolitionist' countries that oppose the death penalty and 'retentionist' States that continue to execute people.

While nearly invisible within the drug control discourse a decade ago, debates on the death penalty have in recent years dominated the United Nations drug regime. Both the United Nations Office on Drugs and Crime and International Narcotics Control Board have moved from silence to public opposition to the practice. Annual meetings of the United Nations Commission on Narcotic Drugs and the 2016 UNGASS have become fora for sometimes heated debates between abolitionist and retentionist governments. At the same time, the UN human rights mechanisms, experts and bodies have slowly begun to embrace considerations of drug enforcement within their mandates, with the Office of the UN High Commissioner on Human Rights playing a particularly vocal role on the death penalty and other abuses linked to drug control.

Despite the growing chorus calling for its abolition, a small and increasingly isolated group of countries continues to kill hundreds of people for drug offences every year (Sander, 2018). Indeed, at the same time that high-level debates on the death penalty for drugs have become more common, many of these retentionist States have stepped up their rates of executions, showing the disconnect that often exists between global policy discourse and the domestic behaviour of States. However, the death penalty for drug offences cannot be dismissed as simply an internal matter for States. Not only do executions for drug offences violate significant international human rights legal protections, as will be explored below, domestic capital punishment laws in many cases cannot be separated from the influence of the international drug control treaty regime. This chapter will explore the question of the death penalty for drug offences and the challenges it presents for the international drug control regime more broadly.

The Death Penalty for Drug Offences in International Law

The application of the death penalty for drug-related offences gives rise to a host of serious human rights concerns. While the use of capital punishment is not absolutely prohibited under international human rights law, its lawful application is subject to significant restrictions and safeguards (United Nations Economic and

Social Council, 1984). The most substantive of these is found in Article 6(2) of the International Covenant on Civil and Political Rights (1966), which states that '[i]n countries which have not abolished the death penalty, sentence of death may be imposed only for the most serious crimes'. Since the Covenant entered into force in 1976, the interpretation of 'most serious crimes' has been refined and clarified by UN human rights bodies in an effort to limit the number of offences for which a death sentence can be lawfully applied (Lines, 2010). Today, it is widely accepted by human rights authorities that the term 'most serious crimes' must be understood to mean crimes involving lethal intent and resulting in death – in other words, intentional killing (Heyns, 2012; United Nations Human Rights Committee, 1993).

The question then becomes, do drug offences (absent those that include violence) meet the threshold of 'most serious crimes' under international human rights law? The clear consensus among the leading human rights authorities is that they do not. The UN Human Rights Committee, the body mandated to interpret the Covenant and monitor its implementation at national level, has on several occasions concluded that drug offences cannot be characterised as 'most serious crimes' (Lines, 2010; United Nations Human Rights Committee, 2005, 2007). This position has been supported by the UN Secretary General (2015), UN Special Rapporteurs on extrajudicial, summary or arbitrary executions (Alston, 2007; Ndiaye, 1997), the former UN Special Rapporteur on torture and other cruel, inhuman or degrading treatment or punishment, Manred Nowak (2009), and the former UN Special Rapporteur on the right of everyone to the highest attainable standard of health (Grover, 2010), among others (United Nations Office of the High Commissioner for Human Rights, 2015; United Nations Working Group on Arbitrary Detention, 2016). This clear legal consensus affirms that the application of the death penalty to drug-related crimes constitutes a violation of the right to life. In recent years, this position has also been adopted by key international drug control bodies, including the United Nations Office on Drugs and Crime (2016) and International Narcotics Control Board (2016).

Another human rights safeguard restricting the lawful application of the death penalty relates to fair trials. Broadly speaking, the death penalty can only be lawfully carried out pursuant to a final judgment by a competent court (International Covenant on Civil and Political Rights, 1966). As former Special Rapporteurs on summary executions and torture, Juan Mendez and Christof Heyns (2015), recently reminded governments, 'in many States where the death penalty is used for drug-related offences, there is not a system of fair trial'. This is most blatant in countries that impose mandatory death penalties for drug offences, but even in countries where this is not required by law, sentencing practices tend to fall far short of international fair trial standards when it comes to drug-related offences. For example, concerns about fair trial norms in China have been raised with regard to confessions made under coercion or torture. Similar allegations have been documented in a number of contexts including, but by no means limited to, Iran, Saudi Arabia and Indonesia (Amnesty International, 2015, 2016). Without this fair trial safeguard, it is impossible to protect against the arbitrary and thus unlawful deprivation of life, which is, with torture and other ill treatment and punishment, absolutely prohibited under customary international law. It also makes it impossible to protect against discrimination.

Indeed, there are deep disparities in how capital drug laws are applied. Very often, foreign nationals comprise a majority or even totality of those sentenced to death and/or executed by the State. In these circumstances, there are major concerns of discriminatory law enforcement practices and sentencing, as well as failures to honour due process norms and provide access to consular assistance (Gallahue, 2011). In 2009, the UN Special Rapporteur on extrajudicial, summary or arbitrary executions, Phillip Alston, observed that:

> the fact that four out of five prisoners awaiting execution on drugs trafficking charges [in Indonesia] are foreigners raises certain questions in terms of possible discrimination in relation to both criminal enforcement and sentencing in drug-related cases.

Indeed, Indonesian national law stipulates that an application for a constitutional review of any provision in law can only be made by an Indonesian national, evidence that discrimination is actually enshrined in law. The result, of course, has been the rejection for constitutional reviews submitted by foreign nationals, mostly in relation to capital drug offences, in clear violation of the obligation to ensure equality before the law and equal protection of the law without discrimination, including on the basis of nationality (Amnesty International, 2015). In 2015, an application for a constitutional review of the legality of this law was submitted on behalf of six individuals on death row, including Myuran Sukumaran and Andrew Chan, two Australian nationals charged with drug trafficking. The first hearing was scheduled for 20 May 2015, but they were executed on 29 April 2015 (Amnesty International, 2015). The terrible hypocrisy is that several States that execute foreign nationals for drug offences, including Indonesia, routinely plead for clemency for their own nationals on death row for drug offences in other countries.

It is worth noting that an increasing number of States, human rights authorities and national, constitutional and regional courts have voiced their opinion that the death penalty is cruel, inhuman and degrading treatment not reconcilable with the inherent right to physical and mental integrity and human dignity (Mendez, 2012a). The former Special Rapporteur on torture, Juan Mendez (2012a, 2012b), has very convincingly argued that the death penalty is increasingly seen in any context to be contrary to an emerging customary norm that the imposition and enforcement of the death penalty is a breach of the absolute prohibition of torture or cruel, inhuman or degrading treatment or punishment. Even if the emergence of this customary norm is still under way, most conditions under which the death penalty is actually applied render the punishment tantamount to torture (Mendez, 2012a).

The Influence of International Drug Control Law on the Growth of the Death Penalty

The death penalty for drug offences is not simply a matter of national concern, evolving separately to and apart from the international drug control regime. For many of the States actively executing drug offenders, the practice is a relatively modern legal development, having adopted these laws from the 1980s onwards. Rather than reflecting long-standing domestic legislation, these policies can instead be linked to the drafting and adoption of the 1988 Convention against Illicit Traffic in Narcotic Drugs and Psychotropic Substances, the third UN drug treaty. Significantly, the 1988 Convention establishes obligations on States to use criminal law and penal sanctions as the primary tool for drug suppression at domestic level. The treaty creates State obligations to criminalise the entire market chain, from production and cultivation, to shipment and sale, to (in some cases) possession for personal use. In political terms, these developments fall within the period of the global 'war on drugs', launched by the United States in the early 1970s, which formed the backdrop for the drafting of the treaty.

We can see evidence of change in State approaches to capital punishment for drugs in this time period. A 2001 report of the UN Secretary-General recorded a more than 50 per cent increase in the number of countries prescribing the death penalty for drugs into domestic law between 1985 and 2000 (United Nations Economic Social Council, 2001). This dramatic increase in States applying capital punishment to drug offences ran exactly opposite to the overall international trend towards the abolition of capital punishment documented during that same period (Hood & Hoyle, 2008; Schabas, 2002). In other words, the number of countries using the death penalty for drugs dramatically increased during the same time when the number of countries using the death penalty for any crimes was dramatically decreasing. This dramatic shift in State practice in a relatively short span of fifteen years reflected developments in international drug control law, and the increasingly punitive nature of the regime throughout the 1970s, as codified in the 1988 drug convention. The irony here is obvious, as many death penalty States were all-too-happy to allow domestic laws to be influenced by the UN drug control treaties, while at the same time claiming that UN human rights treaties that prohibit executions for drug offences represent an inappropriate infringement on domestic affairs.

This relatively recent yet dramatic change in State practice also undermines the common argument that capital punishment for drug offences is a traditional or long-standing approach within the domestic legal systems of these countries. Indonesia, which drew widespread condemnation in 2015 when its new President oversaw several mass executions of drug offenders, is a case that neatly proves the fallacy of this argument. Far from being a longstanding or traditional part of the domestic criminal justice system, the death penalty for drug offences in national law was only established in 1976, and the first person ever executed for drug offences was not until in 1995 (Lines, Barrett, & Gallahue, 2015). Indonesia executed five people in total for all offences between 2009 and 2014, all of those occurring in the year 2013 (Lines et al., 2015). In the other five years, the Government executed no one at all. Yet, in the first few months of 2015, the Government executed 14 people, all for drug offences. How do we explain this pattern? Did Indonesian 'traditions' change between 1995 and 2009, then change again in 2009, and again in 2015? Or did the Government, and Government policy, change?

The 1988 drug treaty also offers a significant, although less explored, window onto of the question of 'most serious crimes'. Most capital drug offences found in national legislation objectively fail to meet the threshold of 'most serious crimes' in international human rights law, as they do not even meet the threshold of most severe offences as defined under international drug control law (Lines, 2016). Article 3 of the 1988 drug treaty proscribes a wide range of activities related to the production, cultivation, trafficking, transportation, possession or purchase of illegal drugs, as well as other offences related to laundering of proceeds from the drug trade. It specifies that while all of these offences are 'grave' and 'serious' in nature, there are additional aggravating elements that may elevate these 'serious' offences to the level the treaty defines as 'particularly serious'. These aggravating factors include participation with domestic or international organised criminal groups, the use of violence or firearms, the involvement of minors and/or the collaboration of public officials. Absent these aggravating factors, none of the 'serious' offences in Article 3 satisfy the 'most serious crimes' threshold within international human rights law, for the simple reason that they do not even meet the highest threshold of criminality within the drug control regime itself (Lines, 2016).

The Death Penalty for Drug Offences in Practice

States that have abolished the death penalty have outnumbered those that retain it since the mid-1990s, and this gap between abolitionist and retentionist countries continues to grow. Today, 72 per cent of States – 141 out of 195 – have abolished the death penalty for all crimes in law or in practice (Amnesty International, 2017a), and trends in State practice, the development of international norms and increasing support for a moratorium suggest that abolition could soon become an obligation under customary international law. Nevertheless, a significant number of people are still put to death each year, a large proportion of which are for drug-related offences. Of the 55 States that continue to apply capital punishment, 33 prescribe the death penalty for drug-related offences in law (Sander, 2018). Of these, at least nine countries still have the death penalty for drugs as a mandatory sanction (Sander, 2018).

The exact number of people executed by the State for drug-related crimes every year continues to be very difficult to track, and estimates cannot be considered comprehensive due to the difficulty of sourcing reliable data. The estimates that are available, however, are alarmingly high. For example, between January 2015 and December 2017, at least 1,320 people are known to have been executed for drug offences, with Iran being responsible for 1,176 – or nearly 90 per cent – of these deaths (Sander, 2018). Indeed, Iran continues to execute more people per capita than any other country in the world, with 2015 marking the highest rate of executions in the country in 25 years. While executions appear to have decreased since then, the numbers remain shockingly high. In fact, January 2017 alone saw the execution of 87 people, which is equivalent to one execution every nine hours (Iran Human Rights, 2017a). Drug offences continue to comprise the majority of executions in the country, even though senior Iranian judiciary officials have themselves admitted that the punishment has failed to reduce drug trafficking in the country (Iran Human Rights, 2016). Importantly, the global estimates above exclude China. While still considered to be the world's top executioner by Amnesty International, the death penalty remains a State secret and reliable figures continue to be impossible to source.

Worldwide, the vast majority of known executions continue to be carried out by just a small handful of countries. Indeed, in 2017, only four countries were known to have executed people for drug offences – China, Iran, Saudi Arabia and Singapore – although hundreds and possibly thousands continue to be sentenced to death in these and several other countries, including Malaysia, Indonesia, Thailand and Vietnam. The countries actively executing people for drug offences comprise what has been termed an 'extreme fringe' of the international community (Gallahue & Lines, 2015). However, important legal and policy developments at the national level suggest that even within this 'extreme fringe' the tide may be shifting.

For example, in Thailand, the National Assembly adopted important legislative amendments to the country's Narcotics Law which took effect in January 2017 (Akbar & Lai, 2017). The reforms introduced reductions in penalties for possession, import/export and production for the sale of drugs, including abolishing the mandatory death penalty for the offence of selling drugs, and include language which will help ensure more proportionate sentencing (Akbar & Lai, 2017; Amnesty International, 2016). In Iran, a critical step towards reducing the use of the death penalty for drug offences was taken in October 2017 when the country's Guardian Council approved a long-debated amendment to the Anti-Narcotics Law that raises the minimum quantity of drugs required to incur capital punishment (Reuters, 2017). Applying to death row prisoners that were charged before the amendment, the new law could help commute the sentences of the estimated 4,000 people on death row for petty drug-related offences (Iran Human Rights, 2017b; Reuters, 2017). And on 30 November 2017, the Malaysian parliament voted to remove the mandatory death penalty for drug offences, giving judges full discretion in sentencing (Channel NewsAsia, 2017). Unfortunately, however, this important legal reform does not apply retroactively (Anand, 2017).

The Death Penalty for Drugs in the Context of Broader Human Rights Violations

While these recent national developments are encouraging, the death penalty for drug offences exists as one example of many serious human rights abuses occurring in the name of drug enforcement and suppression. Since coming to power in June 2016, Philippine President Rodrigo Duterte has carried out a bloody anti-drug campaign that has resulted in the extrajudicial executions of thousands of people accused of using or dealing drugs across the country. It has been claimed that if the current rate of killing continues until Duterte's term ends in 2022, the death toll could reach 60,000 (Murdoch, 2017). Duterte has also taken steps to try to reintroduce the death penalty in the Philippines, making it a legislative priority in Congress. At the time of writing this had not yet gone through and while there has been push back from the Association of South East Asian Nations parliamentarians, the issue is far from being settled domestically. However, as confirmed in the Human Rights Committee's recent General Comment 36 on the right to life, States Parties such as the Philippines that have abolished the death penalty through ratification of the Second Optional Protocol to the Covenant on Civil and Political Rights are barred from reintroducing it (United Nations Human Rights Committee, 2017). Like the Covenant itself, the Second Optional Protocol does not contain termination provisions and States parties cannot denounce it, making the abolition of the death penalty legally irrevocable.

While over 50 governments have condemned these disturbing developments (United Nations Human Rights Council, 2017a, 2017b), others have voiced explicit support for the country's brutal anti-drug campaign (United Nations Human Rights Council, 2017b). The most obvious of these has been Indonesia, where a series of public statements supporting the actions in the Philippines have been made by the Indonesian President, Joko Widodo, as well as other senior government officials. These statements, and Widodo's recent shoot-to-kill order following a series of high-profile drug operations (Soeriaatmadja, 2017), have coincided with an increase in killings in the country (Kline, 2017). Between January and September 2017, 80 suspected drug dealers were killed by police, a sharp increase from the 14 killings in all of 2016 (Sapiie, 2017). Amid this escalation in unlawful killings, Widodo issued a 'shoot-on-sight' policy for drug suspects in October 2017 (Weinberg, 2017). Cambodian Prime Minister Hun Sen, after a state visit by Duterte in January 2017, also launched a crackdown on drugs (Salva, 2017). Although not nearly as violent as Duterte's or Widodo's, it has led to the mass arrest of people who use drugs. As of June 2017, more than 8,000 people had been arrested as part of the sweep and thrown into already severely overcrowded prisons (Salva, 2017). American President Donald Trump also lent his support to Duterte's war on drugs during the ASEAN summit held in November 2017 (PhilStar Global, 2017).

Considering these recent and worrying developments in South East Asia, as well as the explicit support for Duterte's violent campaign voiced by other States, including during the Philippines' recent Universal Periodic Review (United Nations Human Rights Council, 2017), it is possible the Philippines' brutal approach to drugs and culture of impunity could be creating a more tolerant or permissive atmosphere for other States in the region and beyond to adopt similar approaches to drugs (Coca, 2017). At the same time, there could be a surge in retentionist States justifying or legitimising the application of the death penalty for drug offences as the 'judicial', more measured and moderate approach, undoing years of progress and setting a dangerous new precedent (Sander, 2018).

In the context of extreme punishments for drug offences, it is also important to include a brief discussion on the use of corporal punishment, which can be understood as institutionalised physical violence carried out as a disciplinary measure. It has been estimated that over forty countries worldwide maintain corporal punishment as a criminal sanction or as an official disciplinary punishment in different institutional settings (Iakobishvili, 2011). Similar to the opacity around the application of the death penalty for drug offences, it remains quite difficult to obtain reliable data on countries implementing corporal punishment for drug offences in law and in practice. Nevertheless, several States are known to apply the punishment in practice, including but certainly not limited to Malaysia, Iran, Saudi Arabia and Singapore and it is believed that thousands of people convicted of drug offences, including for use and personal possession, are subjected to judicially sanctioned caning, flogging, lashing or whipping every year (Abdorrahman Boroumand Center, 2017; Amnesty International, 2017b; Iakobishvili, 2011).

As the former Special Rapporteur on torture has confirmed, the practice 'can be compared to capital punishment in the sense that, even apart from the physical pain and suffering it might cause, over the last decades it has evolved to be considered a direct assault on the dignity of a person and therefore prohibited by international law' (Nowak, 2009). Indeed, corporal punishment is considered a manifestation of cruel, inhuman and degrading punishment and may even amount to torture depending on the context, both of which are absolutely prohibited under human rights law and recognised as norms of customary international law (Nowak, 2005, 2009). And while the international drug conventions are silent on corporal punishment, nothing can be read within them to permit the application of torture or cruel, inhuman and degrading punishment. In fact, the official commentary on the UN Convention against Illicit Traffic in Narcotic Drugs and Psychotropic Substances confirms that, while the drug conventions allow for 'more strict or severe measures' to be adopted than provided for within their texts, they must be 'subject always to the requirement that such initiatives are consistent with applicable norms of public international law, in particular norms protecting human rights' (Commentary, 1988).

Pulling Back the Curtain: Broader Implications for the Drug Control Regime and 2019

Very few governments actually apply the death penalty for drug offences in practice. They are a small and identifiable group, and they are becoming more and more isolated as explicit opposition to this extreme practice grows. In the last few years, there has been some movement towards removing cooperative assistance to States who continue to execute for drug offences. The UN Office on Drugs and Crimes, for example, stated in a position paper on human rights that if political interventions fail to limit the application of capital punishment, it may have no choice but to employ a temporary freeze or withdrawal of support (United Nations Office on Drugs and Crime, 2012). Similar statements have been made by the European Parliament (2010, para. 65), while the UK, Denmark and Ireland have all pulled funding from Iran's drug control programme due to concerns about the death penalty (RTE News, 2013; The Copenhagen Post, 2013).

Similarly, political support for the abolition of the death penalty is on the rise. Ten years ago, the international drug control regime was largely unconcerned with the application of the death penalty for drug offences. But with the increasing engagement of human rights organisations and mechanisms in drug control issues and forums, the death penalty and other human rights issues have slowly become more visible – and thus increasingly difficult to ignore – within the international drug control regime. For example, never before has the issue received so much attention among Member States at a UN meeting on drug control as at the

UNGASS on the world drug problem convened in April 2016. Although the final UNGASS outcome document was silent on the issue, the death penalty for drug offences was nevertheless one of the most widely and intensely debated issues over the course of the three-day meeting. During the session, over seventy Member States explicitly expressed opposition to the death penalty for drug offences (Sander, 2018).

The tide appears to be shifting. Explicit political support for the abolition of the death penalty for drug offences is rising, and human rights are increasingly recognised as being integral to drug control. But it is not enough for States to simply speak out against capital punishment in the context of drugs and to point fingers at the tiny number of countries that continue to execute people, or apply other inhuman sanctions such as corporal punishment. Rather, governments that rightfully oppose such extreme sanctions must also look honestly at the degree to which their own domestic criminal drug laws reflect, and thereby reinforce, the logic of punitive drug control of which the death penalty is simply the most extreme example.

Corporal punishment and the death penalty for drugs represent the most extreme examples of 'punitive suppression', the logic that the harsher we punish people, the more effectively we will suppress drug use and drug markets (Lines, 2017). Punitive suppression is at the heart of the core UN treaties on drug control, particularly the 1988 Convention. The punishments individual States then choose to impose for drug offences take different forms in different places. While capital and corporal punishment is the norm in a small number of countries, in many others punitive suppression is manifested in other ways, both criminal and administrative. Criminal convictions and incarceration for drugs, mandatory sentencing, felony disenfranchisement, warrantless stop and search policies, mandatory drug testing as a requirement of accessing social welfare or maintaining employment and the legal prohibition of harm reduction services are all far more common internationally than is the death penalty for drugs, yet all these approaches are driven by this same logic (Lines, 2017). This is why the issue of capital punishment for drugs represents a challenge to both retentionist and abolitionist States alike, and indeed to UN drug control agencies such as the UN Office on Drugs and Crime and the International Narcotics Control Board. It also offers a guide for us to understand why the issue has emerged as such a flashpoint in the international arena.

For retentionist governments, the call to end the death penalty for drug offences challenges State power on two plains – the power to control life and death and the power to define moral and social norms around drug use and intoxication. Yet for abolitionist States, the existence of the death penalty for drug offences also poses a challenge to their own domestic drug laws, most of which reflect the same logic of punitive suppression. The clearly extremist and abusive nature of executing people for drug offences pulls back the curtain on the drug control regime as a whole, offering a clear glimpse into the nature of punitive suppression as a policy framework. This, we would argue, explains in part why the issue has come to dominate international drug policy debates – because pulling back that curtain allows us to see clearly the punitive, and often abusive and ineffectual, nature of drug enforcement practices in abolitionist States as well. While we welcome and commend the growing role of States in speaking out against the death penalty, as well as similar statements from both the United Nations Office on Drugs and Crimes and International Narcotics Control Board, we must not lose sight of the degree to which opposition to the death penalty can sit comfortably alongside a defence of the overall drug control regime. This is because, in short, the death penalty makes drug control look bad, and risks bringing the entire global experiment in punitive drug suppression of the past half century into disrepute.

While we absolutely welcome and commend all advocacy for the abolition of the death penalty, the relationship between capital punishment and drug control, and between abolition and drug reform, must be understood within a more complex dynamic. While abolitionist States speaking out against the death penalty are driven by sincerely held human rights principles, absent a similar critique of other forms of punitive suppression within their own domestic laws, these statements can also be viewed as a defence of the wider drug control regime (and the many other abuses, large and small, that take place as a consequence).

However important the cause is, the abolition of the death penalty for drugs does not equal the end of human rights abuses driven by drug enforcement. For this reason, the crucial work of abolishing capital punishment must go hand in hand with broader efforts in all countries to end the use of criminal law and penalties as the policy norm in drug control. Until we acknowledge the flawed logic at the heart of the regime itself, and undo its corrosive effects on drug laws and policies everywhere, we will never end these most extreme practices.

References

Abdorrahman Boroumand Center. (2017, August 21). *Iran's judiciary continues to humiliate and harm citizens with flogging sentences*. Retrieved from https://www.iranrights.org/library/document/3218

Akbar, P., & Lai. G. (2017, February 15). Thailand amends drug law to reduce penalties and ensure more proportionate sentencing. *IDPC Blog*. Retrieved from http://idpc.net/blog/2017/02/thailand-amends-drug-law-to-reduce-penalties-and-ensure-more-proportionate-sentencing

Alston, P. (2007, January). Civil and political rights, including the question of disappearances and summary executions. *Report of the Special Rapporteur on extrajudicial, summary or arbitrary executions to the Human Rights Council*. UN Human Rights Council. UN Doc. A/HRC/4/20.

Alston, P. (2009, 29 May). *Report of the Special Rapporteur on extrajudicial, summary or arbitrary executions*. UN Human Rights Council. UN Doc. A/HRC/11/2/Add.1 (p. 174).

Amnesty International. (2015, October). *Flawed justice – Unfair trials and the death penalty in Indonesia*. London: Amnesty International.

Amnesty International. (2016). *Death sentences and executions*. London: Amnesty International.

Amnesty International. (2017a). *The death penalty in 2016: Facts and figures.* Retrieved from https://www.amnesty.org/en/latest/news/2017/04/death-penalty-2016-facts-and-figures/

Amnesty International. (2017b). *Cooperate or die: Singapore's flawed reforms to the mandatory death penalty.* London: Amnesty International.

Anand, R. (2017, November 30). Parliament removes mandatory death penalty for drug offences, judges to get discretion. *Malaymail Online.* Retrieved from http://www.themalaymailonline.com/malaysia/article/parliament-removes-mandatory-death-penalty-for-drug-offences-judges-to-get#E1OSTwA2sb0QA575.97

Bedau, H. A. (1987). *Death is different: Studies in the morality, law, and politics of capital punishment* (p. 246). Boston: Northeastern University Press.

Channel NewsAsia. (2017, December 1). *Malaysia parliament removes mandatory death penalty for drug offenders.* Retrieved from http://www.channelnewsasia.com/news/asiapacific/malaysia-parliament-removes-mandatory-death-penalty-for-drug-9456748

Coca, N. (2017, July 3). Copy-cat war on drugs in Indonesia. *The New Internationalist.* Retrieved from https://newint.org/sections/agenda/indonesias-drug-war

Commentary on the UN Convention against Illicit Trafficking in Narcotic Drugs and Psychotropic Substances (done at Vienna).(1988, December 20). Art. 3.3.

European Parliament. Resolution of 16 December 2010 on the Annual Report on Human Rights in the World 2009 and the European Union's policy on the matter. *Resolution of the European Parliament.* EUP Doc No P7_TA-PROV(2010)0489, para. 65.

Gallahue, P. (2011). *The death penalty for drug offences: Global overview 2011.* London: Harm Reduction International.

Gallahue, P., & Lines, R. (2015). *Death penalty for drug offences: Global overview 2015 – The extreme fringe of Global Drug Policy.* London: Harm Reduction International.

Grover, A. (2010, August 6). *Right of everyone of the enjoyment of the highest attainable standard of physical and mental health.* Report of UN Special Rapporteur on the right to health, Anand Grover to the United Nations General Assembly. UN Doc. A/65/225, para. 17.

Heyns, C. (2012). *Report of the Special Rapporteur on extrajudicial, summary or arbitrary executions, Christof Heyns, submitted in accordance with resolution 65/208.* UN General Assembly. UN Doc. A/67/275, para. 35.

Hood, R., & Hoyle, C. (2008). *The death penalty: A worldwide perspective* (4th ed.) Oxford: Oxford University Press.

Iakobishvili, E. (2011). *Inflicting harm: Judicial corporal punishment for drug and alcohol offences in selected countries.* London: Harm Reduction International.

International Covenant on Civil and Political Rights. (1966). Adopted and opened for signature, ratification and accession by General Assembly resolution 2200A (XXI) of 16 December 1966, entry into force 23 March 1976, in accordance with Article 49.

International Narcotics Control Board. (2016, August 1). *Press release.* Retrieved from https://www.incb.org/incb/en/news/press-releases/2016/press_release010816.html

Iran Human Rights. (2016, August 30). *Iran judicial official: Death penalty is not a deterrent against drug crimes.* Retrieved from https://iranhr.net/en/articles/2635/

Iran Human Rights. (2017a, February 3). *Iranian authorities execute one person ever 9 hours in January*. Retrieved from https://iranhr.net/en/articles/2783/

Iran Human Rights. (2017b, November 3). *Thousands of Iranian death row inmates to receive sentence reviews under amended drug law*. Retrieved from https://www.iranhumanrights.org/2017/11/thousands-of-iranian-death-row-inmates-to-receive-sentence-reviews-under-amended-drug-law/

Kline, P. (2017, August 23). Duterte's 'drug war' migrates to Indonesia. *Human Rights Watch*. Retrieved from https://www.hrw.org/news/2017/08/23/dutertes-drug-war-migrates-indonesia

Lines, R. (2010). A 'most serious crime?' – The death penalty for drug offences and International Human Rights Law. *Amicus Journal, 12*, 21–28.

Lines, R. (2016, March 3). The death penalty for drug offences: What do the international drug control treaties say about 'most serious crimes'? *Human Rights Centre Blog*, University of Essex. Retrieved from https://hrcessex.wordpress.com/2016/03/03/the-death-penalty-for-drug-offences-what-do-the-international-drug-control-treaties-say-about-most-serious-crimes/.

Lines, R. (2017, May 25). Why pointing a finger at countries with the death penalty for drugs is not enough. *Huffington Post*. Retrieved from https://www.huffingtonpost.co.uk/rick-lines/drug-laws_b_10109286.html.

Lines, R., Barrett, D., & Gallahue, P. (2015). The death penalty for drug offences: 'Asian values' or drug treaty influence? *Opinio Juris*. Retrieved from http://opiniojuris.org/2015/05/21/guest-post-the-death-penalty-for-drug-offences-asian-values-or-drug-treaty-influence/.

Mendez, J. (2012a, August 9). *Interim report of the Special Rapporteur on torture and other cruel, inhuman or degrading treatment or punishment, Juan Mendez*. UN General Assembly. UN Doc. A/67/297.

Mendez, J. (2012b). The death penalty and the absolute prohibition of torture and cruel, inhuman, and degrading treatment or punishment. *Human Rights Brief, 20*(1), 2–6.

Mendez, J., & Heyns, Heyns C. (2015, October 10). *Using the death penalty to fight drug crimes violates international law, UN rights experts warn world day against the death penalty*. Retrieved from http://www.ohchr.org/EN/NewsEvents/Pages/DisplayNews.aspx?NewsID=16581&LangID=E

Murdoch, L. (2017, August 21). This 17-year-old boy killed in Duterte's drug war galvanises the Philippines. *The Sydney Morning Herald Times*. Retrieved from http://www.smh.com.au/world/this-17-year-old-boy-killed-in-dutertes-drug-war-galvanises-the-philippines-20170821-gy0j41.html

Ndiaye, B. W. (1996, December 24). Question of the violation of human rights and fundamental freedoms in any part of the world, with particular reference to colonial and other dependent countries and territories. *Report by the Special Rapporteur on extrajudicial, summary or arbitrary executions*. UN Commission on Human Rights. UN Doc. E/CN/4.1997/60.

Nowak, M. (2005, August 30). *Torture and other cruel, inhuman or degrading treatment or punishment*. UN General Assembly. UN Doc. A/60/316.

Nowak, M. (2009, January 14). Promotion and protection of all human rights, civil and political, economic, social and cultural rights, including the right to development. *Report of the Special Rapporteur on torture and other cruel, inhuman or degrading treatment or punishment*, Manfred Nowak to the UN Human Rights Council. UN Doc. A/HRC/10/44, para. 66.

PhilStar Global. (2017, November 15). *Trump gave biggest support to drug war, says Roque*. Retrieved from http://beta.philstar.com/headlines/2017/11/15/1759140/trump-gave-biggest-support-drug-war-says-roque

Reuters. (2017, August 15). *Iran parliament edges towards softening drug laws to curb executions*. Retrieved from https://www.reuters.com/article/us-iran-drugs-law/iran-parliament-edges-towards-softening-drug-laws-to-curb-executions-idUSKCN1AV109

RTE News. (2013, November 8). *Government ceased anti-drug programme funding over Iran death penalty fears*. Retrieved from https://www.rte.ie/news/2013/1108/485366-ireland-anti-drug-iran/

Salva, A. (2017, May 17). Why are abuse claims in Cambodia's war on drugs being ignored? *This Week in Asia*. Retrieved from http://www.scmp.com/week-asia/politics/article/2094693/why-are-abuse-claims-cambodias-war-drugs-being-ignored

Sander, G. (2018). *The death penalty for drug offences: Global overview 2017*. London: Harm Reduction International.

Sapiie, M.A. (2017, September 19). 80 people killed in police's war on drugs. *Amnesty International. The Jakarta Post*. Retrieved from http://www.thejakartapost.com/news/2017/09/19/80-people-killed-in-polices-war-on-drugs-amnesty-international.html

Schabas, W. A. (2002). *The abolition of the death penalty in international law* (3rd ed.). Cambridge: Cambridge University Press.

Soeriaatmadja, W. (2017, September 18). Jokowi's tough stance on drugs stirs debate. *The Straight Times*. Retrieved from http://www.straitstimes.com/asia/se-asia/jokowis-tough-stance-on-drugs-stirs-debate

The Copenhagen Post. (2013, April 9). *Denmark ends drug crime support*. Retrieved from http://cphpost.dk/news/international/denmark-ends-iranian-drug-crime-support.html

UN Convention against the Illicit Traffic in Narcotic Drugs and Psychotropic Substances (20 December 1988) 1582 UNTS 95.

United Nations Economic and Social Council. (1984). *ECOSOC resolution: Implementation of the safeguards guaranteeing protection of the rights of those facing the death penalty*. Resolution 1984/50.

United Nations Economic and Social Council. (2001, March 20). *Capital punishment and implementation of the safeguards guaranteeing protection of the rights of those facing the death penalty*. UN Doc. E/CN.15/2001/10.

United Nations Human Rights Committee. (1993, July 29). *Concluding observations: Iran*. UN Doc. CCPR/C/79/Add.25, para. 8.

United Nations Human Rights Committee. (2005, July 9). *Concluding observations: Thailand*. UN Doc. CCPR/CO/84/THA, para 14.

United Nations Human Rights Committee. (2007, August 20). *Concluding observations: Sudan*. UN Doc. CCPR/C/SDN/CO/3, para. 19.

United Nations Human Rights Committee. (2017). *General Comment No. 36 on article 6 of the International Covenant on Civil and Political Rights, on the right to life*. Unedited Advanced Version, para. 38.

United Nations Human Rights Council. (2017a). *Report of the Work Group on the Universal Periodic Review*. Philippines. UN Doc. A/HRC.36/12, 18 July 2017.

United Nations Human Rights Council. (2017b, September 11–29). 36th Session. Joint Statement. Item 10.

United Nations Office on Drugs and Crimes. (2012). *UNODC and the protection and promotion of human rights*. Position Paper. Vienna: UN Office on Drugs and Crime.

United Nations Office on Drugs and Crime. (2016, July 29). *Statement by the UNODC executive director on the recent executions in Indonesia*. Retrieved from https://www.unodc.org/unodc/en/press/releases/2016/July/statement-by-the-unodc-executive-director-on-the-recent-executions-in-indonesia.html

United Nations Office of the High Commissioner for Human Rights. (2015, October 10). *Using the death penalty to fight drug crimes violates international law, UN rights experts warn World Day against the death penalty*. Retrieved from http://www.ohchr.org/EN/NewsEvents/Pages/DisplayNews.aspx?NewsID=16581&LangID=E. Accessed on 10 October 2015.

United Nations Working Group on Arbitrary Detention. (2016, April 15). *The Special Rapporteurs on extrajudicial, summary or arbitrary executions; torture and other cruel, inhuman or degrading treatment or punishment; the right of everyone to the highest attainable standard of physical and mental health; and the Committee on the Rights of the Child*. Joint Open Letter on the occasion of the United Nations General Assembly Special Session on Drugs. Retrieved from http://www.ohchr.org/Documents/Issues/Health/UNGASSjoint_OL_HR_mechanisms_April2016.pdf

United Nations Secretary-General. (2015, October 9). *In message for day against death penalty, stresses that it deters neither drugs crimes nor abuse*. Retrieved from https://www.un.org/press/en/2015/sgsm17203.doc.htm

Weinberg, B. (2017, October 6). Indonesia unleashes shoot-to-kill policy on drug suspects. *High Times*. Retrieved from https://hightimes.com/news/indonesia-unleashes-shoot-to-kill-policy-on-drug-suspects/.

Chapter 3

Measuring the 'World Drug Problem': 2019 and Beyond

David R. Bewley-Taylor and Marie Nougier

Abstract

This chapter analyses major issues surrounding the Annual Report Questionnaire (ARQ) – the key mechanism through which the UN collects data on various facets of the world's illicit drug market. As the ARQ is currently under review by the United Nations Office on Drugs and Crime (UNODC), the authors suggest ways to incorporate the gains made at the United Nations General Assembly Special Session (UNGASS) on the World Drug Problem.

The UNGASS Outcome Document has, to certain degree, enabled the international community to move away from the simplistic goals of a drug-free world enshrined in the 2009 Political Declaration and towards a more comprehensive health- and human rights-based approach. The UNGASS has also laid important groundwork for the 2019 Ministerial Segment, where member states will delineate the global drug control approach for the next decade. In this context, the issue of metrics and indicators has a critical political role to play as it will shape how member states will measure progress against their international drug control commitments.

Starting with a review of the 'triple trouble' – poor data quality, low response rates from Member States and other inconsistencies that have long persisted with the ARQ – the chapter moves on to offer substantive critiques on the content of the Questionnaire and ways to better incorporate issues related to health, human rights and development. The chapter concludes by providing guidance on possible synergies with the Outcome Document and the Sustainable Development Goals, bringing international drug control in line with the UN Charter.

Keywords: Metrics and indicators; system-wide coherence; Annual Reports Questionnaire; UNGASS Outcome Document; Sustainable Development Goals; human rights

Collapse of the Global Order on Drugs: From UNGASS 2016 to Review 2019, 65–83

doi:10.1108/978-1-78756-487-920181003

Introduction

Almost two years after the United Nations General Assembly Special Session (UNGASS) on the World Drug Problem, the implications of the resultant Outcome Document (United Nations (UN), 2016) remain unclear and complex. At a structural level, it can legitimately be regarded as a homeostatic text that does much to help prop up the increasingly creaky UN international drug control framework (Bewley-Taylor & Jelsma, 2016). Yet, as member states move to operationalise its key provisions, it is becoming increasingly obvious that the Document has in fact generated considerable concern among what might be called 'status quo countries' seeking to preserve the treaty system in its current form. One need only look at the debates and country statements within the UN's central policy-making body on the drugs issue, the Vienna-based Commission on Narcotic Drugs (CND or Commission) for evidence to support this view (IDPC, 2017c). That prohibition-oriented states like the Russian Federation are investing considerable effort and political capital to argue that the Outcome Document does not supplant previous soft law instruments, particularly the 2009 Political Declaration and Plan of Action (UN, 2009), suggests that the progressive character of the Document exceeds what might have been initially thought as the dust settled in April 2016. Although problematic in many respects, the 2016 instrument does to a certain degree move away from the 2009 Political Declaration's simplistic goal for states to 'eliminate or reduce significantly and measurably' illicit drug supply and demand, the diversion and trafficking of precursors and money laundering. This, it should be recalled, was agreed nearly ten years ago with a target date of 2019. While the operationalisation of many aspects of the Outcome Document merit ongoing scrutiny, key among them is how the international community refines its measurement of what has become known simply and somewhat vaguely as the 'world drug problem'. This is especially so as we approach what has now been agreed to be a high-level ministerial segment of the CND in March 2019 (UNODC, 2017c) and not only what is likely to be an awkward review of progress made against the targets within the Political Declaration but also negotiations regarding how the Commission approaches international drug control in the next decade. Beginning with an overview of the Annual Report Questionnaire (ARQ), the key mechanism by which the UN system collects data on various facets of the state of the world's illicit drug market, this chapter examines the content of the UNGASS Outcome Document in terms of its reference to indicators and some of the problems surrounding the current framework. It then goes on to discuss the increasing attention given to the ARQ within Vienna since the UNGASS before concluding with a critique of the process leading to the meeting of an 'Expert Group' to revise the ARQ; a Group scheduled to meet for the first time in January 2018 (UNODC, 2018).

The ARQ: Triple Trouble

The ARQ has long been core to the UN drug control system's attempts to monitor and better understand the state of the 'world drug problem'. The not unreasonable logic here is that the resultant knowledge will assist national authorities in the design and implementation of effective drug control policies in line with obligations and goals under the international drug control conventions and complementary soft law instruments, including CND resolutions and high-level documents like that emanating from the UNGASS. While non-binding for states, such instruments possess considerable normative power and influence. In terms of hard law, the conventions formally oblige States Parties to provide data each year concerning the situation in their countries to the Secretary General (UNODC, 1961) – in practice the Secretariat of the UN Office on Drugs and Crime (UNODC or Office), the body mandated to assist Member States 'in their struggle against illicit drugs, crime and terrorism (UNODC, 1971). This mechanism dates to the pre-UN foundational era of the international drug control system, including the requirement to submit annual reports from States parties contained within the 1931 Convention for Limiting the Manufacture and Regulating the Distribution of Narcotic Drugs. At various points since 1945, and the transfer of the international control machinery to the UN, the reporting system was reviewed and revised (ECOSOC, 1994; UNODC, 2000). Notably, in December 1999, the CND adopted a 'unified, single questionnaire' that included 'the information required on all action plans and measures adopted by the General Assembly at its twentieth special session', that is to say the 1998 UNGASS on the 'world drug problem' (UN, 1999). More recently, in 2010, the CND endorsed a revised version of the questionnaire:

> to enable the monitoring of and biennial reporting to the Commission on the implementation by Member States of the Political Declaration and Plan of Action on International Cooperation towards an Integrated and Balanced Strategy to Counter the World Drug Problem, as well as for the reporting to the Commission mandated by the three international drug control conventions. (UNODC, 2010a)

The review processes usually involve some form of expert group, for example, the 'open-ended expert group on data collection' mandated by Resolution 53/16 in 2010 (UNODC, 2010b). Of note is the fact that, among other things, this resolution stresses that the ARQ 'should be periodically reviewed in order to have a flexible instrument allowing the reporting of national and emerging drug situations' (UN, 2010b).

Having been revised and streamlined at various points over the years, the ARQ is currently structured in the following way:

- Part I: Legislative and institutional framework.
- Part II: Comprehensive approach to drug demand reduction and supply.
- Part III: Extent and patterns of drug use.
- Part IV: Extent and patterns of and trends in drug crop cultivation and drug manufacture and trafficking.

With United Nations Office on Drugs and Crime (UNODC) acknowledging that sometimes there is insufficient data to provide an 'accurate or comprehensive picture of world drug markets', the Questionnaire is supplemented by a range of other sources. In addition to official national publications, these include the Heads of National Law Enforcement Agencies, the European Monitoring Centre for Drugs and Drug Addiction (EMCDDA), the Inter-American Drug Abuse Control Commission (CICAD) and the Drug Abuse Information Network for Asia and the Pacific (DAINAP) (United Nations Office on Drugs and Crime (UNODC), 2017a).

As UNODC itself notes, there remain considerable problems with the reporting system, particularly regarding the quality of responses from member states. For example, in relation to the ARQ for 2015, the key source of data upon which the UNODC's *World Drug Report 2017* is based, out of 199 potential respondents (including 193 Member States), the Office received only 98 replies to its questionnaire on Part III (down from 101 the previous year) and 101 replies to Part IV (down from 104 the previous year). 'The best coverage', UNODC notes, 'was from Europe (where 80 per cent of the respondents provided a reply), Asia (63 per cent) and the Americas (57 per cent)'. Reflecting one of the major challenges in data collection, in the case of Africa, however, 'only 24 per cent of the Member States replied'. And in the Oceania region, only two out of the 16 countries, responded to the ARQ.

In addition to the response rates themselves, there is significant variation in the quality of data provided. Again, as UNODC recognises in relation to the 2015 Questionnaire, 'the quantity of data provided on illicit drug supply is "significantly better" than that provided on drug demand.' More specifically, '79 per cent of ARQs Part IV were "substantially completed", compared to 67 per cent of ARQs Part III.' 'It should be noted', the Office goes on to say:

> that those ARQs that were more than 50 per cent completed were classed as having been 'substantially filled in', while those having less than 50 per cent completion were classed as 'partially filled in'. (UNODC, 2017a)

Mindful of the complexities and financial cost of data capture, response rates and the quality and completeness of information returned within the Questionnaire are often dependent on frameworks and mechanisms within member states. As understandable as this may be for many countries, variable quality data impact the accuracy of the picture generated, with irregular returns having the potential to influence reported trends 'in a given year' (UNODC, 2017a). Indeed, although the *World Drug Report 2017* states that the 'drug market is thriving' (UNODC, 2017b), as has been discussed at length elsewhere, data gaps and incomplete and poor-quality data sets generate high levels of uncertainty concerning the true state of the 'world drug problem'. This includes a likely underestimation of the scale and complexity of drugs markets in some regions, especially Africa and Asia (IDPC, 2016).

Reducing the levels of uncertainty through an improvement in the quality of the existing data sets clearly remains an ongoing issue of concern; and one that is certainly not new. Writing about data collection in their seminal 1975 book, *The Gentlemen's Club: International Control of Drugs and Alcohol,* Kettil Bruun, Lynn Pan and Ingemar Rexed point out 'the paucity of information in the national reports to the UN' in the early 1970s (Bruun, Pan, & Rexed, 1975). Regarding data 'given to the secretariats' of the Commission and the Division on Narcotic Drugs (a predecessor body of the Office) 'by governments under their treaty obligations', the authors note that this 'information is quite inadequate' and that the 'questionnaires used for such reporting are in need of overhauling'. Interestingly, a key topic of concern raised by research at that point related to 'returns under the heading "drug abuse"'. Here, Bruun et al. (1975) note how a 'systematic study of these reveals the *limited value of the information given*' (emphasis added). Today, while not focussing specifically on drug use, such a perspective is finding increasing resonance. Indeed, while there is a widely held view that gaps in the data pose considerable analytical dilemmas, questions are also being increasingly asked concerning the type and worth of the data that are being collected. Adding another problematising layer to the contemporary challenge, there is clearly a growing disconnect between the current structure and focus of the ARQ and what member states have recently agreed is important when addressing the 'world drug problem'.

Finally, it is also worth mentioning not only the relationship between member states and the data they supply to UNODC but also member state's reactions to data drawn from additional sources. In the first instance, states are able to challenge particular interpretations and forms of presentation within draft versions of the World Drug Report that are perceived to put them in a bad light. However, since countries themselves have supplied the data, complaints are generally difficult to sustain. In such circumstances, anecdotal evidence suggests that irked national officials may be less than cooperative in engaging with the ARQ process in future years. Where annoyance is the result of non-member state data sources, nations are in a position to challenge them and even force UNODC to rewrite offending paragraphs. As occurs at other points within the UN drug control framework, and indeed within the wider UN system of which it is a part, the ability to effect change depends greatly upon the geopolitical and diplomatic muscle of a particular state. This includes its status within the Commission, which is often related to its voluntary financial contributions to the ever cash-strapped UNODC (Bewley-Taylor & Trace, 2006).

Indicators and the Outcome Document: Limited Progress, but some Opportunities

In the lead up to the 2016 UNGASS, it was possible to identify a growing awareness and related discussion within UN for a concerning the increasing inadequacy of the indicators used to assess the state of the illicit global drugs market. This assessment was held not only among sections of civil society but also by some member states (Bewley-Taylor, 2016). Longitudinal analysis of information, contained within the *World Drug Report*, reveals a noticeable and significant shift over recent years to include more data on the negative health consequences of drug use. This is important, since the UNODC's flagship publication does much to set the 'mood music' for discussion in Vienna, with member states often referring to its findings during statements within the CND plenary as well as during discussions in the Commission's Committee of the Whole where resolutions are negotiated. Moreover, the data generated by the ARQ currently feed into the Executive

Director of UNODC's biennial report to the Commission on action taken by states to implement the 2009 Political Declaration and Plan of Action; document that include a set of recommendations for member states (ECOSOC, 2016).

Nonetheless, at the international level, information collected from states via the ARQ remains dominated by a concern for scale and flows, largely process indicators that often tell us more about law enforcement activity than the state of the illicit market. It is plausible to suggest that this preoccupation is the result of a system traditionally premised on the belief that the most effective way to protect the 'health and welfare' of humankind, as laid out in the preamble of the bedrock of the extant international drug control regime, is to shrink the size of and eventually stamp out the illicit market. Such a path-dependent approach, however, is at odds with increasingly widespread and more nuanced market management-oriented perspectives whereby authorities are focussing on reducing the harm associated with not only drug markets themselves but also those policies designed to significantly and measurably reduce the scale of – and ultimately eliminate – them. Consequently, and not unreasonably, during preparations for the New York meeting, there was some hope, again both from some member states and sections of civil society, that the UNGASS would allow for substantive discussion of revised policy objectives accompanied by more sophisticated indicators pertaining to various forms of drug and drug market-related harm. This was particularly so considering both the improved understanding of the dynamics of drug markets and their associated harms and the development of innovative metrics taking place within some member states.

Although often presented as an esoteric and purely technical matter, the political dimension of the issue of indicators soon became clear in the intensity of the negotiations of the Outcome Document – which was to be agreed by consensus. Moreover, as the discussions unfolded, it grew more obvious that many states were willing to side-step what was becoming a contentious issue to secure agreement for other aspects of the draft text. Indicative of this was the loss of a proposed – and on the face of it relatively innocuous – paragraph in a working draft of the Outcome Document that included a call to 'identify quantifiable indicators … in line with the integrated and balanced approach …'. This was shifted to the so-called 'car park', a stand-alone document designated to 'hold' contested language in order to aid the flow of discussions during negotiations and failed to gain sufficient agreement for inclusion in the final text.

That said, some positives must be acknowledged regarding the issue of indicators. Involvement within the formulation process of a range of UN entities beyond the drug control apparatus in Vienna can only be constructive in terms of any future consideration of non-traditional drug policy indicators.[1] Similarly, a move away from the established three-pillar structure laid out in the 2009 Political Declaration ('demand reduction', 'supply reduction' and 'countering money-laundering and promoting judicial cooperation to enhance international cooperation') also offers opportunities for more sophisticated and disaggregated

[1]These included UNAIDS, WHO, UNDP the OHCHR and UN Women.

measurement processes, particularly in relation to access to controlled medicines,[2] a point to which we will return.

In terms of specific metrics, the Document also includes mention of the target to end the HIV epidemic by 2030 'among people who use drugs'. This was the compromise language after agreement could not be reached to recognise that the 2015 target agreed by the international community to reduce HIV transmission by 50 per cent among people who inject drugs had been missed. Furthermore, that the Outcome Document explicitly welcomes the Sustainable Development Goals (SDGs) as 'complementary and mutually reinforcing' to drug control, and recommends 'the use of relevant human development indicators' provides a valuable toe hold for the future development of metrics that not only move beyond law enforcement process indicators but also enhance system-wide coherence on the issue. To be sure, linking new and carefully designed indicators to broader UN objectives, principles and contemporary UN endeavours, such as the Sustainable Development Agenda agreed in late 2015, has the potential to bring international drug control policy more into line with the UN Charter and other instruments, including those concerning indigenous rights – and to better reflect the high-level priorities of the United Nations: achieving human rights, peace and security and development. Any serious discussion of the measurement of drug policy impacts within the broadly defined development domain must read across relevant SDGs indicators (Bewley-Taylor, 2017). Beyond these high-level statements of intent, the Document also mentions, at a more granular level, areas where member states agree to improve data collection. This includes issues that span both the health and organised criminal dimensions of illicit drug markets, and particularly – even though the Questionnaire is not mentioned specifically – areas not covered within the current structure of the ARQ.[3] Furthermore, as discussed below, although problematic in terms of the extant mechanisms, the 2016 text includes some intriguing possibilities in terms of voluntary reporting.

---

[2]The seven headings are Demand reduction and related measures, including prevention and treatment as well as other health-related issues; Ensuring the availability of and access to controlled substances exclusively for medical and scientific purposes, while preventing their diversion; Supply reduction and related measures; effective law enforcement; responses to drug related crime; and countering money laundering and promoting judicial cooperation; Cross-cutting issues: drugs and human rights, youth, children women and communities; Cross-cutting issues in addressing and countering the world drug problem: evolving reality, trends and existing circumstances, emerging and persistent challenges and threats, including NPS, in conformity with the three international drug control conventions and other relevant international instruments; Strengthening international cooperation based on the principle of common and shared responsibility; Alternative development; regional, interregional and international cooperation on development-oriented balanced drug control policy; and addressing socioeconomic issues.

UN. (2016). *Outcome Document of the 2016 United Nations General Assembly Special Session on the World Drug Problem, our joint commitment to effectively addressing and countering the world drug problem*, Thirtieth Special Session, General Assembly, Retrieved from http://www.unodc.org/documents/postungass2016//outcome/V1603301-E.pdf.

[3]See for example Paragraphs 1 (h), 3 (c), 3 (k), 3 (u), 5 (d) and 5 (p).

Discussion of Metrics Since the UNGASS: Increasing Attention on ARQ Revision

As regular observers of the CND will know, in the past few years, the issue of drug policy metrics and indicators has become more prominent (IDPC, 2016). The Commission's 2017 session was no exception. No doubt a combination of the Outcome Document, the, in many ways resultant, increasing prominence of the SDA within drug policy deliberations and the scheduled high-level review in 2019 of the targets set in 2009 contributed to this.

Many states continued to follow the age-old practice of including within statements long lists of figures concerning drug seizures and in some cases, such as India, crop eradication. Although countries including Tanzania, Algeria and Sudan were part of this group, it was those from the Middle East that were particularly noteworthy.

That said, a significant number of other states noted the inadequacies of traditional metrics. For example, the Ambassador to Vienna from Panama highlighted the need for a better framework of indicators beyond those relating to seizures; the UK delegate flagged up the importance of improving impact indicators concerning actions targeting organised crime; and the Netherlands stressed the necessity of new indicators and the need to improve statistics and maintain continuous monitoring of drug markets. A statement from the Norwegian delegate summed up the situation well and highlighted the pressing need to re-visit the data collection mechanisms mandated by member states and operated by the UNODC:

> The process up to and the finalizing of the UNGASS revealed a need to collect better and more reliable data, and towards viewing international drug policy in a more holistic manner. The metrics designed to measure the effectiveness of interventions would profit from more dynamic and sophisticated approaches towards metrics that measure outcomes related to individuals and communities in terms of human rights and development. It now seems timely to review the ARQ such that the UN drug control apparatus is able to capture data relevant to the commitments made in New York, including those relating to the SDGs .... The imperative for such a review is also heightened by the approach of 2019 and the expiration of the targets set by the 2009 Political declaration (IDPC, 2017c).

Such reference to a review of the ARQ echoed that made by the Swiss delegation at the CND intersessional in September 2016. Then, among a range of other issues concerning the Questionnaire and the SDA, Mr. Martin Matter (then Counsellor, Permanent Mission of Switzerland to the United Nations in Vienna) raised an interesting point about states furnishing 'additional information to the CND' to that currently requested by the ARQ, particularly in relation to 'criminal justice policies and practices' and the 'promotion of human rights'. Indeed,

Matter's statement highlighted how the current structure of the Questionnaire made the collection of such information difficult (UNODC, 2016b). This is of particular relevance in relation to Paragraph 4 (h) of the Outcome Document. Under 'Operational recommendations on cross-cutting issues: drugs and human rights, youth, children, women and communities,' this notes that member states:

> Consider, *on a voluntary basis*, when furnishing information to the Commission on Narcotic Drugs pursuant to the three international drug control conventions and relevant Commission resolutions, the inclusion of information concerning, inter alia, the *promotion of human rights and the health, safety and welfare of all individuals, communities and society* in the context of their domestic implementation of these conventions, including recent developments, best practices and challenges (emphases added).

Another statement worthy of note came from the Mexican delegate who, bringing together several themes that emerged during the March meeting, stated that the 'prohibition approach is never going to be enough' with a better way forward involving the measurement of policy impact on individuals' lives as part of a move to 'intersectoral multidimensional strategies'. Building upon positions that had been developing over the course of recent CND sessions, new indicators should, the Mexican delegate claimed, link closely to the work of a range of UN agencies and are essential to achieving progress towards the objectives of the UNGASS Outcome Document.

Interest within Mexico for the metrics issue was also evident in discussions concerning the work of the UN's New York based Statistical Commission (StatComm). Demonstrating a welcome convergence of endeavour across the UN, StatComm presented at its 48th session – the week before the CND – the *Report of the National Institute of Statistics and Geography of Mexico (INEGI) and the UNODC on an international road map to improve drug statistics* (ECOSOC, 2017). Although agreed on for publication some time ago, the report was in many ways a response to the Outcome Document. Discussed at various points during the Commission's 60th session, including within the plenary and side events, it was generally well-received (IDPC, 2017c). Without offering a full critique of the document here, it is fair to say that the international 'Roadmap' certainly adds value to the current discussions, especially in terms of inclusion within the drafting process of other agencies from within and outside the UN (e.g., the World Customs Organization, CICAD, EMCDDA and WHO). Involvement of these bodies can provide different perspectives and expertise and have the potential to 'increase synergies' and 'coordination' in data collection. Nevertheless, the Roadmap arguably remains overly focussed on measuring the scale and flow of drug markets rather than multidimensional harms that result from them, or from misguided repressive drug policies.

All that said, and in terms of the immediate future of the ARQ, probably the key outcome of the March 2017 session of the CND came in the form of resolution 60/1, Preparations for the sixty-second session of the CND in 2019

(UNODC, 2017c). Within this the UNODC was invited, in close cooperation with Member States, to:

> reflect on possibilities to strengthen and streamline its existing data-collection and analysis tools, including improving the quality and effectiveness of the annual report questionnaire, and to report to the Commission on possible ways to enhance these, for consideration by the Commission at its sixty-second session. (UNODC, 2017c)

Having initiated the review process in March, members of the CND also discussed it at the Commission's intersessional meeting in November and the reconvened session the following month. Reiterating the sentiment expressed in March, the Norwegian delegate at the intersessional meeting noted how '… the UNGASS outcome document is a turning point to tackling the world drug problem. It is now time for action, implementation and monitoring.' He then went on to say that, 'We need new metrics and indicators to assess progress. It is timely to review the ARQ so that we can capture data relevant to the commitments agreed in New York' and in relation to the 'SDGs' (IDPC, 2017b).

Within the context of discussions in Vienna, and agreement in Autumn 2017 around the establishment of an 'Expert group Meeting' to meet in January 2018, the UNODC began to organise an 'Expert Consultation' by way of:

> a first step to reflect on ways to improve the current data collection on drugs, including the ARQ, and to discuss activities to support countries in the production of drug relevant statistics, as for example indicated by the Roadmap (VNGOC, 2017b).

Reflecting on both how to 'strengthen and streamline' UNODC-mandated drug data collection tools and on issues around capacity building, the principal outcome of the consultation is intended to be a report submitted to the CND as a 'room document' to inform discussions in March 2018 'on the possible avenues to undertake to improve the quality and availability of drug statistics' (VNGOC, 2017). The same document will be presented to the 49th session of the UN Statistical Commission, also to be held in March 2018, and a final product will be shared at the 62nd CND in March 2019.

Reviewing the ARQ: An Opportunity to Increase Synergies with the Outcome Document

At the time of writing this chapter, December 2017, the precise nature of the work and focus of the 'Expert Consultation' remain fluid. Nonetheless, through the UNODC's welcome engagement with civil society organisations (CSOs), it is becoming clearer how the process is unfolding and where there may be opportunities for states, CSOs and UN agencies based outside Vienna to feed into the revision of the ARQ and bring it more into line with the aspirations of the UNGASS Outcome Document, its calls for an improvement in data capture and movement towards a more rights based approach to drug control more generally. The final section of this chapter, consequently, briefly explores some of the key issues arising from the discussions, giving particular attention to issues that appear to have been omitted.

In December 2017, the UNODC launched an online questionnaire to collect feedback on the ARQ from governments, UN agencies and CSOs. The strategy behind this initiative was that responses to the online questionnaire would then result in a report that would be presented as a background document for the January 2018 meeting. In relation to possible new topics for data collection, the Office's questionnaire selected only seven issues – apparently based on the Statcomm Roadmap: (1) Trends in the composition, production, prevalence and distribution of new psychoactive substances; (2) social, economic and other risk factors encouraging drug use; (3) prevention and countering of drug-related crime and drug supply reduction measures; (4) links between drug trafficking, corruption and other forms of organised crime; (5) money-laundering and illicit financial flows; (6) drug-related criminal activities using the Internet and (7) factors contributing to illicit crop cultivation. These are all relevant issues of interest for the ARQ. Nonetheless, such an approach leaves out several other critical thematic areas for the Questionnaire review process – some directly mandated, others suggested, by the UNGASS Outcome Document.

Human Rights

As noted above, the Outcome Document explicitly calls on member states to 'Consider, on a voluntary basis…the inclusion of information' on a range of issues, including human rights (Paragraph 4 (h)). The Document also promotes more proportionate penalties for drug offences (Paragraph 4 (l)) and alternatives to incarceration (Paragraph 4 (j)). Whether or not member states offer treatment as an alternative to incarceration is already included in the ARQ (Part ii, question 9e). Nonetheless, these two critical issues could be better incorporated within Parts i and ii of the Questionnaire.

The Outcome Document also calls on member states to 'Promote and implement effective criminal justice responses to drug-related crimes to bring perpetrators to justice that ensure legal guarantees and due process safeguards' and 'practical measures to uphold the prohibition of arbitrary arrest and detention and…torture and other cruel, inhuman or degrading treatment or punishment and to eliminate impunity' (Paragraph 4 (o)). Mindful of the high-level commitments made to human rights values within the Document and other texts, it seems important that the updated ARQ reflects these commitments. This might be achieved either as a new 'Human rights' section within the ARQ or by embedding human rights considerations across the various ARQ sections. Additional data (including from CSOs) would most probably need to be considered by UNODC for issues where self-reporting by UN member states to the office may present some difficulties (e.g., impunity, acts of torture and ill-treatment, etc.) – an issue that will need to be addressed in the Expert Group's deliberations. Other UN agencies, notably the Office of the High Commissioner on Human Rights (OHCHR, 2012), have done significant work on developing human rights indicators, and such expertise and experience could be utilised. For instance, the OHCHR might consider drafting regular reports on the impact of drug policies on human rights as a useful tool to feed into the UNODC World Drug Reports.

Gender

The Outcome Document provides a clear mandate for the UNODC to collect gender-disaggregated data across the spectrum of drug policy, stating:

> that targeted interventions that are based on the collection and analysis of data, including age- and *gender-related data*, can be particularly effective in meeting the specific needs of drug-affected populations and communities (preamble, emphasis added).

The Document also promotes non-discriminatory access to health and social services, the need to address the protective and risk factors that make women vulnerable to participation in the illicit drug market, and the specific needs and vulnerabilities of women drug offenders when imprisoned. Currently, the ARQ only requests gender-specific information for alternative development and for the overall prevalence of drug use (but not for other critical issues such as drug injection, related harms and access to services or indeed on any issue related to supply-side activities). Although, as a reading of recent World Drug Reports reveals, the Office has been devoting increasing attention to the issue of gender, the review might consider the inclusion of requests for gender and age-disaggregated data throughout the ARQ. Moreover, it might ask, on a voluntary basis, that member states submit information disaggregated by socio-economic status, race, ethnicity and other categories as appropriate.

Additional UNGASS-related Data Collection

Several new drug-related issues covered in the Outcome Document could also be considered for inclusion within any revised version of the Questionnaire. This might be done both via voluntary reporting by member states to the UNODC (possibly by expanding the 'Additional Comments' sections of the ARQ), or by using the data already being collected by other UN agencies.

For instance, the ARQ currently requests data on HIV, hepatitis and tuberculosis – as well as on interventions such as needle and syringe programmes, opioid substitution therapy and others. Meanwhile, the Outcome Document expands these health issues to include overdose prevention and naloxone distribution (Paragraph 1 (m)). The Expert group might consequently consider requesting member states to report, on a voluntary basis, on progress made towards preventing overdose deaths. Further developing the inter-agency cooperation involved in Statcomm's production of the Roadmap, data collected by other UN agencies on this issue, especially by the WHO, could be included.

Crucially, the Outcome Document dedicates an entire chapter to ensuring adequate availability of controlled substances for medical and scientific purposes.

This is one of the key objectives of the UN drug control treaties and an issue that has been growing in prominence in recent years as research reveals disparities in access to controlled medicines in many parts of the world (Global Commission on Drug Policy, 2015). While this is the case, the current ARQ does not address this issue. Better data are essential both for informing policy action by states to improve access to controlled medicines, to take corrective action when problems with their use occur, and for measuring progress over time. The International Narcotics Control Board (INCB), the 'independent and quasi-judicial monitoring body for the implementation'[4] of the drug control conventions, routinely collects information on the consumption of controlled medicines. It therefore seems reasonable for the Expert Group to consider the use of this valuable data in the future analysis of the world drug situation. In addition, the Group might call upon UNODC to request that, on a voluntary basis, member states report back on progress made towards other relevant questions identified in the Document, in particular removing legislative and technical barriers to accessing controlled medicines and improving training for health-care providers.

Reviewing the Scope of the New Thematic Areas

As noted above, it appears as if only seven possible new topics for data collection have been identified by the Statcomm and UNODC. Among these is 'Social, economic, and other risk factors encouraging drug use'. Available data from the Office itself show that there are no common trends on drug use or the risk factors associated with it – drug use happens across all ages, genders, cultures and political systems. That said, problematic use, drug dependence and drug-related health harms (e.g., HIV and hepatitis C infections, tuberculosis and overdoses) are often concentrated in marginalised, impoverished, conflict-afflicted areas across the globe. Consequently, it may be more relevant for the Expert Group to consider the social, economic and other risk factors around problematic drug use and harms, including poverty, social inclusion, criminalisation, policing, incarceration, gender inequality, armed conflicts and so on.

In addition, it will be recalled that the seventh thematic area listed by the UNODC relates to the 'Factors contributing to illicit crop cultivation'. While these factors are critical, the Outcome Document also commits member states to address 'drug-related socioeconomic issues' related to all supply-side drug control – cultivation, manufacture, production and trafficking – through development-oriented drug policies (Paragraph 7). This appears to be an opportunity for the ARQ to cover broader development concerns in involvement in all illicit drug supply activities – hence contributing to member states' reporting requirements within the 2030 Agenda for Sustainable Development. Furthermore, and as mentioned above, Paragraph 7 (g) of the Document promotes the 'use of relevant human development indicators' – another dataset that could be utilised to support the UNODC's analysis of drug policy issues globally.

[4] International Narcotics Control Board. Retrieved from https://www.incb.org/incb/en/about.html.

Conclusion

Any revision of the ARQ is clearly a complex process; one that involves not only myriad technical challenges but also, and as is likely to become more obvious in the months before March 2019, deeply ingrained political and systemic tensions. While arguably limited in scope, the seven possible new topics for data collection are all fraught with conceptual and methodological dilemmas. As briefly discussed here, both 'Social, economic, and other risk factors encouraging drug use' and 'Factors contributing to illicit crop cultivation' are fiendishly intricate and require a holistic perspective, including the promotion of linkages to the SDGs. Moreover, although not unique within the list, the collection of meaningful data around new forms of drug market such as the dark net and indicators around drug-related corruption will be particularly difficult.

While in some instances, such as crypto-drug markets, a revised ARQ may require the capture of new data, in other instances information might be mined from existing data sets, sets that are already being generated both within the UN system by agencies other than the UNODC and non-governmental organisations (NGOs) (Bewley-Taylor, 2016). For example, in addition to utilising data on controlled medicines collected by the INCB, any revised process might incorporate data from NGOs working in the sector (The Economist, 2015).

In terms of improved cooperation with non-Vienna-based UN agencies, it should be recalled how in its Roadmap, the Statistical Commission concluded that:

> international and regional bodies … *should increase synergies and improve the coordination and their statistical work* in the area of drugs, including with respect to reporting on the indicators and targets related to the Sustainable Development Goals (emphasis added). (ECOSOC, 2017).

In parallel with the ARQ review process, it seems logical therefore for the UNODC to access relevant drug-related information already being collated by other UN agencies and related bodies. This would prevent a significant additional burden on member states for data collection, while promoting more system-wide coherence within the UN for data collection and analysis within their respective mandates. This could include, inter alia, data collected by the WHO,[5] UNAIDS,[6] UNICEF,[7] the INCB,[8] the World Bank,[9] the OHCHR,[10] the Committee on the

[5]WHO. Statistical Information System (WHOSIS). Retrieved from http://www.who.int/whosis/en/.

[6]UNAIDS. *Data*. Retrieved from www.unaids.org/en/dataanalysis.

[7]UNICEF. *Research and Reports*. Retrieved from www.unicef.org/statistics.

[8]International Narcotics Control Board, *Annual Reports*. Retrieved from http://www.incb.org/incb/en/publications/annual-reports/annual-report.html.

[9]World Bank, *Open Data*. Retrieved from http://data.worldbank.org.

[10]OHCHR. *Databases*. Retrieved from http://www.ohchr.org/EN/PublicationsResources/Pages/databases.aspx.

Prevention of Discriminations Against Women,[11] the United Development Programme via the Human Development Index[12] and the SDGs.[13] Mindful of the UNODC's current use of data sets from a range of bodies to complement that generated by the ARQ, such a widening of scope should not be beyond the realms of possibility.

That said, in addition to substantial technical challenges, several fundamental problems can be identified. First, mindful of the increasingly complex and fluid state of the world drug market, it is difficult to reconcile the request within resolution 60/1 to simultaneously 'strengthen' and 'streamline' the ARQ, particularly if many of the existing categories concerning scale and flows are retained. Indeed, although there remains an understandable desire to reduce the burden on member states, particularly since the collection of good quality data is so expensive, it appears as if a better understanding of the 'world drug problem' requires more data, not less. Second, any shifts away from the longstanding interest in flows and scale, as contained within the Outcome Document, raise the sticky twin issues of self-reporting and state sovereignty, including when this involves data from non-state actors. As has been raised elsewhere and mentioned briefly above, that the entire ARQ process is based on self-reporting raises some serious questions. There is certainly something to be said for the view that 'States naturally have an inbuilt bias against reporting failures or poor performance, a problem assumed to be most acute in states or regions of greatest concern' (Rolles et al., 2016).

Reporting poor performance within the domain of human rights, however, goes well beyond the issue of drug policy and the work of the UNODC and an Expert Group. It strikes at the heart of the systemic tension inherent within the UN system: differing perceptions of the appropriate balance between states' obligations and state sovereignty. To be sure, while the language of human rights now permeates soft law instruments (such as the Outcome Document) within the realm of drug policy, there clearly remain substantial differences of view within the international community. These are differences that, while often side-stepped within Vienna, New York, and to a lesser extent Geneva, can be seen to play out within the domestic sphere. As touched upon here, the option of voluntary reporting may be the most realistic first step in capturing states' performance on drug policy vis-à-vis human rights obligations. That some states may choose not to offer information may speak volumes in terms of the creation of new normative standards. Another, or possibly additional, route may be the use of proxy human rights indicators such as incarceration rates for drug-related offences. Ultimately, however, it may be the case that adequate human rights indicators will not fit within anything other than a fundamentally redesigned and reframed ARQ; an unlikely prospect bearing in mind the apparent systemic inertia within Vienna. In such circumstances,

[11]UN Women. *Country Reports*. Retrieved from http://www.un.org/womenwatch/daw/cedaw/reports.htm.

[12]UNDP. Retrieved from www.undp.orgUNDP. *Human Development Index*. Retrieved from http://hdr.undp.org/en/content/human-development-index-hdi.

[13]Sustainable Development Knowledge Platform. *Sustainable Development Goals*. Retrieved from https://sustainabledevelopment.un.org/sdgs.

recourse to other measurement and review mechanisms, including the SDGs and those in Geneva relating to the work of the OHCHR such as the Annual Report, the Universal Periodic Review and Special Procedures mechanisms, may be more realistic options. In whichever part of the UN system the monitoring of human rights outcomes of drug policy takes place, it seems clear that the establishment of a monitoring framework is essential for the operation of a modern and internally coherent international drug control system. Indeed, as Rodrigo Uprimny and Diana Esther Guzman point out, appropriate 'indicators to evaluate drug policies are fundamental' for a human rights approach to the issue area. 'Although current indicators are important to measure some aspects of efficacy of drug policies', they continue, 'supplementary indicators are needed to assure' the fulfilment of 'human rights obligations' (Uprimny & Guzman, unpublished).

Indeed, whatever the route forward, it is becoming increasingly clear that for the language within the Outcome Document to be meaningful, there must be an appropriate set of performance indicators and associated capture mechanisms. On this point, it is worth recalling the words of Bente Angell-Hansen, Norway's Ambassador to Austria and Head of the Norwegian Mission to the United Nations, Vienna. Speaking at a side event at the reconvened session of the CND in December 2017, she evoked the maxim, 'If you have a problem that you don't want to do anything about – don't measure it' (IDPC, 2017a). How states choose to measure or avoid measuring various facets of the world drug problem, the human rights issue prominent among them, looks set to be a key area of concern in the lead up to 2019 and beyond.

References

Bruun, K., Pan, L., & Rexed, I. (1975). *The Gentlemen's Club: International Control of Drugs and Alcohol* (p. 95). Chicago and London: University of Chicago Press.

Bewley-Taylor, D. (2016). *Towards metrics that measure outcomes that matter*. Policy Brief 10, April, Global Drug Policy Observatory, Swansea University. Retrieved from http://www.swansea.ac.uk/media/GDPO%20Metrics%20WEB_FINAL.pdf

Bewley-Taylor, D. R. (2017). Refocusing metrics: Can the sustainable development goals help break the 'metrics trap' and modernise international drug control policy? *Drugs and Alcohol Today*, *7*(2), 98–112.

Bewley-Taylor, D., & Jelsma, M. (2016). *UNGASS 2016: A Broken or B-r-o-a-d Consensus? UN Summit cannot hide a growing divergence in the global drug policy landscape*. TNI-GDPO, Drug Policy Briefing, 45. Retrieved from https://www.tni.org/files/publication-downloads/dpb_45_04072016_web.pdf

Bewley-Taylor, D., & Trace, M. (2006). *The funding of the United Nations Office on Drugs and Crime; an unfinished jigsaw*. The Beckley Foundation Drug Policy Programme, November, Report 11. Retrieved from http://beckleyfoundation.org/wp-content/uploads/2016/04/BF_Report_11.pdf

ECOSOC. (1994). *Development of informational systems on drugs and their abuse*. Resolution 194/3.

ECOSOC. (2010). *Streamlining the annual report questionnaire*. Official records, 2010, Supplement No. 8A, E/2010/28/Add.1, E/CN.7/2010/18/Add.1, Resolution 53/16, pp. 3–4.

ECOSOC. (2016). *Implementation of the political declaration and plan of action on international cooperation towards an integrated and balanced strategy to counter the world drug problem*. CND fifty-ninth session, Item 5 of the provisional agenda, Vienna, 14–22 March.

ECOSOC, Statistical Commission. (2017). *Report of the National Institute of Statistics and Geography of Mexico (INEGI) and the United Nations Office on Drugs and Crime on an international road map to improve drug statistics*. Retrieved from https://unstats.un.org/unsd/statcom/48th-session/documents/2017-12-Drug-Stats-E.pdf

Global Commission on Drug Policy. (2015). *The negative impact for drug control on public health: The Global Crisis of Avoidable Pain*. Retrieved from http://www.globalcommissionondrugs.org/wp-content/uploads/2012/03/GCODP-THE-NEGATIVE-IMPACT-OF-DRUG-CONTROL-ON-PUBLIC-HEALTH-EN.pdf

IDPC. (2016). *IDPC analysis of the UNODC world drug report 2016*. Retrieved from http://fiieserver.idpc.net/library/IDPC-response-to-UNODC-World-Drug-Report-2016_ENGLISH.pdf

IDPC. (2016). *The 2016 Commission on Narcotic Drugs and its Special Session on preparations for the UNGASS on the world drug problem: Report of proceedings* (p. 6). Retrieved from http://idpc.net/publications/2016/07/the-2016-commission-on-narcotic-drugs-and-its-special-segment-on-preparations-for-the-ungass-on-the-world-drug-problem

IDPC. (2017a). *CND blog, Side event: Practices and challenges in relation to data quality and the national capacity to produce drug statistics*. Retrieved from http://cndblog.org/2017/12/side-event-practices-and-challenges-in-relation-to-data-quality-and-the-national-capacity-to-produce-drug-statistics/

IDPC. (2017b). *CND blog, CND Intersessional 17th November: The way forward – Preparations for the sixty-second session of the CND in 2019*. Retrieved from http://cndblog.org/2017/11/cnd-intersessional-17th-november-the-way-forward-preparations-for-the-sixty-second-session-of-the-cnd-in-2019/

IDPC. (2017c).*The 2017 Commission on Narcotic Drugs, Report of Proceedings*. Retrieved from http://fileserver.idpc.net/library/CND-Proceedings-Report-2017_ENGLISH.pdf

Office of the High Commissioner on Human Rights (OHCHR). (2012). *Human rights indicators: A guide to measurement and implementation*. Retrieved from http://www.ohchr.org/documents/issues/HRIndicators/AGuideMeasurementImplementationCompleteGuide_en.pdf.pdf

Rolles, S., Murkin, G., Powell, M., Kusklick, D., Saunter, N. and Slater, J. (2016). *The alternative world drug report* (2nd ed.). Count the Costs of the war on drugs, Transform Drug Policy Foundation (p. 25). Retrieved from http://www.countthecosts.org/alternative-world-drug-report

The Economist. (2015), Quality of death index. Retrieved from http://www.eiuperspectives.economist.com/healthcare/2015-quality-death-index

UN. (1999). Commission on Narcotic Drugs, *Resolution 42/11: Guidelines for reporting on the follow-up to the twentieth special session of the General Assembly*.

Retrieved from https://www.unodc.org/documents/commissions/CND/Drug_Resolutions/1990-1999/1999/CND_Res-42-11.pdf

United Nations (UN). (2009). *Political declaration and plan of action on international cooperation towards an integrated and balanced strategy to counter the world drug problem.* High-level segment of the Commission on Narcotic Drugs, Vienna, 11–12 March, United Nations, New York, NY. Retrieved from https://www.unodc.org/documents/ungass2016/V0984963-English.pdf

United Nations (UN). (2016). *Outcome Document of the 2016 United Nations General Assembly Special Session on the world drug problem, our joint commitment to effectively addressing and countering the world drug problem.* Thirtieth Special Session, General Assembly, Retrieved from http://www.unodc.org/documents/postungass2016//outcome/V1603301-E.pdf

United Nations (UN). (2017). *Commission on Narcotic Drugs, Report on the sixtieth session*, Economic and Social Council, Official Records, 2017, Supplement No., 8.

United Nations Office on Drugs and Crime (UNODC). (1961). *Single convention on narcotic drugs, Article 19.* Retrieved from https://www.unodc.org/pdf/convention_1961_en.pdf

United Nations Office on Drugs and Crime (UNODC). (1971). *Convention on psychotropic substances, Article 16.* Retrieved from https://www.unodc.org/pdf/convention_1971_en.pdf

United Nations Office on Drugs and Crime (UNODC). (2000). *Streamlining the annual reports questionnaire.* CND Resolution 43/1.

United Nations Office on Drugs and Crime (UNODC). (2010a). *Annual General Questionnaires.* Retrieved from https://www.unodc.org/unodc/en/commissions/CND/Sessions-Roundtables-ARQ/Sessions-Roundtables-Arq_ARQ.html

United Nations Office on Drugs and Crime (UNODC). (2010b). Commission on Narcotic Drugs, Report on the reconvened fifty-third session, Economic and Social Council, Official records, Supplement No. 8A, E/2010/28/Add.1, E/CN.7/2010/18/Add.1, Resolution 53/16, pp. 3–4

United Nations Office on Drugs and Crime (UNODC). (2016a). *Action taken by Member States to implement the political declaration and plan of action on international cooperation towards an integrated and balanced strategy to counter the world drug problem.* Report of the Executive Director, E/CN.7/2016/6, Retrieved from https://documents-dds-ny.un.org/doc/UNDOC/GEN/V16/001/27/PDF/V1600127.pdf?OpenElement

United Nations Office on Drugs and Crime (UNODC). (2016b). CND Intersessional Meeting 8th September 2016, Agenda Item 2: Follow-up on the World Drug Problem. (Authors' copy)

United Nations Office on Drugs and Crime (UNODC) (2017a) Methodology. Retrieved from https://www.unodc.org/wdr2017/field/WDR_2017_Methodology.pdf

United Nations Office on Drugs and Crime (UNODC). (2017b). *World Drug Report 2017, Booklet 1 – Executive Summary; Conclusions and Policy Implications* (p. 15).

United Nations Office on Drugs and Crime (UNODC). (2017c). *Commission on Narcotic Drugs resolution 60/1 Preparations for the sixty-second session of the Commission on Narcotic Drugs in 2019.* Retrieved from https://www.unodc.org/documents/commissions/CND/CND_Sessions/CND_60/CNDres_2017/Resolution_60_1_60CND.pdf

United Nations Office on Drugs and Crime (UNODC). (2018). *Expert Working Group on Improving Drug Statistics and Strengthening the Annual Report Questionnaire (ARQ)*. Retrieved from http://www.unodc.org/unodc/en/data-and-analysis/statistics/expert-consultation-on-arq.html

Uprimny, R., & Guzman, D.E. (2017). *Drug policies and human rights*. Unpublished data.

Vienna NGO Committee on Drugs. (2017). *UNODC concept note*. Retrieved from http://vngoc.org/wp-content/uploads/2017/11/UNODC_Concept-Note-on-ARQ_Final-002.pdf

Chapter 4

Improving Access to Internationally Controlled Essential Medicines in the Post-UNGASS, Agenda 2030 Framework

Katherine Irene Pettus

Abstract

This chapter discusses the genealogy and development of the 'access abyss in palliative care and pain relief' affecting 80 per cent of the world's people. It argues that the larger context is an epistemic abyss constituted by incomplete information about the need for controlled medicines for pain relief, and that decades of drug policy based on supply control have prevented development of the necessary knowledge base in many countries. Transnational civil society organisations are working to map and bridge this abyss through education, advocacy and action. Deeper (original) systemic and tensions in the original multilateral drug control narrative produced the current epistemic/clinical abysses and now provide space for more participatory civil society involvement. Where the earlier narrative focussed on a fear-based drive to discipline and punish non-medical use of controlled substances, the evolving (and still contested) 'world drug problem' narrative foregrounds person centred, human rights based, public health approaches to drug policy that explicitly support improved access to internationally controlled essential medicines. Recommended policies can only be operationalised through a concerted 'all hands on deck' effort guided by the international law principle of 'mutual and shared responsibility' for improving access within the context of the 2030 Agenda for Sustainable Development. This calls for enhanced communication, concerted advocacy, collaboration and pluralist praxis to fill the often gaping abyss between 'black letter law' — what is actually written in the drug control conventions — and how member states learn to interpret and operationalise it.

Keywords: Controlled essential medicines; palliative care; drug control; epistemic abyss; clinical abyss; civil society advocacy

---

Collapse of the Global Order on Drugs: From UNGASS 2016 to Review 2019, 85–100

doi:10.1108/978-1-78756-487-920181004

This chapter discusses the genealogy and development of the 'access abyss in palliative care and pain relief' affecting 80 per cent of the world's people (Knaul, 2018). It argues that the larger context is an epistemic abyss constituted by incomplete information about the need for controlled medicines for pain relief, and that decades of drug policy based on supply control have prevented development of the necessary knowledge base in many countries. Transnational civil society organisations are working to map and bridge this abyss through education, advocacy and action. The chapter does not repeat the findings of the now substantial, evidence based, literature that describes the proximate causes of unavailability, inaccessibility and unaffordability of controlled medicines in so many countries (INCB, 2015; Global Commission on Drug Policy, 2015; World Health Organisation (WHO), 2015a). It focusses, rather, on the deeper (original) systemic and narrative tensions in the multilateral drug control narrative that produced the epistemic/clinical abysses in the first place and that now provide space for more participatory civil society involvement (see Dean, Anderson, & Lovink, 2006).

Since the drug control system is member state driven, as will be explained below, participation of more pluralistic and diverse civil society movements in focussed advocacy at all levels of governance expands the quantum of information that was lacking in earlier periods, when civil society participation was minimal but very influential. Where the earlier narrative focussed on a fear-based drive to discipline and punish non-medical use of controlled substances, the evolving (and still contested) 'world drug problem' narrative foregrounds person-centred, human rights based, public health approaches to drug policy that explicitly support improved access to internationally controlled essential medicines. Recommended policies can only be operationalised through a concerted 'all hands on deck' effort guided by the international law principle of 'mutual and shared responsibility' for improving access within the context of the 2030 Agenda for Sustainable Development. This calls for enhanced communication, concerted advocacy, collaboration and pluralist praxis to fill the often-gaping abyss between 'black letter law' — what is actually written in the drug control conventions — and how member states learn to interpret and operationalise it.

Sadly, for patients in need, the system transforming activities that will ultimately improve access to controlled medicines will take time. It is an evolutionary process that entails recalibrating the traditional supply control model of multi-lateral narcotics discourse to one based on evidence and public health ethics. Under this model, governments must *increase* the demand for, and supply of, 'narcotic drugs for medical and scientific purposes' to increase access within their health systems, when for decades they have fought to reduce both demand and supply. Legitimately increasing supply means supporting supply chains that are fit for purpose and preparing an adequately skilled workforce able to relieve patient suffering, while ensuring minimum diversion and misuse of controlled medicines. Civil society advocacy emphasises the fact that states Parties' obligations under the drug control and human rights conventions, and their progress towards the Goals and Targets of the 2030 Agenda for Sustainable Development, are mutually reinforcing elements of this strategy.

Part One: The (Fixed) Legal and Institutional Framework Governing Access to Internationally Controlled Essential Medicines

Internationally controlled essential medicines (or 'controlled medicines') are pharmaceutical products that satisfy two conditions: they are found *both* on the Model List of Essential Medicines compiled by the World Health Organisation (WHO, 2015b) *and* in the 'schedules' appended to two of the three international drug control conventions (United Nations Office on Drugs and Crime (UNODC), 2013). The Model List of Essential Medicines contains 'those that satisfy the priority health needs of the population'. They are selected with due regard to disease prevalence, evidence of efficacy and safety and comparative cost-effectiveness. Essential medicines are intended to be:

> available within the context of functioning health systems at all times in adequate amounts, in the appropriate dosage forms, with assured quality, and at a price the individual and the community can afford. (WHO, 2017)

The WHO Expert Committee on the Selection and Use of Essential Medicines selects the medicines to be included on the Model List on a bi-annual basis, following a deliberative, evidence-based process. The Model List serves as a guide for the development of national and institutional controlled medicine lists. A 2008 WHO study of availability of essential medicines (not under international control) showed an average public-sector availability of only 38 per cent across surveyed countries, forcing patients to buy medicine from the private sector, where treatments are frequently unaffordable (Cameron, Ewen, Ross-Degnan, Ball, & Laing, 2008).

Controlled medicines are 'internationally controlled' when they appear in the schedules appended to the drug control conventions. The Single Convention on Narcotic Drugs (1961/1972) mandates the WHO, through its Expert Committee on Drug Dependence (ECDD), to recommend the level of international control required to (theoretically) on the one hand prevent the non-medical use of substances (some of which are both pharmaceutical products *and* controlled medicines), and on the other to ensure their availability for rational medical use. According to the ECDD webpage, the Committee:

> evaluate[s] the dependence-producing properties and harm to health of psychoactive substances, including the ones with medical use. Recommendations from the ECDD on whether or not these substances should be placed under international control are

> made to the Secretary-General of the United Nations, and are subject to a vote by the United Nations Commission on Narcotic Drugs (CND).[1]

ECDD decisions are supposed to reflect regularly updated, evidence-based deliberations by independent technical experts regarding potential public health harms and benefits of the substances.[2]

In contrast to the WHO's ECDD, which is a technical body, the Commission on Narcotic Drugs (CND) is a political body. As a functional commission of the Economic and Social Council of the United Nations, it consists of UN member states, all of which have their own national agendas, and many of which coalesce into opposing blocs or interest groups around issues of drug control and public health governance. The United Nations Office on Drugs and Crime acts as secretariat for CND, whose regular and intersessional meetings are attended by ECOSOC accredited civil society organisations. CND's mandate, according to its website, is to:

> review and analyse the global drug situation, considering the interrelated issues of prevention of drug abuse, rehabilitation of drug users and supply and trafficking in illicit drugs. It takes action through resolutions and decisions.[3]

The Single Convention explicitly directs the CND to follow the ECDD's recommendations regarding which substances should be listed in the Schedules of the drug control conventions at which level of control.[4] The evolving, treaty-mandated interaction and relationship between these two UN member state bodies — both ostensibly dedicated to the promotion and protection of public health, albeit through different discourses and mechanisms — produces interesting tensions that expose the evolving spectrum of ideological positions and narratives, creating space for productive civil society advocacy.

Medicines on the Model List that are also listed in the schedules for international control include many medicines essential to palliative care practice. They include, but are not limited to, morphine (in multiple formulations), diamorphine (also known as heroin), codeine, oxycodone, fentanyl, methadone (for the relief of severe pain and treatment of substance use disorder) and buprenorphine (also for substance use disorder).[5] The International Association for Hospice and Palliative Care has identified a list of controlled medicines used to treat the main

---

[1]Retrieved from http://www.who.int/medicines/access/controlled-substances/ecdd/en/.
[2]For historical shortcomings of the ECDD process, see Danenberg et al. (2013).
[3]Retrieved from https://www.unodc.org/unodc/en/commissions/CND/Mandate_Functions/Mandate-and-Functions_index.html.
[4]For the mechanics of the scheduling process see Bewley-Taylor, Jelsma, and Hallam (2014).
[5]For the full list see http://www.incb.org/incb/en/narcotic-drugs/Yellowlist_Forms/yellow-list.html and http://www.incb.org/incb/en/psychotropic-substances/green-lists.html (see too note 2).

symptoms for conditions requiring palliative care. These symptoms include anorexia, anxiety, constipation, delirium, depression, diarrhoea, dyspnea, fatigue, nausea and vomiting, pain and respiratory tract secretions.[6]

Tensions arise when individual CND member states, or blocs thereof, reject the recommendations of the WHO ECDD, and table agenda items requesting their CND colleagues to vote to place essential medications that are *not* under international control, in the international schedules. This occurred recently with countries, led by China, asking CND to schedule ketamine, over the WHO's head. Fortunately, owing to concerted civil society organisation (CSO) advocacy with member states, they failed, although they are continuing to pressure ECDD. Ketamine is an anaesthetic medication that is widely used for essential surgery in many Lower and Middle Income Countries, prompting the ECDD to declare that placing it under international control would precipitate a global health crisis (Joshi & Onajin-Obembe, 2016; Nickerson & Attaran, 2015). Although China and its neighbours have ketamine under strict *national* control, elements of their populations are using ketamine illicitly produced in China for non-medical purposes. Similarly, Tramadol is a widely used (because not under international control) 'weak opioid' for the treatment of moderate to severe pain. It is on the WHO Analgesic Ladder, but not the WHO Model List, and *not* under international control. However, although Tramadol is under *national* control in most countries, a pattern of non-medical use in some of those countries has resulted in their governments pressuring the WHO ECDD to recommend to the CND that it be scheduled.[7] So far, ECDD has rejected this pressure because of the widespread global use of Tramadol for pain relief, and the widespread global *un*availability of morphine for pain relief as documented in the Lancet Commission Report (Knaul et al., 2018).

Access to internationally controlled essential medicines will improve in low consumption countries to the extent that the political and technical/scientific UN organisations (the General Assembly, WHO, UNODC, INCB and CND) can develop and adopt a shared narrative that is supported and informed by national and international palliative care associations working with affected populations. The drafters of the Single Convention, through a series of compromises, inadvertently created a system with a 'division of powers' and 'checks and balances' similar to that envisioned by the US founders during that country's constitutional

[6]The list of essential palliative care medicines can be found at http://www.who.int/selection_medicines/committees/expert/19/applications/PalliativeCare_8_A_R.pdf. See also the IAHPC list of essential palliative care medicines https://hospicecare.com/about-iahpc/projects/palliative-care-essentials/iahpc-essential-medicines-for-palliative-care/,

[7]Tramadol is a "weak" opioid on Step Two of the WHO Analgesic Ladder http://www.who.int/cancer/palliative/painladder/en. See 2014 ECDD Report for analysis of Tramadol in response to request for review http://www.who.int/medicines/areas/quality_safety/6_1_Update.pdf; IDPC Note on 2017 Pre-review for 39th Session of ECDD http://fileserver.idpc.net/library/IDPC-advocacy-note_ECDD-39-session.pdf; and The 39th Session recommended Tramadol for critical review at the next session.

drafting period. In the absence of the advice and consent of affected populations and representative civil society organisations, the checks and balances were underdeveloped and could not produce positive public health outcomes. The system often malfunctions, producing tangible health and human rights harms to vulnerable populations, including those that lack access to controlled medicines.

Given more intentional and informed participation of UN organisations, member states, and CSOs, evidence-based arguments that support the evolving narrative can reinforce the often tenuous relationships among them. To the extent that they can participate in the conversations at all levels, civil society voices can legitimise a multilateral ethical framework that prioritises public health and social well-being. The 2030 Agenda for Sustainable Development, at least rhetorically, provides that ethical framework, and the General Assembly has directed all UN Agencies to align their policy agendas with its goals and targets.

Part Two: The (Shifting) Narrative and Political Framework

Cultural and Historical Roots of the Epistemic / Clinical Abyss

The epistemic/clinical abyss that configures the global cartography of untreated pain maps roughly onto the nineteeth and twentieth century cartographies of European and US colonialism, decolonisation and the breakup of the USSR. Likewise, the epigenetic damage of the modern 'war on drugs' can trace its ancestry to the shot-gun marriages between evangelical Anglo-US Christian movements and their governments' imperial and mercantilist ambitions on the high seas (see Tyrrell, 2010). In challenging the industrialisation of opium cultivation imposed by the British Empire, and the profiteering English and American mercantilists, these international religious networks demonised not only the industrialised product but also botanical sources of pain control that had been used by traditional healers and trained medical professionals for millennia, in order to end the 'evil' of 'addiction' (UNODC, 1972: Preamble). Briefly put, the war on drugs would have been unthinkable without the consistent pressure of faith-based organisations in the imperial powers (Pettus, 2016) and the constricted civil society space that resulted in the epistemic abyss.

Religion, medicine and politics were inextricably mixed with the genesis of the imperial US anti-opium crusade and its official inauguration with the 1909 Shanghai Opium Commission. The US Episcopal Bishop to the Philippines, Rev. Charles Brent, convened that meeting with Dr. Hamilton Wright, an American physician. 'Even though he rarely mentioned religion, moralism pervaded his thinking. He believed it necessary to ensure that "God reigns" in Washington and in opium policy' (Tyrrell, 2010). Quoted in the *New York Times*, Dr. Wright called his own country 'The Worst Drug Fiend in the World' (Tyrrell, 2010). Responding in part to Wright's lobbying as well as that of the legal pharmaceutical industry, Congress passed the Harrison Act of 1914, which banned even the medical use of opium, morphine and cocaine, and resulted in the criminalisation of thousands of physicians and patients who were no longer able to legally access what until the Harrison Act were their licit opioid medications.

The evangelist and overseas missionaries' insistence on deploying categories such as sin, evil and slavery to describe 'addiction' allowed stigmatising and exclusionary language to enter into the texts of the multilateral treaties, commentaries and diplomatic discourse that influence narcotics control policies and public attitudes to this day. Just as the Preamble of the cornerstone 1961/1972 Single Convention on Narcotic Drugs describes addiction as 'evil', an Internet search for 'addiction and slavery' generates more than half a million hits. Indeed, the etymology of the word 'addiction', used throughout the official CND and UNODC conventions and texts, is related to 'slavery'.[8]

So as noted above, although civil society organisations of one sort or another have been involved in multi-national narcotics control policy since its inception, very few were involved during the framing of the Single Convention and represented a dominant ideology, rather than today's pluralism of discourses. The original movement to outlaw the international commercial drug trade (largely consisting of Indian opium that was sold to a growing market in China for the benefit of US and UK trading companies) grew out of an explicitly colonial, overtly racist, socio-historical context that associated 'drug use' with non-white 'uncivilised' peoples.[9] The associated legal and civil society narrative policymakers adopted reflects an epistemic deficit, or cognitive disability, that has, until recently, prevented policymakers from apprehending the depth and breadth of the collateral consequences of the dominant supply control narrative (Mills, 1997; Pettus, 2013, Chapter 5).

The supply control narrative inscribed in the Single Convention on Narcotic Drugs (1961, 1972) identifies, classifies and names legally produced, prescribed and distributed *medications* as 'narcotic drugs' and 'psychotropic substances'. It attaches criminal justice sanctions to 'unauthorised' manufacture and distribution of both controlled medicines *and* illicitly produced and marketed 'street drugs'. This international law grants a *de facto* monopoly on production and distribution of controlled medicines to the pharmaceutical industry, labelling non-certified production and distribution 'diversion and abuse', which carried criminal punishment. States Parties and their law-abiding citizens (particularly clinicians) obey the Single Convention and the national laws that implement it[10] on pain of denunciation (by another member state, by INCB, in the General Assembly) and criminal sanctions (under national law). By designating both legal and illegal substances 'narcotic drugs', the Convention, and all the national laws modelled on it, reproduced a fundamental linguistic tension that mirrored the social and political confusion surrounding the healing/harmful properties of the substances. This tension and the accompanying risk, inscribed in countries' codes of civil and criminal law, circumscribes modern clinicians' willingness to learn about and prescribe even the most essential controlled medicines such as morphine for the

[8]Retrieved from https://originofwords.quora.com/Addict-aka-Slave.

[9]See for instance Lusane and Desmond (1991), Baum (1996), Reinarman and Levine (1997), Gordon (1994), Pettus (2013), Chapter 5 for a discussion of this argument and Pettus (2016).

[10]The Single Convention is not a 'self-executing treaty'. See Bewley-Taylor (2002).

control of pain. The vast majority of medical schools do not educate clinicians in the management of severe pain, palliative care, end of life care and palliative pharmacy/medicine. Pharmacists, physicians and nurses can graduate with little or no knowledge of how to appropriately prescribe and use controlled medicines for the multitude of patients that need them.

This epistemic deficit at the national level reveals itself in the annual reports of UN multi-lateral agencies such as CND and INCB. Until very recently, for the past half century or so (since promulgation of the Single Convention in 1961), most UN member states have interpreted the legal framework governing use of, and access to, opioids through the supply control policy lens popularly known as 'the war on drugs' (Quah et al., 2014). Decades of narrative reinforcement of this well-funded 'prohibition narrative' have consistently trumped the much weaker '(regulated) access narrative', making 'narcotic drugs for medical purposes' unaffordable, unavailable and inaccessible for the majority of the world's people.

The original, always fragile and shifting, drug control consensus that produced the Single Convention never intended to restrict availability 'for medical scientific purposes' though (Collins, 2017). It was intended to be a strictly monitored regulatory system to facilitate access to a particular class of pharmaceutical products, while completely restricting access to those same products, and their biotic sources, for *non*-medical use. The global abyss of access to pain medicine actually reflects specific oversights on the part of the founders of that system, which generate unforeseen collateral damage. By not considering or drafting the relevant operational paragraphs to direct states Parties to ensure adequate access to 'narcotic drugs for medical purposes' while drafting specific operational paragraphs for supply control, the founders created the conditions for the epistemic/clinical abyss afflicting so many patients and families today.

Until very recently, the decolonised, developing and post-Soviet bloc member states have had little or no (multi-laterally approved) information or instructions, from WHO or INCB, about how to improve access, and few have understood it as a human rights obligation. There now exist validated guidelines, and curricula for the development of 'balanced policies', and the advocacy task is to make them known and provide basic education to palliative care professionals, as the specialty slowly develops. The institutional profile of these low consumption countries (whose governments are all states Parties to the drug control conventions) tends to be characterised by under resourced public health and education systems, high levels of corruption[11] and increasing prevalence of communicable and non-communicable diseases such as HIV/AIDS, Hepatitis B and C, MDR tuberculosis, cancer, diabetes, heart disease and substance use disorders (all "diseases of the poor"). The WHO has made achievement of Universal Health Coverage, which includes essential palliative care services and medicines, a priority

[11]Low-ranked countries in the corruption indexes: http://www.worldaudit.org/corruption.htm and Transparency International: https://www.transparency.org/country/UGA tend to have low to inadequate consumption levels of controlled medicines as per INCB reports. This is an informal perception of the data that merits further systematic study.

policy. It is also one of the Targets in SDG 3 of Agenda 2030, so should get attention in national capitals if palliative care providers ask to be part of those discussions. Progress will be evident when national drug policies, and guidelines regarding access to controlled medicines, are fit for purpose.

Multi-lateral Advocacy Bridging the Epistemic Abyss: The Road to UNGASS

In 2012, a group of states Parties to the drug control conventions whose populations are most affected by the public health harms generated by strict supply control policies called for new multi-lateral approaches to reduce the high costs of drug market violence, blood-borne diseases, incarceration, untreated pain, corruption, etc. This call resulted in the multi-year process that produced the 2015 UNGASS Outcome Document and 2016 General Assembly Resolution.[12] The governments behind the UNGASS call favoured broad civil society participation in the preparatory phase, and consulted CSOs, networks of affected populations and human rights defenders during the entire process. These governments either have adequate access to controlled medicines in some areas or are now working on improving access as both a human rights obligation and good public policy.

The UNGASS preparations, which involved the development of a new multilateral narrative of evidence-based, public health focussed policy, exposed the contradictions and tensions produced by the original, supply control narrative inscribed in the Single Convention. CSOs, including the official civil society taskforce, partnered with member states, UNODC, the WHO, INCB and academic institutions to evaluate more than 50 years of experience and evidence regarding the effectiveness of drug policies implemented since the Convention was ratified in 1961. The evidence that traditional supply control strategies and ‘drug war rhetoric’ negatively impact medical use of controlled substances, as reflected in the cartography of pain that characterises the abyss in access to controlled medicines, was overwhelming, and led to the drafting of an unprecedented, stand-alone chapter (Chapter Two) in the Outcome Document. This was a far cry from the five lines in Para 19 of the 2009 Political Declaration and Plan of Action.[13]

INCB annual reports and supplements, as well as the 2015 Economist Quality of Death Index (The Economist, 2015), show that countries demonstrating acceptable or improving levels of consumption and access to controlled medicines tend to be in Middle to Upper Income brackets, with established and developing human rights systems, national human rights organisations and reasonably well-functioning judicial systems. That said, it is important to clarify that those countries did not improve access because they identified it as a human rights

[12]Retrieved from https://www.unodc.org/documents/postungass2016/outcome/V1603301-E.pdf.

[13]Retrieved from https://www.unodc.org/documents/commissions/CND/CND_Sessions/CND_52/Political-Declaration2009_V0984963_E.pdf.

obligation.[14] Drivers of improved access are strong health systems, strong civil society participation and a measure of civic trust, democratic elections and political pluralism. Such governments recognise the value of civil society organisations as sources of information and expertise. They are willing to ask CSOs to help them bridge the knowledge abyss that underlies the clinical abyss of access to controlled medicines for pain control.

Countries that opposed the UNGASS process and prefer to maintain the old regime and supply control narrative, tend towards zero-tolerance policies that restrict civil society space and associate drug use with deviance and the potential for civil and political subversion. Since they identify problematic drug use with modern 'liberal' tendencies and expanded civil society space, they cling to the more twentieth century narrative that prioritises attainment of a 'society free of drug abuse' and downplay the importance of human rights and civil society participation. This restricts their information (widens their epistemic gap) about the suffering of those without access to palliative care, especially when their elites go abroad for medical treatment because the health system in their country is sub-standard. Nonetheless, they feel patronised by the neo-colonial narrative of pro-reform drug policy governments and non-governmental organisations.

Fortunately, the narratives of the pro-reform and pro-control camps seem to be converging around the need to improve access to internationally controlled medicines, which is fitting. Even the more traditional or conservative countries recognise the need for palliative care of their older populations and children, once they learn about its benefits from civil society providers. The emerging narrative at CND and other multi-lateral agencies such as the Human Rights Council (HRC), the WHO and the General Assembly, tells these states Parties that they need to strengthen their health workforces to include access to medicines for palliative care, the treatment of pain and substance use disorder. The post-UNGASS narrative, while universal, is always particular and always depends on context and cultural interpretation of the Conventions. The UN ethic of member state equality gives equal weight to the voice of countries and vulnerable communities seeking to improve access of 'narcotic drugs for medical purposes' alongside those that continue to strictly control *non*-medical use of those same, and other, scheduled substances. Left to their own devices, the majority of member states might prefer to ignore the inconvenient ethical obligation to craft policies to improve access for poor patients who produce and consume less of the gross national product when they are dying. It is up to civil society to provide them with the necessary information to convince them of the political salience and economic advantages they will gain once they begin to fulfil that obligation.

Recent CND chairs have used the power of their position to involve civil society in the regular and inter-sessional discussions on drug policy. Since 2016, CSO voices from multi-lateral, officially recognised networks such as the Vienna and

[14]Now also articulated in the OAS Convention on the Human Rights of Older Persons. Retrieved from http://www.oas.org/en/sla/dil/inter_american_treaties_a-70_human_rights_older_persons.asp.

New York NGO Committees on Drugs, and the Civil Society Task Force, are now included in the UNGASS implementation and reporting sessions in the lead up to the High Level meeting in 2019. At the discretion of the Chair, their interventions are scheduled along with those of member states, rather than marginalised and heard only at the end of the session, when time permits. In the current institutional environment member states that otherwise would not listen to non-state actors are being exposed to the expertise of CSOs and providers in a way that would have been unthinkable even five years ago. Of course, many delegations will ignore and reject progressive civil society interventions, depending on their directions from their capitals, but they cannot object to the Chair giving CSOs the floor. This is progress in that it represents more informed global conversation about drug policy, information that is inherently political.

Palliative care providers, through national, regional and international professional associations, are collaborating with patient organisations and other global health CSOs to bridge the epistemic/clinical abyss by developing a whole-of-UN advocacy strategy. A broad spectrum of global drug policy CSO's now partner across a variety of ideological perspectives[15] to advocate directly with member states in capitals and in Vienna, Geneva and New York. This universe of interest groups can provide more fine-grained information to relevant bureaucracies and policymakers regarding the situation on the ground, as well as the legal and ethical obligations to improve access to controlled medicines, among other harm reduction strategies.[16] The organisations network across professional sectors with other concerned partners to develop a compelling, evidence-based, person centred narrative that makes public health and human rights the organising principles of debates about 'the world drug problem'. Their rational request for more cost-effective and ethical policies is gaining traction in countries that are committed to democracy, the rule of law and the protection of human rights (at least at 'home'.)

The policy shift requested by CSOs entails transferring resources from a substance- to a person-centred paradigm in order to strengthen the capacity of health and social service ministries, which traditionally garner the lowest share of national budgets. Key civil society players in this realignment advocating for controlled medicines are the national and regional palliative care organisations that participate with ECOSOC accredited international civil society advocacy networks in the regular meetings and discussions of UN organisations. As part of their strategy to broaden the scope of conflict and discourse, palliative care advocates for improved access to controlled medicines made common cause with the drug policy reform organisations such as the International Drug Policy Consortium and the Global Commission on Drug Policy in the lead up to the High Level Review and Joint Ministerial Statement approved by CND in 2014.[17]

---

[15]The Vienna NGO Committee on Drugs' membership and Board now includes CSOs representing affected populations from many communities in different member states and regions. See www.vngoc.org.

[16]The cornerstone political theory text on interest group theory by Truman (1951).

[17]Retrieved from https://www.unodc.org/documents/drug-prevention-and-treatment/Joint_Ministerial_Statement_2014_High Level_Review_by_the_Commission.pdf.

This issue brought our movements together and helped both to get increased traction at the multi-lateral level.

Current international and regional advocacy strategies to improve access to controlled medicines include coaching colleagues in 'pioneer countries', those that are taking steps to improve access, to assist their counterparts in more fragile states with weak health systems and strong law enforcement presence in the drug markets. Fragile states often restrict civil society space and prevent health professionals from learning the new skills they need to implement the public health approach to drug policy recommended by the 2016 UNGASS Outcome Document. The support of regional and international palliative care associations, funded by progressive philanthropic foundations, is essential to bridge the epistemic/clinical gap in countries where civil society space is restricted and palliative care is not publicly funded, the vast majority. Civil society's right and ability to organise and function democratically is key to constructing the informed national and multi-national narratives that will support publicly funded palliative care.

International, regional and national palliative care advocates are engaging through their networks at the CND, the WHO and HRC to inform member states about how they can help bridge the epistemic/clinical abyss. Their goal is to 'normalise' the global health discourse around access to pain medicine and palliative care and to ensure the routine inclusion of palliative care in the discussions around universal health coverage. This supports the work of national and local associations by weaving a protective normative *pallium*,[18] for healthcare practitioners, just as their clinical care provides a pallium for the patient.

Legitimate CSO advocacy, as noted above, traverses the ideological spectrum of political commitments and engages discursively with member states and multi-lateral agencies across the UN system. Increasing public and policymaker awareness about the issue of the access abyss for controlled medicines prepares the ground for concrete legislative action and budgeting support. The palliative care CSOs generally represent people who cannot, and do not, represent themselves. Whenever possible, as at the January 2018 142nd WHO Executive Board Meeting, their voices are included in plenary interventions when 'non-state actors' are given the floor.

Conclusion: UNGASS 2016, the SDGS, the WHO 13th Programme of Work, and the 2019 High Level Ministerial Meeting

In order to fully bridge the epistemic/clinical abyss of access to palliative care and controlled medicines in the 80 per cent of the world that lacks access, palliative care CSOs must continue aligning the access narrative with a whole range of UN strategy that includes the Goals and Targets of Agenda 2030 and the WHO 13th General Programme of Work. Palliative care advocates will develop joint strategies with drug policy CSOs, global health and faith-based organisations committed

[18]A 'pallium' (Latin) denotes a cloak, protective cover, or mantle. It is the root word of 'palliative'.

to palliative care, and *non*-palliative care CSOs contesting public health harms of neoliberal agendas that prioritise private profit over person-entered public health.[19]

Palliative care is the quintessential, person-centred, public health, clinical practice that leaves no one behind. Paradoxically, few people know about it, or understand its holistic approach, which also requires rational access to internationally controlled essential medicines. Palliative care is an essential service under UHC (Target 3.8 of the SDGs). A new, albeit fragile, rhetorical, normative and juridical *pallium* now lightly covers providers and governments aspiring to improve access to controlled medicines for the relief of pain and palliative care. The International Narcotics Control Board, formerly a bastion of supply side supervision alone, has published two detailed Supplements in recent years[20] and gives considerable visibility to the issue of lack of access to controlled medicines in its public appearances at multilateral meetings (see Tupper & Labate, 2012). UNODC has signed a Memorandum of Agreement with the WHO committing to work together on the public health dimensions of drug control issue, as well as an MOU with the Vienna NGO Committee on Drugs.[21] The disconnect is that the providers on the ground in member states don't know about or understand these developments, or how they relate to their daily practice. The International Association for Hospice and Palliative Care is taking on the task of informing national and regional palliative care associations about the developments in international law and practice through multi-country advocacy workshops involving providers as well as government representatives.

These workshops are essential because member states need to reach out to the *implementers*, the palliative care health workers on the ground, if they are to implement the UNGASS recommendations and achieve the SDG targets that benefit patients and families. Operationalising the recommendations means building political support, finding funding and strengthening community health workforces, which synergises with several Goals and Targets of the 2030 Agenda for Sustainable Development.

Advocates for improved access to controlled medicines in Lower and Middle Income countries will count the 2019 High Level Meeting a success if member states can sustain an honest conversation about the evidence-driven narrative that has developed and the practice shifts that have taken place at all levels of drug policy since they approved the 2009 Political Declaration. As this chapter has

[19]Such as the People's Health Movement: http://www.phmovement.org/.

[20]Report of the International Narcotics Control Board on the Availability of Internationally Controlled Drugs: Ensuring Adequate Access for Medical and Scientific Purposes. (2010). Retrieved from https://www.incb.org/documents/Publications/AnnualReports/AR2010/Supplement-AR10_availability_English.pdf.

Availability of Internationally Controlled Drugs: Ensuring Adequate Access for Medical and Scientific Purposes. (2015). Retrieved from http://www.incb.org/documents/Publications/AnnualReports/AR2015/English/Supplement-AR15_availability_English.pdf.

[21]Retrieved from http://vngoc.org/wp-content/uploads/2017/03/MOU-UNODC-VNGOC_Final-Draft.pdf and https://www.unodc.org/unodc/en/frontpage/2017/January/mou-with-vienna-ngo-committee-on-drugs-stresses-unodcs-commitment-to-forging-partnerships-against-illicit-drugs.html.

argued, these shifts include the broader involvement of civil society at all levels of consultation and implementation (national, regional and international). The meeting will also be a success if the former colonial powers, who were the original architects of the drug control system, acknowledge, not necessarily explicitly, but through substantive consultation and financial support, their shared responsibility for the persistent deficits.[22] Doing so carries the obligation to help strengthen the health systems of their former colonies, upon request, and repair the historical trauma that underlies much of the pandemic of untreated pain.

References

Baum, D. (1996). *Smoke and mirrors: The war on drugs and the politics of failure* (p. 21). Boston, MA: Little Brown.

Bewley-Taylor, D. R. (2002). *United States and international drug control, 1909–1997*. A&C Black, London: UK.

Bewley-Taylor, D., Jelsma, M., & Hallam, C. (2014). *Scheduling in the international drug control system*. Transnational Institute, Amsterdam.

Cameron, A., Ewen, M., Ross-Degnan, D., Ball, D., & Laing, R. (2008). Medicine prices, availability, and affordability in 36 developing and middle-income countries: A secondary analysis. *The Lancet*. doi: 10.1016/S0140-6736(08)61762-6 1; www.thelancet.com. Published online December 1, 2008. https://www.ncbi.nlm.nih.gov/pubmed/19042012

Collins, J. (2017). Rethinking 'flexibilities' in the international drug control system – Potential, precedents and models for reforms. *International Journal of Drug Policy*.

Danenberg, E., Sorge, L. A., Wieniawski, W., Elliott, S., Amato, L., & Scholten, W. K. (2013). Modernizing methodology for the WHO assessment of substances for the international drug control conventions. *Drug and alcohol dependence*, *131*(3), 175–181.

Dean, J., Anderson, J. W., & Lovink, G. (Eds.) 2006. *Reformatting politics: Information technology and global civil society*. London: Routledge.

Global Commission on Drug Policy. (2015). *Global Commission on Drug Policy report "The negative impact of drug control on public health: The crisis of avoidable pain"*. Retrieved from http://www.globalcommissionondrugs.org/reports/the-negative-impact-of-drug-control-on-public-health-the-global-crisis-of-avoidable-pain/

Gordon, D. R. (1994). *The return of the dangerous classes: Drug prohibition and policy politics*. New York, NY: WW Norton.

INCB Supplement. (2015). Availability of Internationally Controlled Drugs: Ensuring Access for Medical and Scientific Purposes. Retrieved from http://www.incb.org/documents/Publications/AnnualReports/AR2015/English/Supplement-AR15_availability_English.pdf

Joshi, G. P., & Onajin-Obembe, B. (2016). The role of ketamine in low-and middle-income countries: What would happen if ketamine becomes a scheduled drug? *Anesthesia & Analgesia*, *122*(3), 908–910.

[22]For a useful discussion see Nollkaemper and Jacobs (2012).

Knaul, F. M., Farmer,P. E., Krakauer, E. L., L. De Lima, L., Bhadelia, A., Jiang Kwete, X., Arreola-Ornelas, H., Gomez-Dantes, O., Rodriguez, N. M., Alleyne, G. A. O., Connor, S. R., Hunter, D. J., Lohman, D., Radbruch, L., Del Rocio Saenz Madrigal, M., Atun, R., Foley, K. M., Frenk, J., Jamison, D. T. & Rajagopal, M. R. (2018). Alleviating the access abyss in palliative care and pain relief-an imperative of universal health coverage: the Lancet Commission report. *Lancet*, *391*(10128), 1391–454. Online October 12, 2017. Open access with registration at: https://www.thelancet.com/journals/lancet/article/PIIS0140-6736(17)32513-8/fulltext .

Lusane, C., & Desmond, D. (1991). *Pipe dream blues: Racism and the war on drugs*. South End Press, Boston.

Mills, C. W. (1997). *The racial contract*. Ithaca, NY: Cornell University Press.

Nickerson, J. W., & Attaran, A. (2015). The Commission on Narcotic Drugs' attempt to restrict ketamine. *The Lancet*, *385*(9971), e19.

Nollkaemper, A., & Jacobs, D. (2012). Shared responsibility in international law: a conceptual framework. *Michigan Journal of International Law*, *34*, 359.

Pettus, K. I. (2013). *Felony disenfranchisement in America: Historical origins, institutional racism, and modern consequences*. SUNY Press.

Pettus, K. I. (2016). Churches and international policy: The case of the "war on drugs," a call to metanoia. *Philosophia Reformata*, *81*(1), 50–69.

Quah, D., Collins, J., Atuesta Becerra, L., Caulkins, J., Csete, J., Drucker, E., & Restrepo, P. (2014). *Ending the drug wars: Report of the LSE Expert Group on the economics of drug policy*. Global Commission on Drug Policy Reports. Retrieved from http://eprints.lse.ac.uk/56706/1/Ending_the%20_drug_wars.pdf.

Reinarman, C., & Levine, H. G. (Eds.). (1997). *Crack in America: Demon drugs and social justice*. Berkeley, CA: University of California Press.

The Economist. (2015). *The 2015 quality of death index. Ranking palliative care across the world*. London: The Economist Intelligence Unit.

Truman, D. (1951). The governmental process. New York: Alfred A. Knopf.

Tupper, K., & Labate, B. C. (2012). Plants, psychoactive substances and the International Narcotics Control Board: The control of nature and the nature of control. *Human Rights and Drugs*, *2*, 17–28. http://www.hr-dp.org/files/2013/12/12/HRDP_Journal_Tupper_Labate.pdf.

Tyrrell, I. (2010). *Reforming the world: The creation of America's moral empire*. Princeton University Press.

United Nations Office on Drugs and Crime (UNODC). (1972). *Single Convention on Narcotic Drugs as amended by the 1972 Protocol amending the Single Convention on Narcotic Drugs 1971*. New York, NY: United Nations.

United Nations Office on Drugs and Crime (UNODC). (2013). *The International Drug Control Convention*. New York, NY: United Nations. Retrieved from https://www.unodc.org/unodc/en/commissions/CND/conventions.html

World Health Organisation (WHO). (2015a). *Guidelines, "Ensuring balance in national policies on controlled substances"*. Geneva, Switzerland: WHO. Retrieved from http://www.who.int/medicines/areas/quality_safety/GLs_Ens_Balance_NOCP_Col_EN_sanend.pdf

World Health Organisation (WHO). (2015b). *Model list of essential medicines*. Geneva, Switzerland: WHO. Retrieved from http://www.who.int/medicines/publications/essentialmedicines/en/

World Health Organisation (WHO). (2017). *Expert committee on the selection and use of essential medicine*. Retrieved from http://www.who.int/selection_medicines/list/en/; http://www.who.int/selection_medicines/committees/expert/21/en/

Chapter 5

The Elephant in the Room: Cannabis in the International Drug Control Regime

Tom Blickman

Abstract

This chapter looks at the past, present and future of international cannabis control required by the UN drug control conventions in the post-2016 United Nations General Assembly Special Session era with an eye on the next High Level Ministerial Segment (HLMS) at the UN Commission on Narcotic Drugs in 2019, and beyond. From a policy analysis perspective, the author meanders through the increasing tendency to legally regulate recreational cannabis markets notwithstanding the obligation enshrined in the UN drug control conventions to limit cannabis exclusively for 'medical and scientific' purposes. Taking into account relevant national and international developments, the chapter describes how the growing discomfort with the status of cannabis and the prohibitive and punitive approach stemming from the international drug control regime went through a process from soft to hard defections of the treaty obligations. The case of the Netherlands demonstrates the difficulty faced by reform-minded states in reconciling their wish for a different cannabis control mechanism with their obligations under international law, resulting in an incomplete regulation of its coffee-shop system, where small amounts of cannabis are tolerated for sale, but where the illicit supply to the shops remained unregulated. Subsequent more wide-ranging reforms to regulate cannabis from seed to sale in Uruguay, several US States and – in 2018 – in Canada, are clearly violating the obligations of the UN drug control conventions. Nevertheless, the HLMS will likely leave the elephant in the room untouched. The emerging paradigm shift regarding cannabis shows that a modernisation of the UN drug control regime is long overdue. This chapter discusses some of the options available.

Keywords: Cannabis; drug policy; international law; United Nations; drug control conventions; drug policy reform

Collapse of the Global Order on Drugs: From UNGASS 2016 to Review 2019, 101–131

doi:10.1108/978-1-78756-487-920181005

Introduction

The emerging acceptance of cannabis – the world's most widely used, internationally controlled recreational psychoactive substance – has led more and more jurisdictions around the world to enact reforms allowing access to cannabis for purposes other than 'medical and scientific' – the only purposes allowed under the 1961 UN Single Convention. These reforms generate tensions between the existing UN drug conventions and law and practice in Member States, which have become the 'elephant in the room' in the UN drug control system, including the 2016 United Nations General Assembly Special Session (UNGASS) on the World Drug Problem – obviously present, but studiously ignored (Bewley-Taylor, Jelsma, Rolles, & Walsh, 2016). Nevertheless, drug policy and international law scholars have started to point out these tensions (Boister, 2016; Hall, 2017). However, nothing in the preparatory process for the next High Level Ministerial Segment (HLMS) at the 2019 UN Commission on Narcotic Drugs (CND) indicates that it will be any different that year.

In the run up to the 2016 UNGASS, the former Deputy Executive Director and Director of Research and Policy of the United Nations Office on Drugs and Crime (UNODC), Sandeep Chawla, a veteran official in the corridors of the UN drug control regime, spelled out the dilemma:

> we may eventually get to the first step to remove what was quite clearly [...] the weakest and the most vulnerable point of the whole control system, which is something that has been obvious for 30 years, but nobody has ever been able to do anything about it, because of the dead weight of multilateral consensus, and that was to include cannabis in the same control regime as heroin and cocaine [...]. That oddity of the system needs to be removed, and the UNGASS can take the first step towards it.' (Chawla, 2014; Ingraham, 2014)

UNGASS 2016: A Missed Opportunity

Sandeep Chawla's cautious optimism about the status of cannabis in the UN drug control system did not come true and the 2016 UNGASS did not address the issue of cannabis. The Outcome Document, negotiated and approved before the actual meeting (Bewley-Taylor & Jelsma, 2016), reconfirmed the outdated commitments of the 2009 Political Declaration, to '[i]ncrease cooperation at all levels and enhance measures to prevent and significantly and measurably reduce or eliminate the illicit cultivation of opium poppy, coca bush and cannabis plant' (UN General Assembly (UNGA), 2016). That was the only specific mention of cannabis in the document.

At that moment, Uruguay had effectively legalised and regulated the non-medical use of cannabis in December 2013 (Walsh & Ramsey, 2016), while in the United States, the states of Colorado, Washington and Oregon had already established legally taxed and regulated cannabis markets and Alaska was finalising preparations to implement the results of its November 2014 ballot initiative. In February 2015, Jamaica had decriminalised the possession of less than two ounces of cannabis, by making it a misdemeanour rather than a felony offence, allowing the sacramental use by Rastafarians, establishing regulations for medical, scientific and therapeutic use while providing a licensing system to regulate 'allowed uses' (Ministry of Justice (Jamaica), 2015). The newly elected Prime Minister of Canada, Justin Trudeau, had announced that cannabis would be legalised and strictly regulated when he won the elections in October 2015. These measures to allow the non-medical and non-scientific use of cannabis are clear contraventions of the 1961 UN Single Convention on Narcotic Drugs.

Nevertheless, the 'dead weight of multilateral consensus' – also known as the Vienna consensus (Boister, 2016; Jelsma & Metaal, 2004), due to the fact that international drug policy is being shaped by the Member States and UN institutions in the Austrian capital – once again prevented an open and honest debate on an issue that will shape the future of the international drug control regime and the relevance of the UN drug control conventions in the coming years. However, in the country statements at the meeting in New York, the wind – or rather the breeze of change was occasionally felt. Canada announced its intention to legalise and regulate, acknowledging that '[w]hile this plan challenges the status quo in many countries, we are convinced it is the best way to protect our youth while enhancing public safety' (UNGASS, 2016a). Jamaica argued that 'the classification of cannabis under the Single Convention is an anomaly', referring in particular to the medical value of the substance (UNGASS, 2016b).

Later that year, in November 2016, that challenge only became more obvious when California, Maine, Massachusetts and Nevada approved ballot initiatives legalising and regulating cannabis for non-medical use. In January 2018, Vermont legalised the possession and use of marijuana, the first state to do so via the legislature, rather than by ballot initiative. Including Vermont, nine US states (plus the District of Columbia) have now chosen some form of legal regulation of cannabis rather than ban it (Walsh, 2016). Despite federal prohibition, more than one in five Americans are now living in states that have opted to legalise cannabis, including the entire west coast, and more states are likely to follow, either via the legislative process or by ballot initiative (Newsweek, 2018). The accommodation of cannabis liberalisation at the state level while federal prohibition continues was made possible by the decision of the Obama administration to allow states to go ahead under certain conditions clarified in the Cole memorandum in August 2013 (Cole, 2013), leaving the issue in a sort of legal grey area. Deputy Attorney General James Cole determined that, amongst other conditions, if states made efforts to prevent the distribution of cannabis to minors, prevent revenues of sales to go to criminal enterprises, diversion to non-regulating states, drug driving and other adverse public health consequences, federal authorities would not intervene, unless state regulation was ineffective and federal enforcement priorities were threatened. In fact, according the professor Neil Boister, the Cole Memorandum *de facto*, if not *de jure*, concedes the existence of a jurisdiction in regulating US states to effectively regulate cannabis markets (Boister, 2016).

In January 2018, President Donald Trump's Attorney General, Jeff Sessions, rescinded the Cole memorandum, reverting to standard US Justice Department guidance regarding prosecution of cannabis-related activities. It remains to be seen how aggressively federal prosecutors may move against state-legal cannabis conduct, but it is already clear that those states that have already chosen to legalise and regulate are not backing away from their new laws. Indeed, Sessions' move to rescind the Cole memorandum, even if it does not generate a new wave of federal enforcement against cannabis, appears to be prompting more urgency from members of Congress from both parties to modernise US federal law on cannabis in ways that explicitly protect state-level legalisation. Time will tell, but early indications suggest that the Trump administration's effort to turn back the clock on state-level cannabis regulation will likely backfire, hastening the day when the US Congress acts to substantially reform federal law (Garvey & Yeh, 2018).

The bottom-up reform by US states weakens the position of the federal government – for decades the effective enforcer of global cannabis prohibition. The United States is currently in no position to stop similar regulatory reform efforts abroad. That will benefit its northern neighbour Canada, which is set to regulate in 2018. Even on the other side of the Atlantic, in Europe, change is in the air. While national governments in Europe are still in a state of denial about the changing policy landscape that is beginning to take shape worldwide, in particular in North America, at the local level the call for regulatory approaches is steadily increasing. Calls for change from local authorities that have to deal with the negative consequences of a persisting illicit cannabis market are still ignored. While historically liberal countries like the Netherlands and Denmark used to defend their policies with a public health argument of a separation of the markets of less and more hazardous drugs, the emphasis has shifted to a public security approach, to counter the public disorder of street dealing, and the involvement of organised crime groups in illicit cultivation and supply (Blickman, 2014).

Soft Defection and the Limits of Latitude

The discontent with the consequences of cannabis' status within the UN treaty system is not new. Over the past 40 years, several countries adapted their policies and moved away from the punitive prohibitions. Successive waves of what might be considered 'soft defection' of the control regime, whereby authorities tried to remain within the flexibility afforded by the treaty framework, but diverged from the prohibitive standard privileged within the conventions, resulted in a 'quiet revolution' of decriminalisation in some US states and European countries since the 1970s (Bewley-Taylor, Blickman, & Jelsma, 2014; Rosmarin & Eastwood, 2012). These waves of soft defection mainly consisted of diminishing or abolishing penal provisions for personal use, possession for personal use, and in some instances the cultivation of a limited amount of plants for personal use.

Most prominent and challenging for the regime was the emergence of the Dutch coffee-shop system after the Netherlands *de facto* decriminalised the use and possession of cannabis in 1976, a symbol of the liberal and public health approach to drugs in Dutch society, and a decades-long outlier internationally, defying the mostly prohibitive and law enforcement-based systems of cannabis control (Boekhout van Solinge, 2017). While eventually more jurisdictions would decriminalise use and possession for personal use, no one went as far as the Dutch in allowing the sale of small amounts in licensed retail shops. However, the will to reform by the Dutch was seriously hampered by the country's obligations under international law.

The revised opium law of 1976 in the Netherlands created a legal distinction between drugs with an unacceptable health risk (such as amphetamines, cocaine and heroin) listed on Schedule I and cannabis products (including hashish) on Schedule II. This led to the implementation of different policies for these two categories of drugs, an approach that came to be known as the 'separation of the markets' for 'soft' and 'hard' drugs (Boekhout van Solinge, 1999). This policy diverged from the scheduling in the 1961 UN Single Convention, where cannabis is listed at the same level as heroin and cocaine. Originally, the Dutch government at the time was even prepared to legalise cannabis (Grund & Breeksma, 2013), according to a government memorandum of January 1974:

> The use of cannabis products and the possession of them for personal use should be removed as soon as possible from the domain of criminal justice. However, this cannot be realized as yet, as it would bring us into conflict with our treaty obligations. The Government shall explore in international consultations whether it is feasible that agreements as the Single Convention be amended in a way that nations will be free to institute, at their discretion, a separate regime for cannabis products. (De Kort, 1994)

The government did indeed initiate consultations. The issue was discussed during a visit of Robert DuPont, the highest U.S. drug policy official in the Ford administration in May 1975. DuPont, who advocated for decriminalisation at home in the U.S., made it clear that amending the Single Convention as desired by the Dutch government could "not be achieved in the near term", and mentioned a time frame of at least 5 to 10 years, due to the inertia of the international bureaucracy. If anything, the US officials noted, the consultations did make clear that Dutch officials were "more aware that the ramifications of the cannabis problem were more complex than they had supposed, and that it could not be dealt with safely or adequately simply by legalizing its use and then forgetting about it", and that "the Dutch will examine with greater care the possible implications of some of the positions it has voiced", in particular towards it neighbours. (US Embassy in The Hague, 1975)

In spite of the fact that the Single Convention had just undergone substantial amendments, laid down in the 1972 Protocol Amending the 1961 Convention, the Dutch government became fully aware that reaching agreement on an amendment allowing more lenient cannabis policies was unrealistic at the time. Meanwhile, possession of small quantities of cannabis was no longer regarded as an offence but as a misdemeanour. Investigation and prosecution were assigned the 'lowest judicial priority'. Police investigation and prosecution of cannabis users were given very low priority, and this led, in practice, to tolerating cannabis possession for personal use. The policy of toleration and inaction is based on the expediency principle in Dutch law, a discretionary option that allows the prosecutor to refrain from prosecution if it is in the public interest to do so. Based on that principle, coffee shops are tolerated when they follow guidelines issued by the Public Prosecutions

Department (Boekhout van Solinge, 2017; Boister, 2016). This tolerance policy extended rapidly to include small-scale sales of cannabis. While the Dutch government never contemplated the institution of coffee shops where small amounts of cannabis would be sold – the policy originally was meant to allow 'house dealers' in popular youth centres – over the years the criteria used to allow tolerated sale of cannabis extended to gradually more commercial enterprises due to court rulings that favoured the emerging coffee-shop system (Boekhout van Solinge, 2017; Grund & Breeksma, 2013). The number of coffee shops where hashish and cannabis were available gradually began increasing from the early eighties onward.

Whereas the front-door policy could be justified by reason of the expediency principle to be one of its 'basic legal concepts' protected in the UN drug control conventions – the Netherlands did make a reservation to safeguard the policy when the 1988 UN Convention against Illicit Traffic in Narcotic Drugs and Psychotropic Substances tightened control provisions – a regulation of the back door was not possible under the regime (Boister, 2016). Due to these limits of latitude in the UN drug conventions (Bewley-Taylor & Jelsma, 2012), the coffee-shop system became a half-baked compromise: cannabis sales were allowed at what became known as the front door of the coffee shop, whereas the supply at the back door was fully illegal and everyone involved pretended not to know where it came from. This 'immaculate conception'[1] of cannabis eventually would lead to problems, since the supply relied on the involvement of organised large-scale Dutch hashish traffickers in the 1980s and 1990s. In 1995, a new Dutch government took office with justice and health ministers in favour of cannabis legalisation. They were committed to end the discrepancy between permitted sales at the coffee shops' front door and the illegal supply at the back door. The original policy intention was that municipalities wishing to experiment with the supply of locally cultivated cannabis to *bona fide* coffee shops could do so if the local triangular consultations between the mayor, the chief public prosecutor and the head of police, agreed, and after consent of the meeting of the prosecutors general at the national level, which was open to the reform. The policy, in fact, was an extension of the expediency principle allowing for regulated sales of cannabis in coffee shops, to the cultivation and supply for the coffee shops (Van Dijk, 1998).

The idea was that a regulated supply could reduce the criminal opportunities for the large Dutch illegal hash traders that had emerged in the 1980s, that were not only supplying the domestic market but were also responsible for a large proportion of the international cannabis trade (Van Dijk, 1998). Those reforms, however, stirred resistance amongst European partners, in particular, the French President Jacques Chirac. He started a campaign against Dutch coffee shops and mobilised political support in Brussels, where European cooperation had been extended to include the area of law enforcement and justice. In the end, the Dutch government, worried about the damage that unilateral legalisation could do to international relations, abandoned the idea of regulating cannabis supplies for

[1]As far as the author knows, Francisco Thoumi, currently a member of the INCB, was the first who coined this depiction.

coffee shops – despite the fact that the chief prosecution office had the regulations ready (Boekhout van Solinge, 2017; Van Dijk, 1998; Lensink & Derkzen, 2013).

The final result, laid out in the 1995 government white paper *Continuity and Change* (GON, 1995), was an accommodation on the cannabis issue. While the original intention to liberate the back door was eliminated, the position of coffee shops in the cannabis market was formally consolidated, becoming the only endorsed cannabis retail selling points operating on the basis of a municipal license. Cannabis supply to coffee shops remained illegal, but new prosecution guidelines were issued to try to shape illegal supply. The design was to reduce cannabis imports of the large criminal networks importing hash in favour of small home growing. Small, non-professional home growers with a five plants maximum got low law enforcement priority, with the intent that many of these small growers would supply the coffee shops. Allowing many of these small growers to supply coffee shops was seen as the second-best option for limiting the opportunities for criminal cannabis groups and organised crime (Boekhout van Solinge, 2017; Van Dijk, 1998).

Once again, the Dutch aspiration for reform was held back by the straitjacket of the UN drug control conventions, as well as European agreements, in particular, the 1990 Schengen Convention implementing the 1985 Schengen Agreement. In the white paper, the government contemplated 'to introduce a state monopoly or a licensing system'. In doing so:

> it would be possible to reduce the role of criminal organisations in coffee shops. The international obligations which the Netherlands has taken upon itself stand in the way of such an approach, however.

The government considered that 'the disadvantages outweigh the practical advantages.' Problems concerning the coffee shops could better be solved within the framework of the UN conventions by 'amending the procedural policies of the Public Prosecutions Department and introducing administrative regulation.' As in 1974, the government considered an international debate on the advantages and disadvantages of the legalisation of cannabis 'desirable'. However, the Dutch contribution to that debate:

> should be made cautiously and with the appropriate awareness of the relativity of Dutch views on the subject. The approach to be adopted should include the establishment of relations with strategic partners abroad. (GON, 1995)

Legal advice to the government on whether the Netherlands could unilaterally decide to legalise the market in cannabis and cannabis products, repealing the provisions making it a criminal offence to cultivate cannabis plants for non-medical and scientific purposes recognised in the 1961 Single Convention, was not encouraging. The conclusion was that both the 1961 Single Convention on Narcotic Drugs and the 1988 UN Convention Against Illicit Traffic in Narcotic Drugs and Psychotropic Substances would have to be denounced, and that there would be little chance to re-access with a reservation on the issues of cannabis (a procedure that would be successfully pursued by Bolivia regarding the traditional use of coca in 2012–2013) due to the fact that a sufficient number of parties (more than one-third in the case of 1961 Convention) would oppose such a reservation (Schutte, 1995).

The European Dimension

Even more complicated were the limitations due to the 1990 Schengen Convention implementing the 1985 Schengen Agreement on the abolition of controls at common borders by some EU member states. EU law regarding cannabis assumes full compliance with the UN drug control conventions, but contrary to those international instruments, the legal advisor concluded that denunciation and re-accession with a reservation to the 1990 Convention were legally not possible (Schutte, 1995). The debate on cannabis legalisation in Europe was thus further complicated by the dimension of European integration, and unlike in 1974, now also had to be pursued within the European legal framework. In an effort to rein in the lenient policies of the Netherlands, Chirac put the 'harmonisation' of drug policy on the European agenda. In 1996, this led to Council Joint Action 96/750/JHA aimed at reinforcing the cooperation of Member States which included a call to approximate their laws to make them mutually compatible to the extent necessary to prevent and combat illegal drug trafficking in the Union, which specifically mentioned measures to counter 'drug tourism' – an obvious reference to foreign buyers in the Dutch coffee shops – and to take the most appropriate steps to combat the illicit cultivation of cannabis, while reiterating that Member States should fulfil their obligations under the United Nations Conventions (EU Council, 1996).

Nevertheless, successive Dutch governments succeeded in ensuring that the 2004 EU Council Framework Decision (2004/757/JHA) on drug trafficking – that replaced Council Joint Action 96/750/JHA – would not commit to changing Dutch policy on the front door coffee shops and the possession of small amounts of drugs for personal use. Like the previous instrument, the Framework Decision only requires legislative action and does not intervene in enforcement and prosecution policies. The established principles of subsidiarity embedded in the European treaty system (to not regulate at EU level what is nationally possible) and proportionality (against any excessive response to a particular problem) were respected (Oostlander, 2004). However, concerning the back door of the coffee shops it did confirm restrictions, given the possible cross-border effects, since each Member State was required to take the necessary measures to ensure that distribution and cultivation of cannabis plants, other than for personal consumption, should be punishable (EU Council, 2004). The European instruments do not specifically focus on the use of cannabis. This is left to the Member States, given that different European countries pursue very diverse policies, from zero tolerance in Sweden to the coffee shop in the Netherlands and decriminalisation in Portugal and the Czech Republic (Blickman, 2016).

The drive towards 'harmonisation' has had policy implications in the Netherlands as the most advanced country in the diverse EU cannabis policy landscape. Amongst senior policy makers in the Netherlands a 'wait and see' attitude became prevalent: any progress would depend on a willingness for change abroad. In the meantime, the Netherlands had no other option than 'to muddle on with its (in)famous coffeeshop system', as one of the officials involved in the 1995 reform attempt put it, for some more years and implement a pragmatic give-and-take policy at the international level, maintaining the status quo as a transitional situation on the road to a possible future administrative regulation (Van Dijk, 1998). Over the years, however, it has led to stricter legislative action in the Netherlands through an array of new instruments in the Opium Act, such as increases in penalties for cannabis offences at the supply side – commercial growing or wholesale selling of cannabis – and for participation in a criminal organisation. The overall effect was a tightening of policies, in particular, regarding the supply of cannabis, and was probably the basis for stronger law enforcement action by a special unit (the Taskforce Tackling Organised Hemp-growing) against illicit cultivation. The European Commission specifically expressed its concerns regarding the problem of the supply of coffee shops by criminal networks (EU Council, 2010).

In the Netherlands itself, this would lead to increasing divergence between the national government, conscious of maintaining its international legal obligations and anxious about its relations with neighbouring countries, and municipal authorities that were confronted with some negative consequences of the policy, leading to increased illicit cultivation at the local level. At the European level, the result was that future national drug policies would be subject to the rule of adhering to the lowest common denominator within the European Union as in the UN drug control system, which means that reform adverse countries are able to obstruct progress towards more liberal cannabis policies in the consensus-oriented policy process based on the restrictive UN drug control conventions that have been incorporated in European legislation (Blickman, 2014).

As far as harmonisation on the user side is concerned, the principle of proportionality and subsidiarity within the EU, which respects the different approaches in European countries due to historical and cultural differences, seems to be gaining momentum (De Witte, 2013). The restriction lies in the possible cross-border effects. In that respect it is interesting to look at the measures taken by the Obama administration after the cannabis regulation in Colorado and the state of Washington. The recently rescinded Cole memorandum gave US prosecutors discretion for non-prosecution of state cannabis regulation under certain conditions, although it is contrary to federal law. One of those conditions is the prevention of 'leaks' of cannabis to states where cannabis is not legal. Another condition is to prevent the proceeds from benefiting criminal associations. If such a measure is possible in a federal state such as the United States – taking into account that the decision to refrain from prosecution under certain conditions is more a policy than a legal decision –why should it not be possible in a confederal context such as the European Union?

A modification of the UN drug treaties regarding cannabis should be reflected in European regulation, which, after all, mainly relies on the international law obligations of the UN treaties. Another possibility in the European context is to get an exception regarding cannabis. An example is the exception that Sweden has stipulated for the use of snus, a kind of a smokeless, moist powder tobacco pouch that you place under your top lip that is traditionally used in the country. When Sweden joined the EU in 1995, Sweden negotiated an exception to the ban on the production and use of snus that applies in the EU. This exemption was confirmed in the new Directive 2014/40/EU (EU, 2014). Whether a country can stipulate an exception retrospectively is not entirely clear, but the reservation made by Bolivia concerning coca in the 1961 Single Convention may create a precedent in international law.

Growing International Disparity in Cannabis Control

Cannabis has not always been the elephant in the room, in particular, when the soft defections of the regime were concerned. Already in 1996, the International Narcotics Control Board (INCB, 1996), the independent and quasi-judicial body for the implementation of the United Nations drug control conventions, aware of the reforms the Netherlands had intended and the formalisation of the coffee shop policy had questioned the Dutch government's 'fidelity to its treaty obligations'. Over the years, the Board had become increasingly critical regarding policies deviating from strict prohibition of the non-medical and non-scientific use of cannabis, in particular in the so-called 'industrial' countries, while pointing to the obvious inconsistency that countries which used to have widespread traditional use, did implement the provision of the UN drug control conventions (Bewley-Taylor, 2014).

The growing disparity in cannabis control measures since the 1990s between mainly western consumer countries and traditional, mostly southern, producer countries led to a clash at the 2002 session of the CND (Bewley-Taylor, 2012; Blickman, 2002). The clash was based on the 2001 annual report of the INCB, which contained strong language about the leniency towards cannabis consumption in some consumer countries. On the Netherlands, for instance, the report said that it:

> continues to maintain a policy, introduced in the 1970s, of tolerating the consumption and sale of cannabis products in so-called 'coffee shops', which is not in compliance with the international drug control treaties. (INCB, 2002a, para. 553)

The report invited the international community 'to take note of and discuss the new cannabis policies in a number of countries and to agree on ways to address that development within the framework of international law' at the CND (INCB, 2002a, para. 228).

On the first day of the CND session, the president of the INCB, Hamid Ghodse, stated:

> In the light of the changes that are occurring in relation to cannabis control in some countries, it would seem to be an appropriate time for the Commission to consider this issue in some detail to ensure the consistent application of the provisions of the 1961 Convention across the globe. (INCB, 2002b)

The INCB report and Ghodse's introductory remarks, reinforced by some behind the scene instigation, led to heated debates at the CND. Morocco, for instance, pointed at the emerging contradiction between the trend towards decriminalisation of cannabis use and a continuing pressure on 'southern' countries to eradicate cannabis with repressive means. Morocco, of course, had a point. Since its independence it had been struggling to control cannabis cultivation, but, instead, it had only increased and most of the hashish produced was smuggled to Europe, making the country the world's largest cannabis producer at the time (Blickman, 2017).

The INCB's 'diligent producer versus the lenient consumer state' discourse (Bewley-Taylor, 2014) contributed to set off the introduction of a resolution at the 2002 CND aiming to limit policy manoeuvre within the treaties. The resolution ultimately was made toothless, but the skirmishing about 'lenient policies' continued at the CND in 2003, remaining unresolved. One of the outcomes of the debate was a request to the UNODC to prepare a global survey on cannabis, which resulted in a special chapter in the 2006 World Drug Report, entitled 'Cannabis: Why we should care', written under the supervision of Sandeep Chawla. In the report, the United Nations Office on Drugs and Crime (UNODC, 2006, p. 155) stated that '[t]he global community is confused about cannabis', and that '[c]oming to terms with cannabis is important because it is, by quite a wide margin, the world's most popular illicit drug'. It further recognised that:

> much of the early material on cannabis is now considered inaccurate, and that a series of studies in a range of countries have exonerated cannabis of many of the charges levelled against it. (UNODC, 2006, p. 156)

It went on to note that '[m]edical use of the active ingredients, if not the plant itself, is championed by respected professionals.'

The report acknowledged that supply reduction is impossible given the potential to grow the plant anywhere and that all past attempts to control availability had failed. In its final conclusion, the report already raised the key issue concerning cannabis today, 10 years ahead of the 2016 UNGASS:

> The world has failed to come to terms with cannabis as a drug. In some countries, cannabis use and trafficking are taken very seriously, while in others, they are virtually ignored. This incongruity undermines the credibility of the international system, and the time for resolving global ambivalence on the issue is long overdue. Either the gap between the letter and spirit of the Single Convention, so manifest with cannabis, needs to be bridged, or parties to the Convention need to discuss redefining the status of cannabis. (UNODC, 2006, p. 186)

Although the distinction between producer and consumer countries regarding cannabis is becoming obsolete – most consumer countries now produce their own cannabis for the domestic market, while consumption in producer countries is often ignored – at the level of UN drug control policy making the difference still exist. While cannabis reform is taking place in what used to be regarded as consumer countries, in traditional producer countries such as Morocco, Afghanistan, Mexico, Lebanon, India and in the Caribbean, amongst others (UNODC, 2017), the debate on reform is lagging behind, at the same time as a multi-billion dollar industry is developing in the United States and Canada.[2] While the sheer money value and increasing economic clout of the industry may help to stem attempts to turn back the clock regarding regulation, it also comes with negative consequences of exaggerated commercialisation. Moreover, in the years ahead, traditional producer countries may risk losing the market share they had in the global illicit market to the increasingly corporatised stock-market listed cannabis industry in North America. If the increasing tensions regarding cannabis in the international drug control regime are not resolved, it will be these traditional subsistence growers in developing countries – as well as the pioneering illicit suppliers in the developed ones (Rodriques, 2017) – that will suffer the consequences of stalemate in the regime. Alternatively, those growers might move to grow other drug producing crops, such as opium; indications are that this might already be happening in Mexico (AP, 2015; Washington Post, 2015).

Bottom-Up Reform

The reform of cannabis control measures is a mainly a bottom-up process, as is evidenced by the developments in the United States. Even in Uruguay and Canada, the process of liberalisation has been greatly affected by civil society and, in the case of Canada, local disobedience by cities and provinces. In the United States, an important breakthrough, after the stalled reforms in the 1970s, was the approval of a ballot initiative in California in 1996 to allow medical cannabis. Apart from the fact that it rehabilitated the medical value of cannabis after years

---

[2]Estimates of the future value of the cannabis market are often speculative. *Cowen and Company,* a prominent investment bank that looked at the short and long-term market potentials for legal recreation cannabis in the United States concluded that it would be worth $50 billion in sales by 2026. See: *Cannabis industry expected to be worth $50 billion by 2026*, Bloomberg, 12 September 2016. Market research by cannabis industry analysts Arcview Market Research, in partnership with *BDS Analytics*, predict that legal cannabis sales to reach $9.7 billion in 2017, a 33 per cent increase over 2016. In 2021, the market will reach $24.5 billion in sales – a 28 per cent annual growth – as more states legalise cannabis for recreational use and existing markets mature in the United States, despite continued federal prohibition. See: *The legal marijuana market is exploding – it'll hit almost $10 billion sales in this year*, Business Insider, 8 December 2017. A report by Ameri Research Inc., a US-based market research and consulting company, estimates that the global legal cannabis market was valued at $14.3 billion in 2016 and is forecast to grow at 21.1 per cent between 2017 and 2024, culminating in 2024 global sales of $63.5 billion. The robust growth of the legal cannabis market is due to the increasing decriminalisation of cannabis products across North America and Europe, according to Ameri Inc. Rising demand of cannabis for both medical and recreational use is a key factor driving the growth. The full potential of the market is not yet realised because of the complex regulatory structures. See: *Legal Marijuana Market Outlook to 2024*, Ameri Research Inc., 21 April 2017: https://www.ameriresearch.com/product/legal-marijuana-market-outlook-2024-depth-market-view-key-categories-recreational-medical-application-pain-management-arthritis-cancer-multiple-sclerosis-alzheimers-regio/.

of reefer madness, because of its lenient implementation the measure amounted to a *de facto* legalisation of recreational cannabis in the state. Over the years, many more states in the United States approved medical cannabis (29 in 2017), although the leniency varied amongst states. In its report for 2010, the INCB commented that it was 'deeply concerned about [the] 'medical' cannabis schemes' that had been introduced in various US states and stated that these:

> control measures applied in those states to the cultivation of cannabis plants and the production, distribution and use of cannabis fall short of the control requirements of the 1961 Convention. (Boister, 2016; INCB, 2011, para. 395)

The process of cannabis normalisation eventually led to the approval of the ballot initiatives for adult recreational use in November 2012 in Washington and Colorado – both states with had previously been implementing rather lenient approaches to the use of medical cannabis – when, in combination with the legislative change in Uruguay, the process of increasing soft defection with the UN drug control regime turned into hard defections (Bewley-Taylor et al., 2014). Europe seems to be lagging behind, reflecting both the fact that national or federal governments are more aware of their international obligations and the diplomatic repercussions of cannabis control reform, whereas local authorities tend to look at the issue from the perspective of resolving public disorder surrounding street dealing, illegal cultivation and involvement of organised criminal groups in the local market (Blickman, 2014).

Nevertheless, in several countries in Europe, local and regional authorities are looking at regulation, also pressured by grassroots movements, in particular the emergence of Cannabis Social Clubs (CSCs) in Spain. The CSC movement started as a limited attempt by cannabis activists at the end of the 1990s, exploring the limits of latitude in Spanish law and the overarching international obligations (Barriuso, 2011; Kilmer, Pardal, Caulkins, & Rubin, 2013), but exploded in 2007–2011 (Marks, 2015), when more commercially driven associations mushroomed in cities such as Barcelona, challenging Amsterdam as the 'cannabis capital' of Europe. In the process, these profit-driven clubs undermined the more careful approach of the activist associations.

The original non-profit clubs cultivating cannabis for personal use on a collective basis operated under strict guidelines – acknowledged by the European Coalition for Just and Effective Drug Policies – to avoid accusations of trafficking, supplying or encouraging use. Clubs should only operate under a collective agreement, with registered members; calculate costs reflecting expected individual use, limiting the amount produced per person intended for immediate consumption, while being closed to the general public; new members were accepted by invitation only. Yet, despite favourable court decisions absolving clubs from prosecution, they are still operating in a legal grey zone, as the conservative central government in Madrid is against the model. The court rulings are regularly accompanied by statements about the imbalance of the prosecutions and the necessity for government regulation to ensure law enforcement and prosecutions target only criminal supply, and not cannabis clubs (Marks, 2015). Police raids on clubs and their plantations remain common, and clubs' representatives have repeatedly asked for a legal regulation to end the uncertainty. Although the exact number of CSCs in Spain is unknown, there may be between 800 and 1,000 CSCs operating in the country (Decorte et al., 2016).

The increase of the clubs and the increasing demands for regulation of the federations of clubs have led to regulation laws by the autonomous regions of the Basque Country, Navarra and Catalonia. However, the Constitutional Court of Spain decided that regulation of the clubs was unconstitutional since the competence to legislate on the issue was in the remit of the central government (La Vanguardia, 2017). Meanwhile, the Supreme Court of Justice did not outright prohibit the clubs, but limited their modus operandi even beyond the already strict regulations designed by the original non-profit associations – in particular regarding the size of the membership – to be in conformity with the jurisprudence on collective consumption, one of the essential features of the legal legitimacy of the clubs. In addition to regional regulation attempts, cities are starting to regulate the clubs with limited administrative rules through municipal bye-laws, increasing the legitimacy of the clubs, but not their legality. The first one was San Sebastian in the Basque Country – which at the time had 23 registered clubs with some 10,000 cannabis users (Diario Vasco, 2014). The local bye-law was approved in December 2014, and entails a formal recognition of clubs as well as the fulfilment of certain obligations by them. 'We had two options,' said a local councillor, 'ignore the existence of these clubs, or attempt to regulate to ensure the reduction of risks from consumption', criticising the current, restrictive national legislation (El País, 2014).

Persuaded that the CSC's are in conformity with the UN drug control conventions, the 'Spanish model' has been copied by activists, and occasionally local authorities, in other EU countries. In Uruguay, the model was included in the 2013 cannabis law, allowing for clubs of between 15 and 45 members, that may cultivate up to 99 plants, but cannot dispense more than 480 g (40 g per month) to each of their members per year (Queirolo, Boidi, & Cruz, 2016; Walsh & Ramsey, 2016). With the exception of Uruguay, the existence or operation of CSC's is disputed, limiting the possibilities for solid regulation. Nevertheless, the self-regulatory non-profit CSC model, although not without its specific problems (Decorte et al., 2016), is increasingly seen as a promising alternative to the mainly commercial regulation arrangements in the United States and the Dutch coffee shop model. The INCB is of the opinion that the CSC's are not consistent with the international obligation to limit cannabis exclusively to medical and scientific purposes (INCB, 2017, para. 188), while others argue that the phenomenon falls within the limits of latitude provided by the Conventions (Bewley-Taylor et al., 2014).

In Belgium, the first CSC appeared in 2006, but the legal foundation remains ambiguous. In September 2017, however, the phenomenon gained legitimacy when the mayor of Mons, former Prime Minister Elio di Rupo, announced he wanted a 'medical and scientific' experiment with a social club, while his party, the Socialist Party (PS), submitted a bill to the Chamber of Representatives proposing a Belgian regulation model within a strict legal framework, either through individual production of cannabis strictly for personal use with a maximum number of plants, or through production and distribution by CSC's on behalf of their members. A CSC movement is also building in the United Kingdom; there are currently probably over 80 clubs (Volteface, 2016a, 2016b). In France, an attempt to have CSCs recognised as non-profit organisations attracted considerable media attention. After an attempt to officially register a club the police responded by detaining the activist and seizing his equipment and records. He was sentenced to a suspended eight-month prison term and fined €2,500 (AFP, 2013). In June 2013 a Tours court decided on the dissolution of the club's federative structure and banned its members from meeting (Libération, 2013). Nevertheless, the debate in France continues, and the new President, Emmanuel Macron, seems to have a more relaxed view on the issue, but concrete measures are still not in sight.

In other European countries cannabis policy reform initiatives are mainly initiated by local authorities. In Germany, some 20 cities are interested in a regulated cannabis market, including Berlin, Bremen, Hamburg and Düsseldorf. The first local authority in Germany to try to force a breakthrough was the Berlin district of Friedrichshain-Kreuzberg in 2013, announcing a pilot project of city-run shops selling cannabis as a means of tackling the growing drug-dealing in the district's Görlitzer Park (Deutsche Welle, 2013). Towns wanting to reform rely on an exemption under paragraph 3 of the German drug law: pilot experiments can be approved if they serve 'scientific and other purposes of public interest'.[3] In order to go forward with pilot projects, an application to the Federal Institute for Medicine and Medicinal Products (*Bundesinstitut für Arzneimittel und Medizinprodukte*—BfArM) should be obtained. An attempt by Friedrichshain-Kreuzberg to obtain such an exemption was, however, declined by the BfArM, in October 2015 (Deutsche Welle, 2015; The Local, 2015). A next attempt by the federal states of Bremen, Berlin and Thuringia to allow for scientific pilot projects before Germany's higher chamber, the *Bundesrat*, failed as well (Weser Kurier, 2017). A similar development took place in Switzerland, where towns or cantons like Geneva, Basel, Bern and Zürich opted for pilot projects, including a model of cannabis clubs or 'cannabis users associations' combined dissuasion commissions – following the decriminalisation model of Portugal – to deal with youth and possible problematic users, were proposed. The Swiss federal government (Federal Council – *Bundesrat*) considers the pilot projects contemplated in different cities as incompatible with the current drug law (Blickman, 2014). In Denmark, Copenhagen city council has forwarded several proposals for a local pilot project but did not receive a go ahead from the national government.

These local initiatives and calls for reform start to get traction at the national level in Europe. In several countries, notably Germany and Italy, legislative proposals have been advanced in national parliaments, although they have been defeated until now (European Monitoring Centre for Drugs and Drug Addiction (EMCDDA), 2017), with the exception of the Netherlands, due to the intensive lobbying of some municipalities and the Dutch Association of Municipalities (VNG). In a report, *Het failliet van het gedogen (Toleration: a bankrupt policy)*, a working group of mayors and aldermen concluded that the policy of toleration was no longer adequate and had become untenable in order to effectively tackle

[3]Paragraf 3 des Betäubungsmittelgesetzes (BtMG): http://www.gesetze-im-internet.de/btmg_1981/__3.html.

the problems, in particular the grip of organised crime groups controlling the supply of cannabis (Meesters, 2015).

> The discussion on cannabis policy has reached an impasse, between proponents and opponents of regulation. We cannot allow the various levels of administration to become bogged down in discussions, while organised crime profits and public health remains insufficiently protected. We call upon all parties to above all employ a pragmatic approach in searching for solutions. We have reached the conclusion that a system of rules for the entire cannabis supply chain offers the best possibilities. We call upon all parties to work in favour of this approach, and subsequently join forces in its further elaboration. This means making choices, further elaborating those choices in a system based on experimentation, and subsequently consistently implementing those choices. Only together can we arrive at a truly effective approach to the problems.

The VNG overwhelmingly supported a legal regulation of a transparent chain of supply to the coffee shops. In February 2017, the lower chamber of the Dutch Parliament approved a bill to allow the regulated supply of cannabis to the back-door of the coffee shops. The bill moved on to the Senate, but in the meantime national elections led to a change in the government coalition. The party that had taken the initiative for the bill entered the four-party government coalition that includes political parties vehemently opposed to the bill and the coffee-shop system.

Nevertheless, an agreement was reached to start experiments with supply:

> The government will introduce legislation, if possible within six months, on uniform experiments with tolerated cultivation of cannabis plants for recreational use. The experiments will be carried out in six to ten large and medium-sized municipalities, with the aim of determining whether and how controlled cannabis can be legally supplied to coffee shops and what the effects of this would be. After these experiments have been independently evaluated, the government will consider what action to take. (GON, 2017)

Still, it seems that the Dutch government tends to think that the experiment will decide whether or not regulation will take place, while the municipalities consider the experiment as a discriminative process on how to best regulate the supply (Dutch News, 2017). The issue is still far from being resolved.

With the exception of the Netherlands, bottom-up initiatives have not (yet?) succeeded. As others have argued (Chatwin, 2007), European cannabis policy might best develop through a model of 'multi-level governance', a rising style of governance in the EU, in particular regarding social policies, in which multiple actors at multiple levels are engaged, and specific details of governance are decentralised and may diversify under EU guidelines. In this model, pragmatic policies are developed at the local level, encouraging greater involvement from citizens – a guiding principle in the EU. 'A system of multi-level governance would allow initiatives to develop at the local level with power following a bottom-up structure,' as opposed to top-down solutions that do not fit local and regional needs. Given the already wide diversity of drug policies in Europe, different local cannabis regulation regimes could then be judged on their effectiveness and leave room for manoeuvre for local authorities (Committee of the Regions (CoR), 2014). Cities and regions that want reform could follow the example set by European towns when they set up the network of European Cities on Drug Policy (ECDP, 1991). In 1990, Amsterdam, Frankfurt, Hamburg and Zürich initiated that network by signing the Frankfurt Resolution, which became the charter of the ECDP, to advocate a more pragmatic, less prohibitionist drug policy including the decriminalisation of cannabis, and initiated a set of innovative harm-reduction measures – such as heroin-substitution programmes, social inclusion through housing-and-work programmes, drug consumption rooms and heroin prescription (Boekhout van Solinge, 1999). The example of the ECDP has shown that it is possible to successfully initiate the adoption of effective harm-reduction strategies at the national and, ever more, the international level (Schardt, 2001).

The Road to 2019

Unless countries opposed to cannabis liberation will start to protest, nothing in the preparatory process at the CND for the next UN HLMS in 2019 indicates that the hard defections from the regime will be addressed at the 2019 HLMS. Despite the fact that California, the world's sixth biggest economy, will have a legal cannabis market as of 1 January 2018 – estimated at $7bn per year by 2020 – and Canada, a G7 country, is set to legalise on 17 October 2018. The liberalisation of cannabis is not just a matter for activists anymore, but a multi-billion-dollar industry with serious financial investments and assets on stock exchanges, while more and more jurisdictions are enticed by the potential lucrative tax revenues. All this, however, has little impact on the containerised proceedings at the UN, where a 'Jurassic system' frozen in time – referring to the outdated UN drug control treaty system, with its roots predating the UN, that lacks a periodic review mechanism in comparison to current systems that allow for modernisation to reflect realities of the times (Bewley-Taylor & Fitzmaurice, 2017; Global Drug Policy Observatory (GDPO), 2014) – is unable to address the issue that will eventually challenge the international drug control system.

Nevertheless, there are developments in the UN system that might force the CND to take a stance. In June 2018, a pre-review of cannabis and cannabis-related substances will be taking place in a 'Special Session on Cannabis' by the Expert Committee on Drug Dependence (ECDD), the World Health Organisation's (WHO) body charged by the 1961 and 1971 Conventions with the scientific and medical review of scheduling proposals. Scheduling, the classification of a substance within a categorised system of controls and restrictions or 'schedules', has to take place in order for the substance to be included in the international control framework of the UN drug control convention shaping the type and intensity of controls to be applied (Hallam, Bewley-Taylor, & Jelsma, 2014). Curiously, a formal review that meets accepted standards and scientific knowledge of the place of cannabis within the Convention has never taken place. As the Committee itself recognised in 2014, 'Cannabis and cannabis resin has not been scientifically reviewed by the Expert Committee since the review by the Health Committee of the League of Nations in 1935' (Expert Committee on Drug Dependence (ECDD), 2014).

Although the scheduling recommendations of the ECDD are generally approved by the CND, the Commission might take a different stance. The CND is allowed considerable flexibility having 'broad discretionary powers' vis-à-vis its acceptance of WHO scheduling recommendations. In principle the CND should accept the scientific findings of the WHO, but it has the possibility to reject a recommendation on 'social or administrative' grounds (Hallam et al., 2014). In other words, the process is still open to differences of interpretation and, consequently, to ideological presumptions of all kinds. The CND may also decide 'by consensus' not to vote, stalling the scheduling process without an explicit rejection, as has happened at the 2007 CND in the case of a ECDD recommendation to change the scheduling status of the cannabis compound dronabinol (Δ^9-tetrahydrocannabinol or THC) from Schedule II to the less restrictive Schedule III in the 1971 Convention on Psychotropic Substances.

In November 2017, the ECDD conducted a pre-review of the cannabis compound cannabidiol (CBD) due to the increased interest from Member States in the use of cannabis for medical indications, including palliative care. The Committee concluded that current information does not justify scheduling of CBD and postponed a fuller review of CBD preparations to June 2018. CBD 'could have some therapeutic value for seizures due to epilepsy and related conditions,' and is unlikely to be abused or create dependence as other cannabinoids such as THC, for instance (ECDD, 2017). Although in its own right CBD is currently not a scheduled substance, but only as a component of cannabis extracts, 'current information does not justify a change in this scheduling position and does not justify scheduling of the substance.' The pre-review reflects the changing positions regarding the medical value of cannabis and its compounds (see for instance Curran, Wiffen, Nutt & Scholten, 2016). It is hard to imagine the process will not lead to some form of rehabilitation of cannabis and the removal of the substance from Schedule IV listing the substances with little or no recognised therapeutic value. Over 40 jurisdictions worldwide (from 16 countries) have already moved to regulate cannabis for medical purposes in one way or another, including Argentina, Brazil, Canada, Chile, Colombia, the Czech Republic, Germany, Israel, Jamaica, Mexico, the Netherlands, Peru, Puerto Rico, the UK, 29 US states and Uruguay. What will happen to recreational cannabis is quite another matter.

Interestingly, scheduling decisions are currently the only ones that are voted upon by the 53 members of the CND,[4] which somewhat corrects the 'dead weight of multilateral consensus'. If it comes to a vote, that will at least identify which Member States will go against the scientific WHO recommendations and on what grounds. Whether or not the issue will appear on the CND agenda before the HLMS in March 2019 remains to be seen, although in specific cases the WHO can rule that a pre-review for a substance is not needed and it can proceed directly to a critical

[4]CND membership as of 1 January 2018: http://www.unodc.org/documents/commissions/CND/Membership/CND_membership_January_2018.pdf.

review (Nougier, 2017). However, due to its contentious nature, the review of cannabis might well take some more time, which will be also less controversial since scheduling recommendations on the basis of a pre-review without the additional scrutiny of a critical review would undermine the scientific basis of the ECDD's scheduling recommendations. Moreover, re-scheduling or de-scheduling cannabis will not be sufficient to allow for fully regulated markets as cannabis is also mentioned explicitly in specific articles within the 1961 and 1988 Conventions. Some form of amendment, modification, or reservation to those treaties is also required (Bewley-Taylor et al., 2016). Meanwhile, the excruciating impasse is likely to continue and, as the delegate of St Vincent and the Grenadines put it at the 2016 UNGASS:

> [f]or this UN process to maintain any semblance of credibility, this week's gathering cannot be another exercise of naïve prescriptions, repetition of failed measures or kicking the can down the road. (UNGASS, 2016c)

Options for Reform

The treaty breaches that may have seemed merely hypothetical only a few years ago are already a reality today, and they will not simply fade away. The accelerating process of local and national reforms has moved cannabis policies beyond the confines of what the UN drug control conventions can legally accommodate. The policy trend towards legal regulation of an adult recreational cannabis market as a more promising and effective model for protecting people's health and safety has changed the drug policy landscape and the terms of the debate beyond the tipping point. The question facing the international community today is no longer whether or not there is a need to reassess and modernise the UN drug control system, but rather when and how to do it. However, the Jurassic nature of the regime will be resisting change for a considerable time, keeping cannabis under international control. As a consequence, while operating outside the confines of international law, the developing regulated markets look set to be closed domestic markets without the possibility of international import and export trade, except for the medical use of the substance.

The result might be that the fast budding multi-billion cannabis industries in the United States and Canada are chasing first-mover advantage to the detriment of the traditional illicit growers in less powerful nations that can ill afford to challenge or ignore international law and its possible repercussions, such as cuts in development aid or exclusion from preferential trade agreements (Bewley-Taylor et al., 2016). Additionally, long-term non-compliance with international law might have serious consequences regarding the banking of the proceeds of cannabis in states with legally regulated markets since it almost certainly violates states' obligation to criminalise money laundering under the 1988 Convention, as well as the UN Convention against Transnational Organised Crime (Boister, 2016). That is why the cannabis market is largely a cash market in the legalising US states, including the payment of local taxes (AP, 2017), despite federal guidelines issued during the Obama administration that intended to give banks a measure of confidence that they will not be prosecuted if they provide services to legitimate cannabis businesses (New York Times, 2014). Attorney General Sessions' decision to rescind the Cole memorandum underscores the continuing uncertainty regarding availability of financial services for the cannabis businesses under state laws, but may intensify efforts in the US Congress to provide a federal legislative remedy for the lack of banking, especially due to concerns over the risks to public safety around a proliferation of cash-only businesses.

In Uruguay, national banks also threatened to withdraw the bank accounts of pharmacies that legally sold cannabis domestically, when US banks, including Bank of America, announced that they would stop doing business with banks in Uruguay that provide services for enterprises engaged in state-licensed cannabis sales (New York Times, 2017). Afraid as they were of losing access to the US banking system, and consequently, due to the central position of the United States in the international financial world, access to the global banking system, Uruguayan authorities are in the process of establishing rules for the creation of new, cash-only points of sale that would not rely on banking access to conduct business.[5]

The 2019 HLMS will not resolve the tensions with the existing UN drug treaties created by the evolving law and practice to regulate legal access to cannabis for purposes other than exclusively 'medical and scientific' in some Member States. Given that stalemate at the international level and the diplomatic nightmare of challenging and formally modernising the regime (Hall, 2017), countries that do want reform need to look at what is possible within the current regime. Simply ignoring the UN drug control conventions, or pretending legal recreational cannabis regulation falls within the 'flexibility' of the current treaties,[6] is not a viable option due to the negative

[5]In the Netherlands, a similar situation occurred when banks started to end relations with coffee shops around 2009, due to new legislation on due diligence as a result of international anti-money laundering obligations. The Finance minister at the time urged the banks to keep current accounts to prevent coffee shops from being forced out of the banking system.

[6]In the run up to the 2016 UNGASS, the U.S. Assistant Secretary for International Narcotics and Law Enforcement Affairs, William Brownfield, unfolded a four pillar strategy intent on sticking with the existing treaties, fostering flexible interpretation to suit changing conditions, tolerating different national strategies and countering transnational criminal networks, in an effort to reconcile obvious breach of the treaties of the federal administration by allowing regulation in its states. Brownfield maintained that the existing treaty framework possessed sufficient flexibility to allow for regulated cannabis markets, with the argument that federal law continues to consider such regulations to be a criminal offence in the entirety of US territory and as such the drug convention obligations are met because the safeguard clauses – parties must carry out the obligations in the convention 'in conformity with the fundamental provisions of their respective domestic legislative systems' or to the party's 'constitutional limitations' – permit such flexibility (Boister, 2016). However, those safeguard clauses only exist for the 1961 Convention, not for the 1988 Convention. Brownfield's flexibility argument's main objective was apparently to 'prevent clear treaty breaches of state-level cannabis legalisation initiatives from triggering an open international debate on treaty reform.' The INCB has made clear statements that Brownfield's interpretation is not valid and that the U.S. state regulation models are not in compliance with the treaties. Brownfield has since acknowledged the INCB's authority in determining whether or not State parties are in compliance (Bewley-Taylor et al., 2016).

consequences it will have on the precarious edifice of international law, which goes beyond the scope of international drug control regime and includes important issue areas such as human rights. International law is supposed to keep arbitrariness by national governments in check, to moderate power struggles in international affairs and to provide public goods (Waibel, 2011). To paraphrase an adage on democracy: no one pretends that international law is perfect or all-wise; indeed, it might be that international law is the worst form of administrating international relations except for all those other forms that have been tried from time to time.

After decades of manifold forms of soft defection, non-compliance, decriminalisation, legal hypocrisy and *de facto* regulation in countries where traditional use is widespread and those nations where cannabis has become popular in the past half century, the state of affairs has now reached a point where *de jure* legal regulation of the entire recreational cannabis market has obtained political acceptability, albeit that it violates outdated provisions of the UN conventions. In the international arena in Vienna and New York tensions are likely to increase between countries engaged in regulatory approaches and those in favour of defending the status quo. The options for those who want reform are difficult, but not impossible. The 'royal' way to go would be for any State party to the convention to notify the UN Secretary General (UNSG) of a projected amendment, including the reasoning behind it. The UNSG than has several options, but, without going into detail,[7] initiating this procedure will likely soon collapse under Chawla's 'dead weight of multilateral consensus', as probably enough parties will oppose such a step to sabotage any chance of an amendment being accepted along the way. Given the multiple possibilities for reform-adverse state parties to stall the process, any state considering reform will think twice about initiating this procedure unless there is a clear majority of signatory parties for support. However, there is no indication that this will be the case in the years to come.

That leaves open the option of procedures that do not require majority approval of all signatory states, but depend on the political will and action of a single state or a like-minded group of states. One of those is the 'Bolivia option' as mentioned above: the procedure of treaty denunciation followed by re-accession with a reservation. Bolivia successfully followed that procedure in the years 2011–2013 regarding the traditional use of the coca-leaf. However, while few countries may be concerned over the ancient practice of coca-leaf chewing, many more will have serious concerns about allowing recreational cannabis markets. Whereas the number of objections to block Bolivia from re-acceding fell short of one-third of all State parties to the Convention (18 while 62 were required), in the case of cannabis that is not a certainty. Making a reservation exempting a particular substance from the convention's general obligation to restrict drugs exclusively to medical and scientific purposes is unambiguously mentioned in the Commentary on the Single Convention as a procedurally allowable option, for coca leaf as well as for

[7]For a detailed description of the procedure, see: Bewley-Taylor et al. (2016). All further options mentioned in this section are taken from the same publication, unless otherwise referenced.

cannabis (United Nations (UN), 1973, p. 476), although a possible conflict with the object and purpose of the treaty as a whole is a matter for legal debate. Acting with a like-minded group of states would increase the viability and legitimacy of such a step and also reduce the vulnerability of a state going this road unilaterally.

Another possibility for reform is an *inter se* modification of obligations regarding cannabis amongst like-minded groups of states parties to the conventions, an option that is not part of the UN drug control conventions but relies on the overarching 1969 Vienna Convention on the Law of Treaties (VCLT) (Bewley-Taylor et al., 2016; Boister & Jelsma, 2017). According to Article 41 of the VCLT, '[t]wo or more of the parties to a multilateral treaty may conclude an agreement to modify the treaty as between themselves alone', as long as it 'does not affect the enjoyment by the other parties of their rights under the treaty or the performance of their obligations' and it is not 'incompatible with the effective execution of the object and purpose of the treaty as a whole' (UN, 1980:article 41(1)). Under the condition that the agreement includes a clear commitment to the original treaty obligations in respect of countries not party to the modification, particularly in relation to deterrence of trade or leakage to prohibiting jurisdictions, this might be the most viable option. Ultimately, if a significant group of like-minded countries would adhere to such an *inter se* agreement, it might evolve into an alternative treaty framework, avoiding the awkward, and under the current circumstances almost impossible, process of approval of amendments to the current regime.

A truly global consensus on cannabis control – if it ever really existed – is now definitely fractured, and a new consensus to replace it is still far away – if it ever will materialise. Therefore, states implementing legal regulated recreational cannabis markets might be forced to remain in temporary non-compliance with the UN drug control conventions, despite good intentions to uphold international law. Instigating a formal procedure to amend or review the current treaty architecture could generate political frictions with some of the most powerful nations in the world, and could even lead to unintended negative outcomes. However, there is no need to postpone the regulation of cannabis at the national level, and there is also no reason to rush to withdraw from the drug control conventions. But instead of recourse to legally deceptive reasoning that the current international legal framework is flexible enough to accommodate the legal regulation of recreational cannabis markets – in spite of its political appeal to avoid or delay tackling the treaty tensions – it would be better to publicly acknowledge that legal regulation will result in an episode of non-compliance with certain treaty obligations. Time is needed to argue for legally sound transition more in line with other domestic and international legal and policy commitments, particularly with regard to public health, child protection and human rights (Walsh, Bewley-Taylor, Jelsma, & Blickman, 2017).

With that in mind, a recent study weighing the obligations of the drug control conventions against positive human right obligations,[8] concluded that, under

[8]Obligations that impose upon a State an obligation to do something, that is, to take some form of action, are norms that impose positive obligations, whereas those that impose an obligation on a State not to do something, are norms that impose negative obligations.

certain conditions, it might be possible for states to regulate cannabis cultivation and trade for recreational use by legalisation in the interests of individual and public health, security and crime control (Van Kempen & Federova, 2016). In order to do so 'in a sincere and convincing manner', a state should 'demonstrate that regulation would constitute a better protection of human rights than a prohibitive approach' that has evolved from the drug control conventions. Under international law, states are compelled to give priority to human rights obligations 'over and above' any conflicting obligations under the UN drug control conventions. However, while generally accepted when negative human rights obligations are concerned, as in the Charter of the United Nations, there is no consensus amongst international law experts when positive obligations deriving from the rights to health, life, physical and mental integrity are concerned. According to the study, further conditions include that regulation must have public support and should be decided through a nationwide democratic process. Other conditions include a closed system to avoid the measure causing inconvenience to foreign countries (such as leakage from the system), as well as an active policy to discourage cannabis use, another primary conditions mainly to satisfy the obligations under the international drug control regime.

The study reinforces the arguments made by Uruguay to justify its decision to go ahead with domestic legal regulation. In fact, Uruguay's rectification was one of the incentives for the study, after a previous study by the same authors, commissioned by the Dutch government at the time, had concluded that legal regulation of the supply of cannabis for Dutch coffee shops was not allowed strictly looking at the UN drug control conventions alone – even coffee shops were not allowed (Van Kempen & Fedorova, 2014). The second study, this time commissioned by Dutch municipalities favouring legal regulation, corrected that conclusion taking into account a broader spectrum of international law. Therefore, the study reinforces the position of states in non-compliance with the UN drug control conventions, supplying convincing arguments to do so. In the absence of a procedure before an international body that could take a concluding decision on the tensions or even conflicts between the drug control and human rights regimes – the current 'quasi judicial' and advisory nature of the INCB thwarts the Board from doing so, unless its mandate and composition would be changed fundamentally[9] – the issue will linger in 'the art of interpretation' that so often epitomises international law (Lines, 2017, pp. 149–151). The positive human rights arguments serve to assist countries where there is political will to regulate. If human rights overrule the drug control obligations that would be a strong argument for breaching them, but it would still only be in accordance with international law if the breaching party subsequently changes its obligations under the drug conventions, via reservation, *inter se* modification or amendment. It remains a policy choice, however.

[9]The INCB mandate whether or not state parties are in compliance only applies to the 1961 and 1971 Convention. The 1988 Convention does not have any monitoring body; disputes about interpretation should be settled through consultation between the State parties themselves or ultimately could be brought to the International Court of Justice for decision (article 32) (Bewley-Taylor et al., 2016). The INCB has no mandate beyond the UN drug control treaties.

Likewise, it will also provide states willing to explore an *inter se* agreement with sound legal arguments to justify that step.

All these options are unlikely to be set in motion before the 2019 HLMS. The meeting in 2019 will evaluate the targets set in the 2009 Political Declaration and Plan of Action 'for States to eliminate or reduce significantly and measurably' the illicit supply and demand of cannabis and other illicit substances (UN, 2009), a target set after the evaluation of the 1998 UNGASS, which had committed to 'eliminating or significantly reducing the illicit cultivation of the coca bush, the cannabis plant and the opium poppy by the year 2008' (Jelsma, 2003). Instead, States are now regulating or starting to regulate the cannabis market. One could argue that regulating is a way to 'significantly and measurably' reduce the *illicit* supply and demand of cannabis, but that is clearly not what States had in mind at the time. The fact that the HLMS will likely leave the elephant in the room untouched might spur reform-minded nations to initiate a mechanism to truly address the issue. The emerging paradigm shift regarding cannabis shows that a modernisation of the UN drug control regime is long overdue, and failing to adapt it to the realities of today will be a scar on the international community's ability to tackle a global issue when required.

References

AFP. (2013). *France cannabis campaigner convicted, fined.* Retrieved from http://www.globalpost.com/dispatch/news/afp/130418/francecannabis-campaigner-convicted-fined. Accessed on April 18, 2013.

Associated Press (AP). (2015). *Mexican opium farmers expand plots to supply U.S. heroin boom.* AP. Retrieved from http://archivo.eluniversal.com.mx/in-english/2015/mexican-opium-farmers-100966.html. Accessed on February 2, 2015.

Associated Press (AP). (2017). *California proposes armored cars to transport pot tax money*, AP. Retrieved from http://uk.businessinsider.com/ap-california-proposes-armored-cars-to-transport-pot-tax-money-2017-11. Accessed on November 7, 2017.

Barriuso Alonso, M. (2011). Cannabis Social Clubs in Spain: A normalizing alternative underway. *TNI Series on Legislative Reform of Drug Policies Nr. 9.* Retrieved from http://druglawreform.info/images/stories/documents/dlr9.pdf. Accessed on January 2011.

Bewley-Taylor, D. (2012). *International drug control: Consensus fractured* (pp. 200–206). Cambridge: Cambridge University Press.

Bewley-Taylor, D. (2014). The INCB and cannabis: From description to condemnation. In: Bewley-Taylor, D., Blickman, T., & Jelsma, M. (2014). *The rise and decline of cannabis prohibition: The history of cannabis in the UN Drug Control System and options for reform.* Amsterdam, The Netherlands: Transnational Institute & Global Drug Policy Observatory. Retrieved from http://druglawreform.info/images/stories/documents/Rise_and_Decline_Web.pdf.

Bewley-Taylor, D., Blickman, T., & Jelsma, M. (2014). *The rise and decline of cannabis prohibition: The history of cannabis in the UN Drug Control System and options for reform.* Amsterdam, The Netherlands: Transnational Institute & Global Drug Policy Observatory. Retrieved from http://druglawreform.info/images/stories/documents/Rise_and_Decline_Web.pdf

Bewley-Taylor, D., & Fitzmaurice, M. (2017). *The modernization of treaty regimes: The contrasting cases of International Drug Control and Environmental Regulation.* Working Paper presented at the 'Cannabis Regulation and the UN Drug Control Treaties' Expert Seminar in Amsterdam, 26–28 October 2017. Retrieved from http://www.swansea.ac.uk/media/ModernizationofTreatyRegimesWkngPaper.pdf

Bewley-Taylor, D., & Jelsma, M. (2012). The limits of latitude: The UN drug control conventions. *TNI Series on Legislative Reform of Drug Policies*. Retrieved from http://druglawreform.info/images/stories/documents/dlr18.pdf. Accessed on March 18, 2012.

Bewley-Taylor, D., & Jelsma, M. (2016). UNGASS 2016: A Broken or b-r-o-a-d consensus? *TNI Drug Policy Briefing 45*. Retrieved from http://www.druglawreform.info/images/stories/documents/DPB_45_04072016_web.pdf. Accessed on July 2016.

Bewley-Taylor, D., Jelsma, M., Rolles, S., & Walsh, J. (2016). *Cannabis regulation and the UN Drug Treaties. Strategies for reform.* Transnational Institute. Retrieved from http://www.druglawreform.info/images/stories/documents/cannabis%20regulation%20and%20the%20un%20drug%20treaties_june%202016_web.pdf. Accessed on June 2016.

Blickman, T. (2002). European Cannabis policies under attack. *TNI Briefing*. Reviewed from http://www.druglawreform.info/en/issues/cannabis/item/2400-european-cannabis-policies-under-attack. Accessed on April 2002.

Blickman, T. (2014). Cannabis policy reform in Europe: Bottom up rather than top down. *TNI Series on Legislative Reform of Drug Policies*. Reviewed from http://www.druglawreform.info/images/stories/documents/dlr28.pdf. Accessed on December 28, 2014.

Blickman, T. (2016). Nederland is klaar om te reguleren; nu de landelijke politiek nog. *Socialisme & Democratie, 73*. Retrieved from http://druglawreform.info/images/stories/documents/SD_artikel_Tom_Blickman.pdf. Accessed on August 4, 2016.

Blickman, T. (2017). Morocco and Cannabis: Reduction, containment or acceptance, *TNI Drug Policy Briefing 49*. Retrieved from http://druglawreform.info/images/stories/documents/DPB_49_eng_web.pdf. Accessed on March 2017.

Boekhout van Solinge, T. (1999). Dutch drug policy in a European context. *Journal of Drug Issues*, *29*(3), 511–528. Retrieved from //www.cedro-uva.org/lib/boekhout.dutch.html

Boekhout van Solinge, T. (2017). The Dutch model of cannabis decriminalization and tolerated retail. In Savona, E. Kleiman, M. & Calderoni. F. (2017). *Dual markets: Comparative approaches to regulation* (pp. 145–170). Cham (Switzerland): Springer.

Boister, N. (2016). Waltzing on the Vienna Consensus on Drug Control? Tensions in the International System for the Control of Drugs. *Leiden Journal of International Law*, *29*(02), 389–409. 10.1017/S0922156516000078

Boister, N., & Jelsma, M. (2017). *Inter se modification of the UN Drug Control Conventions: An exploration of its applicability to legitimise the legal regulation of cannabis markets.* Working Paper presented at the Expert Seminar on 'Cannabis Regulation and the UN Drug Control Treaties', Amsterdam, 26–28 October 2017.

Chatwin, C. (2007). Multi-level governance: The way forward for European illicit drug policy? *International Journal of Drug Policy*, *18*(6), 494–502.

Chawla, S. (2014). *Presentation at International Impacts of the U.S. Trend towards legal marijuana*. Brookings Institution, Washington, DC. Retrieved from https://www.brookings.edu/wp-content/uploads/2014/10/20141017_legal_marijuana_transcript.pdf. Accessed on October 17, 2014.

Cole, J. M. (2013). *Guidance regarding marijuana enforcement*. Office of the Deputy Attorney General, U.S. Department of Justice. Retrieved from https://www.justice.gov/iso/opa/resources/3052013829132756857467.pdf. Accessed on August 28, 2013.

Curran, H. C., Wiffen, P., Nutt, D. J., & Scholten, W. (2016). *Cannabis and cannabis resin: Pre-review report*. DrugScience. Retrieved from http://www.drugscience.org.uk/assets/files/WHOcannabisreport.pdf. Accessed on October 2016.

Committee of the Regions (CoR). (2014). *A charter for multilevel governance in Europe was adopted by the EU Committee of the Regions in April 2014*. Retrieved from http://cor.europa.eu/en/activities/governance/Pages/charter-for-multiLevel-governance.aspx

Decorte, T., Pardal, M., Queirolo, R., Boidi, M. F., Sánchez Avilés, C., & Parés Franquero, O. (2016). Regulating cannabis social clubs: A comparative analysis of legal and self-regulatory practices in Spain, Belgium and Uruguay. *International Journal of Drug Policy*, *43*(2017), 44–56.

De Kort, M. (1994). The Dutch cannabis debate, 1968–1976. *Journal of Drug Issues*, *24*(3), 417–427 (quoting a Memorandum [Nota] of 4 January 1974 in the Nederlandse Staatscourant (Netherlands State Gazette), No. 5, 8 January 1974).

Deutsche Welle. (2013). *Cannabis cafes could set up shop in Berlin*. Retrieved from http://www.dw.de/cannabis-cafes-could-set-up-shop-in-berlin/a-17089498. Accessed on September 16, 2013.

Deutsche Welle. (2015). *Berlin district loses marijuana legalization bid*. Retrieved from http://www.dw.com/en/berlin-district-loses-marijuana-legalization-bid/a-18762857. Accessed on October 5, 2015.

De Witte, F. (2013). Sex, drugs & EU law: The recognition of moral and ethical diversity in EU law. *Common Market Law Review*, *50*, 1545–1578.

Diario Vasco. (2014). *Donostia se convierte en la primera localidad en regular los clubes sociales de cannabis*. Retrieved from http://www.diariovasco.com/20140430/local/san-sebastian/donostia-convierte-primera-localidad-201404301314.html. Accessed on April 30, 2014.

Dutch News. (2017). *Councils call for more experimental approach to cannabis production*. Retrieved from http://www.dutchnews.nl/news/archives/2017/11/councils-call-for-more-experimental-approach-to-cannabis-production/. Accessed on November 27, 2017.

Expert Committee on Drug Dependence (ECDD). (2014). *Cannabis and cannabis resin: Information document*. WHO, 36th meeting, Geneva, 16–20 June 2014. Retrieved from http://www.who.int/medicines/areas/quality_safety/8_2_Cannabis.pdf

Expert Committee on Drug Dependence (ECDD). (2017). *Cannabidiol (CBD), pre-review report*. WHO, 39th meeting, Geneva, 6–10 November 2017.

El País. (2014). *Una ventana abierta a la marihuana*. Retrieved from http://ccaa.elpais.com/ccaa/2014/11/30/paisvasco/1417370065_986474.html. Accessed on December 1, 2014.

European Cities on Drug Policy (ECDP). (1991). *1st Conference: European Cities at the Centre of Illegal Trade in Drugs*. Retrieved from http://www.ecdp.net/ or http://www.realitaeten-bureau.de/en_news_04.htm

European Monitoring Centre for Drugs and Drug Addiction (EMCDDA). (2017). *Cannabis legislation in Europe: An overview* (pp. 23–25). Luxembourg: Publications Office of the European Union. Retrieved from http://www.emcdda.europa.eu/system/files/publications/4135/TD0217210ENN.pdf

EU Council. (1996). *Joint action 96/750/JHA*. Retrieved from http://eur-lex.europa.eu/legal-content/EN/ALL/?uri=uriserv:OJ.L_.1996.342.01.0006.01.ENG. Accessed on December 17, 1996.

EU Council. (2004). *Framework decision 2004/757/JHA*. Retrieved from http://eur-lex.europa.eu/legal-content/EN/TXT/?uri=CELEX:32004F0757. Accessed on October 25, 2004.

EU Council. (2010). *Report from the Commission on the implementation of Framework Decision 2004/757/JHA laying down minimum provisions on the constituent elements of criminal acts and penalties in the field of illicit drug trafficking, Secretary-General of the European Commission, 5200/10*. Retrieved from http://www.eumonitor.eu/9353000/1/j9vvik7m1c3gyxp/vj6ipizg4suj. Accessed on January 26, 2010.

EU Council. (2014). *EU directive 2014/40/EU*. Retrieved from https://ec.europa.eu/health//sites/health/files/tobacco/docs/dir_201440_en.pdf. Accessed on April 3, 2014.

Garvey, T., & Yeh, B.T. (2018). *Attorney General's memorandum on federal marijuana enforcement: Possible impacts*. Congressional Research Service, 10 January 2018.

Global Drug Policy Observatory (GDPO). (2014). *International Law and Drug Policy Reform*. Report of a GDPO/ICHRDP/TNI/WOLA Expert Seminar, Washington, DC, 17–18 October 2014. Retrieved from http://druglawreform.info/images/stories/documents/Expert_Seminar_Report_-_International_Law__Drug_Policy_Reform.pdf

GON. (1995). Ministerie van Binnenlandse Zaken, Ministerie van Justitie, Ministerie van Volksgezondheid, Welzijn en Sport (1995). *Het Nederlandse drugbeleid; continuïteit en verandering*, Tweede Kamer, vergaderjaar 1994–1995, 24077, nrs. 2-3. For an English translation see: *Drugs policy in the Netherlands: Continuity and change*. Retrieved from http://www.emcdda.europa.eu/system/files/Ministerie%20VWS%20%281995%29%20Continuity%20and%20Change%2C%20Dutch%20drug%20policy.pdf

GON. (2017). Coalition agreement 'Confidence in the future'. Retrieved from https://www.kabinetsformatie2017.nl/binaries/kabinetsformatie/documenten/verslagen/2017/10/10/coalition-agreement-confidence-in-the-future/coalition-agreement-2017-confidence-in-the-future.pdf. Accessed on October 10, 2017.

Grund, J. P., & Breeksema, J. (2013). *Coffee shops and compromise: Separated illicit drug markets in the Netherlands*. Global Drug Policy Program, Open Society Foundations, July 2013.

Hall, W. (2017). The future of the international drug control system and national drug prohibitions. *Addiction*, *112*. 10.1111/add.13941

Hallam, C., Bewley-Taylor, D., & Jelsma, M. (2014). Scheduling in the international drug control system, *TNI Series on Legislative Reform of Drug Policies 25*. Retrieved from https://www.tni.org/files/download/dlr25_0.pdf. Accessed on June 2014.

International Narcotics Control Board (INCB). (1996). *Report of the International Narcotics Control Board for 1995*. New York, NY: INCB/United Nations, para. 350. Retrieved from http://www.incb.org/documents/Publications/AnnualReports/AR1995/AR_1995_E.pdf

International Narcotics Control Board (INCB). (2002a). *Report of the International Narcotics Control Board for 2001*. New York, NY: INCB/United Nations. Retrieved from http://www.incb.org/incb/en/publications/annual-reports/annual-report-2001.html

International Narcotics Control Board (INCB). (2002b). Statement by Professor Hamid Ghodse, President of the International Narcotics Control Board, at the Forty-fifth session of the Commission on Narcotic Drugs, Vienna, March 11–15. Retrieved from http://www.incb.org/documents/Speeches/Speeches2002/45_CND.pdf

International Narcotics Control Board (INCB). (2011). *Report of the International Narcotics Control Board for 2010*. New York, NY: INCB/United Nations.

Ingraham, C. (2014). How marijuana legalization in Colorado and Washington is making the world a better place, *The Washington Post*, Wonkblog. Retrieved from https://www.washingtonpost.com/news/wonk/wp/2014/10/17/how-marijuana-legalization-in-colorado-and-washington-is-making-the-world-a-better-place/. Accessed on October 17, 2014.

Jelsma, M. (2003). Drugs in the UN system: The unwritten history of the 1998 United Nations General Assembly Special Session on drugs. *International Journal of Drug Policy 14*(2). Retrieved from http://www.druglawreform.info/images/stories/documents/unwritten.pdf

Jelsma, M., & Metaal, P. (2004). *Cracks in the Vienna Consensus: The UN Drug Control Debate*. WOLA Drug War Monitor. Retrieved from http://druglawreform.info/images/stories/wolabrief.pdf. Accessed on January 2004.

Kilmer, B., Kruithof, K., Pardal, M., Caulkins, J. P., & Rubin, J. (2013). *Multinational overview of cannabis production regimes*. Rand Europe/WODC/Dutch Ministry of Security and Justice. Retrieved from http://www.rand.org/content/dam/rand/pubs/research_reports/RR500/RR510/RAND_RR510.pdf

La Vanguardia. (2017). *El TC dice que los clubes de cannabis no pueden ser regulados por las CCAA*, 21 December 2017. Retrieved from http://www.lavanguardia.com/vida/20171221/433796160950/el-tc-dice-que-los-clubes-de-cannabis-no-pueden-ser-regulados-por-las-ccaa.html

Libération. (2013). *Les Cannabis Social Clubs partent en fumée*. Retrieved from http://www.liberation.fr/societe/2013/06/20/les-cannabis-social-clubs-partenten-fumee_912628. Accessed on June 20, 2013.

Lensink, H. & Derkzen, S. (2013). Internationaal is reguleren van wiet geen probleem, Vrij Nederland, Amsterdam, 2 December 2013. Retrieved from https://www.vn.nl/internationaal-is-reguleren-van-wiet-geen-probleem/.

Lines, R. (2017). *Drug control and human rights in International Law*. Cambridge: Cambridge University Press.

Marks, A. (2015). The legal landscape for Cannabis Social Clubs in Spain. Observatorio Civil de Drogas. Retrieved from http://observatoriocivil.org/wp-content/uploads/2015/03/OC-2015-3-The-legal-and-Socio-Political-Landscape-for-Cannabis-Social-Clubs-in-Spain.pdf

Meesters, M. (2015). *Het failliet van het gedogen. Op weg naar de cannabiswet*, VNG, October 2015. An English summary is available from https://vng.nl/files/vng/rapport_werkgroep_cannabisbeleid_engels.pdf

Ministry of Justice (Jamaica). (2015). *Dangerous Drugs Amendment Act 2015 Fact Sheet*. Retrieved from http://moj.gov.jm/sites/default/files/Dangerous%20Drugs%20Amendment%20Act%202015%20Fact%20Sheet_0.pdf

Newsweek. (2018). Marijuana legalization 2018: Which states might consider cannabis laws this year?, *Newsweek*. Retrieved from http://www.newsweek.com/marijuana-legalization-2018-which-states-will-consider-cannabis-laws-year-755282. Accessed on January 2, 2018.

New York Times. (2014). *U.S. issues marijuana guidelines for banks*. Retrieved from https://www.nytimes.com/2014/02/15/us/us-issues-marijuana-guidelines-for-banks.html. Accessed on February 14, 2014.

New York Times. (2017). *Pot was flying off the shelves in Uruguay. Then U.S. banks weighed in*. Retrieved from https://www.nytimes.com/2017/08/25/world/americas/uruguay-marijuana-us-banks.html. Accessed on August 25, 2017.

Nougier, M. (2017). *Contribution for the pre-review of CBD and Tramadol at the 39th WHO Expert Committee on Drug Dependence*. IDPC Advocacy Note. Retrieved from http://files.idpc.net/library/IDPC-advocacy-note_ECDD-39-session.pdf. Accessed on November 2017.

Oostlander, A. M. (2004). *Report on the proposal for a Council Framework Decision laying down minimum provisions on the constituent elements of criminal acts and penalties in the field of drug trafficking, Justice and Home Affairs, Committee on Citizens' Freedoms and Rights, A5-0095/2004*. Retrieved from http://www.europarl.europa.eu/sides/getDoc.do?pubRef=-//EP//TEXT+REPORT+A5-2004-0095+0+DOC+XML+V0//EN. Accessed on February 23, 2004.

Queirolo, R., Boidi, M. F., & Cruz, Cruz (2016). Cannabis clubs in Uruguay: The challenges of regulation, *International Journal of Drug Policy*, *34*, 41–48.

Rodriques, C. (2017, December 29). I grow pot in California for a living. I'm worried about legalization. *The Washington Post*. Retrieved from https://www.washingtonpost.com/opinions/will-small-marijuana-farmers-like-me-be-wiped-out-when-pot-goes-legal-in-california/2017/12/29/b54cd99c-ec25-11e7-b698-91d4e35920a3_story.html

Rosmarin, A., & Eastwood, N. (2012). A quiet revolution: Drug decriminalisation policies in practice across the globe. London: Release. In 2016 and updated version was published. Retrieved from https://www.release.org.uk/publications/drug-decriminalisation-2016

Schardt, S. (ed.). (2001). *European Cities on Drug Policy. Cooperation and community consensus. The multi-agency approach to effective local drug policies*. Frankfurt am Main, Germany: European Cities on Drug Policy. Retrieved from http://www.realitaeten-bureau.de/documents/commcoop-ECDP_002.pdf

Schutte, J. J. E. (1995). The legal implications of legalising cannabis and cannabis products, GON (1995). *Drugs policy in the Netherlands: Continuity and change*, Annex III. Retrieved from http://www.emcdda.europa.eu/system/files/Ministerie%20VWS%20%281995%29%20Continuity%20and%20Change%2C%20Dutch%20drug%20policy.pdf

The Local. (2015). *Cannabis coffee shops given red light in Berlin*. Retrieved from https://www.thelocal.de/20151005/cannabis-shops-given-the-red-light-in-berlin. Accessed on October 5, 2015.

United Nations (UN). (1973). *Commentary on the Single Convention on Narcotic Drugs, 1961*. New York.

United Nations (UN). (1980). *Vienna Convention on the Law of Treaties*, Vienna, May 23, 1969, United Nations Treaty Series *1155*(18232).

United Nations (UN). (2009). *Political Declaration and Plan of Action on international cooperation towards an integrated and balanced strategy to counter the world drug problem*. High-level segment Commission on Narcotic Drugs, Vienna, 11–12 March 2009. Retrieved from https://www.unodc.org/documents/ungass2016/V0984963-English.pdf

UN General Assembly (UNGA). (2016). *A/S-30/L.1, Our joint commitment to effectively addressing and countering the world drug problem*. UNGA. Retrieved from https://daccess-ods.un.org/TMP/1073419.00467873.html. Accessed on April 14, 2016.

United Nations General Assembly Special Session (UNGASS). (2016a). *Statement by Canada at the 2016 UNGASS*. New York. Retrieved from http://statements.unmeetings.org/media2/7657386/canada-eng-.pdf. Accessed on April 20, 2016.

United Nations General Assembly Special Session (UNGASS). (2016b). *Statement by Kamina Johnson Smith*. Minister of Foreign Affairs and Foreign Trade of Jamaica, at the 2016 UNGASS. New York. Retrieved from http://statements.unmeetings.org/media2/7657400/jamaica.pdf. Accessed on April 20, 2016.

United Nations General Assembly Special Session (UNGASS). (2016c). Statement by H. E. Camillo M. Gonsalves, Minister of Economic Planning, Sustainable Development, Industry, Information and Labour of St Vincent and the Grenadines, at the 2016 UNGASS, New York. Retrieved from http://statements.unmeetings.org/media2/7657555/saint-vincent-and-the-grenadines.pdf. Accessed on April 21, 2016.

United Nations Office on Drugs and Crime (UNODC). (2006). *World Drug Report 2006*.

United Nations Office on Drugs and Crime (UNODC). (2017). *World Drug Report 2017: Market analysis of plant-based drugs*. Retrieved from https://www.unodc.org/wdr2017/field/Booklet_3_Plantbased_drugs.pdf

U.S. Embassy in The Hague. (1975). Visit of US Drug Abuse Officials To Neths, Confidential Cable, 19 May 1975 (Document Number: 1975THEHA02525); available at https://archive.org/details/StateDeptcable1975-232930

Van Dijk, J. J. M. (1998). The narrow margins of the Dutch drug policy: A cost-benefit analysis. *European Journal on Criminal Policy and Research*, *6*(3), 369–393. Retrieved from https://pure.uvt.nl/portal/files/1000726/Narrow.pdf

Van Kempen, P.H., & Fedorova, M. (2014). *Internationaal recht en cannabis. Een beoordeling op basis van VN-drugsverdragen en EU-drugsregelgeving van gemeentelijke en buitenlandse opvattingen pro regulering van cannabisteelt voor recreatief gebruik (International law and cannabis. An assessment of municipal and foreign views in favour of regulating cannabis cultivation for recreational use based on UN Narcotic Drugs Conventions and the EU legal instruments in anti-drugs policy)*. Deventer, Netherlands: Kluwer. An executive summary in English is available from https://www.wodc.nl/binaries/2411-summary_tcm28-73399.pdf

Van Kempen, P. H., & Fedorova, M. (2016). *Internationaal recht en cannabis II. Regulering van cannabisteelt en -handel voor recreatief gebruik: positieve mensenrechtenverplichtingen versus VN-drugsverdragen (International law and cannabis*

II. Regulation of cannabis cultivation and trade for recreational use: positive human rights obligations versus UN Narcotic Drugs Conventions), Deventer, Netherlands: Wolters Kluwer. An executive summary in English is available from http://www.ru.nl/publish/pages/797876/internationaal_recht_en_cannabis_ii_-_english_summary.pdf

Volteface. (2016a). *The story of the UK's Cannabis Social Clubs*. Retrieved from http://volteface.me/features/story-of-ukcsc/. Accessed on June 23, 2016.

Volteface. (2016B). *UK's Cannabis Social Clubs come of age*. Retrieved from http://volteface.me/features/ukcsc-general-meeting/. Accessed on November 8, 2016.

Waibel, M. (2011). Demystifying the art of interpretation. *The European Journal of International Law*, *22*(2). Retrieved from http://www.ejil.org/pdfs/22/2/2155.pdf

Walsh, J. (2016). *Silver linings: U.S. State votes to legalize cannabis boost reform opportunities in the Americas*. WOLA Commentary. Retrieved from https://www.wola.org/analysis/silver-linings-u-s-state-votes-legalize-cannabis-boost-reform-opportunities-americas/. Accessed on November 2016.

Walsh, J., Bewley-Taylor, D., Jelsma, M., & Blickman, T. (2017). Yes, legalizing marijuana breaks treaties. We can deal with that. *Ipolitics*. Retrieved from https://ipolitics.ca/2017/12/11/yes-legalizing-marijuana-breaks-treaties-not-problem/. Accessed on December 11, 2017.

Walsh J., & Ramsey, Ramsey (2016). Cannabis regulation in Uruguay: An innovative law facing major challenges. *Journal of Drug Policy Analysis*. *11*(1). DOI: 10.1515/jdpa-2015-0007

Washington Post. (2015). *Losing marijuana business, Mexican cartels push heroin and meth*. Retrieved from https://www.washingtonpost.com/world/the_americas/losing-marijuana-business-mexican-cartels-push-heroin-and-meth/2015/01/11/91fe44ce-8532-11e4-abcf-5a3d7b3b20b8_story.html. Accessed on January 11, 2015.

Weser Kurier (2017). *Bundesrat lehnt Cannabis-Antrag ab*. Weser Kurier, July 8 2017, Bremen, Germany Retrieved from https://www.weser-kurier.de/startseite_artikel,-bundesrat-lehnt-cannabisantrag-ab-_arid,1622416.html.

Chapter 6

Drug Policy in the Russian Federation: Do Control Policies Produce More Harm than Drugs?

Mikhail Golichenko, Anya Sarang, Khalid Tinasti and Isabela Barbosa

Abstract

The United Nations General Assembly Special Session on drugs has provided countries with internationally agreed recommendations to adapt their drug policies for more efficiency and better outcomes. This chapter focusses on the Russian Federation's role in international drug policy, through an analysis of its national approaches and their design, as well as on its diplomatic efforts at the bilateral and multilateral levels to oppose drug policy reform. A systematic review of peer-reviewed, grey literature, policy documents, UN reports and news reports on the country's response to drugs internally and externally was conducted between September and December 2017. Despite its efforts to oppose drug policy reform and the prioritisation of public health, the Russian Federation faces major epidemics of imprisonment and HIV. Internationally, while it has not been successful in addressing the ongoing reforms in Europe and the Americas, it has been effective in preserving its international priorities by opposing harm reduction and maintaining the prohibition paradigm at the multilateral level.

Keywords: Russian Federation; drug policy; HIV and AIDS epidemic; imprisonment epidemic; opioid substitution therapy; Commission on Narcotic Drugs

Introduction

In the post-United Nations General Assembly Special Session on drugs 2016 era, the divide in the design and implementation of national drug policies has deepened,

Collapse of the Global Order on Drugs: From UNGASS 2016 to Review 2019, 133–149

doi:10.1108/978-1-78756-487-920181006

with some countries reviewing their health or criminal justice responses, others moving towards the legalisation of narcotics, while the remainder continue with the escalation of their war on drugs. Although the transnational nature of the response to drugs is recognised globally to address organised crime and money laundering, elements related to demand reduction are not consensual among the UN member states. With this globally changing policy landscape, and the retreat of the United States from its position of the major advocate for the war on drugs, the Russian Federation has maintained its fierce opposition to drug use, production and trafficking. This opposition, based on the three international drug control conventions, is showcased in the national policies of the Russian Federation, and is highlighted through its diplomatic activity to tackle the current wave of reforms taking place in the Americas and in Europe.

Such opposition to review policies based on the total prohibition of drugs was implemented through the last century, and it benefited from popular support, policymakers' commitment and the presence of funding for the law enforcement in charge of drug control. As a result, a country that bans some treatment options and opposes harm reduction services is facing major prison overcrowding, significant HIV, hepatitis and tuberculosis epidemics, as well as the appearance of new dangerous psychoactive substances. Moreover, the efforts to eradicate drugs, with high levels of legal criminalisation and social stigma towards people who use drugs (as reported: misuse by law-enforcement agencies of the drug withdrawal syndrome to obtain confessions, misuse of social and medical status as reasons for arrest of people who use drugs, and extrajudicial violence, including sexual violence against women who use drugs (Golichenko & Sarang, 2013; Lunze, Cheng, & Samet, 2016) have resulted neither in a reduction of demand for drugs, nor in success in reducing their supply.

This chapter, divided into two parts, reviews the national drug policies of the Russian Federation and the public health and imprisonment epidemics it generated. It discusses the origins of the repressive drug control regime in the Russian Federation since the Soviet Russia until the dismantling of the drug control service in 2016. The second part reviews the activism of the Russian diplomacy to propagate its policies regionally and internationally, as well as its current positions in the post-United Nations General Assembly Special Session on drugs in 2016 and how it attempts to undermine the outcome document negotiated in the said special session.

Part 1: Russian Drug Laws and their Enforcement as Drivers of Multiple Epidemics

Drug policy in the Russian Federation is heavily underpinned by the notion of using punishment as a response to drugs – an approach that is hardly unique to the country. Although this approach was formed largely during the Soviet era (between 1960 and 1990), it has certainly developed some troubling features after the collapse of the Soviet Union, when the Russian Federation faced a significant increase in supply of heroin from Afghanistan in the 1990s and the rise in injecting drug use (Hamers & Downs, 2003). Some authors have commented on the 'securitization' of drug policy discourse in Russia in recent years (Marshall, 2014), but the drugs issue has for the last century been treated not only as a law-enforcement prerogative but also as a particular threat to national security and the social order. From as early as the 1920s, Soviet authorities considered drug trafficking among the most serious crimes against the state, alongside conspiracy against the state, espionage and high treason (Декрет ВЦИК, 1913). Later, in the 1960s, the term 'serious crimes' appeared in the UN Drug Conventions, but there is no evidence of the Soviet influence in this regard. Drug trafficking was also considered an allegation to be dealt with as a form of counter-revolutionary activity subject to prosecution before the Revolutionary Tribunals (Декрет ВЦИК, 1920). Soviet Russia's Criminal Codes of 1922,[1] 1926 and 1960 contained provisions related to trafficking in narcotic drugs with no provisions related to the prohibition concerning the dissemination of drug information (what later appear as 'drug propaganda') or incitement to use narcotic drugs.[2] Before 1960, criminal sanctions for drug trafficking were part of the 'economic crimes' section of the Criminal Code – drug crimes per se were never punishable by the death penalty. The criminal liability for simple possession of drugs without the intent of trafficking, for incitement to drug use, and for running drug use facilities (drug dens), as well as administrative liability for non-medical use of drugs, were only introduced in Russia in 1974.[3]

The Emergence of the Current Drug Control Policies

Drug use has always been a much stigmatised social phenomenon, which was deemed inconsistent with Soviet society and therefore non-existent, despite statistical and medical data suggesting the contrary (Panin, 2003). This alleged inconsistency, as well as the official assertion that drug use did not exist in the Soviet state, may help explain why drug use and simple possession were not criminalised for roughly 50 years following the founding of the USSR. Yet paradoxically, despite this official position, research suggests that drug use was most probably harshly addressed by repressive measures, especially during Stalin's 'Great Terror' of 1936–1938 (Latypov, 2012). Some indirect evidence suggests that Stalin's Gulag harboured many people who used drugs.[4] Given the political nature of

---

[1]Article 140d regarding cocaine and opium trafficking was introduced in 1924. There were no provisions regarding other drugs defined in law as 'narcotics', other than cocaine and opium.

[2]Criminal Codes of other Soviet Union Republics contained similar provisions.

[3]For a detailed overview of the Soviet Russia drug laws and regulations, please read Kalachev (2001).

[4]For example, the 1987 Soviet movie 'Kholodnoye Leto 53-go' (A Cold Sumer of 1953) tells a story about a group of prisoners released as part of a large amnesty of thousands of prisoners from the Gulag after Stalin's death in 1953. In one scene, the group of prisoners enters a private house and finds a box with medications; one prisoner rushes to the box screaming 'codeinchik' (codeine). After a short battle, the group leader takes tablets for himself and swallows them with an expression of relief on his face.

the dictatorship at that time, people who used drugs could be prosecuted for any anti-Soviet behaviour or acquisitive crimes, thus the criminal justice system could deal with people who use drugs having no special legal provisions concerning drug use or even possession of drugs with no intent to supply. From the late 1930s to the beginning of the 1970s, drug dependence was officially declared to be 'nearly completely liquidated', which also led to the absence of accessible literature about drug use in the Soviet Union (Latypov, 2012) and little development of any organised system of ostensible treatment for drug dependence as a health condition.

There is no exact answer to what triggered the development and toughening of drug laws from 1960 onward. Perhaps there was an interplay of several factors, such as the overall reform of criminal laws (the new Criminal Code of the Russian Soviet Federal Social Republic was adopted in 1960, Уголовный кодекс РСФСР, 1960), the USSR's active participation in drafting and promoting the 1961 Single Convention on Narcotic Drugs and later the 1971 UN Convention of Psychotropic Substances, as well as the growing problem of alcohol and drug addiction in many USSR republics. The interplay of these factors could be the reason for the incremental changes in criminal law, such as the introduction of coercive treatment for alcohol and drug dependent people, and later the criminal liability for the offences related to drug use. Regardless of the exact reasons, the main features of the current punitive drug control system in the Russian Federation were introduced in the 1960s and 1970s.

It is against this backdrop that, in the 1970s, the field of drug dependence treatment — or 'narcology' as it is referred to in Russia — began to emerge within a framework already heavily influenced by a criminal justice mindset. In other words, with the emergence of the discipline of narcology in the 1970s, there was a more open recognition of the reality of drug use, even if it was still caught up in politicking of the day. Thus the new discipline was already born out of and into a system that was heavily punitive and surveillance-oriented in its approach. Methods for treating drug dependence differed little from those already adopted for treating alcohol dependence – that is, 'treatment' in the so-called 'treatment labor centres' under the supervision of police. When drug use – and particularly problematic drug use – increased significantly in Russia after the dissolution of the USSR, the narcological system turned out to be woefully unprepared to handle the dramatically increased number of people identified, whether correctly or not, as requiring treatment.

The last 15 years have also seen other important developments in drug law and the machinery for its enforcement in Russia. The system continues to evolve, although its predominant emphasis remains on prohibition and prosecution, and key evidence-based health interventions for problematic drug use remain inaccessible and even legally prohibited. In 2003–2004, the federal Parliament (Duma) enacted amendments to the Criminal Code and other drug laws decriminalising possession of up to 10 daily doses of any prohibited narcotic substances (e.g., up to 1 g of heroin). Corresponding to this legal reform, more than 40,000 people in prison for related offences were released. Tragically, many died during the first weeks after release because of limited access to effective drug dependence treatment and the existence of only a few harm reduction programmes operated by non-governmental organisations (NGOs) in some municipalities, none of which were equipped to provide interventions (e.g., the opioid antagonist naloxone) to prevent fatal overdoses, naloxone being a prescribed medication which is legally restricted for free distribution by harm reduction programmes run by NGOs.[5]

Also in 2003, the Russian government created the Federal Drug Control Service (FDCS), reporting directly to the President of the Russian Federation. The FDCS was created after the Federal Tax Police was disbanded. Most former tax police officers became drug law-enforcement police. With no background or training in drug offences, these officers found the easiest targets for prosecution in people who use drugs; and migrants. The situation did not change significantly until June 2016, when the government closed the FDCS and reassigned drug enforcement functions to the Ministry of Home Affairs, thus bringing drug control back to the sole responsibility of the police. The recent police and judicial statistics demonstrate that the situation on the ground has not changed significantly since this institutional change.

The Public Health Epidemic

The drug treatment system was and remains archaic under the extensive influence of famed physicians. People such as Professor Eduard Babayan, former representative of the USSR, and later the Russian Federation, on the International Narcotics Control Board,[6] played a significant role through the 1998 federal law in ensuring that Russia imposed a federal legal ban on the use of any controlled substitute for treatment of drug dependence, and thus effectively subjecting under criminal prohibition the opioid substitution therapy (OST) for those with opioid dependence (e.g., through the use of methadone or buprenorphine). It is to be noted that the use of Tramadol – a synthetic opioid analgesic – is allowed as substitution treatment for in- and out-patients with severe abstinence syndrome, for up to ten days. The ban of substitution therapy with methadone and buprenorphine stands in stark contrast to the successful experience of such treatment options in many countries worldwide (World Health Organisation, 2009), as well as widespread recommendations from various international expert bodies, both as an important treatment option for opioid dependence and as a key element

---

[5]Naloxone is an opioid antagonist that blocks and reverses the depression of the central nervous and respiratory systems caused by opioids such as heroin. The medication is administered on an emergency basis shortly following an overdose to prevent death and may be administered intravenously, injected into a muscle or via a nasal spray.

[6]The INCB was established by the UN Single Convention on Narcotic Drugs of 1961. It describes itself as 'the independent and quasi-judicial body for the implementation of the United Nations drug control conventions'. (See the INCB website at http://incb.org/incb/en/about/mandate-functions.html.) It monitors states' implementation of this convention and the other UN drug control treaties, and offers its views and its recommendations regarding whether states are in compliance with their treaty obligations.

to support HIV prevention and treatment among people using heroin or other opioids (Gowing, Farrell, Bornemann, Sullivan, & Ali, 2011).

The Russian Federation faces an expanding HIV epidemic driven by drug injection, with more than 1 million people infected, an almost twofold increase from 2010, and estimated to reach 3 million people by 2020 (Osborn, 2016). Among the 100,000 new HIV cases reported in 2015, 57 per cent were among people who inject drugs (PWID) (Виткин, 2016). Eastern Europe and Central Asia have by far the highest prevalence of injecting drug use globally, with 1.27 per cent and 0.72 per cent of the population aged 15–64 respectively (UNODC, 2016). The Russian Federation is the country with the highest number of citizens injecting drugs, with an estimated 1.5–3 million PWID (Clark, 2016) of whom 20 per cent live with HIV and between 60 per cent and 90 per cent are infected with hepatitis C, while tuberculosis is the main cause of death among people living with HIV in the country (Heimer, Eritsyan, Barbour, & Levina, 2014; Tsui et al., 2016). The current HIV and AIDS epidemic has been building up over time. From 1995 to 2001, the rate of new HIV infections doubled every six to twelve months (United Nations Development Programme, 2004) and by 2002 an estimated 93 per cent of people living with HIV were PWID (Central and Eastern European Harm Reduction Network, 2002).

To respond to this alarming situation, the government approved a national HIV/AIDS strategy for the period 2010–2020. However, the strategy does not include evidence-based approaches to prevent HIV among PWID, with policies limiting access to NSP, banning OST, limiting opiate dependence treatment to Naltrexone (medication usually used to treat alcohol dependence) or very restrictive use of tramadol, and large investments in education, testing and communications campaigns (Правительство Российской Федерации, 2016; Черных, 2016).

Health authorities have not generally objected to the dominance of law-enforcement measures in Russian drug policy, and have not sought to pursue approaches or implement programmes that would deviate in any significant way from an enforcement-focussed approach (Golichenko & Ka Hon Chu, 2018). In the area of drug control, many doctors who had seemed to be more oriented towards a health-based and evidence-based approach to drug treatment, have gradually changed their views to reflect the more repressive orthodoxy.[7] For

[7]For example, Evgeny Bruin, a Chief Drug Treatment Doctor since 2009, used to favour a concept of substitution therapy for drug dependence treatment. In 1994, he patented a substitution therapy method with use of tramadol. However, from 2009, since his appointment as a Chief Drug Treatment Doctor, he became a strong opponent of substitution therapy (information about a patent certificate is in Сошников, С., Власов, В. В., Граница, А., Сосунов, Р., Смирнов, А., Владимиров, С. (2011). Контент-анализ запатентованыых методов лечения наркологических расстройств в России. Неврологический вестник. Журнал им. В.М. Бехтерева. 2011. № 4. С. 3-7.) Tatyana Klimenko, an Advisor to the Minister of Health and former senior staff member of Serbsky Center used to accept substitution therapy provided that the sound rehabilitation system is in place in Russia (интервью Татьяны Клименко газете Московской Комсомолец «Нас ждет сопротивление наркологов». 9 августа 2012 года.). However, since her appointment as an advisor to

example, in 2011 the Chief Drug Treatment Doctor announced his endeavor to create a four level system of 'social pressure' in order to respond to the drug problem (Курская, 2011). The first level of this system is the so-called early detection of drug use by means of school and work place testing[8]; the second level is voluntary drug treatment; the third level is compulsory treatment by referral from the criminal justice system; the fourth level is compulsory treatment within the criminal justice system. In fact, this system started taking shape in 2010 when the first school and work place drug testing laws were introduced in the Duma, eventually being passed in 2013. That same year, the Duma amended the Criminal Code to provide for suspended sentences for people with drug dependence convicted of a minor drug offence or an acquisitive crime for the first time. The Code of Administrative Offences was also amended to provide for compulsory treatment as an alternative for punishment for non-medical use of drugs; for drug testing of suspects committing administrative drug offences; while non-compliance with a court order regarding compulsory treatment is an administrative offence. Thus the four levels of the 'social pressure' system have been gradually shaped. As part of this system the Ministry of Home Affairs coordinates the 'social rehabilitation' and the 'resocialization' of people who use drugs.[9]

---

the Health Ministry in 2012, she is now a strong opponent of substitution therapy. In 2015, commenting on the applications of three Russian citizens who challenged the Russian ban on OST in the European Court of Human Rights, Ms Klimenko stated firmly that OST shall remain banned and foreign attempts to bring this treatment to Russia should receive 'a-symmetric response' from the Russian Government (Марина Юдкевич. «Дела пациентов из Татарстана ушли в Европейский суд». Газета Вечерняя Казань. 30.04.2015). Alexander Kozlov, a former Deputy Chief of Department at FDCS and current Chief Treatment Doctor at the Moscow Psychiatry Institute, used to give fair accounts regarding the need to introduce OST in Russia (Kozlov, Polunina, & Davydov, 2007; Оценка динамики клинико-психопатологических и психосоциальных характеристик пациентов с опийной зависимостью / Т.В. Клименко, А.А. Козлов, С.А. Игумнов [и др.] // Медицинская психология в России: электрон. науч. журн. – 2016. – N 2(37). Retrieved from http://mprj.ru). In 2014, he co-authored a pseudo-scientific report regarding OST program in Crimea which eventually led this program to abrupt termination (report Kozlov, Mandibura and Klimenko. Another co-author of this report was a senior drug treatment doctor from Crimea Evgeny Mandibura. For many years, he was an active supporter of OST in Ukraine and Crimea; he was running the largest OST cites in Crimea. However, as soon as Crimea was annexed by the Russian Federation in 2014, he turned into an opponent of his own program in Crimea (Klimenko et al., 2014).

[8]The FDCS supported school drug testing. See Interview with Victor Ivanov. «Иглы без разума. Наркополиция закрывает ночные клубы, где обнаружены наркотики». Иван Егоров. Российская газета. Retrieved from http://www.rg.ru/2010/02/04/igly.html; 'Тестировать на употребление наркотиков необходимо с 11 лет - ФСКН'. RAPSI. 20 November 2012. Retrieved from http://rapsinews.ru/incident_news/20121120/265438175.html; Interview with Victor Ivanov. «Иглы без разума. Наркополиция закрывает ночные клубы, где обнаружены наркотики». Иван Егоров. Российская газета. Retrieved from http://www.rg.ru/2010/02/04/igly.html

[9]See Указ Президента РФ от 10 июля 2014 г. N 507

The Imprisonment Epidemic

In July 2016, there were 650,633 prisoners in the Russian Federation (including more than 52,622 women, about 8 per cent of the total prison population).[10] These figures include the total number of adults and minors in correction facilities and pre-trial detention. With a population of 146.5 million people,[11] the Russian Federation incarcerates 444.1 inmates per 100,000 people. This places Russia as the second most incarcerating country in the world, after the United States (Institute for Criminal Policy Research, 2016). The number of inmates per capita is comparable to the number of secondary school teachers, which is of 719.5 teachers per 100,000 people.[12] The application of Russia's drug laws accounts for a very substantial proportion of this high prevalence of imprisonment. At the end of 2015, of the 525,056 adult prisoners (including about 52,600 women), 134,245 (including 16,999 women) had been convicted for drug-related offences – nearly 1 in 4 overall, and nearly 1 in 3 of incarcerated women.

There is no precise data concerning pro rata numbers of migrants/non-citizens among people convicted for drug offences, and/or ethnic profiles of these people. There is no racial profiling data in the Russian judicial statistics.[13] At the same time, information which was available on the website of the FDCS before it was closed in April 2016 suggested that the racial factor plays an important role in law-enforcement of high-profile drug dealers: in August 2015, all the people convicted as 'extremely dangerous drug dealers' were people of non-Slavic origins (FDCS, 2015).

The accusatory bias in criminal proceedings is an additional important factor which is reported by researchers of the criminal justice system in Russia. Due to this bias, charges supported by prosecutors, especially more serious charges, very rarely end with acquittals (Volkov, Paneyakh, Titaev, & Primakov, 2010). All drug charges are charges supported by prosecutors, and the majority of drug-related offences are considered serious crimes. Thus, the accusatory bias plays a

[10]Official statistics available on the website of the Federal Penitentiary Service of the Russian Federation. No data are available about the number of prisoners identifying as transgender. Retrieved from http://www.fsin.su/structure/inspector/iao/statistika/Kratkaya%20har-ka%20UIS/. Accessed on November 27, 2017.

[11]According to the official Russian statistics agency Rosstat. Retrieved from http://www.gks.ru/wps/wcm/connect/rosstat_main/rosstat/ru/statistics/population/demography. Accessed on November 27, 2017.

[12]According to the official Russian statistics agency Rosstat. Retrieved from http://www.gks.ru/free_doc/new_site/population/obraz/o-obr2.htm. Accessed on November 27, 2017.

[13]Police statistical cards, which police must fill in for every criminal case, have an entry for 'nationality'. Information in this entry is 'according to information from a person', so it usually means citizenship. For example, an ethnic Caucasian will most probably will appear as 'Russian' if he/she carries a Russian passport. The publicly available judicial and police statistics do not include information on ethnicity. The so-called prison census (last done in 2009) does not reflect the ethnic profile of prisoners incarcerated for drug offences. Police statistics only reflect the number of crimes committed by foreign citizens; and against foreign citizens. It is unclear why ethnic information is not included in official statistics.

significant role in criminal proceedings on drug offences. It should be noted that the number of convictions for drug offences has remained stable, between 110,000 and 130,000 annually, since 1999, including following the creation of the FDCS in 2003.[14] Similarly unchanged is the proportion of crimes related to drug use and drug trafficking (two-thirds of convictions each year are for offences related to drug use and the remaining third for crimes related to drug trafficking),[15] as well as the bulk of annual heroin seizures (UNODC, 2015).

The most significant decrease of registered drug offences was in 2004 due to the amended criminal laws when the daily doses were introduced into the Criminal Code, and the threshold amount for the possession of all drugs for the purpose of criminal liability was lifted. However, in 2006, these amendments were repealed, which resulted in growing numbers of registered drug offences.

The closing of the FDCS in April 2016 did not lead to a significant change in the number of recorded drug crimes. From January to November 2017, police registered 194,800 drug offences. During the same period in 2015, both police and the FDCS registered 218,900 drug-related offences (Ministry of the Interior, 2018). The fluctuations in the number of registered offences do not follow the fluctuations in annual drug seizures (UNODC, 2015). In fact, the highest number of registered drug offences occurred in 2014, when police statistics showed that 253,000 registered drug offences does not correspond to any increase in seizures. The bulk of seizures of all type of drugs took place in 2004, at the same time as the lowest number of registered drug offences, 150,000. In 2004, the newly created FDCS could not be more efficient than it was in the following years. And yet, 2004 was the most successful year in terms of drug seizures. The number of registered drug offences might rather suggest that the FDCS officers incrementally gained skills in arresting people who use drugs and petty drug traffickers, who most likely were drug users themselves. There is no evidence that police changed this practice after the closing of the FDCS in April 2016.

Part 2: The Russian Position at the International Level

This national situation mirrors the international drug policies of the Russian Federation. As a Global Player, a regional power and a permanent member of the UN Security Council, the country uses multilateral and bilateral fora and relationships to address drug-related issues and their trans-national nature. The second part of this chapter focusses on the firm defence by Russia of a law-enforcement-based

[14]Data from the court statistics for 2015 of the Supreme Court Judicial Department. Retrieved from www.cdep.ru; Note for the State Council 2002 (Справка к Заседанию президиума Государственного совета № 23 «О состоянии и мерах противодействия злоупотреблению наркотиками и их незаконному обороту» 24 сентября 2002 года. Retrieved from http://archive.kremlin.ru/text/stcdocs/2002/09/30599.shtml) and the Statistics of the Supreme Court Department. Retrieved from www.cdep.ru.

[15]Official courts statistics available on the Supreme Court Judicial Department website. Retrieved from www.cdep.ru.

approach derived from the three international drug control conventions (The Single Convention on Narcotic Drugs of 1961, the Convention on Psychotropic Substances of 1971 and the United Nations Convention against Illicit Traffic in Narcotic Drugs and Psychotropic Substances of 1988) (UNODC, 2013) through various diplomatic tactics and channels. Within the United Nations, the Russian Federation has been, in the pre- and post-UNGASS 2016 period, a strong promoter of the entities and assemblies mandated by the Conventions to guide the design and implementation of drug laws and policies. The country has been continuously trying to close the debates on drug policy, including its specific health or development components such as harm reduction, in other UN fora or forums such as the World Health Assembly (WHA), the Joint Programme on HIV/AIDS and the Human Rights Council. Such an approach had as its goal to monopolise discussion on drugs in the Commission on Narcotic Drugs (CND). The Russian Federation has also used its other regional and global fora to influence the outcome of other nations' drug policies, and to find allies to adopt its priorities in the multilateral system. The country has used its influence in the G8 and the BRICS; tried to build its own international coalitions against some forms of treatment (OST); and attempted to use its move from a global recipient to donor of international aid before the recent decline of its economy.

The UN: CND, General Assembly and WHA

The CND, the UN Member State assembly with a mandate to discuss solely international drug control policies, is the multilateral body in charge of the negotiations of international commitments to 'combat' drugs. It was the forum in which the UNGASS 2016 outcome document was negotiated and finalised, being simply approved by the General Assembly at the opening of the Special Session. It is also the body that is charged with the review, in 2019, of the decennial 2009 political declaration and the plan of action to address drugs, despite the fact that it had failed to review the mid-term implementation of these same documents in 2014, adopting a document that was unable to provide any elements on the current situation of drug use, reduction in demand or supply and provided a set of contradictory targets – between health protection and drug enforcement – for the future (Commission on Narcotic Drugs, 2014).

During the pre-UNGASS preparatory process, the CND requested Member States to provide their contributions through their regional groups. Such a tactic was beneficial to the status quo, and in ensuring that the contributions would be limited to the big players in the diplomatic space. To illustrate this point, one should remember the political dynamics within the UN regional groups, which have not been reformed or reviewed since the creation of the UN. Through the EE group,[16] the Russian Federation has shared its priorities for the UNGASS.

[16]The Eastern Europe Group (EE), which includes the Russian Federation, used to group the European countries of the former Soviet space, and today still includes 11 central and eastern European countries currently members of the European Union (EU), which adopt EU positions rather than those of the EE group.

The country called for the use of the three drug conventions as the cornerstone of drug policies, reminded that reducing the production, use and trade of drugs have not been achieved, and that the appearance of new psychoactive substances and the questioning of the effectiveness of the current international control system by some other governments and civil society are exacerbating factors of these shortcomings. The Russian contributor added that this, in return, makes the achievement of a drug-free world more important and that the outcome of the UNGASS should concentrate on reducing the demand and supply of drugs by focussing on the traditional supply reduction and law-enforcement approaches (Commission on Narcotic Drugs, 2015).

In the post-UNGASS period, and after the adoption of the UNGASS outcome document that introduced four new pillars to the international drug control system (access to controlled medicines; human rights and youth; new challenges; alternative development) (United Nations, 2016), the Russian Federation was focussing its efforts on limiting the significance of this international agreement and calling for the strengthening of the 2009 political declaration and plan of action, arguing its supremacy over the UNGASS document through a valid procedure in line with the General Assembly's resolution requesting the organisation of the UNGASS (United Nations, 2012). Moreover, Russia has showed its determination to contest any progress towards health-based interventions by blocking a decision item at the WHA in May 2016, a month after UNGASS, which requested WHO to draft a health sector strategy on drugs. Such a strategy is a non-binding, regular procedure that allows WHO to provide countries with technical expertise to address a specific health-related issue. In informal negotiation meetings, the aggressive approach of the Russian Federation and its allies to counter this decision item has created a rare situation in diplomatic forums, pushing representatives of other countries to share their irritation for such non-diplomatic action never seen before in discussion later in the Committee A plenary (World Health Organisation, 2016).

A Strategic Use of Economic Multilateral Forums? From the G8 to the BRICS

Abundant literature has discussed the Russian Federation's influence on national policies in Eastern European and Central Asian countries (EECA), and in particular the country's interest in regional cooperation to reduce supply with the objective of consolidating efforts to fight drug trafficking (Csete & Pearshouse, 2007). While today the Russian Federation is considered as a regional leader in many strategic areas of cooperation, the extent of its influence in the region is somehow contrasted by national policies and practises in the drug policy field. In fact, Uzbekistan and Turkmenistan are the only other countries in EECA to ban harm reduction services and substitution treatments.

In the pre-UNGASS period, Russia's interventions and discourses at the G8 and the BRICS illustrated the ability of the country to use foreign relations as a tool for pushing cooperation against drugs as a main priority. In early 2014, and as the Russian Federation assumed the presidency of the G8 for the year and was expected to host the Leaders' Summit in Sochi, it laid out five priorities for its presidency, with the first being 'Cooperation in the fight against drugs' with a Ministerial meeting on countering drugs, which was put forward above issues such as fighting terrorism, conflict resolution, disaster risks and global health security (ФСКН, 2014). This priority given to address drug trafficking was put to an end by the Ukrainian crisis and the annexation of Crimea by the Russian Federation in March of the same year, leading to the interruption of its participation in the G8 (Waterfield, 2014).

In 2015, as the hosting nation of the BRICS Summit in Ufa, Russia, the Russian Federation held meetings of the anti-drug agencies and experts in Moscow, before aligning its position with the other four countries, calling for the international drug conventions to be the basis for drug policies; reaffirming their commitment to the 2009 political declaration; and creating mechanisms of interaction in countering drugs (BRICS, 2015). Similarly, in August 2015, the Russian Federation aimed to create an international anti-substitution therapy coalition to oppose the recognition of the effectiveness of methadone, an controlled medicine included in WHO's list of medicines that countries must deliver to their citizens in need, in reducing the harms related to heroin injection (Козлов & Козичев, 2015). This coalition mainly attracted countries of the Gulf Cooperation Council and neighbouring Uzbekistan and Turkmenistan. Other global or regional players, such as China or Iran, which adopted repressive drug policies similar to those of the Russian Federation, do nevertheless implement OST on a large scale. In December 2017, the Russian Federation hosted a meeting of members of parliaments from 43 countries, such as Iran, Pakistan, Uzbekistan, Tajikistan, Afghanistan, and Philippines. Participants agreed to oppose drug law reforms and to develop joint treaties to counter-balance the trend in some countries to legalise substances such as cannabis (Litavrin, 2017). Interestingly, these efforts are undertaken by the Russian Federation ahead of the 2019 review of the decennial political declaration and plan of action at the CND.

Funding as Soft Power: From Recipient to Donor

During the Cold War, the Soviet Union provided massive amounts of foreign aid for several decades, but the Russian Federation became a recipient country in the 1990s (Provost, 2011). Taking advantage of its economic growth in the early 2000s, Russia prepared its re-emergence as a provider of development assistance. The re-emergence as a donor country, officially confirmed in 2006 during the St Petersburg Summit of the G8, was among Russia's strategies to leverage its power regionally and internationally, and to regain a place in the global order. Russia presented its aid strategy 'Concept for Russia's Participation in International Development Assistance' (Ministry of Finance of the Russian Federation, 2011), adopted in 2007. This policy calls for a more consistent approach to international development to help strengthen the country's international position (Government of the Russian Federation, 2014).

Using international health development aid as an instrument of foreign policy is not new. RusAID was initially designed by the Ministry of Health to be Russia's leading agency for the delivery of bilateral aid, following the examples of

USAID and DFID, among others. But in 2008, Rossotrudnichestvo (the Russian development cooperation) was established under the Ministry of Foreign Affairs. Today, RusAID is presented as a:

> Regional Program for providing technical aid to countries of Eastern Europe and Central Asia on prophylaxis, control and management of HIV and AIDS and other infectious diseases, according to which Russia is currently aiding its neighboring countries, such as Armenia, Kyrgyzstan and Tajikistan in strengthening their potential to establishing efficient controls to reveal, treat and prevent HIV, sexually-transmitted infections (STIs), viral hepatitis and other parenteral diseases.

The programme is presented as 'the only source of technical aid aiming to cope with HIV/AIDS epidemics supported by the government of the Russian Federation as a donor in the countries of EECA/CIS' (RusAID, 2013).

In 2009, during the global financial crisis, Russia's development aid contributions amounted to $785 million and experienced a significant decrease to $472 million in 2010 (Provost, 2011). The situation of the Russian Federation as an international donor, able to sustain its international objectives against OST and harm reduction, worsened after the fall in the prices of raw materials, the annexation of Crimea, the extreme costs of the Winter Olympic Games in Sochi and the impact of the international economic sanctions. These serious economic shortcomings represented a barrier for the Russian strategy as the country did not have sufficient funds to back its international ambitions on drug policy (Galeotti, 2015).

Conclusion

As this chapter has highlighted, the Russian Federation has been one of the most prominent stakeholders in the design and implementation of prohibition-based drug control since the adoption of the first international drug control convention in the 1960s. Through its national, regional and international drug policies, it supported the American-invented 'war on drugs'. This approach, which is still unsuccessful in achieving its own goals while it benefits from large funds to repress people using or involved in drug trafficking, as well as from popular support of voters, did not result in the reduction of the supply of or demand for drugs.

In the last few years, the Russian Federation has gained more prominence in international drug policies, with the weakening of the international power of the United States, no longer able to address its own unprecedented national opioid epidemic, or to explain in international fora the current wave of legalisation of cannabis for medical or recreational purposes in some States, in contradiction of federal laws. This prominence of the Russian Federation can be seen in the UNGASS outcome document, where OST has been referred to as 'medication-assisted therapy', with harm reduction not being mentioned; through the maintenance of the traditional language of supply reduction; and especially by systematically preceding the progressive and new language in the resolution by the mention 'in accordance with national legislation'.

Nevertheless, the human cost the Russian Federation pays for its ill-management of drug injecting drug use, with high rates of overdoses and the highest increases in HIV through drug injection as a mode of transmission worldwide, make its current policies unsustainable. While the government's populist discourses on its attachment to traditional values, and of drug use being a foreign depravation attempting to corrupt its citizens are still popular, the realities of the impact of its HIV crisis and the human cost of imprisonment on its economy and future will have to be faced. Unfortunately, a century of fierce rejection of evidence-based policies to put drugs under control and to allow people who use drugs or those dependent on drugs to be functional citizens cannot be reversed easily. Nevertheless, the authorities will have to review their policies to redress their economy and to renew the trust between the state services and the most vulnerable populations; it is not just expected to happen in the foreseeable future.

References

English Language

BRICS. (2015). VII BRICS Summit: 2015 Ufa Declaration, BRICS, July 9, 2015, Ufa. Retrieved from www.en.brics2015.ru/load/381158. Accessed on December 8, 2016.

Central and Eastern European Harm Reduction Network – CEEHRN. (2002). *Injecting drug users, HIV/AIDS treatment and primary care in Central and Eastern Europe and the Former Soviet Union, July 2002*, p. 6.

Clark, F. (2016). Gaps remain in Russia's response to HIV/AIDS. *The Lancet*, *388*(10047), 857–858.

Commission on Narcotic Drugs. (2014). Joint Ministerial Statement of the 2014 High-Level Review by the Commission on Narcotic Drugs of the Implementation by Member States of the Political Declaration and Plan of Action on International Cooperation towards an Integrated and Balanced Strategy to Counter the World Drug Problem. UNODC, Vienna.

Commission on Narcotic Drugs. (2015). The Russian Federation proposals for the UN General Assembly Special Session on the World Drug Problem to be held in 2016. Comprehensive Package of Contributions Input for Preparation UNGASS Outcome Document Submitted through the UNGASS Board Members, 11 September 2015, Vienna.

Csete, J., & Pearshouse, R. (2007). *Dependent on rights: Assessing treatment of drug dependence from a human rights perspective* (pp. 24–25). Canadian HIV/AIDS Legal Network.

Galeotti, M. (2015). *Narcotics and nationalism: Russian drug policies and futures*. Washington, DC: Brookings Institution.

Golichenko, M., & Sarang, A. (2013). Atmospheric pressure: Russian drug policy as a driver for violations of the UN Convention against torture and the International

Covenant on Economic, Social and Cultural Rights. *Health Human Rights*, *15*(1), E135–E43.

Golichenko, M., & Ka Hon Chu, S. (2018). Human rights in patient care: Drug treatment in Russia. *Public Health Reviews* (39: 12.).

Government of the Russian Federation. (2014). The Russian Federation's State Policy in the Area of International Development Assistance, Decree No. 259 of the President of the Russian Federation of April 20, 2014. Moscow. Retrieved from http://www.mid.ru/en/foreign_policy/official_documents/-/asset_publisher/CptICkB6BZ29/content/id/64542. Accessed on November 17, 2017.

Gowing, L., Farrell, M. F., Bornemann, R., Sullivan, L. E., & Ali, R. (2011). Oral substitution treatment of injecting opioid users for prevention of HIV infection. *Cochrane Database of Systematic Reviews 8*, Art. No.: CD004145; Committee on Economic, Social and Cultural Rights. "Concluding observations of the Committee on Economic, Social and Cultural Rights: The Russian Federation." E/C.12/RUS/CO/5 May 20, 2011, para 29.

Hamers, F. F., & Downs, A. M. (2003). HIV in central and eastern Europe. *Lancet*, *361*(9362), 1035–1044.

Heimer, R., Eritsyan, K., Barbour, R., & Levina, O. S. (2014). Hepatitis C virus seroprevalence among people who inject drugs and factors associated with infection in eight Russian cities. *BMC Infectious Diseases*, *14*(Suppl. 6), S12.

Institute for Criminal Policy Research. (2016). *World prison brief*. Retrieved from http://www.prisonstudies.org/world-prison-brief. Accessed on October 26, 2017.

Kalachev, B. (2001). *Narcotics in Russia. Phase four – Soviet State*. Electronic book. Retrieved from www.narkotiki.ru.

Klimeko, T. et al. (2014). Preliminary assessment of the drug situation, measures to close down programs 'substitution therapy' for people with opioid dependence and optimization of anti-drug activity service in the republic of Crimea and Sevastopol city. *Narcology Journal*, *5*.

Kozlov, A. A., Polunina, A. G., & Davydov, D. M. (2007). Brain disintegration in heroin addicts: The natural course of the disease and the effects of methadone treatment. *Journal Heroin Addiction and Related Clinical Problems*, *9*(2), 17–26.

Latypov, A. (2012). *On the road to 'H': Narcotic drugs in Soviet Central Asia*. Washington, DC: George Washington University.

Litavrin, M. (2017). No to any humanization: How state Duma discussed drug policy. [Максим Литаврин. Никакой гуманизации: как в Госдуме обсудили наркополитику]. Retrieved from https://openrussia.org/notes/716900/. Accessed on December 5, 2017.

Lunze, K., Raj, A., Cheng, D. M., & Samet, J. H. (2016). Sexual violence from police and HIV risk behaviors among HIV-positive women who inject drugs in St. Petersburg, Russia – A mixed methods study. *Journal of International AIDS Society*, *19* (4 Suppl. 3).

Marshall, A. (2014). From drug war to culture war: Russia's growing role in the global drug debate. Swansea: Swansea University. Retrieved from http://www.swansea.ac.uk/gdpo/files/GDPO%20Russia%20Article-1.pdf. Accessed on October 12, 2017.

Ministry of Finance of the Russian Federation. (2011). *Presidential Document: The Concept of Russia's Participation in International Development Assistance: Overview*. Moscow: Ministry of Finance.

Ministry of the Interior (2018). Statistics of the Ministry of the Interior. Retrieved from https://мвд.рф

Osborn, A. (2016, January 21). Russia at AIDS epidemic tipping point as HIV cases pass one million – official. *Reuters*, . Retrieved from http://uk.reuters.com/article/uk-russia-aids-idUKKCN0UZ2AN. Accessed on October 31, 2016.

Panin, S. (2003). Drug use in Soviet Russia (1917–1920). *Questions of History*, *8*, 129–134. (Панин С.Е. Потребление наркотиков в Советской России (1917–1920-е годы) Вопросы истории. 2003. № 8. С. 129–134.)

Provost, C. (2011). The rebirth of Russian foreign aid. *The Guardian*, London. Retrieved from https://www.theguardian.com/global-development/2011/may/25/russia-foreign-aid-report-influence-image. Accessed on November 15, 2017.

RusAID. (2013). *The program for technical aid to countries of Eastern Europe and Central Asia on prophylaxis, control and management of HIV and AIDS and other infectious diseases (2013–2015)*. Retrieved from http://en.rus-aid.ru/about-project/about-project/. Accessed on November 15, 2017.

Tsui, J. I., Ko, S. C., Krupitsky, E., Lioznov, D., Chaisson, C. E., Gnatienko, N., & Samet, J. H. (2016). Insights on the Russian HCV care cascade: Minimal HCV treatment for HIV/HCV co-infected PWID in St. Petersburg. *Hepatology, Medicine and Policy*, *1*(13), 1–7.

United Nations Development Programme. (2004). *Reversing the epidemic: Facts and policy options. HIV/AIDS in Eastern Europe and the Commonwealth of Independent States* (p. 16). Bratislava, Slovakia: UNDP.

United Nations. (2012). *General Assembly Resolution 67/193. International cooperation against the world drug problem*. New York, NY: United Nations.

United Nations. (2016). *General Assembly Resolution S-30-1, Our joint commitment to effectively addressing and countering the world drug problem*. New York, NY: United Nations.

UNODC. (n.d.). *Mandate and functions of the Commission on Narcotic Drugs*. Retrieved from http://www.unodc.org/unodc/en/commissions/CND/Mandate_Functions/Mandate-and-Functions_index.html. Accessed on November 6, 2017.

UNODC. (2013). *The international drug control conventions*. Vienna, Austria: UNODC.

UNODC. (2016). *World drug report 2016*, Vienna, Austria: UNODC.

UNODC. (2015). *Statistics about drug seizures*. Vienna, Austria: UNODC.

Volkov, V., Paneyakh, E., Titaev, K., & Primakov, D. (2010). *The accusatory bias in the criminal proceeding: the prosecutor factor. Analysis of statistics*. Saint-Petersburg, Russia: European Institute.

Waterfield, B. (2014, March 24). G8 suspends Russia for annexation of Crimea. *The Telegraph*. Retrieved from http://www.telegraph.co.uk/news/worldnews/europe/russia/10720297/G8-suspends-Russia-for-annexation-of-Crimea.html. Accessed on December 2, 2016.

World Health Organization. (2009). *Guidelines for the psychosocially assisted pharmacological treatment of opioid dependence*. Geneva, Switzerland: WHO.

World Health Organization. (2016). *Live web stream from Sixty-ninth World Health Assembly (WHA69)*. Retrieved from http://www.who.int/mediacentre/events/2016/wha69/webstreaming/en/. Accessed on November 7, 2017.

Russian Language

Виткин, Б. (2016). Борьба со СПИДом в России стала заложницей ультраконсерватизма, ИноСМИ. *Ru, 10 August*, Retrieved from http://inosmi.ru/social/20160810/237506365.html. Accessed on November 23, 2016. (Vitkin, B. The Struggle against AIDS in Russia became a hostage to ultra-conservatism InoSMI.Ru.)

ФСКН (2015). Retrieved from http://mybiblioteka.su/tom2/5-41899.html. Accessed on October 26, 2017.

Декрет ВЦИК от 20 июня 1919 года «Об изъятиях из общей подсудности в местностях объявленных на военном положении». Retrieved from http://base.consultant.ru/cons/cgi/online.cgi?req=doc;base=ESU;n=17452

Декрет ВЦИК от 18 марта 1920 года «О революционных трибуналах». Retrieved from http://base.consultant.ru/cons/cgi/online.cgi?req=doc;base=ESU;n=16940;fld=134;dst=100021;rnd=0.4151172328274697. Accessed on November 10, 2017.

Козлов В, Козичев Е. (2015). У метадона появился геополитический противник, Коммерса́нтъ, 6 August. Retrieved from http://kommersant.ru/doc/2782912. Accessed on October 31, 2016.

Курская, А. (2011). Социальный прессинг против наркомании. РИА Новости. Retrieved from http://ria.ru/analytics/20110516/375468514.html. Accessed on December 2, 2017.

Клименко, Т., Козлов А., Понизовский П., Мандыбура А. (2014). Предварительная оценка наркологической ситуации, меры по закрытию программ заместительной терапии лиц с опиоидной зависимостью и оптимизации деятельности наркологической службы в Республике Крым и в городе федерального значения Севастополе. Наркология. N5.

Правительство Российской Федерации. (2016). Об утверждении Государственной стратегии противодействия распространению ВИЧ-инфекции в России на период до 2020 года и дальнейшую

перспективу, 20 October, Retrieved from http://government.ru/docs/24983/. Accessed on November 2, 2016. (Government of the Russian Federation, 'On the approval of the State Strategy to Counteract the Spread of HIV Infection in Russia for the Period to 2020 and Further Prospects'.)

Уголовный кодекс РСФСР от 27 октября 1960 г. (УК РСФСР). Retrieved from http://base.garant.ru/10107062/16/#block_22402#ixzz4FB2tmVRR. Accessed on October 27, 2017.

ФСКН (2014). Федеральная служба Российской Федерации по контролю за оборотом наркотиков: 2014: *Anti-Drug Cooperation*. Position paper of *anti-drug* agenda within the frames of the Presidency of the G8. Federal Drug Control Service, Moscow.

Черных, А. (2016). Правительство не изыскало новых средств для ВИЧ, Коммерсантъ, 26 October, Retrieved from http://kommersant.ru/doc/3126109. Accessed on November 2, 2016. (Chernykh, A. 'The Government did not find new funds for HIV', Kommersant.ru.)

Chapter 7

Consensus and Contradictions in ASEAN: An Analysis of Southeast Asia At and After UNGASS 2016

Ricky Gunawan and Gloria Lai

Abstract

In the years leading up to United Nations General Assembly Special Session (UNGASS), Southeast Asia drew the attention of the drug policy world because of its refusal to drop the goal of becoming a drug-free region and for the extreme methods used in striving to achieve it. This chapter presents an analysis of the official positions taken by governments in the regional body known as the Association of Southeast Asian Nations from before until after the UNGASS in the context of one of the most punitive drug policy environments in the world and offers a perspective on what we could expect from them in 2019.

Keywords: ASEAN; drugs; UNGASS 2016; drug policy; Asia; Southeast Asia

Introduction

In the years leading up to United Nations General Assembly Special Session (UNGASS), Southeast Asia drew the attention of the drug policy world because of its refusal to drop the goal of becoming a drug-free region and for the extreme methods used in striving to achieve it, namely, execution of people mandatorily sentenced with the death penalty for trafficking even small amounts of drugs (e.g., 15 g of heroin is the threshold quantity in Singapore) and compulsory detention

Collapse of the Global Order on Drugs: From UNGASS 2016 to Review 2019, 151–165

doi:10.1108/978-1-78756-487-920181007

of people who use drugs in the name of rehabilitation.[1] This chapter presents an analysis of the official positions taken by governments in the region from before until after the UNGASS in the context of one of the most punitive drug policy environments in the world and offers a perspective on what we could expect from them in 2019.

A 'Drug-free' ASEAN: An Increasingly Hollow Slogan

The hard stance against drugs taken by the Association of Southeast Asian Nations (ASEAN) has been well established, dating back to 1976 when it adopted the *ASEAN Declaration of Principles to Combat the Abuse of Narcotics Drugs*.[2] This Declaration contained language that took on a similar tone to the Preamble of the *UN Single Convention on Narcotic Drugs 1961*,[3] stating that 'the abuse of narcotic drugs and psychotropic substances is fraught with social and economic danger to mankind' and committing themselves to 'intensify its vigilance and preventive and penal measures with regard to illicit traffic in drug[s]'. Over the following decades, ASEAN has followed up this Declaration with a plethora of other Declarations and Statements committing to a zero-tolerance approach to drugs. At its fifth ASEAN Summit in 1995, ASEAN – for the first time – expressed its policy goal to 'further enhance cooperative efforts against drug abuse and illicit trafficking […] with the aim of creating a drug-free ASEAN'.[4]

In July 1998, ASEAN member states reiterated their commitment to creating a drug-free ASEAN by 2020, a target year that was first stated at the Second Informal Summit of ASEAN Heads of State/Government in December 1997.[5] At the 33rd ASEAN Ministerial Meeting on Drug Matters (AMMD) in July 2000, ASEAN member states agreed to bring forward their target year for realising a drug-free ASEAN to 2015, to emphasise the urgency for action in reducing the use and supply of drugs. Later in 2009, the *ASEAN Work Plan on Combating Illicit Drug Production, Trafficking, and Use (2009–2015)* was adopted.[6] Until present, ASEAN has adamantly retained their tough on drugs position and pursuit for a drug-free zone, despite the failure of ASEAN countries to make any progress towards becoming drug-free (attested to by UNODC reports of expanding drug markets year after year)[7] and with no regard to reforms taking place in other countries.

---

[1]Csete et al. (2016). Retrieved from http://www.thelancet.com/journals/lancet/article/PIIS0140-6736(16)00619-X/fulltext?code=lancet-site.
[2]ASEAN Declaration of Principles to Combat the Abuse of Narcotics Drugs Manila, 26 June 1976.
[3]Single Convention on Narcotic Drugs, 1961–INCB (1961).
[4]Bangkok Summit Declaration of 1995 Bangkok, 14–15 December 1995 (2012).
[5]1998 Joint Declaration for a Drug-Free ASEAN (1998).
[6]ASEAN Work Plan on Combating Illicit Drug Production, Trafficking and Use 2009–015 (2017).
[7]IDPC advocacy note a drug-free ASEAN by 2015: Comments on the final assessment from a civil society perspective (2014). See also, A drug-free ASEAN by 2015: Comments on the final assessment from a civil society perspective (2017).

ASEAN on the Road to UNGASS 2016

Given ASEAN's long history and unwavering position on drugs, one could simply predict the positions it would take on issues such as legalisation, decriminalisation, harm reduction, abolition of the death penalty and other human rights issues at the UNGASS in 2016. At the 4th AMMD in Malaysia in October 2015, the Ministers endorsed a common ASEAN position to be reflected in their official statements at the 59th session of the Commission on Narcotic Drugs (CND) a month before UNGASS in April 2016. They stated that this ASEAN position 'will reaffirm ASEAN's commitment to a zero-tolerance approach in realising its aspiration for a Drug-Free ASEAN, and to the three international drug control conventions, which should continue to serve as the basis for the world drug policy',[8] and proposed that member states include the following key points in their country statements at UNGASS:

- A zero-tolerance approach against drugs: 'Zero-tolerance means that we strongly commit to suppress and eliminate the scourge of drugs and condemn its abuse in our society.'
- A comprehensive and balanced approach towards drugs, involving both demand and supply reduction efforts.
- Support the centrality of the international drug conventions and stand firm against drugs, including being resolute against calls to legalise controlled drugs.
- Sovereign right of each country to 'decide on the best approach to address the drug problem in their country, taking into account the historical, political, economic, social and cultural contexts and norms of its society'.
- Ready to work with other regions, 'as part of a global collaborative effort to address and mitigate the scourge of illicit drugs'.
- Support the role of the CND, 'as the principal policymaking organ of the United Nations on matters of international drug control and as the governing body of the UNODC's drug programme.'[9]

At the 59th CND session, ASEAN delivered a statement which confirmed the common position agreed at the AMMD in 2015, and said that member states 'have prevented the scourge of drugs from overwhelming our communities, crippling our economies and robbing our youths of their future.'[10] ASEAN also said that it 'remains united in our core commitment to a drug free vision' as it is 'acutely aware of the disastrous effects of drugs, not just on the drug abuser and the society at large, but also on national security and development.' It further referred to drug policy reforms taking place in some countries to decriminalise or legalise the use

[8]The 4th ASEAN Ministerial Meeting on Drug Matters 29 October 2015, Langkawi, Malaysia Chairman's Statement (2015).

[9]Position statement endorsed and adopted by the 4th ASEAN Ministerial meeting on drug matters 29 October 2015, Langkawi, Malaysia (2015).

[10]ASEAN Statement at the 59th Session of the Commission on Narcotic Drugs Special Session on UNGASS Preparations, 14–16 March 2016 (2016).

of drugs, and stated that while they respected those measures in the light of their domestic situations, such approaches should not be imposed on other countries.[11]

In their country statements, ASEAN member states echoed the ASEAN position. Singapore,[12] Indonesia[13] and Malaysia,[14] for example, all communicated the same message of being committed to their drug-free goals, a balanced approach in addressing their drug problems and emphasising their different characteristics which thereby require them to resolve their problems in their own way. However, Thailand took a distinctive position from other ASEAN governments. Although it expressed support for ASEAN's position against the idea of 'legalisation of dangerous drugs and decriminalisation for serious offence[s] of major drug traffickers', Thailand acknowledged that their domestic policy had proven to be insufficient in addressing their drug problems and suggested that 'drug users should receive treatment and rehabilitation, not incarceration.'[15]

ASEAN-esque and ASEAN-ish Positions at UNGASS 2016

At UNGASS, the ASEAN position once again reiterated its 'core commitment to a drug free vision'.[16] In a statement delivered by Malaysia on behalf of the member states, the ASEAN position referred to the key points agreed to at the AMMD in October 2015, with the objective 'to protect individuals and families from the dangers of drugs, wean abusers off their addiction and protect the security' of ASEAN.

In their individual country statements, Indonesia and Malaysia emphasised some of the agreed key points from the ASEAN position in saying that there is no one-size-fits-all approach to drug control and that it is 'the sovereign right of every government and its citizens to decide what is best for them.' Indonesia further stated that 'no one should generalise failure to deal with the drug abuse in his or her own territory as the failure of every country to tackle the world drug problem.'[17]

[11]ASEAN Statement at the 59th Session of the Commission on Narcotic Drugs Special Session on UNGASS Preparations, 14–16 March 2016 (2016).
[12]Singapore Statement at the 59th Session of the Commission on Narcotic Drugs Special Session on UNGASS Preparations, 14–16 March 2016 (2016).
[13]Statement by the Head of Delegation of the Republic of Indonesia H.E. Ambassador Rachmat Budiman Permanent Representative of the Republic Indonesia at the 59th Session of the Commission on Narcotic Drugs Vienna, 14–22 March 2016 (2016).
[14]Malaysia's Statement 59th Session of the Commission on Narcotic Drugs (2016).
[15]59th Session of the Commission on Narcotic Drugs (CND) Statement by His Excellency General Paiboon Koomchaya Thai Minister of Justice, the Special Segment of the General Assembly on the World Drug Problem to be held in 2016 on Monday 14 March 2016, 10.00–13.00 hrs. Plenary Hall, M-Building, Vienna International Center Vienna, Republic of Austria (2016).
[16]Statement on behalf of the ASEAN and National Statement by the Honourable Mr. Nur Jazlan Mohamed, Deputy Minister of Home Affairs of Malaysia at the 30th Session of the Special Session of the General Assembly on the World Drug Problem, New York, 19 April 2016 ().
[17]Statement by the Head of Delegation of the Republic of Indonesia H.E. Ambassador Rachmat Budiman at the 30th Session of the United Nations Special Session on the World Drug Problem (UNGASS), New York, 19–21 April 2016 (2016).

In 2015, despite widespread international condemnation and strong diplomatic pressure, Indonesia carried out two rounds of executions and killed 14 people who were convicted of drug offences. This subsequent international criticism shaped Indonesia's interventions at UNGASS. While Indonesia emphasised the importance of the promotion and protection of human rights and fundamental freedoms, it appeared to qualify that by saying this should be 'undertaken in a balanced manner' and 'the rights of the victims of drug related offences [...] should be considered as an important element in the formulation of global drug policy.'[18] Their latter remarks seem to be an attempt to justify and legitimise their use of the death penalty for drug offences.

As expected, other individual country statements shared the same ASEAN-esque message. Singapore repeated that every country should develop their own drug policy, reiterated their commitment to a balanced and tough approach to both supply and demand reduction, as well as opposition to harm reduction – a position based upon the belief that 'drugs will destroy' Singapore.[19] They also outlined some of their achievements, including 'no drug havens, no no-go zones, no drug production centres, no needle exchange programmes' apparently to demonstrate that this tough stance on drugs has enabled Singapore to build a safe and secure country.

Thailand[20] and the Philippines[21] echoed ASEAN's opposition to the idea of legalising controlled drugs. Thailand's reiterated the point made in their statement at the CND in the previous month that while they did not agree with decriminalisation for serious offences, 'drug users should receive treatment and rehabilitation, not incarceration.' Thailand's implicit support for decriminalisation of drug use (i.e., that people who use drugs should not be criminalised or imprisoned) seemed at odds with the overall ASEAN position as well as that of other ASEAN member states. In another point of departure from other ASEAN governments, the Philippines specifically stated that it 'does not support the imposition of capital punishment for drug-related offences – or for any other criminal offense.' A position that changed dramatically with the election of a new president in 2016.

Vietnam offered another point of contrast from ASEAN member states, by stating that 'drug control solutions should be balanced between supply reduction, demand reduction and harm reduction.'[22] Whether or not harm reduction programmes implemented in Vietnam are in line with human rights is a separate issue, but to have the phrase 'harm reduction' mentioned in an ASEAN member state's statement at UNGASS was an interesting highlight.

---

[18]Statement by the Head of Delegation of the Republic of Indonesia H.E. Ambassador Rachmat Budiman at the 30th Session of the United Nations Special Session on the World Drug Problem (UNGASS), New York, 19–21 April 2016 (2016).
[19]Singapore Statement at Plenary Session UNGASS 2016 (2016).
[20]Permanent Mission of Thailand to the United Nations (2016).
[21]Statement of the Honorabe Emmanuel Caparas Secretary of Justice United Nations General Assembly Special Session on the World Drug Problem, 20 April 2016 (2016).
[22]Keynote speech by H.E. Sen.Lt. Gen Le Quy Vuong Vice Minister of Public Security – S.R of Vietnam at UNGASS 2016 – 19-21/4/2016 (2016).

By looking at the statements issued by ASEAN as a whole, or by individual member states of ASEAN, at ASEAN meetings on drug matters, CND, and UNGASS, one can conclude that ASEAN's has a resolute position on being tough against drugs. There are key qualities that almost all member states share. Some of these qualities are actually not unique to drug policy positions around the world – but it also reflects an ASEAN way of dealing with social and public policy issues. The principles of non-intervention and respecting state sovereignty are an example, where in the area of drug policy it is translated into the 'no one-size-fits-all' phrase commonly used by member states to express their view that no other government can dictate how ASEAN member states should approach their drug problems, both regionally and nationally. However, despite the commonalities in their drug policies, including their policy goals of creating a drug-free society in their respective countries and ASEAN region, it appears there are some significant points of divergence that warrant further elaboration.

First, ASEAN has long been known for its strict adherence to the principle of consensus building. However, as could be seen from the CND and UNGASS when it comes to individual country statements, there are positions taken that may not fully align with the ASEAN consensus position. For example, the ASEAN consensus position maintains support for policies that achieve a balance between supply and demand reduction without any mention of harm reduction. While Singapore was vocal against the concept of harm reduction in their statements at CND and UNGASS, and countries that adopt harm reduction programmes (i.e., Indonesia, Thailand and Malaysia) did not mention the words 'harm reduction' in their statements, Vietnam appeared quite brave in stating at UNGASS that they have adopted 'harm reduction' measures. This dynamic indicates that although ASEAN position statements repeatedly refer to zero-tolerance approaches that strive only for drug-free goals; in practice, they seem like hollow phrases given that member states do not necessarily abide with that position, regardless of whether they speak out about them or not.

Second, the ASEAN position taken at UNGASS to distance itself from decriminalisation reforms elsewhere in the world contrasts with the position taken by Thailand against the incarceration of people who use drugs. Thailand also diverged from other member states in referring to the use of disproportionate penalties for all drug offences, and the resulting consequence of overcrowded prisons without being able to effectively address drug-related problems in the country. This divergence could be explained at least partly by noting that Thailand has by far the largest prison population in ASEAN, with the majority of detainees held for drug offences.[23]

Third, in stating their opposition to use of the death penalty for drug offences (and other crimes), the Philippines positioned themselves in the same camp as the European Union and other abolitionist countries vis-à-vis Indonesia, Singapore, Vietnam and Malaysia. Although the Philippines' position changed after

[23]Csete et al. (2016). Retrieved from http://www.thelancet.com/journals/lancet/article/PIIS0140-6736(16)00619-X/fulltext?code=lancet-site.

the UNGASS, following the election of a new administration that aims to re-introduce the death penalty, this does not change the fact that they were willing to speak out in support of their minority position within ASEAN.

After the UNGASS: Human Rights Violations Driving Further Divergences in ASEAN

While executions for drug offences in Indonesia were amongst the human rights violations that triggered the most outrage amongst civil society and some governments in the lead up to UNGASS, they were eclipsed by subsequent events. First, Indonesia resumed executions later in 2016 with the killing of four people on death row for drug trafficking offences in July.[24] But then, Rodrigo Duterte became elected as the President of the Philippines in May 2016.[25] The key pillar of his election campaign was a promise to eradicate drugs and crime by killing all those suspected of using or supplying drugs, and other crimes.[26] Even before his inauguration as president in June 2016, the killings had already begun by both vigilantes and police. By the end of 2017, non-government organisations and media outlets estimate the number of unlawful killings to have reached over 6,000–12,000, with ongoing impunity as evidenced by the fact that as of December 2017, there had not been a single conviction for any of the killings.[27] In addition, over one million people were coerced into registering themselves with local authorities as a person that has used or dealt drugs, already overcrowded prisons drastically worsened following ballooning rates of arrest and incarceration for drug offences and the Philippines' Congress began considering a legislative bill to re-instate the death penalty for mostly drug offences.[28]

An indication of the ability of ASEAN member states to influence each other could be seen in the subsequent crackdown on drugs launched by Cambodia in January 2017, following Duterte's visit to Cambodia in December 2016, thereby marking the start of the Philippines' chairmanship of ASEAN that year.[29] Cambodia's crackdown emphasised the arrest and detention (rather than the killing) of people allegedly suspected of using or dealing drugs, resulting in an estimated 17,800 people arrested in 2017 with over 50% targeted for solely drug use.[30] The influence of the Philippines' drug war could also be seen in Indonesia, where approving statements of killing suspects pursued during drug enforcement operations by Indonesia's President Jokowi and drug control agency chief Budi Waseso underscored the increasing numbers of people killed during such operations in 2017.[31]

[24]Amnesty International (2017).
[25]BBC News (2016).
[26]BBC News (2016).
[27]UN Office of the High Commissioner for Human Rights (2016), Amnesty International (2017) and Singh & Human Rights Watch News (2017).
[28]*New York Times* (2017), CNN Philippines (2017) and ABC News (2017).
[29]The Diplomat (2017).
[30]Reuters (2017) and *The Phnom Penh Post* (2018).
[31]McRae (2017).

The scaling up of violence in the name of drug control in parts of Southeast Asia was unexpectedly contradicted by drug policy reform dialogues and processes featuring decriminalisation of drug use, proportionality of sentencing and reducing use of the death penalty in other countries in the region. In Thailand, where debate about reforms to ensure proportionate sentencing and reduce incarceration was initiated in 2014 by HRH Princess Bajrakitiyabha and later catalysed by Minister of Justice Paiboon Khumchaya, the UNGASS appeared to provide the government with further authoritative justification for reform.[32] In the *ASEAN Drug Monitoring Report 2016*, published in August 2017, Thailand stated that:

> as a result of the UNGASS 2016, Thailand is revising a new paradigm of national drug control policy, instead of focussing on drug suppression, which caused problems of overcrowded prisons and quality of treatment access. The new paradigm shift will emphasize public health related issues, human rights approaches and treatment services, rather than drug suppression, especially when dealing with drug users and addicts. These users and addicts are regarded as patients not criminals.[33]

Thailand's 'new paradigm of national drug control policy' began to take shape with one set of amendments to the drug law passed in January 2017, which reduced penalty ranges and reliance on mandatory sentencing by enabling judges more discretion in determining sentences for drug offences including use of the death penalty.[34] Further amendments to the drug laws are expected in 2018 to introduce a range of alternatives to incarceration for judges to consider during sentencing and to shift more responsibility for responding to drug use and dependence to the Ministry of Health, amongst other reforms. Although much more work is needed to ensure the implementation of reforms in accordance with principles of public health, human rights and the rule of law, Thai government agencies are engaging in drug policy debate about ongoing reforms that is to some extent inclusive of civil society. Similarly, in Myanmar, amendments to the drug law had been under consultation involving a wide range of stakeholders including civil society, people who use drugs and UN agencies since 2016, covering proposals to reduce penalties and decriminalise the use of drugs.[35] Amendments to the drug law and Myanmar's first National Drug Control Policy were adopted in February 2018, which resulted in the removal of a compulsory requirement for people who use drugs to register themselves (with criminal penalties for those who fail to do so), but not the removal of criminal penalties for possession of drugs for the purpose of personal use.[36]

[32]Fordham and Lai (2016).
[33]ASEAN Narcotics Cooperation Centre (2016).
[34]Akbar and Laomanutsak (2018).
[35]Drug Policy Advocacy Group (2017).
[36]R. Cachia (2018). https://www.tni.org/en/article/will-myanmar-complete-its-transition-towards-an-evidence-based-approach-to-drug-control.

At the end of 2017, Malaysia adopted legal reforms to remove the death penalty as a mandatory sentence, allowing judges discretion to determine the sentence for drug trafficking cases instead.[37] Following Vietnam's decision in 2015 to reduce the number of drug offences that can lead to a death penalty sentence,[38] these shifts appear to reflect a growing acknowledgement in parts of the region, with the glaring exception of the Philippines and to some extent Indonesia, that use of the death penalty for drug offences is problematic and increasingly unacceptable.

ASEAN Positions Taken Post-UNGASS

As 2015 was the deadline that ASEAN had set for itself to become a drug-free region, as well as the end of its 2009–2015 ASEAN Work Plan against drugs, it could have been a timely opportunity for ASEAN to conduct an open review of the effectiveness of its drug control strategy to inform development of a revised strategy in parallel with the UNGASS process. ASEAN tasked the UNODC to conduct the final assessment of implementation of the Work Plan, but it was not a transparent process and closed to civil society engagement. In the new *ASEAN Work Plan on Securing Communities Against Illicit Drugs 2016–2025* adopted in October 2016, it refers to the conclusions of the UNODC report on the final assessment relating to the proliferation of methamphetamine and new psychoactive substances (a common theme highlighted in the official statements made by ASEAN member states), and the need to 'evolve from a one-dimensional control approach to multi-dimensional management approaches'.[39]

The new ASEAN Work Plan adopted for 2016–2025 retains the ultimate goal of achieving a drug-free ASEAN as well as several typical components on drug prevention campaigns and reducing illicit manufacturing and trafficking by increasing the number of operations, investigations, seizures and arrests. However, it also appears to seek to address the UNODC's recommendation to broaden its approach to drugs, by including components such as:

- Managing drug-related risks by reviewing national drug control plans and identifying challenges and enhancing partnerships between public and private sectors and civil society organisation in response to drug use.
- Engaging other government agencies with responsibility for education, health, social matters and home affairs to address various aspects of drug control.
- Working towards the improvement of access to equitable justice for all individuals in the ASEAN region while respecting the sovereignty, national legislation and policies of each country. This is to be achieved through ensuring financial and technical resources to meet the demands of an equitable system of justice and strengthening the capacity of the criminal justice system particularly drug enforcement officers.

---

[37]Anand (2017).
[38]*Global Times* (2015).
[39]Association of Southeast Asian Nations (ASEAN, 2016).

- Improving levels of governance by adopting a transparent approach in the enforcement of drug laws.
- Adopting evidence-based treatment protocols based on international standards in treatment.

The broader scope of components, and the activities outlined to implement them, potentially provides a platform for drug policy processes to facilitate more open, inclusive dialogue on the effectiveness and ineffectiveness of existing strategies, along with their negative consequences. This apparent relative openness, combined with active national debates on proposals for decriminalising drug use in at least Myanmar and Thailand, seems to contrast with Singapore's resistance against reform in the region and relentless crusade to insist on a unified ASEAN position 'strongly against drugs' and 'committed to ASEAN's shared vision of a region free of drug abuse', as well as opposing harm reduction (their focus is on 'harm prevention' instead).[40]

In perhaps an effort to entrench the principles and actions agreed in the UNGASS Outcome Document, the ASEAN Regional Forum (an entity involving the participation of many governments around the world in addition to ASEAN member states)[41] adopted in August 2017 a statement on *Enhancing Cooperation in Addressing and Countering the Drug Problem* that emphasised the UNGASS outcomes as representing the most recent consensus and forming part of the basis of work towards the '2019 UN-CND Ministerial Segment'.[42] The statement also reiterated several measures agreed in the UNGASS Outcome Document including medication-assisted therapy and injecting equipment programmes, voluntary participation of individuals in treatment programmes, alternative measures to conviction and punishment and proportionate sentencing policies.

While in practice at country-level, Thailand, Malaysia, Myanmar, Vietnam and Indonesia are already implementing or proposed to implement aspects of the UNGASS outcome document relating to harm reduction interventions, alternatives to conviction and punishment and proportionate sentencing, it appears only Thailand, Malaysia and Vietnam openly spoke about such efforts at the CND annual session and inter-sessional meetings in 2017.[43] Thailand's Minister of Justice spoke on his government's efforts to shift to a health-based response to drugs, especially methamphetamines given high levels of use in the country (as elsewhere in the region), and its legal reform process to ensure proportionate sentencing to reduce prison overcrowding and avoid sending people who use drugs to prison. Vietnam referred to its efforts to develop treatment and care for people who use drugs, including methadone maintenance treatment programmes.

---

[40]Central Narcotics Bureau Singapore (2017).

[41]The ASEAN Regional Forum comprises participant countries from ASEAN and other parts of the world: Australia, Bangladesh, Brunei Darussalam, Cambodia, Canada, China, Democratic People's Republic of Korea, European Union, India, Indonesia, Japan, Lao PDR, Malaysia, Mongolia, Myanmar, New Zealand, Pakistan, Papua New Guinea, Philippines, Republic of Korea, Russia, Singapore, Sri Lanka, Thailand, Timor-Leste, United States, and Viet Nam.

[42]ASEAN (2017).

[43]CND Blog (2017).

While Malaysia continued to refer to its commitment to ASEAN's drug-free goals and opposition to legalisation, it also highlighted its efforts to facilitate provision of voluntary treatment, rehabilitation and harm reduction programmes and surprisingly at the CND inter-sessional meeting in November 2017 spoke about its plans for decriminalisation so that people who use drugs can avoid prosecution, along with the legal amendments to remove mandatory sentencing of the death penalty.

In defensive mode due to on-going human rights violations relating to the death penalty and unlawful killings at home, Indonesia and the Philippines emphasised principles of sovereignty and non-intervention at the CND in 2017, while insisting that they respect human rights in their drug control responses. As it had done at UNGASS together with Singapore and China, Indonesia attempted to interpret human rights standards on its own terms at the CND annual session in March 2017, stating that the rights of victims of drug dealers should be respected, thereby implying that the rights of people suspected of drug supply offences should not be respected.

In terms of official positions taken at CND amongst ASEAN member states in 2017, Singapore seemed quite alone in stressing its harm prevention strategy featuring education on the harms of drugs, mandatory treatment and rehabilitation programmes and tough penalties and enforcement. Given the uniqueness of its size, wealth and governance system, it should indeed be expected that Singapore's position would differ from most of its regional neighbours. It is when Singapore insists on a unified ASEAN position that it seems odd. The remaining ASEAN member states, Laos, Brunei and Cambodia, did not make official statements at CND in 2017, likely because they did not attend as is typically the case.

Looking Towards 2019: Political Tensions May Suppress Cracks in the ASEAN Consensus

With several countries in Southeast Asia expected to hold national elections in the lead up to the 2019 high-level meeting (Cambodia, Malaysia and Thailand in 2018 and Indonesia in 2019), the drug policy environment for the region is tense. Political leaders in Cambodia and Indonesia could well be expected to escalate already violent and punitive drug control measures to secure populist support. Proposals for reform in Malaysia and Thailand could come to a halt or delayed until after elections, when newly elected leaders could decide on whether to proceed with drug policy reforms towards measures such as decriminalisation. Even where reform eventuates, as in Myanmar, or where support for harm reduction continues as is the case in Vietnam and Malaysia, such countries may not choose to break with consensus and promote reforms or harm reduction in the lead up to and at the 2019 high-level segment.

The ongoing impunity for unlawful killings in the Philippines could perhaps drive reform-minded member states towards distinctive policy positions, but at a time when the space for civil society to protest against government policies is diminishing (especially in the Philippines, Vietnam, Cambodia and Thailand where governments are growing increasingly authoritarian),[44] the prospects seem slim.

[44]Pepinsky (2017).

However, the UNGASS certainly seems to have helped to open dialogue on drug policy reform in parts of ASEAN, leading to deepening fractures in any ASEAN consensus on drug control. Further, analysis of official positions taken during 2017 do not appear to show overwhelming enthusiasm for a unified ASEAN stance that rails against any drug policy reform and health-led policies. The tentative divergences on crucial issues such as harm reduction, abolition of the death penalty and decriminalisation of drug use over the past four years indicate that even within ASEAN's seemingly strict adherence to the zero-tolerance principle, there are openings for drug policy reformers to promote change. On the issue of harm reduction, it may be just a matter of time that Indonesia and Malaysia will make statements in support of the harm reduction approach at drug policy fora – like Vietnam did at UNGASS. The key to pursuing this objective is for advocates to rigorously seek to influence government positions at the domestic level. On the issue of proportionality, Thailand has some role to play within the region. The fact that their drug policy has resulted in negative consequences such as overcrowded prisons because of high numbers of drug offenders is actually a shared problem with Indonesia, Malaysia, Cambodia and the Philippines. Emphasising the need to foster regional cooperation led by Thailand may be a key to unlock further opportunities to influence reform of country-level drug policies in ASEAN. And if these concerted efforts take place synergistically, ASEAN's unrealistic pursuit of a drug-free region that began more than forty years ago just might come to an end.

References

1998 Joint Declaration for a Drug-Free ASEAN. (1998). Retrieved from https://cil.nus.edu.sg/wp-content/uploads/formidable/14/1998-Joint-Declaration-for-a-Drug-Free-ASEAN.pdf

ABC News. (2017, September 20). *Philippine prisons overflowing with hungry inmates as Duterte's drug war intensifies*. Retrieved from http://www.abc.net.au/news/2017-09-20/philippine-prisons-overflowing-as-war-on-drugs-intensifies/8959448

Akbar, P., & Laomanutsak, P. (2018, January 15). *A sprint through a year of policy developments in Thailand*. Retrieved from http://idpc.net/blog/2018/01/a-sprint-through-a-year-of-drug-policy-developments-in-thailand

Amnesty International. (2017). *Annual report 2016/2017*. Retrieved from https://www.amnesty.org/en/latest/research/2017/02/amnesty-international-annual-report-201617/

Amnesty International. (2017, April 11). *Death sentences and executions 2016* (p. 21). Retrieved from https://www.amnesty.org/en/documents/act50/5740/2017/en/.

Anand, R. (2017, November 30). *Parliament removes mandatory death penalty for drug offences, judges to get discretion*. Retrieved from http://www.themalaymailonline.com/malaysia/article/parliament-removes-mandatory-death-penalty-for-drug-offences-judges-to-get#UDhilvBxcD9AtzAJ.99

Association of Southeast Asian Nations (ASEAN). (2016). *The ASEAN work plan on securing communities against illicit drugs 2016–2025, adopted in October 2016, 1–2*. Retrieved from http://asean.org/storage/2016/10/ASEAN-WP-on-Securing-Communities-Against-Illicit-Drugs-2016-2025-FINAL.pdf

Association of Southeast Asian Nations (ASEAN). (2017). *ARF statement on enhancing cooperation in addressing and countering the drug problem*. Retrieved from https://www.asean2017.ph/wp-content/uploads/9.ARF-Statement-on-Enhancing-Cooperation-in-Addressing-and-Countering-the-Drug-Problem_Adopted.pdf

ASEAN Narcotics Cooperation Centre. (2016). *ASEAN drug monitoring report 2016* (p. 128). Retrieved from https://aseannarco.oncb.go.th/ebook/B0063/index.html

ASEAN Statement 59th Session of the Commission on Narcotic Drugs Special Session on UNGASS Preparations 14–16 March 2016. (2016). Retrieved from https://www.unodc.org/documents/commissions/CND/CND_Sessions/CND_59/Statements_16_March_AM/20_ASEAN.PDF

ASEAN Work Plan on Combating Illicit Drug Production, Trafficking and Use 2009–2015. (2017). Retrieved from http://asean.org/storage/2017/07/Doc-1-ASEAN-WP-on-Combating-Illicit-Drug-Production-2009-2015.pdf

Bangkok Summit Declaration of 1995 Bangkok, 14–15 December 1995. (2012). Retrieved from http://asean.org/?static_post=bangkok-summit-declaration-of-1995-bangkok14-15-december-1995

BBC News. (2016, May 10). *Philippines election: Maverick Rodrigo Duterte wins presidency*. Retrieved from http://www.bbc.com/news/world-asia-36253612

BBC News. (2016, September 30). *Philippines President Rodrigo Duterte in quotes*. Retrieved from http://www.bbc.com/news/world-asia-36251094

Central Narcotics Bureau Singapore. (27 July 2017). *38th meeting of ASEAN senior officials on drug matters 2017*. Retrieved from https://www.cnb.gov.sg/NewsAndEvents/News/Index/38th-meeting-of-asean-senior-officials-on-drug-matters-2017

CND Blog. (2017). Retrieved from http://cndblog.org/

CNN Philippines. (2017, March 22). *Palace: Drug surrenderees surpass million marks*. Retrieved from http://cnnphilippines.com/news/2016/12/31/Drug-surrenderees-reach-one-million.html

Csete, J., Kamarulzaman, A., Kazatchkine, M., Altice, F., Balicki, M., Buxton, J., … Beyrer, C. (2016). Public health and international drug policy. *The Lancet*, *387*(10026), 1427–1486, 1432, 1444, 1445, 1454. doi: 10.1016/S0140-6736(16)00619-X

The Diplomat. (2017, December 10). *What did the Philippines' Duterte achieve in Cambodia?* Retrieved from https://thediplomat.com/2016/12/what-did-the-philippines-duterte-achieve-in-cambodia/

Drug Policy Advocacy Group. (2017). *Guiding drug law reform in Myanmar*. Retrieved from https://www.tni.org/en/publication/guiding-drug-law-reform-in-myanmar

Fordham, A., & Lai, G. (2016). Is drug decriminalisation on the cards for Thailand. *Volteface*. Retrieved from http://volteface.me/features/thailand-drug-decriminalisation/

Global Times. (2015, November 27). *Vietnam passes amended Penal Code, removing death penalty for 7 crimes*. Retrieved from http://www.globaltimes.cn/content/955326.shtml

IDPC advocacy note a drug-free ASEAN by 2015: Comments on the final assessment from a civil society perspective. (2014). Retrieved from http://fileserver.idpc.net/library/IDPC-advocacy-note_2014-ASEAN-drug-strategy.pdf.

Keynote speech by H.E. Sen.Lt. Gen Le Quy Vuong Vice Minister of Public Security – S.R of Vietnam at UNGASS 2016 – 19-21/4/2016. (2016). Retrieved from http://statements.unmeetings.org/media2/7657442/vietnam.pdf

Malaysia's Statement 59th Session of the Commission on Narcotic Drugs. (2016). Retrieved from https://www.unodc.org/documents/commissions/CND/CND_Sessions/CND_59/Statements_15_March_AM/05_Malaysia.PDF

McRae, D. (2017, November 28). *Indonesia's fatal war on drugs*. Retrieved from http://www.eastasiaforum.org/2017/11/28/indonesias-fatal-war-on-drugs/

New York Times. (2017, March 1). *Philippines moves closer to reinstating death penalty*. Retrieved from https://www.nytimes.com/2017/03/01/world/asia/philippines-death-penalty.html

Pepinsky, T. (2017, November 4). Democracy isn't receding in Southeast Asia, authoritarianism is enduring. *East Asia Forum*. Retrieved from http://www.eastasiaforum.org/2017/11/04/democracy-isnt-receding-in-southeast-asia-authoritarianism-is-enduring/

Permanent Mission of Thailand to the United Nations. (2016). Retrieved from http://statements.unmeetings.org/media2/7657420/thailand.pdf

The Phnom Penh Post. (2018, January 19). *Necessary' drug crackdown to continue*. Retrieved from http://www.phnompenhpost.com/national/necessary-drug-crackdown-continue

Position statement endorsed and adopted by the 4th ASEAN Ministerial meeting on drug matters 29 October 2015, Langkawi, Malaysia. (2015). Retrieved from http://www.asean.org/storage/2015/10/Position-Statement-on-Drugs-endorsed-and-adopted-by-the-4th-AMMD-on-29-October-2015-Langkawi-Malaysia.pdf

Reuters. (2017, February 8). *Cambodia promises harsher drug crackdown as arrests soar*. Retrieved from https://www.reuters.com/article/uk-cambodia-drugs/cambodia-promises-harsher-drug-crackdown-as-arrests-soar-idUKKBN15N18Z.

59th Session of the Commission on Narcotic Drugs (CND) Statement by His Excellency General Paiboon Koomchaya Thai Minister of Justice, the Special Segment of the General Assembly on the World Drug Problem to be held in 2016 on Monday 14 March 2016, 10.00–13.00 hrs. Plenary Hall, M-Building, Vienna International Center Vienna, Republic of Austria. (2016). Retrieved from https://www.unodc.org/documents/commissions/CND/CND_Sessions/CND_59/Statements/07_Thailand.PDF

Singapore Statement at Plenary Session UNGASS 2016. (2016). Retrieved from http://statements.unmeetings.org/media2/7657384/singapore.pdf

Singapore Statement 59th Session of the Commission on Narcotic Drugs Special Session on UNGASS Preparations 14–16 March 2016. (2016). Retrieved from https://www.unodc.org/documents/commissions/CND/CND_Sessions/CND_59/Statements_14_March_PM/01_Singapore.PDF

Single Convention on Narcotic Drugs, 1961 – INCB. (1961). Retrieved from https://www.incb.org/documents/Narcotic-Drugs/1961-Convention/convention_1961_en.pdf

Singh, P. (2017, December 7) Human Rights Watch News. Smokescreen Justice for 'Drug War' Deaths in the Philippines (pp. 295 -296). Retrieved from https://www.hrw.org/news/2017/12/07/smokescreen-justice-drug-war-deaths-philippines

Statement by the Head of Delegation of the Republic of Indonesia H.E. Ambassador Rachmat Budiman Permanent Representative of the Republic Indonesia at the 59th Session of the Commission on Narcotic Drugs Vienna, 14–22 March 2016. (2016). Retrieved from https://www.unodc.org/documents/commissions/CND/CND_Sessions/CND_59/Statement_15_March_PM/03_Indonesia.pdf

Statement by the Head of Delegation of the Republic of Indonesia H.E. Ambassador Rachmat Budiman at the 30th Session of the United Nations Special Session on the World Drug Problem (UNGASS), New York, 19–21 April 2016. (2016). Retrieved from http://statements.unmeetings.org/media2/7657409/indonesia.pdf

Statement of the Honorabe Emmanuel Caparas Secretary of Justice United Nations General Assembly Special Session on the World Drug Problem 20 April 2016. (2016). Retrieved from http://statements.unmeetings.org/media2/7657389/philippines.pdf

Statement on behalf of the Association of Southeast Asian Nations (ASEAN) and National Statement by the Honourable Mr. Nur Jazlan Mohamed, Deputy Minister of Home Affairs of Malaysia at the 30th Session of the Special Session of the General Assembly on the World Drug Problem, New York, 19 April 2016. (2016). Retrieved from http://statements.unmeetings.org/media2/7657354/malaysia.pdf

The 4th ASEAN Ministerial Meeting on Drug Matters 29 October 2015, Langkawi, Malaysia Chairman's Statement. (2015). Retrieved from http://asean.org/storage/2016/10/Chairmans-Statement-of-the-4th-AMMD-ADOPTED.pdf

UN Office of the High Commissioner for Human Rights. (2016, August 18). *UN experts urge the Philippines to stop unlawful killings of people suspected of drug-related offences*. Retrieved from http://www.ohchr.org/EN/NewsEvents/Pages/DisplayNews.aspx?NewsID=20388

Chapter 8

Deconstructing the Islamic Bloc: The Middle East and North Africa and Pluralistic Drugs Policy

Maziyar Ghiabi

Abstract

States in the Middle East and North Africa (MENA) have historically leaned towards conservative, reactionary models of drugs policy. The combination of authoritarian forms of government, whether dynastic monarchies (Morocco, Jordan and Persian Gulf countries), semi-military republics (Syria, Egypt and Algeria) or religiously sanctioned republics (Iran), with the strong influence of Islamic law and norms, has signified that the region has enforced strict forms of drug prohibitions. For that matter, the region is home to cultural and social norms that are less permissive than in other regions of the world: for instance, with regard to premarital sex, homosexuality, clothing, alcoholic drinks and freedom of expression. This image of the MENA region is often overplayed by media commentators and Western scholars, especially in the field of drugs policy. The almost total absence of studies of drugs policy or drugs history in the MENA, excluding works in epidemiology, speaks well about the oblivion to which the region has been relegated over the last decades. The chapter provides first a background on the main questions regarding MENA drugs policy, looking at the historical developments in drug regulations and drug trends. Then, it discusses the current policies that operate across the region and, if pertinent, the prospects of policy development. When necessary, the argument refers to contextual elements that have influenced the direction in national and transitional drugs policy. Conscious of the fact that the MENA is as vast and diverse as a continent, I have opted to focus on three paradigmatic cases (Iran, Lebanon and Saudi Arabia), which provide an adequate geographical and thematic coverage of the MENA drugs policy. The three cases cover different aspects

Collapse of the Global Order on Drugs: From UNGASS 2016 to Review 2019, 167–189

doi:10.1108/978-1-78756-487-920181008

of today's MENA drugs policy spectrum, from draconian repressive measures to progressive harm reduction programmes. Taken in their geographical dimension one can appreciate the variety and difference that exists within the MENA region, therefore supporting one of the key objectives of this chapter, which is to provide a nuanced analysis of drugs policy against the grain of homogenising and culturally reductive approaches.

Keywords: Middle East and North Africa; Western Asia; Authoritarian States; conservativism; policy development; drug policy

Introduction: A Hundred Years of Drug Prohibition

In 1924, Mohammad El Guindy, the delegate representing Egypt at the Second International Opium Conference of the League of Nations in Geneva, made a vigorous campaign against *hashish*. He called for *hashish*'s inclusion in the list of controlled substances, insisting on the depravity of its users and the surfacing of the problem of *hashishism,* which endangered social cohesion in Egypt and beyond (League of Nations, 1925). Emphasising the risk for mental health, the Egyptian representative made the case for a cannabis prohibition, supported by the Turkish counterpart, which in vein of the new nationalist sentiments gaining momentum in Istanbul was eager to abandon old Orientalist pastimes in favour of new modern consumption.[1] Eventually, El Guindy's proposal was included in the Geneva Convention, thus imposing strict control measures (and subsequent repressive penalties) on cannabis. Egypt itself led the anti-cannabis campaign, adopting in 1926 strict criminal procedures for drug offenders, with up to three years' imprisonment for drug possession, and established the first anti-narcotic police force worldwide (Nahas, 1985).

Less than a hundred years later, in 2016, on the occasion of the United Nations General Assembly Special Session (UNGASS) on Narcotic Drugs, another Egyptian, Ambassador Khaled Shamaa, chaired the preparatory board in Vienna leading to the special session. Formerly head of the Commission on Narcotic Drugs (CND), Shamaa adopted a less than cooperative approach in the discussions with civil society, impeding efforts to include in the final declarations innovative language and ideas about international drugs policy. His chairmanship represented the status quo camp within the spectrum of the international drug control machine (Rolles, 2017). Again Egypt – and the Middle Eastern conservative camp – had built up support for international prohibitionist policies.

States in the Middle East and North Africa (MENA) have historically leaned towards conservative, reactionary models of drugs policy. The Egyptian case illustrates well this genealogical trait, which over the 10 successive decades seems to have changed in inconspicuous ways. The combination of authoritarian forms

[1]Kemal Mustafa 'Ataturk', the new president in Turkey following the fall of the Ottoman Empire in 1922, was a moderniser and westerniser, who had a good taste of alcoholic drinks and cigarettes, as opposed to opium and narghilés.

of government, whether dynastic monarchies (Morocco, Jordan and Persian Gulf countries), semi-military republics (Syria, Egypt and Algeria) or religiously sanctioned republics (Iran), with the strong influence of Islamic law and norms, has signified that the region has enforced strict forms of drug prohibitions. For that matter, the region is home to cultural and social norms that are less permissive than in other regions of the world: for instance, with regard to premarital sex, homosexuality, clothing, alcoholic drinks and freedom of expression.[2]

This image of the MENA region is often overplayed by media commentators and Western scholars, especially in the field of drugs policy. The almost total absence of studies of drugs policy or drugs history in the MENA, excluding works in epidemiology, speaks well about the oblivion to which the region has been relegated over the last decades. Scholarly publications on this topic have been limited to those cases, which are relevant to European drug strategies, notoriously the Moroccan case for influx of hashish in the EU (Afsahi, 2009, 2015; Chouvy & Afsahi, 2014), and the Afghan opium route, which alone represents alone ca. 80–90% of the world opiate supply (World Drug Report, 2010, 2016).

Analysing drugs policy in the MENA is equivalent to looking into a continent's drugs policy. The differences in history, society, politics and culture are so great that they impede a coherent analysis. Although most of the region is inhabited by Muslim majority populations, Islam is not the only feature of the region. Apart from differences in Islamic denominations (Shi'a, Sunni, etc.), there is the input of culture (Arab, Turkish, Persian, Kurds, Jews and many other groups) and economics (oil-rich, oil-poor, migrant, labour intensive, etc.). The MENA has also undergone significant transformations over the last two decades. From the recent civil wars in Syria, Libya and Yemen and the massive flow of refugees, to the US-led wars on Afghanistan and Iraq, the region has experienced epochal changes, including in drugs phenomena. The unprecedented level of human displacement, only a small proportion of which has reached Europe, has modified existing social and political conditions in many countries. They have also affected in dramatic ways laws and trends with regard to drugs.

This untold story in the global narrative about drugs policy is part and parcel of this chapter's objective. To do so, the chapter provides first a background on the main questions regarding MENA drugs policy, looking at the historical developments in drug regulations and drug trends. Then, it discusses the current policies that operate across the region and, if pertinent, the prospects of policy development. When necessary, the argument refers to contextual elements that have influenced the direction in national and transitional drugs policy. Conscious of the fact that the MENA is as vast and diverse as a continent, I have opted to focus on three paradigmatic cases, which provide an adequate geographical and thematic coverage of the MENA drugs policy. The three cases cover different aspects of today's MENA drugs policy spectrum, from draconian repressive measures to progressive harm reduction programmes. Taken in their geographical dimension

[2]At the same time, social norms are also changing generation after generation, especially in some countries, such as Iran, Lebanon and Turkey.

one can appreciate the variety and difference that exists within the MENA region, therefore supporting one of the key objectives of this chapter, which is to provide a nuanced analysis of drugs policy against the grain of homogenising and culturally reductive approaches.

These cases are the Islamic Republic of Iran, for it tops the world's rank for opiate users, opiate seizures, drug-related death sentences and it has among the most developed programmes of harm reduction; Lebanon, for it is a small country which has experienced great civil society activism in drugs policy and is currently discussing decriminalisation, besides being a transit for cannabis and fake Captagon pills[3]; Saudi Arabia, for it represent the reactionary bastion of the region's drugs policy while also experiencing a surge in consumption of amphetamine-type stimulants (ATS) and it adopts an emblematic case of religious prohibition. The three countries together provide paradigmatic cases for the understanding of MENA drugs policy. Iran and Saudi Arabia are influential countries, respectively, in the Levant (Iraq, Syria and Lebanon) and in the Arabian Peninsula and Sunni-majority states (Kuwait, Bahrain, UAE, Qatar and Oman). Lebanon instead is a multiconfessional state, where different religious communities partake in the political process. Through the discussion of different themes, such as harm reduction, death penalty, civil society participation and drug policy reform, the chapter intends to cast light on a new dimension of international drugs policy, that of the MENA region, in light of the UNGASS 2019. Eventually, the chapter aims at demonstrating how Islam is not a key (and exclusive) element in shaping MENA drugs policy.

The chapter results from the author's research in the Middle East over the last five years. It combines fieldwork research, interviews and participant observation in Iran (2012–2017) and Lebanon (2013, 2015, and 2017), with systematic literature review and discourse analysis in both English, Arabic, French and Persian newspapers and reports. The latter covers also the case of Saudi Arabia, where the author was not able to carry out on-the-ground fieldwork and/or directly interview key stakeholders.

Prevalence and Trends in Drugs in the Modern MENA

Narcotics, in the form of cannabis and opium, entered the European, Western imagination notably from the Orient. Tales of dreamy and fabulous smoking sessions are rich in the literature and travellers' accounts of the last three centuries. The image of Oriental decadence was in part also the result of the idea that narcotic drugs were a commodity commonly used on the southern and eastern coasts of the Mediterranean Sea. This holds water even when one comes to know that the Arabic and Persian word for opium, *afyun*, actually comes from the Greek *opion* (the poppy juice) or that in Southern Italy the use of the poppy was

[3]Fake Captagon pills are made of a chemical combination, which uses elements contained in the original pharmaceutical product, adding other stimulant substances, under the brand name of Captagon.

widespread in peasant communities in the last five centuries (Barba, Belperio, & Porciello).

Today, cannabis, opium, heroin and ATS are the most commonly used drugs in the region.[4] While the first two have been part of local traditions and pharmacopeia, heroin and ATS are substances that gained popularity, respectively, in the 1980s and the 2000s.[5] The lack of clear data remains a major obstacle in understanding regional trends in drug use, as most MENA countries do not reveal national statistics. In part this is due to a lack of systematic data collection, which prevents a solid critical assessment. When data are collected, it is produced under political constraints and it tends to fit political narratives, including when data collection is done by international organisations such as the UNODC. In the following section, I discuss the trends and prevalence of drug use in Iran, Lebanon and Saudi Arabia.

Iran: From Opium to Meth

In Iran, opium has been used since time immemorial, with its recreational use becoming mainstream towards the early twentieth century. By the late 1970s, heroin became widely available, following the incremental activities of Turkish narcotics traffickers (Gingeras, 2012, 2013) as a consequence of Iran's ban on opium production in 1955 (Ghiabi, 2018a). A more dramatic shift in consumption pattern arrived in the early 2000s, when increasing numbers of former opiate users shifted to methamphetamine, known in Iran under the name of *shisheh* ('glass'). In less than a decade, meth had become an increasingly popular drug in Iran, consumed in quantities that may not be that dissimilar to opiates (Ghiabi, 2018). This event represents a historical transition from crop-based substances to synthetic ones, even though the shift may not be permanent and data, as mentioned earlier, are not systematic. Its implications for policy are also crucial as I elucidate in the latter part of this chapter.

Changes in drug phenomena have been paralleled by changes in policy. Iran was the only opium producing country to introduce domestic regulations on drug use after the Opium Conventions in Shanghai (1909) and The Hague (1911) (Ghiabi, 2018a). Although opium represented an important economic asset for the modernising plans of the Pahlavi monarchy, by 1955 its government had introduced a legislation prohibiting poppy cultivation and opium consumption. The decision was justified not on Islamic grounds, the Pahlavi being a secular ruling family; public health and modernisation plans were given as rationales of the ban (which was heavily subsidised by the United States). About fifteen years later, in 1969, in light of the failure of the prohibition policy, the government reversed its drugs policy and approved one the world's most comprehensive maintenance systems

[4]Khat (aka *qat*) is a stimulant drug common in Yemen and the Horn of Africa. See Carrier et al. (2017).

[5]I leave out the use and abuse of pharmaceutical products, such as Ritalin and Prozac, for reasons of space and pertinence. See Behrouzan (2015).

for opiates. Almost 200,000 people were registered in the opium provision plan set up by the government.

The law envisioned the provision of opium vouchers to all registered users who manifested physical malaise, including drug dependency, or were over 60 years of age (Ghiabi, 2018a). Following the Islamic Revolution of 1979, the policy was abruptly reversed. The Islamic Republic adopted a stanch prohibitionist policy, with draconian measures against drug traffickers and, at times, drug consumers (Ghiabi, 2014). The approach remains the basis of Iran's drugs policy to today, even though very important changes have occurred during the 2000s. In particular, faced with a severe HIV/AIDS epidemic at the end of the 1990s, the Iranian government first piloted and then scaled up a nationwide programme of needle exchange (NEP) and opiate substitution treatment (OST), including in prisons. (The prison NEP has now terminated after the evaluation of the pilot programme.)

Data on drug use remain vague and unreliable. Between the 1990s and 2017, the Iranian government declared the number of drug users in the country to be fixed at 1,325,000, with 90% of them men. There are around 200,000 injecting drug users, according to the government. This puts the prevalence of drug use in the age range between 15 and 65 at more than the 2.65% of the population estimated up to 2016 (DCHQ, 2016). This statistical inertia is contested on a regular basis by public officials from the Ministry of Health, the Welfare Organisation as well as media, declaring that the number of drugs users has dramatically increased. Unofficial statistics put the number between three and five million drug users (Eskandarieh, Jafari, Yazdani, Hazrati, & Saberi-Zafarghandi, 2014; Moghanibashi-Mansourieh & Deilamizade, 2014). Anecdotal accounts from the urban life of Iranians suggest that the number may be closer to the higher end of the range. Eventually in June 2017, the DCHQ announced a revision of the data, setting the total number of 'addicts' at 2,808,000 people, without providing further details.

Cannabis has gained great popularity among bourgeois urban youth, while cannabis resin, *hashish*, is more popular with working class and heterodox religious groups, such as the *dervish*. Another substance that had become popular since 2000 is *kerak*, a heroin-based substance, the name of which is reminiscent of the North American *crack*. Methamphetamines too are now consumed in large amounts, with women representing a key consumer group of this substance. Supply is guaranteed by local laboratories set up across the Iranian plateau, despite systematic efforts by Iranian anti-narcotic officials to curb their activities. As such, Iran has again become a producing country of drugs, after the successful eradication of poppy cultivation carried out by the Islamic Republic in the 1980s (Ghiabi, 2014).

Saudi Arabia: Captagon and Boredom

Saudi Arabia, which is by far the most populous and influential Kingdom of the Gulf Cooperation Council (GCC), is a paradigmatic case for MENA drug policy conservativism. Historically reluctant to introduce policy change in social and cultural fields, the Arab kingdoms of the Persian Gulf regard drug consumption and drug trafficking through moralistic and securitising frames. In terms of history of consumption, the Arabian Peninsula has not had a comparable history to that of the Iranian plateau. Narcotic use emerged concomitant to the modernisation process during the second part of the twentieth century, parallel to the increase in oil revenues. By the turn of the millennium, the Islamic codes reigning in Saudi Arabia, which are the most austere in the MENA region, were juxtaposed with a significant rise in ATS use and heroin consumption (Alam-Mehrjerdi, Roya, & Kate, 2016). The lack of transparency in the publication of data makes it very difficult to discern the prevalence of drug use. The increasing flux of narcotics and stimulants generated in Syria is sign of the substantial demand for stimulants among Saudis citizens, together with the fact that the Persian Gulf kingdom has developed into a key transhipment point (Robins, 2013). The *World Drug Report* announced in 2010 that more than half of the world's 24.3 metric tonnes of amphetamine were sized by Saudi authorities (World Drug Report, 2010), data that were described by a UNODC official as 'absolutely phenomenal' (CNN, 2010). It is not clear whether this seizure is due exclusively to transit dynamics or if it is justified by domestic consumption.

The royal family has at times been accused of involvement in the illegal drug trade. In 1999, a Saudi Prince was accused of having smuggled two tonnes of cocaine from Venezuela to France. He was convicted by a French court in 2007 in absentia, as he sought shelter back in the Kingdom. In 2015, amidst the rage of the Syrian civil war, another Saudi Prince was arrested in Beirut when his plane – belonging to the royal family – was found with more than two tonnes of fake Captagon pills and large amounts of cocaine (*The Independent*, 2015). In origin, Captagon is a pharmaceutical stimulant, fenetylline, produced in the 1960s to treat hyperactivity, narcolepsy and depression (BBC, 2015), later banned because of its addictive nature. The label has been used by local producers in Syria and Lebanon to indicate a substance containing amphetamine, caffeine and other psychoactive elements, which had been used across the region (and especially in the Arabian Peninsula) for its stimulant effect. Allegedly, the substance is also used in combat by jihadi fighters in order to keep awake over the long hours of confrontation and to resist fear during their often-suicidal assaults. In 2016, the executive director of the UNODC announced that ISIS and al-Nusra Front had smuggled the chemical substance used in Captagon production (UNODC, 2015).

WikiLeaks cables have revealed the large-scale use of ATS, such as Captagon, in Saudi Arabia's elite circles, despite all intoxicating substances being forbidden by the country's Islamic law (Foreign Policy, 2015). Given the lack of data, the reasons for the increase in use can be inferred from the country's very strict social norms, which prohibited cinemas, public display of inter-sex sociality, clubs, etc. Stimulant use such as ATS enables to cope with boredom, while being less noticeable than cannabis, alcohol and opiates. Among women, there are reports of Captagon use for weigh loss purposes, given that 44% of Saudi women are clinically obese (VOA, 2015).

Lebanon: Hashish, ATS and Civil War

Lebanon has historically been the producing hub for cannabis in the MENA region, together with Morocco, both of which supplied European countries.

A small country with roughly six million people, it has been at the heart of regional politics in the last 100 years. Colonial mandates, the rise (and fall) of Arab nationalism, Israeli intervention and occupation, civil war and high-level political assassinations have characterised the history of this small Mediterranean country. Some of these events have intertwined with peculiar developments in drugs economy and culture. During the years between the two World Wars, Lebanese, and, generally, Arab traders built up networks of opium and hashish supply that cut across North Africa and the Mediterranean (Marshall, 2012). Later these networks matured in what Marshall named the 'Lebanese Connection', a transnational route supplying premium quality heroin, connecting Beirut to Marseille, and from the French port to the Atlantic shores of North America.

In terms of domestic consumption, these illegal activities seemed to bear little influence. Hashish remained a drug consumed sparsely among traditional rural communities and later among Westernised urban dwellers, especially in the vibrant intellectual life of Beirut. Opiates had some medical use, but no widespread opiate culture had emerged. This changed during the long and excruciating civil war, which divided Lebanon between 1975 and 1990. By the early 1980s, traditional cannabis cultivation in the Be'eka Valley had been replaced by the more lucrative poppy, a transition which lasted up to the signing of the peace treaty which ended the Lebanese civil war in 1990 (Interview with Elie Aaraj, 2017). During that period, local laboratories transformed the opium sap into heroin, shipping it outside the country for (or to) Western markets. Funnelling large amount of monies to the Lebanese warlords was one reason behind this shift; hence, heroin became a drug of choice among the combatants. In response to the widespread violence within urban and rural communities, militiamen of different confessions and ideologies had acquired a taste for heroin, as a coping mechanism to the everyday violence of civil war (Interview with Elie Aaraj, 2017).[6] Around 120,000 people died in the conflict, which needs to be added to the mass internal displacement of people in the south, during the Israeli occupation (Traboulsi, 2007).

By the early 1990s, there was an acknowledgement of the extent of heroin abuse, which effected the HIV spread in the later decade. As I describe later, this provided the justification for the first steps towards reforms in drugs policy and the introduction of harm reduction. Since the outbreak of the Syrian civil war in 2011, there has been a dramatic rise in ATS production, which originates in the region straddling Syrian and Lebanon. Fake Captagon pills are the most notorious version of this drug, but other ATS are also consumed across Lebanon. The lack of data does not allow a clear assessment, but fieldwork observation in poorer districts of Beirut (e.g. Bourj Hammoud) and the Northern region of Lebanon (Tripoli's Tabbaneh) confirmed that consumption of Captagon has surged over the last five years (Interview with Skoun workers; Participant observation with Soins Infirmiers et Developpement Communautaire - SIDC). The latter

[6]Elie Aaraj, at a time a social worker, was among the first to organise health and welfare services for people with substance abuse problems and/or infected with HIV/AIDS.

area is also known for hosting radical Islamist groups and, given its geographical proximity to the Syrian border, it is object of high security measures by the Lebanese army (The Daily Star, 2016). Recent reports have also indicated a rise of ATS consumption among Syrian refugees in Lebanon; however, one should be cautious of these reports, as Syrians are increasingly subject to scapegoating in Lebanese public discourse (Al-Araby, 2015).

The MENA region is going through important transformations in terms of drug phenomena. These are connected to changing drug cultures as in the rise of stimulant drugs in the place of traditional narcotic substances, but they are also the result of geopolitical and socioeconomic processes, caused by conflicts and large-scale displacement. When the US-led military alliance attacked Afghanistan in 2001, the production of opium skyrocketed for the following decade, flooding the Middle East and Europe with unprecedented quantities of narcotics (Chouvy, 2009; Farrell & Thorne, 2005). The invasion of Iraq in 2003 left a geopolitical void at the heart of the region. Replaced by illegal smuggling networks, the void represented an opportunity like no other for traffickers of all sorts, including drug traffickers. A similar situation has been engendered by the brutal civil war in Syria. With the crumbling of state institutions and territorial disintegration, Syria has become a main site for the production and smuggling of illicit good, with drugs representing a highly remunerative business for insurgent groups. Conflicts have not only affected drug routes. They bear upon consumption trends too. With mass scale human costs and psychological traumas, the use of drugs looms large in the region as a latent question.

Policy and Policy Developments *vis à vis* Drugs

In this section, I discuss the existing policies on illegal drugs in the three cases under analysis. Given the diversity of the three cases, I intend to highlight different policy elements, such as the use of the death penalty, harm reduction strategies, civil society participation and the potential for policy development. In brief, while Iran and Saudi Arabia have adopted the death penalty for drug trafficking charges, they differ substantially with regard to harm reduction strategy and drug policy experimentation. Lebanon, in contrast, provides the paradigm for civil society participation and the emergence of a reform-oriented mind-set in a multiconfessional setting. The three cases together provide a new perspective on MENA drugs policy in view of the 2019 UNGASS meeting.

Islamic Republic of Iran: Death Penalty, Harm Reduction and Legalisation?

Iran's drugs policy exists in a paradoxical situation, where severe punishments coexist with welfare services to drug (ab)users.[7] The authorities have resorted

[7]For the use of category of (ab)user see Ghiabi (2018).

systematically to the application of the death penalty for drug trafficking, armed smuggling and recurring drug offences, at least up to 2017. The country applied the capital sentence in at least 567 cases in 2016, which decreased from the 2015 data of 977 (Amnesty International, 2017). Roughly, 80% of these are due to drug trafficking charges. The prison population too mainly consists of drug offenders, with about 50% of all inmates being accused of drug crimes and 65% considered drug abusers (Tasnim, 2016). Proximity to Afghanistan, which produces about 80–90% of the world's opiate supply, puts Iran at the heart of global transit routes towards the West (BBC, 2013).

Iranian legislation considers drug use a crime. Therefore, possession of illicit substances is punished per se, as it is the consumption of prohibited substances. One distinguishing element in the legislation is the category of 'public intoxication' (*tajahor*). For instance, if a person is found intoxicated in the public place, but with no drugs, he/she is considered guilty of a crime. In practice, this notion targets impoverished drug users and migrant populations, especially the two million Afghan refugees who live in Iran following the USSR invasion of Afghanistan in the 1980s, and then the US invasion of Afghanistan in 2001. People accused of public intoxication can be sentenced to a few months' incarceration or, since the approval of the 2010 Drug Law reform, to mandatory treatment in a state-run rehab treatment centre. If state-run centres are incapable of providing treatment services, the convicted addict can seek subsidised treatment in private, charitable centres. In practice, there is very little or no judicial supervision for these convictions and the application and follow up process is haphazard and inconsistent.

Cultivation, production and concealment of illicit drugs are punished with monetary fines for the first two offences; incarceration is considered if found guilty for a third time; and the death penalty if the offender commits the crime four times (but the law is not applied since 2017). Possession and transportation have heavier fines, lashes and prison sentences for over 50 g of opium and hashish and 1 g of heroin, meth and ATS (Anti-Narcotic Law of IRI 2010). Armed trafficking is punished with the death sentence, a law that applies selectively to the southeast region of Baluchistan, from where most of the opiate flux passes.[8] The use of the death sentence has had de facto no impact on drug trafficking. Iran has topped the world's ranking for drug seizures since the 1980s and, despite its draconian measures, it has been praised for its commitment to the War on Drugs by the UN Office on Drugs and Crime (Fars, 2013). However, it has also been the target of international campaigns against the death penalty, led by Amnesty International and Human Rights Watch. In 2013–2014, one of these campaigns brought to an end the international cooperation programme that supported Iran's supply and demand reduction (Christensen, 2017). Among its unintended consequences was the halt of international donations for Iran's harm reduction plan, which targeted Afghan refugee population (Interview with UNODC official, 2015).

[8]It could be argued that the punishment for armed trafficking is not so much a question of trafficking as a question of armed resistance to state authority, which in the Islamic Republic is punished with the capital sentence.

In the summer of 2017, the Iranian Parliament approved a draft reform that would abolish the death penalty for non-violent drug charges. This was further upheld by the Head of Judiciary, Ayatollah Sadegh Amoli-Larijani, in January 2018 in a speech to regional and provincial prosecutors. Despite systemic resistance by conservative members of the political establishment and some popular resentment against the provision, the upper echelon of the state is keen to see this step accomplished. With this policy development, Iran could see the number of death sentences diminish dramatically while being brought back from the international isolation that this policy has caused. Indeed, one can see how the reassessment of the death penalty is part of a broader debate around drugs policy reform, as I discuss in the following paragraphs.

The other facet of Iran's drugs policy is a comprehensive harm reduction strategy, which is arguably the most developed in the MENA and one of the most dynamic worldwide. According to official statistics, in 2016 almost 800,000 people were admitted to the treatment and harm reduction services, with around 412,671 and 83,649 being treated respectively with methadone and buprenorphine substitution programmes.[9] There are more than several thousand non-governmental organisations (NGO) working in this sector, including users-led groups, charitable foundations, women-led associations, advocacy and research centres as well as very active research centres. It is not surprising that Iran has the highest number of Narcotic Anonymous members worldwide after the United States (The Fix, 2014). Iranian researchers actively participated in the epidemiological and medical studies around drug abuse and infectious diseases.

Harm reduction policy was adopted in the 2000s in response to a severe HIV/AIDS epidemic that originated in prisons. Results were encouraging and more than a decade later the rate of HIV transmission through injecting had decreased significantly. This prompted the government and state apparatus to legitimise harm reduction within the General Policy of the Islamic Republic, a blueprint which emanated from the highest political authority, the Supreme Leader Ayatollah Ali Khamenei. Beside the provision of clean needles and methadone, the Iranian authorities also introduced an opium tincture programme. Opium tincture is a liquid solution derived directly from opium sap. It is generally administered to elderly opium smokers (over 60 years of age). While around 90% of methadone clinics are private (supervised by the Ministry of Health and Medical Research), opium tincture is dispensed only in state-run clinics (DCHQ, 2016).

From an ideological viewpoint, the introduction of opium tincture can be the gateway to broader reforms around illicit drugs. Opium had long been stigmatised and associated to the *ancien regime* of the Shahs. Yet, the shift among Iranian consumers to harder drugs such as heroin and more problematically methamphetamine has led the authorities to reconsider their previous position on traditional drugs such as opium and cannabis. Recently, top officials of

---

[9]These data have been criticised by some practitioners because of the poor reporting structures and the potential of double-counting for people who visit more than one clinic. Nonetheless, the social scope of methadone clinics can be simply observed by their very visible and capillary public presence in Iranian towns and cities.

the Drug Control Headquarters, Iran's umbrella agency for illicit drugs, have expressed the need to 'shift from industrial drugs to traditional drugs', meaning that drugs policy should facilitate consumption of opiates and decrease meth use (ILNA, 22/1/2017; IRNA, 7/11/2011). This is justified on a practical ground: opiates can be managed through the country's well-developed harm reduction system, whereas synthetic ('industrial', *san'ati*) drugs, i.e. methamphetamine, cannot be targeted by classical harm reduction approaches. Among the proposals that have been taken into considerations, the most radical is that of a 'state management of drug consumption and supply'. The proposal, initially formulated at Tehran's International Conference on Addiction Sciences in September 2015, envisages the direct and comprehensive involvement of state institutions in the spheres of cultivation, production, supply and consumption of drugs. The substances that have been considered under this model are opium and cannabis, but the model could potentially apply to other derivatives, such as heroin. In the two years following the proposal, the debate reached parliament and had been amply analysed in the media and policy venues. The primary objective clearly remains that of cutting off the interests of criminal organisations and reducing the costs of drug use, which in Iran stands at an exorbitant level. This would occur in parallel with the establishment of safe injection rooms for heroin users, a pilot programme that is currently under way in the capital, Tehran.

What is more interesting is that these proposals did not arise from engagement with international drug reformers, as it often happens in the context of Latin American countries or in North America. Of course, policy makers in Iran looked at outside models and evaluated the feasibility of alternatives to criminalised approaches. However, the policy developments occurred through indigenous discussions and without much reference to international counterparts, leaving Iran at the fringes of international drugs policy debate.

Lebanon: The Syrian Conflict, Dysfunctional State and Decriminalisation of Drug Use?

The Lebanese state has been generally described as dysfunctional and ineffective (Hudson, 1985). Organised around multiple sectarian lines and subject to geopolitical contention between regional and international powers, Lebanese politics is often regarded as an undiscernible miasma. Of course, this affects in significant ways also its drugs policy. With legislative duties regularly bogged down by polarising divides with the Parliament, Lebanon has not been capable of updating its response to changing drug phenomena over the last forty years (Bigo & Laurent, 1991). Moreover, political parties along the spectrum have been accused of cashing in on the lucrative drug trade. This connection is a legacy of the time of the civil war when different factions used drug trafficking to support the costs of war. Connection between drug producing families and political elites is given as an undisputable fact and it has hampered systematic discussions of drug policy reform. The laxity of enforcement with regard to cannabis growers and large-scale money laundering confirm this side of the story.

Much of Lebanon's drugs policy needs to be understood in light of regional developments. With the war in Syria, drug producers – of both cannabis and Captagon – sought to take advantage of the new security threat posed by Islamic State and jihadi terrorists, to increase production levels. With law enforcement focussed on terrorist threats, the drug economy experienced a great boost, which was further funnelled by new land routes via Syria to the European and Persian Gulf markets (*The Daily Star*, 2014). However, in 2017, a change in geopolitical balance has impinged upon this business. Limited stability on Syria's western front and increased domestic stability, the Lebanese anti-narcotic strategy has re-focussed on cannabis cultivation and ATS production. Targeting cultivated lands in the Be'eka Valley and laboratories of Captagon production across the country has brought about a drop in the trade (*The Daily Star*, 2017). Some cannabis producers, for instance, have turned to vineyard cultivation, which is a comparatively remunerative and strongly supported by the authorities. But Cabernet cannot be a viable alternative to cannabis. Shi'a cannabis growers, who have historically been occupied in this business, are likely to continue with the old business model, as wine production is traditionally considered an un-Islamic alternative, while there is no such stigma on cannabis.[10]

It is not the first time that cannabis growers had experienced a decline (*The Daily Star*, 2014). This industry has gone through some structural change since 2011. With more than two million Syrian refugees seeking shelter in Lebanon, landowners hired a cheap workforce from this reserve migrant army. Syrian men and women and adolescents take part in the cannabis harvest, which pays an average of $12–20 per day (Reuters, 2015). Indeed, cannabis is entrenched in Lebanese political economy. This is also acknowledged by public officials and influential politicians. For example, in 2014, the Minister of Agriculture, Akram Chehayeb, called for the legalisation of cannabis farming as an alternative to the haphazard booms and busts that exist today. 'We are conducting studies on how to organise this type of agriculture so that it becomes monitored by the state, and thus the state can buy the harvest and export it to the countries that need it.... This agricultural product is in demand worldwide for pharmaceutical production' (*The Daily Star*, 2014). His suggestion was limited to cannabis cultivation and it was aimed at stabilising the state relation with the cultivators, which often had escalated in armed confrontation.

Walid Jumblatt, a long-term Druze political leader and Member of Parliament, has also made a case for cannabis legalisation, in terms of cultivation but also with regard to domestic medical use. A key historical figure in the leftist camp, Jumblatt's call has found some institutional support. Economists spoke in favour of the developmental benefits of cultivation for impoverished areas in the north and east with a return of at least $400 million to the state budget and $2 billion to the wider economy (Reuters, 2014), whereas progressive NGOs

[10]This is despite drug scholarship in the Islamic world says that all drugs are seen as haram, 'illegal', in Islam. The statement is both discursively and theoretically incorrect.

rode the tide calling for drug decriminalisation. Even members of the Shi'ite Resistance Movement Hezbollah have expressed cautious interest in a reform of the current law, arguing that cultivators' interests cannot be left out of the picture (In-door discussions at the Lebanese Parliamentary Session on Human Rights, 2017).

Cultivation and consumption of cannabis is not the only field in which Lebanese drug policy is being debated. The Narcotics Law of 1998 is the main legal text in dealing with drug use and addiction. In the text, it is agreed that consumption of drugs is illegal and must be punished. However, the text also includes the option of treatment as an alternative to prison, which should be supervised by an ad hoc Addiction Committee. According to a study carried out by the NGO Skoun, the great majority of people convicted for drug use were not offered the option of treatment. In fact, the Addiction Committee had been activated only in 2013, about 15 years after the approval of the law. Up to 2013, people charged with drug use received sentences that varied between a few months to several years of incarceration (IDCP, 2011, Interview with Nadya Mikdash, 2017). Between 2009 and 2013, about 11,000 people were arrested for drug abuse, with poor communities being the primary target of the Internal Security Forces (ISF). Even following the creation of the Addiction Committee, only 110 individuals out of several thousands were given the choice between prison and treatment (NOW, 2014). The criminalisation approach also leads to negative results on broader public health. Hospitals tend to notify the ISF on overdose cases (NOW, 2014; Interview with Nadya Mikdash, 2017), which prevents people from seeking treatment in case of health complication.

Double standards are the rule in Lebanon. Prosecutors systematically release drug offenders who belong to wealthy and well-known families, even when their cases involved large-scale trafficking networks (Al-Akhbar, 2013). These inequalities have been the subject of grassroots and lobbying work by several NGOs. Civil society organisations are one of the progressive faces of Lebanon's drug policy. The leading actors in this field are Skoun, which provides welfare consultation and primary medical care to drug users, beside lobbying in favour of drugs policy reform; Ajam, which works in the contexts of prisons and assist drug abusers, and their families during and following their release; SIDC, which operates psychological services and primary harm reduction in popular neighbourhoods; and the Middle East and North Africa Harm Reduction Association, the region's hub for drug policy reform.

The NGOs provide harm reduction services to drug users, including methadone substitution. In the absence of a programmatic engagement by public institutions, the NGOs fill the void. One feature of Lebanese civil society is its great activism. Advocacy and lobbying are used in order to introduce new debates in the public sphere. For example, a recent parliamentary meeting was convened around decriminalisation of drug use after Skoun and Legal Agenda's public campaign. A draft proposal amending the 1998 Law was sent to Parliament and it was discussed at a roundtable hosted in the parliament's Human Rights Committee. The proposal included the adoption of alternatives to incarceration for drug users, with an emphasis on individual cases rather than a one-size-fits-all mandatory treatment. The proposal was met with opposition from the Head of anti-Narcotics, Ghassan Chamseddine, who accused it of being a disguise for condoning recreational drug use (*The Daily Star*, 2017). The draft proposal received the support of the Ministry of Health.

The extent of drug use in Lebanon remains unclear. The capital, Beirut, remains the only place in the country where people seeking treatment can find welfare support, often through private channels. In the south, the territory is mostly dominated by the political branch of the Hezbollah movement. Anecdotal information hints at a recent rise in substance abuse in the southern countryside, especially following the return of militia fighters from the civil war in Syria, where Hezbollah has had a decisive role in fighting both Syrian rebel forces and Islamic State units. The social dimension of drug abuse is covered up by the organisation, but media affiliated to Hezbollah as well as Hezbollah-elected municipalities have recently adopted more nuanced approaches towards drug abuse (Interview with Mayor of Nabatiyyeh, 2017). The moral stigma of drug use is downplayed, medicalisation is used as an interpretative frame and religious recovery is stressed as a palliative support but not a panacea (Interview with Mayor of Nabatiyyeh, 2017). The militant movement has also been open to further reform of drug laws, including the possibility of decriminalisation. Whether this is influenced by the 'progressive' stance of Hezbollah's ideological patron, the Islamic Republic, is unclear. Opposed to medicalisation and decriminalisation are groups belonging to the religious therapeutic movement. The most influential are Oum al-Nour, a Christian Maronite charity, and Cenacle de la Lumière, founded by a Christian mission, which reject OST programmes and call for a 'a drug-free world' (CDLL, n.d.). There are similarities with Pentecostal groups in Latin America, with 'religio-therapy' being on the rise in the MENA.

In conclusion, the Lebanese case demonstrates how policy development about illicit drugs is not simply impinged by Islamist discourses or, for that matter, religious ideology. It is the result of broader political questions, which touch upon the role and strength of the state and the capacity to engage with political cadres among civil society groups.

Saudi Arabia: Princes, Foreign Workers and the Status Quo

In 2016, Saudi Arabia was elected to the board of the United Nations Human Rights Committee. After China and Iran, Saudi Arabia ranks third in the world for the number of executions. Drug offenders constitute half of the overall number of executions, which between 2014 and 2015 numbered about one in every two days. Of the 1,072 people executed between 1985 and 2015, about 48.5% were foreign nationals, a fact that is evidence of the selective punishment applying to criminal prosecution – and particularly drug offences – in the country (Amnesty, 2015). After all, as mentioned earlier in the chapter, Saudi princes have repeatedly been caught with huge quantities of illicit drugs, without facing charges. Drug (ab)use has also prompted significant power shifts: in summer 2017, the dismissal of Mohammd bin Nayef (MbN), then Crown Prince, was allegedly justified by

King Salman and his favourite son Mohammad bin Salman (MbS), because of his painkiller addiction (Reuters, 2017). Following an Al-Qaeda attack in his palace in 2009, MbN had lived with chronic pain, which he treated with morphine and other painkillers. Unable to get off the drug even following special treatment in Switzerland, the King used his substance disorder to dismiss him in favour of MbS (Middle East Eye, 2017).

Beyond the palace, Saudi domestic legislation targets the large community of foreign workers, which numbers above nine million of the country's 32 million population, 30% of the entire population). Western workers are not generally targeted by this policy; they can access alcohol and drugs as long as they consume it in strictly private settings or at the underground party scene connected to the Saudi royal family. According to an Amnesty International researcher in Saudi Arabia, many of the execution sentences come 'arbitrarily', based on local governors' considerations of the total number of punishment or as a deterrent against crimes such as drug offences (*The Independen*t, 2013). On the moderately positive side, the Saudi anti-drug law maintains the anonymity of convicted drug users (Al-Shazly & Tinasti, 2016), given the strict moral code that exists in Saudi society. This probably saves the face of more prominent drug offenders.

Discrimination and repression of drug consumption is further complemented by the Saudi authorities' approach to HIV/AIDS and people living with HIV (PLHIV). The country has implemented a screening programme to identify the presence of HIV, making it a national priority. Saudi harm reduction policy, however, consists in the deportation of PLHIV, if these are foreign nationals, or in their arrest and punishment, if Saudi citizens. Budgetary allocation is also concentrated in furtherance of this screening policy, which de jure and de facto criminalises PLHIV. Calls from international and regional advocacy organisations, such as MENAHRA, have fallen on deaf ears. Locally, there are no effective civil society groups engaging in drugs policy debates; hence, there is no political interest in introducing harm reduction (MENAHRA, 2017).

The national legislation on illicit drugs was approved in 2005, mostly reinstating the status quo prohibition, which includes also that of alcoholic drinks. As said earlier, ATS represent the bulk of drug consumption in Saudi Arabia, although there are no clear data on this subject (Robins, 2016). ATS seizure comprises up to 25% of global seizures, which itself indicates the huge demand for stimulants in the peninsula (*World Drug Report*, 2009), though this may also be due to Saudi Arabia being a transhipment point between Southeast Asia and Europe. The number of people admitted to treatment for ATS abuse has also steadily increased since the year 2000. For example, a specialised treatment hospital (Dammam) has seen a ninefold increase between 1998 and 2006 (*World Drug Report*, 2009). Availability of treatment is very limited and, at the top end of the class hierarchy, it may occur in private clinics or, more likely, abroad (Camino Recovery, n.d.). Residential and in-patient detoxification are the sole option for opioid users, with three centres being available (Alam-mehrjerdi, 2016). Foreign workers cannot access treatment; if they are found consuming or being addicted to drugs, they are jailed or deported (AbuMadini, Rahim, Al-Zahrani, & Al-Johi, 2008; Bassiony, 2013). Detoxification remains the only available option in Saudi Arabia. The country's powerful theologians, who are charged with the approval of domestic legislation, have declared harm reduction practices, such NEP and OST, not compatible with Islamic Law (*shari'a*). Despite the recent attempts at introducing timid social reforms, such as the right to drive for Saudi female citizens, it is unlikely for there to be a major step for future development in drugs policy.

It is not only the strict interpretation of Islamic law that prevents policy development. Saudi Arabia remains one of the few absolute monarchies on the planet. The narrowly top-down structure of power exits in an enormous and complex state bureaucracy, which has weak technical expertise and relies on foreign consultants for key tasks. This lack of local knowledge/expertise remains a major impediment to the formulation of localised responses to changing drug phenomena, such as the current ATS spike. In a short time, the hidden ATS using population might require a more drastic intervention, which might put the authorities in Riyadh face to face with controversial decisions and the need to acknowledge publicly the failure of strict prohibition. This is further exacerbated by the quasi-absence of independent civil society and pressure groups, a fact that widens the gap between those in power and the social dynamics of drugs. This remains a structural void within the Saudi political ecosystem, despite recent promises of reforming Saudi society by the Crown Prince Mohammad Bin Salman, a rhetorical call that so far has resulted in the concentration of power in his own hands and the arrest of dissident voices.

Conclusions

Islam alone is not the source of drug policy conservativism in the MENA. Islamic countries have adopted different measures and strategies, partly because of their local drug environments, partly because of public order considerations. It is a matter of fact that Islamic jurisprudence considers intoxication as a problematic affair, but situational interpretation remains a key to the judgement. It is superficial to argue that Islam considers drugs as *haram*, 'religiously prohibited', as several commentators on the subject, including scholars from the Muslim world, have argued (Kamarulzaman & Saifuddeen, 2010). There is ample flexibility in interpreting what is legal and what is prohibited, and interpretation remains a prerogative of the jurists' hermeneutical approach, which in certain cases is updated from time to time. Substances (and acts) that are *haram* for one jurist may not be so for another. More cogently, in Islamic jurisprudence, it is the circumstances that make something *haram* or *halal*, not the object, the act, the substance per se. Reconsidering under what circumstances narcotics and stimulants are *haram* or not is a key track for investigating drug policy development in the region and the position of Muslim majority countries in the international scene. Medicalisation of formerly illegal drugs may be the potential outcome of the acceptance of new circumstances under which drug use is legitimated.

In the Islamic Republic of Iran, for example, methadone, a narcotic substance, and opium tincture are legitimately administered to registered users, with the approval of religious authorities. Recent studies have also suggested that there is potential acceptance among religious scholars of medical cannabis use (Ghiabi et al., 2018). More importantly, one should be remindful that strict drug prohibition was initially adopted during the rule of secular-minded regimes in the MENA, as exemplified by Egypt's anti-narcotic strategy under Jamal 'abd al-Nasser, Pahlavi Iran's ban on opium in 1955 or Turkey's successive ban on opium (Ghiabi, 2018a; Robins, 2016). Prohibition of drugs in the first place occurred using the language of modernisation (and westernisation). It addressed opium *also* because the poppy was seen as an inherently backward Oriental crop, which impeded the leap forward towards the future (Ghiabi, 2018a). That said, it is equally important to bear in mind that public codes of morality in Muslim majority countries tend to condemn 'intoxication' regardless of the substance consumed, whether legal or prescribed. Accordingly, ordinary police forces have the authority to reprimand or punish people found intoxicated, including with non-scheduled substances.

The logistics of police intervention varies as the powers of the police in the Middle East – and worldwide – tend to be discretionary, especially vis à vis illegal drugs. The parameters at play here are influenced by perceptions of class, social status, ethnic identity and public appearance as well luck and statistical opportunism, in cases where law enforcement needs to boost up arrest numbers. To some extent, this same logic applies to the provision of harm reduction programmes in those contexts where it is the law of the land. For example, in the Islamic Republic of Iran, there is a marked discrepancy between the quality and extent of harm reduction in the capital Tehran and the periphery (a fact that is valid beyond harm reduction). Harm reduction has been scaled up nationwide and; it is available across Iran's major cities (Mashhad, Shiraz, Kerman, Yazd, Tabriz) as well as major provincial towns. However, in the spatially extensive countryside, provision of services remains scant and perfunctory. A similar pattern is found in Lebanon where harm reduction is mainly restricted to Beirut, the capital.

In Saudi Arabia, the application of the law is even more drastically informed by power considerations, with members of the ruling elite (a numerous group of individuals) benefitting from exemptions from the draconian drug laws and special access to treatment in foreign private clinics. Despite the media frenzy over the Crown Prince Mohammad bin Salman's supposedly 'progressive' take on social issues, the kingdom maintains an austere approach towards substance use.

One should be careful in interpreting as Islamic each and every policy development that occurs in the MENA region, since this approach ignores historical transformations and complex social dynamics in the last 100 years. After all, 'a drug-free world' is a slogan embraced by strongly secular states such as the former Soviet Union and the People's Republic of China as well as by many Christian groups across the world (Ghiabi, 2018b). This too should make drug policy scholars re-think their engagement with the MENA region and the Islamic world at large. As stated earlier, governments in the Islamic world may re-evaluate the category of *haram* and the circumstances under which it applies, but in order for this to happen, there is need for a political avant-garde which opens up the public debate around illegal drugs. In countries where this debate exists, such as Iran and Lebanon, policy development has the potential to succeed.

If one needed to position the three countries under analysis along a continuum of drugs policy, the result would be the following: at the conservative/regressive end of the line, there would be Saudi Arabia, where reform of drugs policy remains unlikely or even unthinkable (Middle East Eye, 2017; Reuters, 2017); Lebanon would share the centre/moderate ground, with a potential shift towards reform, although hampered by geopolitical instability and lack of state resources and coherence; the Islamic Republic of Iran would be located on the progressive end, especially in light of the abolition of the death penalty for drug traffickers and the debate about state regulation of cannabis and opiates, and a maintenance system for heroin users through safe injection sites. A key element remains state capacity and the ability to project legislative reforms across the social body and spatial territory of drugs policy. To this, one should add also the readiness of social agents to reproduce policy reforms through civil society endeavours which legitimate organically changes in policy.

Reforms at the domestic level in Iran and Lebanon might not lead to a new stance in the international settings. The Islamic Republic of Iran has been consistent in its rhetorical condemnation of illicit drugs and; in this stance, it shares the vision of the Saudi counterparts. Part of this duplicity between international rhetoric and domestic dynamics is the result of differing views among public officials. While Iran is often represented by security and law enforcement officials at the CND and UN venues, at the domestic level the debate is enlivened by the participation of academics, scientists and the medical community, who have a nuanced understanding of the 'drug problem'. Were Iran and Lebanon to introduce new policies with regard to cannabis and opium – including state cultivation, recreational use or maintenance plans – they might be accused of breaking the international drug conventions. In the current geopolitical climate, they might be further isolated both vis à vis regional prohibitionist countries (Egypt, GCC and Turkey) and internationally (Russia, China and the United States).

However, there is no coordinated stance among the three case studies when it comes to international negotiations. Iran and Saudi Arabia are at odds on many fronts and narco-diplomacy cannot bridge their disputes for the time being. Lebanon remains in between these two countries and the relative push for reform at the domestic level can hardly turn into a clear-cut diplomatic stance. Diplomatic inertia remains the easiest way forward in all the three cases and, per extension, across the MENA and Islamic world. But this should be confused with an Islamic block and a monolithic drugs policy model.

Change in drugs policy is obstinate and slow, until it takes place as a breakthrough. That applies to the Middle East too.

References

AbuMadini, M. S., Rahim, S. I., Al-Zahrani, M. A., & Al-Johi, A. O. (2008). Two decades of treatment seeking for substance use disorders in Saudi Arabia: Trends and patterns in a rehabilitation facility in Dammam. *Drug and Alcohol Dependence*, *97*(3), 231–236.

Afsahi, K. (2009). *Les producteurs de cannabis dans le Rif-Maroc: Étude d'une activité économique à risque*. Ph.D. thesis, Université de Lille 1, Villeneuve-d'Ascq, France.

Afsahi, K. (2015). Are Moroccan cannabis growers able to adapt to recent European market trend? *International Journal of Drug Policy*, *26*(3), 327–329.

Al-Akhbar. (2013, May 30). Lebanon: Drug Ring Exposes Corruption of Justice System. Retrieved from http://english.al-akhbar.com/node/15959

Alam-mehrjerdi, Z., Roya, N., & Kate, D. (2016). Opioid use, treatment and harm reduction services: First report from the Persian Gulf region. *Journal of Substance Use 21*(2) (2016), 217–223.

Al-Araby. (2015, August 17). Addiction Rife among Syrian Victims of War. Retrieved from https://www.alaraby.co.uk/english/features/2015/8/17/addiction-rife-among-syrian-victims-of-war

Al-Shazly, F., & Khalid, T. (2016). Incarceration or mandatory treatment: Drug use and the law in the Middle East and North Africa. *International Journal of Drug Policy 31*(2016), 172–177.

Amnesty International. (2017). *Death sentences and executions 2016*. London. Retrieved from https://www.amnesty.org/en/documents/act50/5740/2017/en/

BBC News.com. (2013, November 13). Afghanistan opium harvest at record high - UNODC. Retrieved from http://www.bbc.com/news/world-asia-24919056

BBC News.com. (2015, November 2). Lebanon charges Saudi prince with drug smuggling. Retrieved from http://www.bbc.com/news/world-middle-east-34700489

Behrouzan, O. (2015). Writing Prozāk Diaries in Tehran: Generational anomie and psychiatric subjectivities. *Culture, Medicine, and Psychiatry*, *39*(3), 399–426.

Belpiero, M. (2014). *Il Fiore Perduto: La cultura del Papaver somniferum nell'area del Mediterraneo*. Ph.D. thesis, Università di Genoa, Genoa, Italy.

Bigo, D., & Annie, L. (1991). Guerre et drogue au Liban. Entretien avec Antoine Boustany. *Cultures & Conflits*, *03*(1991), 99–104.

Chawla, S. U. (2010). World drug report 2010. New York, NY: United Nations Publication.

Camino Recovery. (n.d.). Drug Alcohol Rehab Saudi Arabia. Retrieved from https://www.caminorecovery.com/drug-alcohol-rehab-saudi-arabia. Accessed on November 3, 2017.

Carrier, N., & Klantschnig, G. (2018). Quasilegality: khat, cannabis and Africa's drug laws. *Third World Quarterly*, *39*(2), 350–365.

CDLL (n.d.). About us. Retrieved from http://www.cenacledelalumiere.org/about.php. Accessed on February 1, 2018.

Chouvy, P. A. (2009). *Opium: Uncovering the politics of the poppy*. Cambridge, MA: Harvard University Press.

Chouvy, P. A., & Afsahi, K. (2014). Hashish revival in Morocco. *International Journal of Drug Policy*, *25*(3), 416–423.

Christensen, J. B.. (2017). Human rights and wrongs in Iran's drug diplomacy with Europe. *The Middle East Journal 71*(3), 403–432.

CNN (2010, June 23). Does Saudi have world's biggest amphetamine habit? Retrieved from http://edition.cnn.com/2010/WORLD/meast/07/23/middle.east.drugs.amphetamine/index.html

DCHQ. (2016). *Drugs Policy in Iran*. Tehran: DCHQ Publications. Retrieved from http://dchq.ir/en/images/portal-e/reports/dc2016.pdf

Eskandarieh, S., Jafari, F., Yazdani, S., Hazrati, N., & Saberi-Zafarghandi, M. B. (2014). Compulsory maintenance treatment program amongst iranian injection drug users and its side effects. *International Journal of High Risk Behaviors & Addiction, 3*(4).

Farrell, G., & Thorne, J. (2005). Where have all the flowers gone? Evaluation of the Taliban crackdown against opium poppy cultivation in Afghanistan. *International Journal of Drug Policy, 16*(2), 81–91.

Fars. (2013, December 28). UNODC Envoy Hails Iran for Anti-Drug Campaign Efforts. Retrieved from http://en.farsnews.com/newstext.aspx?nn=13921007001465

Foreign Policy. (2015, October 26). Saudi Arabia's Royal Drug Problem. Retrieved from http://foreignpolicy.com/2015/10/26/saudi-arabias-royal-drug-problem/

Ghiabi, M. (2015). Drugs and revolution in Iran: Islamic devotion, revolutionary zeal and republican means. *Iranian Studies 48*(2), 139–163.

Ghiabi, M. (2018). Maintaining disorder: the micropolitics of drugs policy in Iran. *Third world quarterly, 39*(2), 277–297.

Ghiabi, M. (2018a). The opium of the state: Local and global drug prohibition in Iran, 1941–1979. In Alvandi R. (Ed.), *The age of Aryamehr: Late Pahlavi Iran and its global entanglements*. London: Gingko Press.

Ghiabi, M. (2018b). Spirit and being: interdisciplinary reflections on drugs across history and politics. *Third World Quarterly, 39*(2), 207–217.

Ghiabi, M., Maarefand, M., Bahari, H., & Alavi, Z. (2018). Islam and cannabis: Legalisation and religious debate in Iran. *International Journal of Drug Policy, 56*, 121–127.

Gingeras, R. (2012). Poppy politics: American agents, Iranian addicts and Afghan opium, 1945–80. *Iranian Studies, 45*(3), 315–331.

Gingeras, R. (2013). Istanbul confidential: Heroin, espionage, and politics in cold war Turkey, 1945–1960. *Diplomatic History, 37*(4), 779–806.

Hudson, M. C. (1985). *The precarious republic: Political modernization in Lebanon*. London: Random House.

IDCP. (2011, June 20). Lebanese Drug Law between Text and Implementation. Retrieved from http://idpc.net/publications/2011/07/lebanese-drug-law-between-text-and-implementation

Interview with Elie Aaraj. (2017). Director of the Middle East and North African Harm Reduction Association (MENAHRA), Beirut.

IRNA. (2011, July 7). علل تغییر الگوی مصرف مواد مخدر از سنتی به صنعتی. The cause behind the shift in consumption model from traditional to industrial drugs. Retrieved from http://www.irna.ir/fa/News/2000241559

Kamarulzaman, A., & Saifuddeen, S. M. (2010). Islam and harm reduction. *International Journal of Drug Policy 21*(2), 115–118.

League of Nations. (1925). Records of the Second Opium Conference – Volume I – Plenary Meetings Text of the Debates, Geneva, 17 November 1924–19 February 1925.

Marshall, J. (2012). *The Lebanese connection: Corruption, civil war, and the international drug traffic*. Palo Alto, CA: Stanford University Press.

MENAHRA. (2017) *Harm reduction in the MENA*. Retrieved from http://www.menahra.org/en/menahra-publications/publications

Middle East Eye. Saudi Mohammad bin Nayef deposed over painkiller drug addiction (2017, July 19). Retrieved from http://www.middleeasteye.net/news/saudis-mohammed-bin-nayef-deposed-over-painkiller-drug-addiction-report-379525031.

Moghanibashi-Mansourieh, A., & Deilamizade, A. (2014). The state of data collection on addiction in Iran. *Addiction*, *109*(5), 854–854.

Nahas, G. G. (1985). Hashish and drug abuse in Egypt during the 19th and 20th centuries. *Bulletin of the New York Academy of Medicine*, *61*(5), 428.

NOW. (2014, June 26). Lebanon's war on drugs. Retrieved from https://now.mmedia.me/lb/en/reportsfeatures/553371-lebanons-war-on-drugs.

Reuters. (2014, May 20). Lebanon's cannabis farms flourish while army looks away. Retrieved from https://www.reuters.com/article/us-lebanon-cannabis/lebanons-cannabis-farms-flourish-while-army-looks-away-idUSKBN0E01CG20140520

Reuters. (2017, 19 July). Addiction and intrigue: Inside the Saudi palace coup. Retrieved from https://www.reuters.com/article/us-saudi-palace-coup/addiction-and-intrigue-inside-the-saudi-palace-coup-idUSKBN1A41IS

Robins, P. (2013). *Middle East drugs bazaar: Production, prevention and consumption*. Oxford: Oxford University Press

Robins, P. (2016). *Middle East drugs bazaar: production, prevention and consumption*. Oxford: Oxford University Press, 2016.

Rolles, S. (2017). Reflection on the UN General Assembly Special Session on drugs: One year on. *Drugs and Alcohol Today*, *17*(2), 74–80.

Tasnim. (2016, October 5). فایده‌ای ندارد. ۵۶ درصد زندانیان معتادند/بازداشت معتادان هیچ 65% of prisoners is addicted. Arresting addicts is no utility. Retrieved from https://www.tasnimnews.com/fa/news/1395/07/14/1204138/65

The Daily Star. (2014, December 9). Lebanon agriculture minister urges legalization export of cannabis. Retrieved from http://www.dailystar.com.lb/News/Lebanon-News/2014/Dec-19/281649-lebanon-agriculture-minister-urges-legalization-export-of-cannabis.ashx

The Daily Star. (2016, October 26). Tripoli Captagon Bust highlights rising trend. Retrieved from http://www.dailystar.com.lb/News/Middle-East/2016/Oct-26/378178-tripoli-captagon-bust-highlights-rising-trend.ashx

The Daily Star. (2017, 25 March). Lebanon police bust drug trafficking network. Retrieved from http://www.dailystar.com.lb/News/Lebanon-News/2017/Mar-25/399180-lebanon-police-bust-drug-trafficking-network.ashx

The Fix. The Needle and the Crescent: the remarkable rise of NA in Iran. (2014, July 4). Retrieved from http://www.thefix.com/content/Iran-Narcotics-Anonymous-phonemoneon-Lavitt2099).

The Independent. (2013, October). Saudi Arabia: how the kingdom treats the people its is going to execute. Retrieved from http://www.independent.co.uk/news/world/middle-east/saudi-arabia-how-the-kingdom-treats-the-people-it-is-going-to-execute-a6692671.html

The Independent. (2015, 27 October). Saudi prince caught up in drugs bust: lucky the incident happened in Beirut. Retrieved from http://www.independent.co.uk/voices/saudi-prince-caught-up-in-drugs-bust-lucky-the-incident-happened-in-beirut-a6711076.html

Traboulsi, F. (2007). *A history of modern Lebanon*. London: Pluto Press.

UNODC. (2010). World Drug Report 2010 (United Nations Publication, Sales No. E.10.XI.13UNODC. (2015). 'Remarks at 32nd International Drug Enforcement Conference', June 2, 2015. Retrieved from https://www.unodc.org/unodc/en/speeches/2015/remarks-at-the-32nd-international-conference-on-drugs--cartagena-.html

United Nations Office on Drugs and Crime. (2016). World Drug Report 2016 (United Nations publication, Sales No. E.16.XI.7.

VOA. (2015, November 6). Captagon breaking bad in Saudi Arabia. Retrieved from https://www.voanews.com/a/captagon-breaking-bad-in-saudi-arabia/3044225.html

Chapter 9

Breaking Ranks: Pioneering Drug Policy Protagonism in Uruguay and Bolivia

Jonas von Hoffmann

Abstract

Both Bolivia and Uruguay broke ranks with the global drug prohibition regime by introducing novel drug policies. State control of the production and supply of coca and cannabis represents a clear departure from both the spirit and the letter of the international drug conventions. Although, the rationale, processes and outcomes of policy change were distinctive in many regards, this chapter posits that there are conceptual resemblances. In both countries, the leadership of a charismatic and idiosyncratic president has to be considered. Furthermore, in both countries, mobilisation and activism were also decisive. Lastly, in both countries novel drug policy responded to specific problems that decision-makers faced. Approaching drug policy reforms in Bolivia and Uruguay in terms of personal leadership, mobilisation and policy problems provides a useful analytical first-cut to assess the continuity and change in drug policy observable elsewhere. Additionally, scrutinising the reasons and motivations for undertaking drug policy reform also allows to better understand each country's behaviour on the international stage.

Keywords: Drug policy reform; Latin America; Bolivia; Uruguay; Coca; Cannabis

In 2011, Bolivia took the unprecedented step of withdrawing from the United Nations (UN) Conventions, to later re-join with a reservation for the coca leaf. In doing so, it followed-up on already having instituted 'social control' of coca leaf production domestically. In 2013, Uruguay legally regulated its domestic cannabis market. Both Uruguay and Bolivia, then, are examples of the group of countries

Collapse of the Global Order on Drugs: From UNGASS 2016 to Review 2019, 191–216

doi:10.1108/978-1-78756-487-920181009

'establishing open drug markets' (Klein & Stothard, Introduction). Both small Latin American nations undertook their pioneering drug policy reforms during a time that has seen an increased questioning of *status quo* drug policy (Fordham & Haase, Chapter 1). Both broke ranks by challenging the logic and consensus underlying the long-dominant prohibitionist global drug policy regime (Bewley-Taylor, 2012).

Despite this, there are substantive differences between the changes in drug policy in Uruguay and Bolivia. First, cannabis and coca are different substances. Their position in the international drug commodity chain and the social significance in each country are not easily comparable. Additionally, Bolivia and Uruguay pursued distinct strategies and goals on the international stage. Bolivia had tried for years to 'legalise' the coca leaf, pro-actively challenging the Conventions, whereas Uruguay reactively devised a defence to shield its cannabis reform. Uruguay sought changes *within* and Bolivia *of* the global drug control regime.

Unsurprisingly, there are differing specific reasons when it comes to why each country pursued innovative drug control policies. Despite this, the present chapter posits that there are conceptual resemblances. In both countries, the leadership of a charismatic and idiosyncratic president has to be considered. While no account is complete without contemplating Evo Morales and José 'Pepe' Mujica's personal involvement, in both countries reforms were not simply the result of 'top-down' processes, but mobilisation and activism were also decisive. Furthermore, in both countries, novel drug policy responded to specific problems that decision-makers faced.

Substantiating this argument, the chapter proceeds as follows, dealing with the Bolivian and Uruguayan cases in turn. First, it describes the elements of drug policy. Second, it scrutinises the countries' actions on the international stage. Third, it presents the reasons for drug policy reform in a structured, yet inevitably incomplete, way by assessing the contribution of personal leadership, pressure through mobilisation and the *problematique* represented by coca or cannabis, respectively. The conclusion draws together the various strands of these arguments, highlighting both the differences and similarities of Uruguay and Bolivia's pioneering drug policy protagonism that led them to break rank with global drug prohibition.

Drug Policy Protagonism in Bolivia

With the election of Evo Morales in 2005, Bolivia's drug policy markedly changed (Farthing & Kohl, 2014; Grisaffi, 2016; Ledebur & Youngers, 2006). In contrast to previous forced eradication, the Morales administration promoted cooperative coca reduction to reduce the amount of coca destined for the illicit cocaine market (Farthing & Kohl, 2010, 2012; Grisaffi & Ledebur, 2016). The 'coca yes, cocaine no' policy is shaped by the leaf's centrality in indigenous cultures, rooted in respect for indigenous rights, and based on the inclusion of coca growers (Farthing & Kohl, 2012; Farthing & Ledebur, 2015; Telleria Escobar, 2013).

The goal of the Morales' government was to take back control over the country's drug policies, as part of a broader effort to 'nationalise' and 'decolonise' Bolivian politics (Roncken & de Acha, 2015). Bolivia turned from being a passive recipient of coca control policies to becoming its 'own anti-narcotics policy maker' and 'active player' in the international arena, trying to promote the global acceptance of the coca leaf (Hesselroth, 2015, p. 91).

Coca and its Forced Eradication

The coca leaf has been grown in Bolivia for millennia, for use in traditional medicine, social interactions, spiritual rituals and commercial trade (Farthing & Ledebur, 2015; Rivera Cusicanqui, 2011; South, 1977). Bolivia is a country in which coca consumption is so prevalent that 'even soldiers chew the leaf during coca eradication missions' (Farthing & Ledebur, 2004). Coca cultivation is not only culturally important but also represents an important economic activity (Farthing & Kohl, 2005).

Despite the importance of the coca leaf, subsequent Bolivian governments have attempted to eradicate its cultivation. As part of the US-led 'war on drugs', Bolivia has implemented policies to limit and destroy coca cultivation and cocaine production (Painter, 1994). As Farthing and Ledebur (2004) note, 'Washington dictates how the war on drugs will be fought in Bolivia and controls the purse strings.' For the United States, supply-side anti-narcotic policies in the form of eradication have been the weapon of choice (Boville, 2004). With the collaboration of domestic elites, repressive and draconian anti-drug policies were implemented (Menzel, 1997).

In 1988, Law 1008 came into effect, which delineated which coca in what areas would be designated for eradication (Congreso Nacional, 1988). On one hand, Law 1008 recognised traditional uses and domestic consumption of the coca leaf and established 12,000 hectares as 'traditional growing zones'. On the other hand, it called for the eradication of any other cultivation in 'transitional' and 'illicit' zones. Thus, while coca grown in the *Yungas*, east of La Paz, was mostly left alone, coca fields in the *Chapare* region have been frequently targeted.

This forced eradication has led to manifold violent confrontations between coca growers and eradicators (Kohl & Farthing, 2001). Temporary gains in eradicated coca resulted in well-documented human rights violations (HRW, 1996; Petterson & Mackay, 1993; Williams, 1997). Overall, however, counternarcotic programs in Bolivia have had little impact on region-wide cocaine production or prices and purity in consumer countries (Laserna, 2011).

A Novel Approach: Social Control

Once in power, president Morales' administration laid out its new coca policy in the *Estrategia de lucha contra el narcotráfico y revalorización dela hoja de coca* (2006). The strategy has several notable elements. First, it raised the ceiling of permitted coca production to 20,000 hectares, and, second, extended permitted coca cultivation to the *Chapare* region. By not being required to eradicate their coca bushes before providing development aid, coca growers have been afforded greater flexibility in experimenting with planting alternative cash crops (Grisaffi, 2016). The new approach included promises of increasing demand for alternative coca products, such as tea, flours, and toothpastes to absorb cultivated coca leaves (Ledebur & Farthing, 2014).

The central element of the new policy is 'social' or 'community' control. Coca growers agree to eliminate coca, in excess of the *cato*, an area of 1,600 m^2, and cooperate with authorities. This 'innovative community-led control scheme' works to limit the amount of coca cultivated based on voluntary 'rationalisation' (Farthing & Kohl, 2010, p. 198). Coca grower organisations are enlisted to limit cultivation. Rather than seeing them as enemies, the Morales administration gives them an integral role in self-policing (Farthing & Kohl, 2010, 2012; Farthing & Ledebur, 2015). As a government representative explained: 'We decided to leave the machine guns, the bullets and the bombs behind. We opted to include coca growing communities in the debate and analysis that created our policies' (cited in Ledebur & Farthing, 2014).

The active participation of coca growers is a key to the success of 'social control' and has greatly enhanced their sense of policy ownership, with many *cocaleros* 'describing community control of coca as "theirs"' (Farthing & Ledebur, 2015, p. 27). With good reason, coca growers perceive the policy as something they have fought and died for (Grisaffi, 2016). Cooperative control makes the whole community responsible for limiting coca cultivation to the *cato*. Formal and informal sanctions are imposed by the coca growers to eliminate coca exceeding the permitted amount (Farthing & Kohl, 2014). Non-compliance has both material and reputational consequences (Grisaffi, 2016). As one *cocalero* states: 'If you go to the town hall and your union has not respected the *cato*, it's like having a criminal record. No one will meet with you' (cited in Farthing & Ledebur, 2015, p. 35).

Further measures bolster 'social control'. A sophisticated system of biometric registration, satellite surveillance of coca plots, titling of land and registration of parcels has accompanied community control (Farthing & Ledebur, 2015; Grisaffi & Ledebur, 2016; Ledebur & Youngers, 2012). Many of those in charge of coca policy have a background as cultivators (Farthing & Ledebur, 2015) and remain close to the *cocaleros* (Grisaffi, 2016). The importance of coca for the Morales administration is further highlighted by the new 2009 constitution, which establishes in Article 384 that 'the state will protect traditional coca as cultural patrimony, natural resource representative of Bolivia's biodiversity and matter of social cohesion' (Asamblea Constituyente, 2009).

Although it has minimised the involvement of the military, social control has not led to the cessation of fighting cocaine production and trafficking (Farthing & Kohl, 2010; Grisaffi, 2016; Ledebur & Youngers, 2012). Part and parcel of the new approach to coca is the clear distinction between coca and cocaine. Embodied by the notion of 'coca sí, cocaina no', Bolivia has tried to minimise the harms generated by supply-side counter-narcotic programmes, while at the same time continuing to combat cocaine production (Farthing & Kohl, 2012).

While Bolivia has been strongly criticised by the United States and continuously been 'decertified' (Pearson & Grisaffi, 2014), the United Nations Development Programme (UNDP) and the European Union have praised Bolivia's efforts to reduce and control coca cultivation (Youngers & Ledebur, 2015). Many observers share such positive assessments, pointing not only to the reduction of areas under coca cultivation but also the reduction of violence associated with coca control (Farthing & Kohl, 2012; Farthing & Ledebur, 2015; Ledebur & Youngers, 2013). While Bolivia's new drug policy is 'no panacea' (Farthing & Kohl, 2012, p. 493), Bolivian drug policy innovation has helped curtail the negative consequences of forced eradication, made growers valued policy share-holders and has largely succeeded in controlling cultivation.

Taking on the Conventions

On the international level, Bolivia has long been critical of the treatment of coca by the international drug conventions and has sought the acceptance of the legal cultivation of the coca leaf and traditional uses. In international fora, Bolivia argued that there was a need to re-examine coca's status as a dangerous narcotic under the UN Conventions and took its message of 'coca yes, cocaine no' around the world, campaigning to elicit support (Ledebur & Youngers, 2008b; Lorenzo & Rodriguez, 2011). However, both attempts to reclassify the coca leaf and efforts to amend the Single Convention were unsuccessful (Bewley-Taylor, 2016; Jelsma, 2011; Metaal et al., 2006).[1] Influential actors in international drug control, such as the International Narcotics Control Board (INCB) and the United States were staunchly opposed to any changes (Ledebur & Youngers, 2008b).[2] However, simply rejecting it did not make Bolivia's initiative disappear.

Having failed with these previous efforts, the Morales administration changed tack. Instead of attempting to achieve 'a high degree of legal change' by changing the international classification of coca, Bolivia now aimed at 'a lower degree of legal change' by gaining acceptance of domestic coca cultivation and chewing (Pfeiffer, 2013, p. 307). In June 2011, Bolivia became the first country in the world to withdraw from the Single Convention (Bewley-Taylor, 2016; Kim, 2014; Telleria Escobar, 2013). At the same time that Bolivia formally denounced and exited the Single Convention, the Andean nation announced that it would apply to re-accede with a reservation allowing for the traditional use of the coca leaf. To make its case, the Bolivian government argued that it was correcting a historical

[1]For instance, in 2009, Bolivia presented a proposal to delete provisions on coca leaf chewing from the Single Convention, emphasising that it represented 'a sociocultural practices and rituals of the Andean indigenous peoples […] closely linked to [their] history and cultural identity' (Bolivia, 2009). However, 21 countries opposed, and thereby prevented the amendment (Pfeiffer, 2013).

[2]For instance, the 2007 INCB report noted its 'concern' and urged Bolivia to 'formulate and implement … programs aimed at eliminating coca leaf chewing' (INCB, 2008, p. 38). At the 2008 CND, a US delegate stated: 'Coca should be limited as is the case with any other narcotic drug.' (cited in Ledebur & Youngers, 2008b).

mistake, followed the mandate of its new constitution to protect coca chewing as an ancestral practice, and was in line with international treaties calling for the respect for indigenous rights (Boister, 2016).[3]

Four months after denouncing the 1961 Single Convention, Bolivia applied for re-accession (Bolivia, 2011). In doing so, Bolivia followed the proper procedures (Hesselroth, 2015). However, its re-accession was far from a foregone conclusion, as the United States led the opposition to re-joining with a reservation (Ledebur & Youngers, 2012). The United States argued that greater coca production would invariably lead to greater availability of cocaine (Pfeiffer, 2013). Other opponents maintained that Bolivia's efforts would significantly weaken the integrity of the treaties (Youngers, 2013). Despite the vocal opposition of some, a largely silent majority accepted Bolivia's exception. As only 15 countries formally objected to Bolivia's re-accession, the path was cleared for Bolivia to re-join the treaty with a reservation in January 2013 (Boister, 2016). While this represented a symbolic triumph for Bolivia, coca remains illegal outside its borders and is still classified as dangerous narcotic for the rest of the world (Farthing & Kohl, 2014; Ledebur & Youngers, 2013; Telleria Escobar, 2013).

Explaining Drug Policy Protagonism in Bolivia

The emergence of alternative coca policies in Bolivia has elicited much academic attention (Farthing & Kohl, 2010, 2012; Grisaffi, 2010, 2016, 2017; Grisaffi & Ledebur, 2016; Hesselroth, 2015; Ledebur & Youngers, 2013; Norman, 2017; Ramirez & Youngers, 2011; Roncken & de Acha, 2015; Telleria Escobar, 2013). Some ascribe reforms of coca control policies – implicitly or explicitly – to Evo Morales. Morales himself has done much to bolster the perspective of himself as the foremost champion of coca. The coca leaf has long been an important element not only of his rhetoric but also his 'often larger than life' theatrics (Farthing & Kohl, 2014, p. 4). On the international stage, Morales has repeatedly chewed coca leaves in front of perplexed delegates during his speeches (Brocchetto, 2012). In another instance, he recommended the Pope chew coca (Gorbea, 2016). He has long been outspoken in his support of coca and would customarily finish speeches with the *cocaleros'* battle cry in Quechua: '*¡Kausachun coca, wanyachun yanki!*' ('Coca live, Yankee die').

Other authors argue that coca growers' pressure on a sympathetic administration was a key for Bolivia's shift in drug policy. For instance, Norman (2017, p. 37) argues that changes 'resulted from the *cocaleros*' rise to power', and Ochoa (2014, p. 2) contends that *cocaleros* 'altered national coca policies along the way' to power. However, while the Morales administration has promised to be open and

---

[3]In the case of coca cultivation, eradication seems to be incompatible with the respect for and protection of traditional cultural practices of indigenous populations (Pfeiffer, 2013). The 2007 United Nations Declaration on the Rights of Indigenous Peoples establishes several rights that can be construed as defending traditional uses of coca (UN, 2008) and provided Bolivia a powerful argument to make its case (Kim, 2014).

inclusive in its decision making (Anria, 2013; Crabtree & Chaplin, 2013; Harten, 2013), the degree to which Morales is accountable to the movements that brought it to power has been questioned (Grisaffi, 2013; Oikonomakis & Espinoza, 2014; Zuazo, 2010). There are signs that the Morales administration has used 'a mixture of top-down, behind closed door decisions and more participatory elements of direct democracy' (Harten, 2013, p. 203) and has taken decisions 'without much consultation' (Farthing & Kohl, 2014, p. 154). Grisaffi (2017, p. 60) notes that 'rank and file members [of the coca unions] frequently complain that these days "everything comes from the top down ... and it's all Evo, Evo, Evo"'.

A smaller set of authors have highlighted that the specific configuration of Bolivia's 'social control' of coca is the result of a policy conundrum: Morales' personal preferences and demands from coca growers had to be brought in line with requirements of the international community to avoid diversion of coca cultivation to the production of cocaine (Grisaffi, 2010; Ledebur & Youngers, 2008a; Oikonomakis & Espinoza, 2014). Confronted by this problem, the Morales administration came up with the solution of 'coca sí, cocaina no' to both allow the cultivation of coca and the eradication of cocaine (CONALTID, 2006).

Compañero Evo's Personal Leadership

There is tendency to see Bolivia's drug policy from a top-down perspective; as the direct effect of Morales' efforts. While there is a general tendency of speaking of 'Evo's Bolivia' (Farthing & Kohl, 2014), many accounts of Bolivia's drug policy emphasise his personal leadership and protagonism. Efforts to change Bolivia's approach to coca have been called 'Evo Morales' crusade' (Alzamora, 2017), and his 'quest' and 'mission' (Otis, 2011). The country re-acceding the Single Convention in 2013 is characterised as Morales 'winning a victory' (Neuman, 2013) and 'scoring one for the coca leaf' (Rueda, 2013). The coca leaf definitively holds a special importance for Evo Morales. He has grown coca himself, continues to chew the leaf and experienced the violence related to forced eradication first hand (Grisaffi, 2017; Harten, 2013; Sivak, 2010). While he has been personally deeply involved with changing Bolivia's drug policy, and, despite being President, has retained his role as leader of the coca grower's union, it is too facile to see the issue simply as one of personal policy preferences and 'top-down' process.

The Cocaleros' Pressure for Reform

There has long been important pressure from below for alternative coca control policies. *Cocaleros* organised and mobilised to contest the government's anti-coca policies in the 1980s. Criminalisation and eradication of coca cultivation and the concomitant violence led to the formation of strong resistance (Ochoa, 2014). Repressive counter-narcotic programmes created the context of violence from which Bolivia's organised coca growers originate (Castillo Gallardo, 2004; Grisaffi, 2017; Salazar Ortuño, 2012). From initially defending their coca crops, *cocaleros* formed a social movement, launched a political party, and helped elect their leader to be Bolivia's first indigenous President.

The *cocaleros* succeeded in transforming their struggle into a national issue by framing it as resistance against foreign hegemony and defence of traditional values and gained control over rural and labour unions (Grisaffi, 2010; Healy, 1991; Ochoa, 2014). In the process, coca was transformed from being 'no different from any other crop that was grown' (Grisaffi, 2010, p. 432), to a central element of the identity of Bolivia's indigenous population (Mala, 2009).

Cocaleros have relied on hunger strikes, road blockades and protest marches to install the issue of coca on the agenda (Castillo Gallardo & Durand, 2008; Kohl & Farthing, 2001; Spedding, 2004). The most notable instance of successfully pressuring the government occurred in 2004. Reeling from social protests and high levels of unpopularity, President Carlos Mesa agreed to negotiate with the *cocaleros* and allowed them to grow a limited amount of coca known as a *cato* (Farthing & Ledebur, 2004). At least temporarily, President Mesa suspended eradication of 3,200 hectares of coca cultivation (Metaal et al., 2006), thereby changing the direction of Bolivia's drug policy and creating the basis on which the Morales administration would eventually build its novel coca control policy.

However, this success was an exception rather than the rule and reflected the influence coca growers had attained by the mid-2000s. Over the years, subsequent Bolivian governments mostly evidenced intransigence, reacting either with violence or ignoring coca growers' demands (Kohl & Farthing, 2001). To supplement their protest campaign, the *cocaleros* 'in an effort to resist and to defend their right to coca production, deepened their political organization' (Oikonomakis & Espinoza, 2014, p. 292). *Cocaleros* formed a 'political instrument' to compete on the electoral stage and their interests. The *Movimiento al Socialismo* (MAS) emerging in the 1990s, eventually became the country's dominant political force. Its leader, Evo Morales, was elected President in 2005.

'*Cocaleros* gave birth to the MAS' (Anria, 2013, p. 23) and, in turn, the MAS acted as the 'political wing of the *cocalero* unions' (Norman, 2017, p. 30). As political representatives of the coca growers began to occupy elected offices, their presence in formal electoral politics gave *cocaleros* greater visibility and influence. Their 'political instrument' enabled them to challenge drug policy both in the halls of power and in the streets. Although there are indications that, once in power, the Morales administration has grown increasingly distant from its movement roots (Zuazo, 2010), *cocaleros* continue to play an outsized role in national politics. 'Of all the social sectors in Bolivia, President Morales has paid most attention to the concerns of his powerbase located in the *Chapare*' (Grisaffi, 2013, p. 57). The *cocaleros* and their concerns are key for the Morales administration, as they represent a crucial part of the 'support base of the government' (Mala, 2009, p. 112) and constitute its 'core constituencies.' (Anria, 2013, p. 23).

From Problem to Solution: 'Coca Sí, Cocaina No'

The dilemma that the Morales administration faced in designing alternative coca control policies is that 'the coca leaf has gone from being a potent symbol of indigenous identity and anti-imperial resistance to something that has to be controlled' (Grisaffi, 2010, p. 427). Morales and his administration have found themselves between a rock and hard place, 'caught between the demand of their support bases (in *Chapare* especially) to protect coca cultivation and the pressures from the international community to reduce it' (Oikonomakis & Espinoza, 2014, p. 300). Bolivia had to find a way of 'balancing pressures from the international community with the demands of its coca growing constituents' (Ledebur & Youngers, 2008a).

While delivering for *cocaleros*, Morales has had to devise a strategy that allows the government to fight cocaine-production and trafficking, control coca cultivation and prevent an unfettered expansion of not just coca cultivation but cocaine production, thereby being portrayed as a 'narco-state'.[4] This dilemma has long been recognised by Evo Morales: 'There cannot be zero coca, but nor can there be unregulated cultivation of coca … a portion is diverted into drug-trafficking' (BBC News, 2012). Indeed, the Morales government has been at pains to point out that it would not abdicate from its responsibilities to fight cocaine production and trafficking (Hesselroth, 2015). As Vice President Felipe Cáceres highlighted: 'We don't shirk our international obligations. Instead, we proposed a coherent policy, based on our new constitution that fundamentally respects indigenous human rights' (cited in Ledebur & Farthing, 2014).

The required solution would have to be a compromise between the demands of the international community and an important domestic constituency. At the heart of the solution, the Morales government devised, was 'its commitment to Bolivia's international responsibilities regarding drug trafficking while decreasing the violence formerly associated with fighting the "drug war" in Bolivia' (Farthing & Kohl, 2010, p. 210), by clearly distinguishing between coca and cocaine and relying on 'social control' and cooperation rather than adversarial policies and forced eradication. This policy of '*coca sí, cocaina no*' represented Bolivia's pioneering drug policy.

Drug Policy Protagonism in Uruguay

On 20 December 2013, President José 'Pepe' Mujica signed Uruguay's new cannabis legislation into law, establishing complete state control and regulation of cannabis along the commodity chain. Thereby, Uruguay became the first country in the world to legally regulate cannabis from seed to smoke. Uruguayan cannabis regulation has been called 'noteworthy' and 'innovative' (Cerdá & Kilmer, 2017), not only for the process by which it became the law of the land but also its contents (Pardo, 2014; Sanjurjo Garcia, 2014; Walsh & Ramsey, 2015). In terms of process, cannabis reform cleared the legislative process after long and arduous debates (von Hoffmann, 2015c). Uruguay's cannabis reforms 'was approved by politicians, not the voters' (Cerdá & Kilmer, 2017, p. 118). In fact, politicians

[4]Bolivia was deemed to have become a 'narco-state' after the *coup d'état* by Luis García Meza in 1980 because he had close links to drug traffickers (Menzel, 1997). The Morales administration has been acutely aware that being linked to 'narco-traffickers' would do the 'worst damage' possible to its domestic and international legitimacy (Ledebur & Youngers, 2012, p. 12).

from the governing *Frente Amplio* acted against the will of the voters, as public opinion was strongly opposed to making cannabis legally available (Cruz, Queirolo, & Boidi, 2016).

Legally Regulating Cannabis from Seed to Smoke

In terms of substance, Uruguay's new cannabis legislation, as established by *Ley 19.172* and subsequent regulation, encompasses the production, sale and consumption of recreational cannabis. Any cannabis user is legally required to register with state authorities for either one of the exclusive methods of access of cannabis: home cultivation, collective cultivation or commercial sales. Those registered with the government are allowed either grow up to six plants at home, become members in newly formed cannabis social clubs, or buy up to 40 g of cannabis per month in pharmacies (Ley 19.172, 2013 and Decreto Reglementario CM/847, 2014). A newly established government institution, the *Instituto de Regulación y Control del Cannabis* (IRCCA), was established to implement, control and monitor cannabis reform.

Uruguay thus represents a 'middle ground approach to cannabis supply' that falls somewhere between a prohibition and a commercial model (Cerdá & Kilmer, 2017, p. 118). Law 19.172 is 'commercially restrained' with minimal interest in raising tax revenue, rather giving 'a significant role to the state on matters of drug regulation and commercialization' (Walsh & Ramsey, 2015, p. 8). The government tightly controls cannabis production and sale, *inter alia* by setting the price and purity of cannabis being sold, establishing a set of requirements for cannabis social clubs (15–45 members growing up to 99 plants), prohibiting any advertisement and carrying out educational campaigns to reduce cannabis use. Despite the law's 41 pages, cannabis legislation and regulations left many important questions unanswered, to be figured out subsequently.

The Implementation and Effects of Cannabis Reform

Depending on whom one asks, implementation has been 'methodical', 'cautious' and 'deliberate' (Cerdá & Kilmer, 2017; Kreher, 2016; Ramsey, 2016), or an 'improvised' and 'half-baked' mess (Cher, 2016; *El Observador* Editorial, 2016; *El País* Editorial, 2016; Haberkorn, 2014). On some level, slow roll-out has had to do with Uruguay '[f]inding itself in unchartered territory' (Walsh & Ramsey, 2015, p. 12). Simply, there were few experiences to draw on, and it is an inherently complex process to set up and regulate a newly established market and production infrastructure (Pardo, 2015). On another level, there are indications that hesitant implementation might have had to do with the well-documented reservations of newly elected President Tabare Vazquez about legally regulating cannabis (Draper & Müller Sienra, 2017). While the registration of home cultivation and cannabis clubs began in 2014 (von Hoffmann, 2015a), the licensing of cannabis cultivation for commercial sales took longer than anticipated (Ramsey, 2016). When selling cannabis in a handful of locations was finally implemented in July 2017, 'pot was flying off the shelves' until sales were derailed by US banking regulations, which prohibit managing proceeds from illicit narcotics (Londoño, 2017).

The lofty aspirations of Uruguay's 'experiment' in cannabis legislation have been difficult to translate into practice. Regulations on cannabis clubs have been found to be highly burdensome, bringing their long-term viability into question (Queirolo, Boidi, & Cruz, 2016). The mutual exclusivity of home cultivation, club membership and commercial sales and initial uncertainty about the handling of private data, have not helped to incentivise cannabis consumers to register with the government (Ramsey, 2016). Considering these difficulties and delays, it is still too early to say much that is meaningful about the results of cannabis reform in Uruguay. As of late 2017, the legal regulation of recreational cannabis remains a policy in gestation, with the most important part only recently coming online and the extent of implementation being limited. 'It is far too early to draw all of the conclusions whether Uruguay's cannabis law is meeting all of its objectives; indeed the feature of the law that is likely to be most important – commercial sales of cannabis at pharmacies – has yet to be implemented' (Ramsey, 2016, p. 41). Thus, it still remains to be seen what the long-term effects of Uruguay legally regulating cannabis will be.

Shielding Cannabis Reforms from International Criticism

Uruguay has long maintained that it does not want to serve as a 'model' for other countries (Canepa, 2014) and has largely refrained from taking bold, proactive action in the international arena (Alvarez, Pose, Lujan, 2017). The Uruguayan government sought 'to find alternative interpretations of international law' (Arraras & Bello-Pardo, 2014, p. 185), rather than trying to upend the international drug control system (Alvarez et al., 2017). Instead of attempting to change the conventions, denounce and re-accede as Bolivia had done, Uruguay tried to carve out a space *within*, by presenting a novel interpretation and defence of its legally regulated cannabis market.

Uruguay benefitted from and capitalised on an international 'window of opportunity' for drug policy reform (Alvarez et al., 2017, p. 22). Over the previous years, there had been substantial change behind the facade of the international prohibition regime, as the international 'consensus' underwriting international drug control had 'fractured' (Bewley-Taylor, 2012). International and regional debates about drug policy reform reached unprecedented intensity, and the traditional sponsor of international drug prohibition was less inclined to maintain and defend the regime, at least in terms of cannabis, changing the costs for countries contemplating cannabis legalisation (von Hoffmann, 2016b). Traditionally, the assumption has been that violating the terms of the global drug prohibition regime would incur the wrath of the international community and have severe material or reputational repercussions (Andreas, 1999). Yet, this did not occur in Uruguay's case.

Crucially, in contrast to its traditionally vocal role as a stalwart defender and enforcer of global prohibition (Bewley-Taylor, 2002; Bewley-Taylor, Blickman, & Jelsma, 2014; Nadelmann, 1990), the United States remained remarkably silent on Uruguay's cannabis reform process (von Hoffmann, 2016b).[5] The lone voice decrying Uruguay's action was the INCB, which has long played a pivotal role in restricting policy experimentation and perpetuating the status quo (Bewley-Taylor, 2012; Bewley-Taylor & Trace, 2006; Reinarman, 2003). The INCB's criticism mattered little, though, without the United States providing the necessary backup: the 'watchdog' that barked could not bite.[6]

In order to defend its cannabis reform, 'the government implemented an international strategy to justify its initiative, generate alliances and contain potential criticism' (Alvarez et al., 2017, p. 37). Uruguay's behaviour was predominantly reactive and defensive, the country did not strive to change the international drug conventions, but rather to advance an alternative interpretation that allowed its cannabis reform to co-exist with(in) the global drug prohibition regime.[7] Diego Cánepa's (2013, 2014) intervention at subsequent CND meetings and Luis Porto's (2014) speech at the INCB meeting are instructive of Uruguay's argument.[8]

The Uruguayan government's argument on the international level was twofold. First, it was not *liberalising,* but rather *regulating* cannabis control, which was an experimental response to domestic circumstances, not a model for the rest of the world (Valdomir, 2015). Second, it was honouring a more important set of international conventions on human rights, by reducing drug-related violence and respecting the rights and liberties of its citizens (Arraras & Bello-Pardo, 2014). These arguments were 'decisive to persuade the international and regional

[5]Recent domestic cannabis reforms in the United States had undermined its ability and credibility to criticise other countries for doing essentially the same (Alvarez et al., 2017; Arraras & Bello-Pardo, 2014; Valdomir, 2015).

[6]In March 2013, the INCB's annual report 'notes with deep concern a proposal by the Government of Uruguay'. (2013, p. 36) In June of 2013, INCB President Raimond Yans remarked that legally regulating cannabis 'would be in grave contravention of the drug control conventions and would have negative, far-reaching consequences for the functioning of the entire drug control system' (2013, p. 2). In December 2013, the conflict between the INCB and the Uruguayan government escalated (Jelsma, 2013). Yans compared Uruguay's attitude to that of 'pirates' and President Mujica pushed back, defending the cannabis bill and calling Yans a hypocrite (von Hoffmann, 2016b).

[7]As interviews of Alvarez et al. (2017) reveal, there were internal debates about going further and denouncing the conventions. However, this argument lost out to those arguing for a more cautious and limited approach.

[8]At the 2013 CND, Diego Cánepa (2013) justified Uruguay's initiative, arguing that 'our country has the right to attack head-on the economic foundations of narcotrafficking through the regulation, control and taxation of the cannabis market.' At the 2014 CND, highlighting that cannabis reform was a measure to control the cannabis market and combat drug-trafficking, Cánepa (2014) remarked that 'we are convinced that our policies are clearly encapsulated in the spirit of the conventions.' Rather than following 'rigid and inflexible' measures, Uruguay was experimenting 'with great responsibility' with an alternative drug control, designed not to negatively affect neighbouring countries. In a 2014 presentation to the INCB, Vice-minister of Foreign Affairs Luis Porto (2014) emphasised that the other measures Uruguay was undertaking to control drugs in its boarders, gave it 'the background and moral authority in the matter for our government to exercise its sovereignty in the initiative to responsibly regulate the cannabis market.'

community' and 'created a legitimising narrative' (Alvarez et al., 2017, p. 51). They were meant defensively to justify and explain domestic cannabis reform not to promote cannabis legalisation internationally. In sum, Uruguay did not pursue a 'complete break with the international drug regime' (Arraras & Bello-Pardo, 2014, p. 186), rather it reactively defended its domestic reforms trying to carve out a space within the existing treaty framework.

Explaining Drug Policy Protagonism in Uruguay

There is no shortage of accounts of Uruguay's novel and perplexing cannabis reform process and outcome (Arraras & Bello-Pardo, 2014; Draper & Müller Sienra, 2017; Garat, 2012, 2015; Sanjurjo Garcia, 2013). Several studies argue that Uruguay's drug policy reform was largely a 'top-down' process (Boidi, Cruz, Queirolo, & Bello-Pardo, 2015; Cruz et al., 2016; Repetto Gonzalez, 2014). For these authors, cannabis was legally regulated in Uruguay because President José Mujica decided to do so. While Mujica's 'leading role on the issue' was crucial for cannabis reform, such a 'top-down' approach does not pay sufficient attention to the 'bottom-up' pressure exerted by cannabis activism, which dates back over a decade and first established cannabis reform as an issue in the public agenda (Aguiar & Muñoz, 2007). Several studies conclude that 'bottom-up' campaigning and pressure made an important contribution to cannabis reform (Filardo, Aguiar, Musto, & Pieri, 2012; Lemos, 2014; Rivera-Velez, 2017). A third set of authors highlight the importance of a pressing policy problem confronting the Uruguayan government: rising fears and preoccupation with perceived drug-related insecurity (Castro, 2014; Repetto Gonzalez, 2014; Viscardi, 2016). The most enlightening studies address the complexity of the Uruguayan case by considering and untangling the multiple interactions of political calculations, social mobilisation, legislative politics and prominence of a pressing policy problems (Aguiar & Musto, 2015; Castro, 2014; von Hoffmann, 2015c). The following discussion assesses the personal leadership, social mobilisation pressure and problem-centric arguments in turn.

Pepe Mujica's Personal Leadership

Uruguayan President José 'Pepe' Mujica always stood out among world leaders. His appearance, demeanour and personal story were refreshingly different (Israel, 2014). What further endeared him to the international audience was his purported role in progressive reforms on same-sex marriage, abortion and cannabis (Combs, 2014; Fairbanks, 2015; Goni, 2014; Rodriguez Tarditi, 2012). Famously, he had declared that 'Someone has to be the first [to legalise cannabis]' and was willing to take the necessary steps (*El Observador*, 2012a). Many journalists and analysts have ascribed Uruguay's cannabis reform to 'its architect', the pioneering 'pro-pot President' (Kim, 2013; Jordan, 2014; McKay, 2014; Valencia, 2015). The reform, then, is 'his', as '*he* legalised cannabis' (Bartlett, 2015). While there is kernel of truth to this, and Mujica's personal willingness to consider and support cannabis reform were vital, he was more a pragmatic than a principled reformer, responding to pressures and trying to address an important problem bedevilling the country.

No doubt, without President Mujica the story of drug policy reform in Uruguay would have unfolded differently.[9] Nevertheless, his role in cannabis reform was more ambiguous and complicated than assumed by those subscribing to a 'top-down' explanation. In fact, Mujica was rather sceptical of drug policy reform. He disavowed having ever smoked cannabis, and disapproved of cannabis use (Draper & Müller Sienra, 2017). For him, drug users were '*nabos* [idiots]'. (*El Pais*, 2013). For Mujica (2012), cannabis reform had to be done for purely instrumental reasons. He supported it as measure against drug trafficking. While this, *per se*, does not diminish his importance in the process of cannabis legalisation, it is important to consider that it was preceded by both protest and proposals, and came in response to a pressing policy problem (von Hoffmann, 2015c).

For someone purportedly responsible for cannabis reform, Mujica's involvement was mostly superficial. The Executive did not fully assume ownership of the reform process, rather it left the bulk of the work to be done, and the details to be figured out, to Parliament (Draper & Müller Sienra, 2017). The reform bill (2012) the Executive presented in August 2012 was intentionally vague, consisting of only one article. While individual public servants, such as *Junta Nacional de Drogas* (JND) secretary Julio Calzada, became instrumental for the reform process (Garat, 2015), the lack of Mujica's personal involvement is reflected by the fact that he did not meet with the key legislator working on cannabis reform until after its passage (Sabini, 2014).

At times, Mujica even undermined the reform process making statements that hurt, rather than helped, move it along. For instance, shortly after announcing the intention to legally regulate the cannabis market, President Mujica cast doubts on the prospects of the initiative, when he stated: 'If 60% of the country do not support us, we are toast [*se va al mazo*]' (*El Observador,* 2012b). This statement was especially damaging as public opinion polls showed widespread rejection of the initiative (Cruz, Boidi & Queirolo, 2018, 2016). In late 2012, cannabis reform appeared on track and Legislators intended to have the project finalised and approved before the new year (Nuñez, 2014). Yet President Mujica put cannabis reform on hold, announcing: 'The decision is not mature, that is why I stopped it' (*El Pais*, 2012). His principal reason was the continued lack of popular support. While he still supported drug policy reform, the President reiterated the necessity to persuade the population, setting up a daunting obstacle to be overcome by cannabis reformers (Draper & Müller Sienra, 2017).

Mobilising for Cannabis Reform

Alarmed by the possibility of drug policy reform derailing, international and domestic activists met in early 2013 to design a communication strategy in order to advance the debate and achieve a greater level of public support (Collazo,

[9] Had the executive not announced its support, the best-case alternative scenario would have been the passage of a previously introduced bi-partisan *autocultivo* bill (Bango, 2014). The *Estrategia* substantially changed the dynamic, scope and prospects of drug policy reform, giving it new impetus and importance. According to Sebastian Sabini, it 'changed the terms of debate of what was discussed in Parliament' (Sabini, 2014).

2014; Hetzer, 2015; Machado, 2014). The result of the meeting was the creation of a professional communication campaign (Hetzer & Walsh, 2014). *Regulación Responsable* was born with the purpose of selling the reform to a sceptical public. While the campaign was unsuccessful at changing public opinion, it was more successful in framing cannabis reform as 'regulation', signalling momentum, and establishing that there was some societal support for reform (Draper & Müller Sienra, 2017; Garat, 2015; Lemos, 2014). With their organised, vocal and timely activity, proponents offset the unorganised and diffuse opposition of the 'silent majority' that rejected cannabis reform. Thus, cannabis activists fought on two fronts for cannabis legalisation in Uruguay, to persuade the public, and to advise and influence the drafting of the bill.

Uruguayan Cannabis activism was not new, but began in earnest in 2005, when the first-ever-pro-marijuana demonstration was held in Montevideo. The march was crucial for the emergence of social mobilisation around cannabis in Uruguay (Aguiar & Muñoz, 2007; Draper & Müller Sienra, 2017; Lemos, 2014). The seed of cannabis activism had been planted and began to grow. In 2007, between 6,000 and 7,000 people took to the streets to demand cannabis legalisation (Lemos, 2014). These manifestations gave cannabis reform a new level of visibility and weight. Because of social mobilisation, the debate on drug policy reform had gained increased prominence in the electoral campaign of 2009 (Garat, 2012). During the presidential primaries, Mujica said that the topic had been brought to his attention by social mobilisation, while he was open to cannabis reform but did not consider it a priority (Cabrera, 2009).

The arrest of cannabis growers became a *cause célèbre* for the cannabis movement and gave new urgency to demands for cannabis reform (Draper & Müller Sienra, 2017). In early 2011, Alicia Castilla was arrested for growing cannabis plants in her house. Argentinean-born Castilla was a 66-year-old writer, who was vocal on the benefits of cannabis, gave the long-criticised contradictions of decriminalisation a concrete human face. The imprisonment of 'the grandma with the plants' garnered widespread attention and demands for her freedom became a rallying cry for mobilisation (Aguiar, 2014; Blanco, 2014; Vaz, 2014).

Around the same time, especially activists from pro-cannabis organisation *Proderechos* began working with legislators to draft a cannabis reform bill and to advance the debate (Draper & Müller Sienra, 2017). In recently elected, young legislators, such as Sebastián Sabini and Nicolas Núñez, they found politicians open to cannabis reform (Collazo, 2014; Nuñez, 2014; Sabini, 2014). In 2011, their work in parliament resulted in a cannabis reform bill, contemplating allowing *autocultivo* [home cultivation]. In August 2011, a national debate on drug policy brought together activists, experts and policymakers to exchange ideas (Lemos, 2014). The fact that cannabis activists were sitting across the table from decision makers to discuss cannabis reform, shows how far they had come since 2005.

Years of activism and linkages with policy makers helped Uruguay's cannabis activists to have a seat at the table when cannabis reform was proposed by the government in 2012. Cannabis activists successfully clamoured for the inclusion of *autocultivo*, which the government wanted to exclude (Draper & Müller Sienra, 2017). Activists were not only crucial for shaping the contours of cannabis reform but also in assuring the reform's passage. Calzada (2014) considered the formation and activities of a varied 'group in favour of regulation' indispensable, Aguiar (2014) referred to the important contributions of a 'legalizing coalition', and Lemos (2014, p. 15) wrote about the 'formation and consolidation of a coalition of movements and actors'. At least in part, cannabis reform succeeded in Uruguay because of these efforts and 'bottom-up' pressure.

Drug-related Insecurity: A Problem to be Solved

An important part of understanding Uruguay's pioneering cannabis reform is the context of perceived drug-fuelled insecurity. In response, the Mujica administration sought out-of-the-box thinking and solutions to a pressing problem confronting the government and society. Insecurity came to be understood as being about drug consumption and trafficking and, thereby, crucially influenced the decision to pursue cannabis reform (Draper & Müller Sienra, 2017; Repetto Gonzalez, 2014; Viscardi, 2016).

Pasta base de cocaina (PBC) [cocaine base paste], or simply *pasta base,* radically changed Uruguay's approach to drug policy after it took hold in the early 2000s (Aguiar & Pais, 2010). While always consumed by a relatively small number of users, *pasta base* captured the imagination of lawmakers and wider society (Suarez, 2014). The media helped to construct an image of a society under siege by violent drug traffickers and users (von Hoffmann, 2015b). 'Lateros' smoking *pasta base* were seen as responsible for a plethora of societal ills (TNI, 2006). 'From the point of view of the population the association of PBC-transgression is direct and the substance is blamed for the level of disorder and insecurity' (Folgar, 2006, p. 182). *Pasta base,* then, became construed as the 'scourge' of Uruguayan society, directly contributing to the public's sensation of rising insecurity and lack of effective state responses.

Although by comparison still one of the safest and securest countries in a region rife with high levels of crime and violence (UNDP, 2013), perceptions of insecurity in Uruguay increased to alarming levels (Paternain, 2012). By 2012, public security had become the predominant political issue (Draper & Müller Sienra, 2017). According to opinion polls, insecurity had become the principal concern of Uruguayans (Bottinelli, 2012). Especially, internal conflicts between drug-dealers and gangs, so-called '*ajustes de cuenta*' [score-settling] received widespread attention. A point-blank murder in the restaurant *La Pasiva* on 17 May 2012, which was caught on tape, shocked Uruguayans, as television channels repeated the gruesome footage *ad nauseam.* The media was battering Mujica's administration for the supposed deterioration of security (Draper & Müller Sienra, 2017). The government was seen as not having an effective response to this 'crisis' of drugs and crime (Castro, 2014). The administration perceived public insecurity as its blind spot and reason why it was haemorrhaging support (Garat, 2015). Something had to be done.

On 20 June 2012, Minister of Defence, Eleuterio Fernández Huidobro revealed that the Uruguayan government planned to legally regulate the cannabis market. Cannabis reform was only one among fifteen measures of the unveiled *Estrategia por la vida y convivencia* (2012b). Overall, the strategy was not at all 'soft on drugs', as it included tougher sentences for dealing drugs and increased policing (Walsh & Ramsey, 2015). Huidobro (2012a) presented cannabis reform as way to improve public security and weaken drug gangs, stating: 'We think that the prohibition of certain drugs is creating more problems for society than the drug itself'.

In sum, for the Uruguayan government, drug policy reform was about fighting drug trafficking and thereby improving security (Viscardi, 2016). The problems of drugs and crime had become 'synonymous' (Castro, 2014, p. 28). Consequentially, drug policy reform was conceived 'from and through a lens of security' (Repetto Gonzalez, 2014, p. 14). In Mujica's words: 'the grave problem is narcotrafficking, not marijuana' (CNN, 2012). He emphasised that 'the idea is not to liberate', rather, 'to the contrary, to control'. He explained that this was only one of the measures intended to 'reduce the number of crimes in Uruguayan cities'. Cannabis legalisation, then, was not initiated out of principled but pragmatic reasons, to solve a pressing problem. The overarching goal of the *Estrategia* was to regain the initiative in the field of public security and reduce drug-related crime with decisive, if controversial, action.

Conclusion

Bolivia and Uruguay broke ranks with the global drug prohibition regime by introducing novel drug policies. State control of the production and supply of coca and cannabis represents a clear departure from both the spirit and the letter of the Conventions, which establish that states have 'to limit exclusively to medical and scientific purposes the production, manufacture, export, import, distribution of, trade in, use and possession of drugs' (UN, 2013, p. 30).

As outlined above, both the rationale, processes and outcomes of policy change were distinctive in many regards. However, going beyond merely cataloguing these differences, the chapter suggests a unifying heuristic to explain policy protagonism. Going beyond the cases of Uruguay and Bolivia, thinking in terms of personal leadership, mobilisation and policy problems might provide a useful analytical first-cut to assess the continuity and change in drug policy observable elsewhere.

Scrutinising the reasons and motivations for undertaking drug policy reform also allows for better understanding of each country's international behaviour. While Bolivia proactively pursued a strategy of 'hard' defection, Uruguay reactively defended its cannabis policy and engaged in 'soft defection' (Bewley-Taylor, 2012). The former sought changes *of* the Conventions, willing to leave and re-accede, the latter aimed to remain and reform the treaty body from *within*. Nonetheless, both countries advanced arguments for their breaking with the global drug prohibition regime that invoked other treaty obligations. In effect, they leveraged increasingly discussed contradictions and inconsistencies of global drug prohibition with international human rights law and respect for indigenous rights (Bewley-Taylor, 2005; Boister, 2016; Lines, 2011; Pfeiffer, 2013).

Although both Uruguay and Bolivia are among the most prominent examples of alternative approaches to drug policy, only Uruguay assumed a leading role in the UNGASS process (Tokatlian & Comini, 2016). It spearheaded efforts to include topics such as respect for human rights and the legal regulation of cannabis in the international debate (von Hoffmann, 2016a). Contending that 'the most appropriate measure … is the regulation and control of the market', Uruguay hoped to 'break with the single mindedness and open up new perspectives on how to address the global drug problem' (JND, 2015, p. 9). While UNGASS ultimately failed to usher in a paradigm change, Uruguay and Bolivia have forged ahead to break ranks with the global drug prohibition regime. Whatever comes after the 2016 UNGASS, the pioneering protagonism in Uruguay and Bolivia will remain to represent instances of 'actually existing' alternative drug control policies

References

Aguiar, S. (2014). Co-founder *Proderechos*. Interview with author, September 5 & 24, 2014, Montevideo, Uruguay.

Aguiar, S., & Muñoz, C. (2007). *Movimiento por la legalización del Cannabis*. Grupo de Estudios Urbanos y Generacionales. Montevideo: Universidad de la Republica.

Aguiar, S., & Musto, C. (2015). El rayo verde: Regulación de la mariguana en Uruguay, 297–316. In B. Caiuby Labate & T. Rodrigues (Eds.), *Drogas, politica y sociedad en America Latina y el Caribe*. Mexico City: Centro de Investigación y Docencia económicas (CIDE).

Aguiar, X., & Pais, A. (2010). *Rostros que se hacen humo*, 1–95. Montevideo: Junta Nacional de Drogas.

Alvarez, N., Pose, N., & Lujan, C. (2017). La política internacional de la regulación del cannabis en Uruguay. Un análisis de la respuesta uruguaya a los desafíos y oportunidades del régimen internacional de drogas. *Desafíos*, *29*(2), 19–59. doi: 10.12804/revistas.urosario.edu.co/desafios/a.5223

Alzamora, M. (2017, March 30). Bolivian President Evo Morales' crusade: De-vilifying the coca leaf. Retrieved from http://www.drugpolicy.org/blog/bolivian-president-evo-morales-crusade-de-vilifying-coca-leaf. Accepted on November 18, 2017.

Andreas, P. R. (1999). When Policies Collide: Market Reform, Market Prohibition, and the Narcotization of the Mexican Economy, 125–142. In R. H. Friman & P. R. Andreas (Eds.), *The Illicit Global Economy and State Power*. Lanham, MD: Rowman & Littlefield Publishers.

Anria, S. (2013). Social movements, party organization, and populism: Insights from the Bolivian MAS. *Latin American Politics & Society*, *55*(3), 19–46. doi:10.1111/j.1548-2456.2013.00201.x

Arraras, A., & Bello-Pardo, E. D. (2014). *Inventando Caminos Cannabis Regulation in Uruguay,* 173–197. In R. Zepeda & J. D. Rosen (Eds.), Cooperation and Drug Policies in the Americas. New York, NY: Lexington Books.

Asamblea Constituyente (2009). Constitución Pólitica del Estado Plurinacional de Bolivia. La Paz: Estado Plurinacional de Bolivia.

Bango, J. (2014). Legislator Frente Amplio. Interview with author, September 9, 2014. Montevideo, Uruguay.

Bartlett, E. (2015, March 2). 8 Reasons why we'll miss Jose Mujica, Uruguay's maverick president. *The Independent*. https://www.indy100.com/article/

8-reasons-why-well-miss-jose-mujica-uruguays-maverick-president--e1t_MupEpl. Accessed on November 21, 2017.

BBC News. (2012, July 9). Bolivia's Evo Morales re-elected coca growers leader. Retrieved from http://www.bbc.com/news/world-latin-america-18768929. Accessed on November 18, 2017.

Bewley-Taylor, D. R. (2002). United States and International Drug Control, 1909–1997. New York, NY: Continuum International Publishing Group.

Bewley-Taylor, D. R. (2005). Emerging policy contradictions between the United Nations drug control system and the core values of the United Nations. *International Journal of Drug Policy*, *16*(6), 423–431. doi: https://doi.org/10.1016/j.drugpo.2005.06.007

Bewley-Taylor, D. R. (2012). International Drug Control. New York, NY: Cambridge University Press.

Bewley-Taylor, D. R. (2016). Coca and cocaine: The Evolution of International Control. In *Roadmaps to regulation coca, cocaine, and derivatives*. The Beckley Foundation.

Bewley-Taylor, D. R., Blickman, T., & Jelsma, M. (2014). *The rise and decline of cannabis prohibition*. TNI/GDPO.

Bewley-Taylor, D. R., & Trace, M. (2006). *The International Narcotics Control Board: Watchdog or guardian of the UN drug control conventions?* The Beckley Foundation.

Blanco, L. (2014). Activist *AECU*. Interview with author, August 29, 2014, Montevideo, Uruguay.

Boidi, M. F., Cruz, J. M., Queirolo, R., & Bello-Pardo, E. D. (2015). Marijuana Legalization in Uruguay and Beyond, 1–12. Latin American Marijuana Research Initiative (LAMRI) Report. FIU College of Arts & Sciences - School of International and Public Affairs.

Boister, N. (2016). Waltzing on the Vienna consensus on drug control? Tensions in the international system for the control of drugs. *Leiden Journal of International Law*, *29*(2), 389–409. doi: https://doi.org/10.1017/S0922156516000078

Boliva. (2011). *Instrument of Accession to Single Convention on Narcotic Drugs, 1961*. United Nations.

Bolivia. (2009). *Proposal of Amendments by Bolivia to Article 49, Paragraphs 1 (c) and 2 (e)*. United Nations.

Bottinelli, E. (2012). Principales Preocupaciones De Los Uruguayos, 2–8. Montevideo: *Instituto Factum*.

Boville, B. (2004). The Cocaine War in Context: Drugs and Politics. New York, NY: Algora Publishing.

Brocchetto, M. (2012, March 13). Bolivia's morales to UN: Legalize coca-leaf chewing. Retrieved from http://edition.cnn.com/2012/03/13/world/americas/bolivia-morales-coca/. Accepted on November 18, 2017.

Cabrera, S. (2009, March 10). Legalizar la marihuana es otro tema para la campaña. *El Pais*.

Calzada, J. (2014). Secretary (JND). Interview with author, September 19, 2014, Montevideo, Uruguay.

Canepa, D. (2013). Intervención del Jefe de Delegación de Uruguay.

Canepa, D. (2014). Intervenciòn del Jefe de Delegación de Uruguay.

Castro, G. (2014). From punishment to markets: Social movements, the state, and legal Marijuana in Uruguay. Paper presented at the APSA Conference.

Castillo Gallardo, M. (2004). Movimiento cocalero en Bolivia. Violencia, discurso y hegemonía. *Gazeta De Antropologia*, *20*, 1–10.

Castillo Gallardo, M., & Durand, A. (2008). Movimiento cocalero, política y representación: los casos boliviano y peruano. In F. Garcia (Ed.), *Identidades, etnicidad y racismo en America Latina* (pp. 47–72). Quito: Facultad Latinoamericana de Ciencias Sociales (FLACSO).

Cerdá, M., & Kilmer, B. (2017). Uruguay's middle-ground approach to cannabis legalization. *International Journal of Drug Policy*, *42*, 118–120. doi: https://doi.org/10.1016/j.drugpo.2017.02.007

Cher, L. (2016, March 21). Uruguay's Half-Baked Marijuana Experiment. *Foreign Policy*. http://foreignpolicy.com/2016/03/21/uruguay-marijuana-legalization/.

CNN. (2012, August 26). José Mujica: "El problema grave es el narcotráfico, no la marihuana". Retrieved from http://cnnespanol.cnn.com/2012/08/26/jose-mujica-el-problema-grave-es-el-narcotrafico-no-la-marihuana/. Accessed on March 8, 2015.

Collazo, M. (2014). Activist *Proderechos*. Interview with author, September 26, 2014. Montevideo, Uruguay.

Combs, C. (2014, May 21). How the world's poorest president became the most popular public figure on the internet. Retrieved from http://mic.com/articles/89669/how-the-world-s-poorest-president-became-the-most-popular-public-figure-on-the-internet. Accessed on December 10, 2014.

CONALTID. (2006). *Estrategia de lucha contra el narcotráfico y revalorización dela hoja de coca, 2007 – 2010*. La Paz: Estado Plurinacional de Bolivia.

Congreso Nacional. (1988). Ley No. 1008 - Ley del regimen de la coca y sustancias controladas. La Paz: Estado Plurinacional de Bolivia.

Crabtree, J., & Chaplin, A. (2013). *Bolivia*. London: Zed Books.

Cruz, J. M., Queirolo, R., & Boidi, M. F. (2016). Determinants of public support for marijuana legalization in Uruguay, the United States, and El Salvador. *Journal of Drug Issues*, *46*(4), 308–325. doi: https://doi.org/10.1177/0022042616649005

Cruz, J. M., Boidi, M. F., & Queirolo, R. (2018). Saying no to weed: Public opinion towards cannabis legalisation in Uruguay. Drugs: Education, Prevention and Policy, 25(1), 67–76. http://doi.org/10.1080/09687637.2016.1237475

Draper, G., & Müller Sienra, C. (2017). *Marihuana oficial*. Montevideo: Sudamericana.

Editorial. (2016a, August 22). Complicado "porrito". *El Pais*.

Editorial. (2016b, November 3). Fracaso de la marihuana legal. *El Observador*.

El Observador. (2012a, June 21). Mujica: "Vamos a controlar". *El Observador*.

El Observador. (2012b, July 11). Mujica se va "al mazo" si 'el 60% no respalda'liberalizar la marihuana. *El Observador*.

El Pais. (2012, December 18). Mujica mandó frenar proyecto de ley sobre ventade marihuana. *El Pais*.

El Pais. (2013, June 24). Mujica calificó de "nabos" a los adictos a las drogas. *El Pais*.

Fairbanks, E. (2015, February 5). Jose mujica was every liberal's dream President. He Was too good to be true. *New Republic*.

Farthing, L., & Kohl, B. (2005). Conflicting agendas: The politics of development aid in drug-producing areas. *Development Policy Review*, *23*(2), 183–198. doi: 10.1111/j.1467-7679.2005.00282.x

Farthing, L., & Kohl, B. (2010). Social control: Bolivia's new approach to coca reduction. *Latin American Perspectives*, *37*(4), 197–213. Retrieved from http://www.jstor.org/stable/25700540

Farthing, L., & Kohl, B. (2012). Supply-side harm reduction strategies: Bolivia's experiment with social control. *International Journal of Drug Policy*, *23*(6), 488–494. doi: https://doi.org/10.1016/j.drugpo.2012.06.004

Farthing, L., & Kohl, B. (2014). *Evo's Bolivia*. Austin, TX: University of Texas Press.

Farthing, L., & Ledebur, K. (2004). The Beat Goes on: The U.S. war on coca. *NACLA Report on the Americas*, *38*(3), 34–41.

Farthing, L., & Ledebur, K. (2015). *Habeas Coca*. New York, NY: Open Society Foundation (OSF).

Filardo, V., Aguiar, S., Musto, C., & Pieri, D. (2012). La marihuana provoca esquizofrenia. Espacio público y drogas en Uruguay. In Varios (Ed.), *Aporte universitario al Debate Nacional sobre Drogas* (pp. 119–170.). Montevideo: Universidad de la Republica.

Folgar, L. (2006). De lata y lateros: usuarios de PBC y sus mundos de sentido. *Anuario De Antropología Social y Cultural en Uruguay*, 177–183.

Gabinete de Seguridad. (2012a). Conferencia de Prensa. Retrieved from http://www.presidencia.gub.uy/sala-de-medios/audios/conferencia-prensa-gabinete-seguridad-dia-20

Gabinete de Seguridad. (2012b). *Estrategia por la vida y la convivencia*. Montevideo: República Oriental del Uruguay.

Garat, G. (2012). Marihuana y otras yerbas. Montevideo: Debate.

Garat, G. (2015). *El Camino*. Friedrich Ebert Stiftung and Junta Nacional de Drogas.

Goni, U. (2014, November 16). Uruguay's beloved Pepe bows out to spend time with his beetle and three-legged dog. *The Guardian*. http://www.theguardian.com/world/2014/nov/16/uruguay-jose-mujica-humble-president/print.

Gorbea, G. (2016, April 15). Bolivia's President suggested the Pope Try Coca. Retrieved from https://news.vice.com/article/bolivia-president-suggested-the-pope-try-coca. Accessed on November 18, 2017.

Grisaffi, T. (2010). We are originarios … "We just aren't from here": Coca leaf and identity politics in the chapare, Bolivia. *Bulletin of Latin American Research*, *29*(4), 425–439. doi: 10.1111/j.1470-9856.2010.00385.x

Grisaffi, T. (2013). "All of us are presidents": Radical democracy and citizenship in the Chapare Province, Bolivia. *Critique of Anthropology*, *33*(1), 47–65. doi: https://doi.org/10.1177/0308275X12466681

Grisaffi, T. (2016). Social Control in Bolivia: A Humane Alternative to the Forced Eradication of Coca Crops. In B. Caiuby Labate, C. Cavner, & T. Rodrigues (Eds.), *Drug Policies and the Politics of Drugs in the Americas* (pp. 149–166). London: Springer.

Grisaffi, T. (2017). From the grassroots to the presidential palace: Evo Morales and the coca growers' union in Bolivia. In S. Lazar (Ed.), *Where Are the Unions Workers and Social Movements in Latin America, the Middle East and Europe* (pp. 44–63). London: Zed Books.

Grisaffi, T., & Ledebur, K. (2016). Citizenship or repression? Coca, eradication and development in the Andes. *Stability: International Journal of Security and Development*, *5*(1), 1–19. doi: http://doi.org/10.5334/sta.440

Haberkorn, L. (2014, August 1). Uruguayan pot marketplace may go up in smoke. *The Miami Herald*.

Harten, S. (2013). *The rise of Evo Morales and the MAS*. London: Zed Books.

Healy, K. (1991). Political Ascent of Bolivia's Peasant Coca Leaf Producers. *Journal of Interamerican Studies and World Affairs*, *33*(1), 87–121. Stable URL: http://www.jstor.org/stable/166043.

Hesselroth, A. (2015). The decolonization of Bolivia's antinarcotics policy? *Bolivian Studies Journal/Revista De Estudios Bolivianos*, *21*, 59–99. doi: https://doi.org/10.5195/bsj.2015.134

Hetzer, H. (2015). Latin America Director *DPA*. Interview with author, January 9, 2015, via Skype.

Hetzer, H., & Walsh, J. M. (2014). Pioneering Cannabis Regulation in Uruguay. *NACLA Report on the Americas*, *47*(2), 33–35. Washington: North American Congress on Latin America.

HRW. (1996). Bolivia under pressure: Human rights violations and coca eradication. New York, NY: Human Rights Watch.

International Narcotics Control Board (INCB). (2008). *Report of the International Narcotics Control Board for 2007*. INCB.

International Narcotics Control Board (INCB). (2013). *Report of the International Narcotics Control Board for Report 2012*. INCB.

Israel, S. (2014). *Pepe mujica: El presidente*. Montevideo: Planeta.

Jelsma, M. (2011). Lifting the ban on coca chewing. *TNI Series on Legislative Reform of Drug Policies*, *11*, 1–8. Amsterdam: Transnational Institute.

Jelsma, M. (2013, December 17). INCB vs Uruguay: The art of diplomacy. Retrieved from http://druglawreform.info/en/weblog/item/5214-incb-vs-uruguay-the-art-of-diplomacy. Accessed on March 4, 2015.

Jordan, C. (2014, April 15). President José Mujica, a Latin American political pioneer. *Council on Hemispheric Affairs (COHA)*. http://www.coha.org/president-jose-mujica-a-latin-american-political-pioneer/. Accessed on April 20, 2015.

Junta Nacional de Drogas (JND) (2015) *Uruguay Realiza Aporte Innovador en Abordaje De La Temática De Las Drogas*. Montevideo: JND.

Kim, A. (2014). The plight of Bolivian coca leaves: Bolivia's quest for decriminalization in the face of inconsistent international legislation. *Washington University Global Studies Law Review*, *13*(3), 559–583. Retrieved from https://openscholarship.wustl.edu/law_globalstudies/vol13/iss3/13

Kim, V. (2013, July 24). Uruguay's pro-pot President admits he's "never tried it". Retrieved from http://www.thefix.com/content/uruguay-president-marijuana-never-tried-it91962. Accepted November 25, 2014.

Kohl, B., & Farthing, L. (2001). The Price of Success: Bolivia's War Against Drugs and the Poor. *NACLA Report on the Americas*, *35*(1), 35–41. Washington: North American Congress on Latin America.

Kreher, D. (2016). *Uruguay, a dos años de la aprobación de la ley que regula el cannabis*, 1–53. Iglesia Evangélica Protestante de El Salvador (IEPES).

Laserna, R. (2011). *El fracaso del prohibicionismo*. La Paz: Fundacion Vincente Pazos Kanki.

Ledebur, K., & Farthing, L. (2014). To the Beat of a Different Drum: Bolivia's Community Coca Control. *NACLA Report on the Americas*, *47*(2), 51–55. Washington: North American Congress on Latin America.

Ledebur, K., & Youngers, C. A. (2006). Bolivia's Coca Policy Walks a Tightrope, 1–6. NACLA. Https://nacla.org/news/bolivias-coca-policy-walks-tightrope. Accessed on November 14, 2017.

Ledebur, K., & Youngers, C. A. (2008a). *Balancing Act: Bolivia's Drug Control Advances and Challenges*, 1–9. Washington: WOLA and AIN.

Ledebur, K., & Youngers, C. A. (2008b). The Coca Debate: *Headed toward Polarization or Common Ground?,* 1–6. Washington: WOLA and AIN.

Ledebur, K., & Youngers, Youngers C. A. (2012). *Bolivian drug control efforts: Genuine progress, daunting challenges*, 1–24. Washington: WOLA and AIN.

Ledebur, K., & Youngers, C. A. (2013). From Conflict to Collaboration: An Innovative Approach to Reducing Coca Cultivation in Bolivia. *Stability: International Journal of Security and Development*, *2*(1), 1–11. DOI:http://doi.org/10.5334/sta.aw.

Lemos, F. (2014). Coalición por la transformación de la política de drogas. In D. Collazo (Ed.), *Uruguay se planta* (pp. 15–28). Montevideo: Estuario Editora.

Lines, R. (2011). Deliver us from evil? – The single convention on narcotic drugs, 50 years on. *International Journal on Human Rights and Drug Policy*, *1*, 3–13. Retrieved from SSRN: https://ssrn.com/abstract=1837554

Londoño, E. (2017, August 25). Pot was flying off the shelves in Uruguay. Then U.S. Banks Weighed In. *The New York Times*.

Lorenzo, A. G., & Rodriguez, J. A. (2011). La hoja de coca en Bolivia ¿Un dilema de la Convención de Viena o la defensa del akulliku? *Revista Andina De Estudios Politicos*, *7*, 1–22.

Machado, S. (2014). Activist (Proderechos). Interview with author, September 29, 2014. Montevideo, Uruguay.

Mala, S. (2009). El movimiento "Cocalero" en Bolivia durante los años 80 y 90: Sus causas y su su desarrollo. *Revista Esbocos*, *20*, 101–117. doi: http://dx.doi.org/10.5007/2175-7976.2008v15n20p101

McKay, T. (2014, December 9). One year after Uruguay legalized marijuana, here's what it's become. Retrieved from https://mic.com/articles/106094/one-year-after-uruguay-legalized-marijuana-here-s-what-it-s-become#.kFvA8fhV5. Accessed on December 4, 2017.

Menzel, S. H. (1997). *Fire in the Andes*. Lanham, MD: University Press of America.

Metaal, P., Jelsma, M., Argandoña, M., Soberon, R., Henman, A. R., & Echeverria, X. (2006). Coca yes, cocaine, no? *TNI Drugs & Conflict,* 13, 1–20. Amsterdam: Transnational Institute.

Mujica, J. (2012, December 26). Una ley contra el narcotráfico. Retrieved from http://www.presidencia.gub.uy/wps/wcm/connect/Presidencia/PortalPresidencia/Comunicacion/comunicacionNoticias/ley-contra-narcotrafico. Accessed on November 14, 2014.

Nadelmann, E. A. (1990). Global prohibition regimes: The evolution of norms in international society. *International Organization*, *44*(4), 479–526. Retrieved from http://www.jstor.org/stable/2706851

Neuman, W. (2013, January 11). Bolivia: Morales wins victory as U.N. agrees to define some coca use as legal. *The New York Times*.

Norman, S. V. (2017). Social movements, unions, and drug policy in Bolivia. Paper presented at the annual meeting of the Latin American Studies Association 2017, Peru, Lima.

Nuñez, N. (2014). Diputado *Frente Amplio*. Interview with author, September 9, 2014, Montevideo, Uruguay.

Ochoa, U. D. (2014). *The political empowerment of the cocaleros of Bolivia and Peru*. New York, NY: Palgrave Macmillan.

Oikonomakis, L., & Espinoza, F. (2014). MAS and the Movements That Brought It to State Power. In R. Stahler-Sholk, H. E. Vanden, & M. Becker (Eds.), *Rethinking Latin American Social Movements: Radical Action From Below*, (pp. 285–305). London: Rowman & Littlefield.

Otis, J. (2011, March 23). On a mission to legalize coca. Retrieved from https://www.pri.org/stories/2011-03-28/mission-legalize-coca. Accessed on November 19, 2017.

Painter, J. (1994). *Bolivia and Coca: A Study in Dependency*. Tokyo: United Nations University Press.

Pardo, B. (2014). Cannabis policy reforms in the Americas: A comparative analysis of Colorado, Washington, and Uruguay. *International Journal of Drug Policy, 25*(4), 727–735. 10.1016/j.drugpo.2014.05.010

Pardo, B. (2015, September 25). Legal marijuana? Much easier said than done. Retrieved from http://www.eldailypost.com/trade/2015/09/legal-marijuana-much-easier-said-than-done/

Paternain, R. (2012). *Uruguay: Inseguridad, delito y estado*. Montevideo: Ediciones Trilce.

Pearson, Z., & Grisaffi, T. (2014, September 19). Washington snubs Bolivia on drug policy reform, again. Retrieved from http://fpif.org/washington-snubs-bolivia-drug-policy-reform/. Accessed November 21, 2014.

Petterson, B., & Mackay, L. (1993). *Human rights violations stemming from the "War on Drugs" in Bolivia*. Cochabamba: Andean Information Network.

Pfeiffer, S. (2013). Rights of indigenous peoples and the international drug control regime: The Case of traditional coca leaf chewing. *Goettingen Journal of International Law, 5*, 287–324. doi: 10.3249/1868-1581-5-1-pfeiffer

Poder Ejecutivo. (2012). *Proyecto de Ley*. Presidencia de Uruguay. Republica Oriental del Uruguay.

Poder Legislativo. (2013). Ley 19.172. Republica Oriental del Uruguay.

Porto, L. (2014). *Discurso de subsecretario de relaciones exteriores ante JIFE*. Ministerio de Relaciones Exteriores de la Republica de Uruguay.

Presidencia de Uruguay. (2014). Reglementación CM/847. Republica Oriental del Uruguay.

Queirolo, R., Boidi, M. F., & Cruz, J. M. (2016). Cannabis clubs in Uruguay: The challenges of regulation. *International Journal of Drug Policy, 34*, 41–48. doi:10.1016/j.drugpo.2016.05.015

Ramirez, S., & Youngers, C. A. (2011). *Drug policy in the Andes*. Washington: The Carter Center.

Ramsey, G. (2016). *Getting Regulation Right: Assessing Uruguay's Historic Cannabis Initiative*. Washington: Washington Office on Latin America *(WOLA)*.

Reinarman, C. (2003). Geo-political and cultural constraints on international drug control treaties. *International Journal of Drug Policy, 14*(2), 205–208. doi: https://doi.org/10.1016/S0955-3959(03)00010-0

Repetto Gonzalez, L. (2014). Regulación del cannabis en Uruguay: ¿un asunto de seguridad? Entrada y mantenimiento en agenda de un problema de política pública. Paper presented at the Segundo Congreso Internacional de la Asociación Mexicana de Ciencia Política.

Rivera Cusicanqui, S. (2011). Coca: An indigenous commodity and its paradoxes. *ReVista – Harvard Review of Latin America*, Volume XI, 1 (Fall), 21–25.

Rivera-Velez, L. (2017). La agenda de derechos en Uruguay. Del movimiento social a las políticas públicas en el gobierno de José Mujica. *Nuevo Mundo, Mundo Nuevos*. Retrieved from http://journals.openedition.org/nuevomundo/70657

Rodriguez Tarditi, S. (2012). South America's unsung political hero – Uruguay. Retrieved from http://monocle.com/monocolumn/2012/south-america-s-unsung-political-hero/. Accessed on March 12, 2014.

Roncken, T., & de Acha, G. M. de J. (2015). La política de drogas en Bolivia: Un proceso de cambio marcado por continuidades, 231–254. In B. Caiuby Labate & T. Rodrigues (Eds.), *Drogas, politica y sociedad en America Latina y el Caribe*. Mexico City: Centro de Investigación y Docencia económicas (CIDE).

Rueda, M. (2013, January 12). Evo Morales Scores One for the Coca Leaf. Retrieved from http://abcnews.go.com/ABC_Univision/evo-morales-scores-coca-leaf/story?id=18195230. Accessed on November 18, 2017.

Sabini, S. (2014). Legislator *Frente Amplio*. Interview with author, September 22, 2014. Montevideo, Uruguay.

Salazar Ortuño, F. (2012). De la coca al poder. Buenos Aires: Consejo Latinoamericano de Ciencias Sociales (CLACSO).

Sanjurjo Garcia, D. (2013). El Cambio en Las Políticas De Estupefacientes: El Ejemplo De Uruguay. *Revista Jurídica Universidad Autónoma De Madrid, 27*, 291–311.

Sanjurjo Garcia, D. (2014). Análisis del proyecto de ley de regulación del Mercado de cannabis en Uruguay. *Circunstancia, XII*(35), 1–22.

Sivak, M. (2010). *Evo Morales*. New York, NY: St. Martin's Press.

South, R. B. (1977). Coca in Bolivia. *Geographical Review, 67*(1), 22–33.

Spedding Pallet, A. (2004). The Cocalero Movement and Drug Policy in Bolivia. *TNI Drugs & Conflict*, (10), 4–13. Amsterdam: Transnational Institute.

Suarez, H. (2014). Director observatorio Uruguayo de drogas. Interview with author, September 10, 2014, Montevideo, Uruguay.

Telleria Escobar, L. (2013). Bolivia y la despenalización de la hoja de coca como estrategia de cambio. *URVio – Revista Latinoamericana De Seguridad Ciudadana*, (13), 95–107. doi: https://doi.org/10.17141/urvio.13.2013.1184

TNI. (2006). Paco Under Scrutiny: The cocaine base paste market in Argentina, Uruguay and Brazil. *TNI Drugs & Conflict*, (14), 1–14. Amsterdam: Transnational Institute.

Tokatlian, J. G., & Comini, N. (2016). "Guerra contra las drogas": ¿Se puede modificar el paradigma internacional? América latina en UNGASS 2016: Un impulso restringido, una cumbre anodina. *CIDOB Notes Internacionals*, (149), 1–5.

United Nations (UN). (2007). *United nations declaration on the rights of indigenous peoples*. UN.

United Nations (UN). (2013). *The international drug control conventions*. UN.

United Nations Development Programme (UNDP). (2013). *Informe Regional de Desarrollo Humano 2013–2014*. UNDP.

Valdomir, S. (2015). "Alguien tiene que ser el primero." *Nueva Sociedad*, (255), 106–116.

Valencia, R. (2015). After Mujica: Can Uruguay Maintain Its Progressive Model? World Politics Review. https://www.worldpoliticsreview.com/articles/17262/

after-mujica-can-uruguay-maintain-its-progressive-model. Accessed on May 7, 2016.

Vaz, J. Activist AECU. Interview with author, September 16, 2014, Montevideo, Uruguay.

Viscardi, N. (2016). Políticas de seguridad en Uruguay: Un análisis a través la Ley de Regularización del Cannabis. Paper presented at the 2016 Congress of the Latin American Studies Association.

von Hoffmann, J. (2015a). Assessment of the first year of the legally regulated cannabis market in Uruguay. *GDPO Situation Analysis* (pp. 1–8). Swansea: Global Drug Policy Observatory. https://www.swansea.ac.uk/media/Uruguay%20Situation%20Analysis.pdf

von Hoffmann, J. (2015b). Legitimizing legalization or restricting reform? The media's role in Uruguay's drug policy reform process. Paper presented at the SLAS Conference 2015.

von Hoffmann, J. (2015c). *The politics of drug policy reform: "Legalizing" cannabis in Uruguay*. MPhil Thesis, University of Oxford, Oxford.

von Hoffmann, J. (2016a). De Palabras y Hechos: The rhetoric and reality of cannabis reform in Latin America (2009–2016). Paper presented at the ISSDP Conference 2016.

von Hoffmann, J. (2016b). The international dimension of drug policy reform in Uruguay. *International Journal of Drug Policy*, *34*, 27–33. doi: https://doi.org/10.1016/j.drugpo.2016.04.015

Walsh, J., & Ramsey, G. (2015). *Uruguay's drug policy: Major innovations, major challenges*. Washington: Brookings.

Williams, J. (1997). Waging the War on Drugs in Bolivia. *WOLA Background Paper* (pp. 1–41). Washington: Washington Office on Latin America (WOLA).

Yans, R. (2013). Statement by Mr. Raymond Yans, President, International Narcotics Control Coard. Delivered at the special event of the fifty-sixth session of the Commission on Narcotic Drugs launch of the United Nations Office on Drugs and Crime world drug report, on the occasion of the International Day against Drug Abuse and Illicit Drug Trafficking. Vienna: International Narcotics Control Board (INCB).

Youngers, C. A. (2013, February 12). Bolivia officially returns as a party to the 1961 single convention on narcotic drugs. Retrieved from https://www.wola.org/analysis/bolivia-officially-returns-as-a-party-to-the-1961-single-convention-on-narcotic-drugs/. Accessed November 19, 2017.

Youngers, C. A., & Ledebur, K. (2015). Building on Progress. *WOLA Research Report* (pp. 1–21). Washington: Washington Office on Latin America (WOLA).

Zuazo, M. (2010). ¿Los movimientos sociales en el poder? *Nueva Sociedad*, *227*, 120–135.

Chapter 10

The Netherlands, Portugal and the Czech Republic: Political Perceptions and Legal Realities

Danilo Ballotta and Brendan Hughes

Abstract

In Europe, the Netherlands, Portugal and the Czech Republic are the countries increasingly portrayed as having the most 'progressive', 'liberal', or even 'radical' drugs policies in Europe. In a post-United Nations General Assembly Special Session (UNGASS) 2016 period and with the 2019 UN target date approaching, the EU and these countries within are bound to play a key role in the definition of an international drug policy for the next decade. This chapter analyses how the perceptions of these countries match against the drugs legislations and how they fit into the overall EU drug policy approach.

Keywords: Legislation; policy; drug use; Commission on narcotic drugs; UNGASS

Introduction

In Europe, a number of countries are increasingly lauded for their drug policies by commentators supporting an outlook that usually involves lower penalties for drug offences and, if any response is necessary from the state, one more directly aimed at improving the health of the user. In the authors' experience of monitoring drug laws and policies – and commentaries on them – around the EU for more than 15 years, the Netherlands, Portugal and the Czech Republic are the countries most often portrayed as having the most 'progressive', 'liberal' or even

Collapse of the Global Order on Drugs: From UNGASS 2016 to Review 2019, 217–231

doi:10.1108/978-1-78756-487-920181010

'radical' drugs policies in Europe. There are various definitions of what a policy is. The European Monitoring Centre for Drugs and Drug Addiction (EMCDDA, 2017a, 2017b, 2017c, 2017d, 2017e) uses the definition that it is the combination of the laws, the political directions, and the public expenditure on a particular topic.[1] We suggest in this case, though, that it is used broadly as a synonym for laws only, and so our main focus will be on the perceptions and the wording of the laws.

So, if all three countries (claim to) have laws in compliance with the United Nations Drug Conventions and the EU Drug Strategy, how are they seen in the public perception? We suggest it is the following aspects: the Netherlands' paradigm-shifting 'coffee shop policy' has evolved since the 1970s which has, in essence, created a de-facto licit market for cannabis nationwide; Portugal is known as the first country to decriminalise use of all drugs in 2001, with a gradual improvement in key public health markers, including a drop in overdose deaths; and the Czech Republic is also known as having recently decriminalised drug possession offences, and is often referred to as liberal, as well as developing a comprehensive strategy that addresses most licit and illicit addictive behaviours together.

This chapter will analyse how these perceptions match against the drugs legislations of these countries; and how they fit among their European peers.

The Netherlands

The Perception

'Cannabis is legal in the Netherlands/Amsterdam'. The Netherlands is often considered as a country of liberal policies, with various examples: drugs, sex work, same-sex marriage, abortion and euthanasia.

The Background

Following the recommendations of the governmental expert commissions led by Hulsman and Baan in 1972, proposing to introduce a 'risk scale' based on medical, pharmacological, sociological and psychological data, Dutch law was fundamentally amended in 1976, introducing the version currently in force. Accordingly, the 1976 Opium Act, codifying these principles, distinguished between drugs presenting unacceptable risks (unofficially called 'hard drugs') and other drugs (unofficially called 'soft drugs', mainly cannabis products).

The underlying arguments defended by the commissions' experts for not arresting individual drug users referred to the counterproductive potential of criminal law in this area. The idea of not arresting individual drug users unless

[1]'Drug policy is the overall direction and approach taken by a government to address (illicit) drug issues. It encompasses the whole system of laws, regulatory measures, courses of action and funding priorities concerning (illicit) drugs put into effect by a government or its representatives'. EMCDDA (2017), Policy evaluation topic overview at http://www.emcdda.europa.eu/publications/topic-overviews/policy-evaluation.

they cause social nuisance or show criminal behaviour became a well-established policy practice (Cohen, 1994). This is detailed mainly by guidelines issued by the Office of the Public Prosecutor ('the Opium Act Directive'). The penal provisions set in the framework of the drugs laws must be understood in this context.

Around this time, coffee shops (cannabis sales outlets licensed by the municipality) gradually emerged as the 'official/unofficial' sale points of cannabis, albeit under strict conditions. Coffee shops were and still are officially tolerated with the goal of separation of the markets – the attempt to keep young people, who experiment with cannabis, away from other drugs and provide a safe space for sale and use. The sale of small quantities of cannabis in coffee shops is still technically an offence, but prosecution proceedings are only instituted if the operator or owner of the shop does not meet certain criteria issued by the Prosecutor General, discussed below. However, since 2000, governments have placed further restrictions on coffee shops, and the number of them in the Netherlands has been steadily reducing over that time. For example, one priority of a more recent Dutch Government was combating the nuisance and crime associated with coffee shops. With this aim, a scheme to convert coffee shops into closed clubs with registered members was trialled, but then dropped in 2012. From January 2013, coffee shops can only legally be used by residents of the Netherlands on production of an identity card or residence permit. Municipalities may also introduce restrictions such as the minimum distance from schools.

The Current Policy

Drug use itself is not an offence in the Netherlands, even if there are situations when the use of drugs is prohibited and punishable; for example, in schools and on public transportation.

As far as the possession of drugs for personal use is concerned, the maximum penalty for possessing cannabis not exceeding 30 g is one month imprisonment and/or a €2,300 fine. Possession of maximum of 5 g of cannabis will see the drug being confiscated, but will not lead to investigation or prosecution. Using drugs without causing a social nuisance or showing criminal behaviour is accorded a low priority by prosecutors and police. This policy extends to other drugs. Anyone found in possession of a small amount of list I (i.e., 'hard') drugs intended for personal use will generally not be prosecuted, though the police will confiscate the drugs and inform a care agency. Recent prosecutor guidelines set out fines of €375 for possession of 1 g or double that for 5 g of hard drugs for first offenders; for cannabis, possession of 5–30 g may be fined €75.

Possession of cannabis or other drugs for commercial purposes is considered a more serious offence and will be prosecuted subject to prosecutor guidelines. Production of cannabis up to 100 kg is liable for a recommended 10 months in prison for a first offence, while if the substance is not cannabis the maximum penalty is eight years. The maximum penalties can be increased by one-third if the same crime has been committed more than once.

The directives for offences against the Opium Act indicate how to proceed with regard to criminal investigation, prosecution and penalties for each drug-related offence. Among the guidelines are those indicating the quantities to be considered as a 'small quantity of drugs' for personal use, above, and the conditions of running of the coffee shops:

- no more than 5 g per person may be sold in any one transaction, and no more than 500 g of stock to be kept;
- no hard drugs may be sold;
- drugs may not be advertised;
- the coffee shop must not cause any nuisance;
- they are not allowed to sell alcoholic beverages;
- no drugs may be sold to minors (under the age of 18), nor may minors be admitted to the premises;
- non-residents of the Netherlands may not be allowed to enter or purchase.

Implementation and enforcement of the residency rule varies by municipality. A proposal to limit coffee shop sales to cannabis products with THC levels under 15% remains pending while enforcement issues are addressed.

The Mayor may order a coffee shop to be closed when the criteria are being disregarded (Article 13a of the Opium Act), and municipalities may determine whether to allow coffee shops to operate within their boundaries or not. They may also impose additional rules.

A particular form of waiver of prosecution is the possibility of transaction. All criminal offences that are penalised with less than six years of imprisonment (in current practice, this means 90% of all criminal cases) and additionally all minor offences can be processed and settled by the Public Prosecutor by offering the suspect to redeem the case. This means that the Public Prosecutor proposes to the suspect to pay a certain sum of money or to fulfil certain other conditions. In exchange, the Public Prosecutor will not bring the case to court. The penalty asked for by the Public Prosecutor cannot exceed the fine set for the criminal offence.

An evaluation of the Dutch drug policy in 2009 found that the coffee shops were the main source of cannabis for users, the markets for soft and hard drugs remained separate and adult cannabis use was relatively low compared to other European countries, even if those countries have no such outlets and apparently have strict criminal sanctions for users. However, underage use was high (whether due to coffee shops, greater acceptance of use or other factors), there was serious nuisance from drug tourism, such as public consumption and parking congestion in border towns, and the sector had become increasingly commercialised and of interest to organised crime. The more recent legal developments described above took place partly in response to this evaluation. There is still no ability to regulate the product being sold, either for potency or for contaminants, though in 2012 the government stated its intention to classify cannabis products with potency higher than 15% THC as 'list 1' substances, meaning they would not be tolerated in coffee shops. This has not yet been implemented due to the practical difficulties of testing such products; they cannot be tested at source as no production is permitted, but testing user doses at retail level would be prohibitively expensive.

The latest development, following an election in March 2017 and new coalition agreement of October 2017, is that the coalition will agree to allow trials of tolerated cultivation in six to 10 municipalities to stock the coffee shops and thus move the production out of the shadows; product regulation might then be developed.

The Opium Act Directive is only a guidance and only addresses half of the supply issue: no cultivation or import is tolerated, which makes the supply of the coffee shops an official blind spot. What started as a minor policy of tolerance has grown to become a major industry, with many shops selling much more per day than their agreed maximum stock of 500 g, introducing potent strains of cannabis (with associated health risks for users) and no form of quality control; currently regulated by illegal market forces rather than the state. Various restrictive measures have been taken since the evaluation of 2009, but it is only as recently as October 2017 that we start to see a national attempt to solve the issue by other means.

The Broader Context

For years, the Dutch system has been subject to detailed analysis and commentary on its coffee shop policy. Two other approaches in Europe have also attracted media attention. The first is 'Pusher Street' in Christiania, an alternative lifestyle commune in Copenhagen, Denmark, that has also existed since the 1970s; this 'street' also offers a form of supply that has been more or less tolerated under certain governments or city administrations, but with a turbulent existence, often being raided and even voluntarily shut down by residents. Again, supply has been taken over by organised crime. In recent years, Copenhagen City Council has made three proposals to introduce a regulated cannabis market in the city, including state cultivation of cannabis, with designated and regulated retail premises. So far, the proposals have not been accepted by national governments. The second is the model of 'cannabis clubs' that have become prevalent particularly in some areas of Spain over the last 10–15 years, based on the principle that if one plant is tolerated for one person's personal use, then a collection of plants belonging to a group of owners, who share the cannabis produced, should also be tolerated. In many of these clubs, it seems that new 'members' are permitted to join, some after paying a fee, effectively making the clubs cannabis supply systems to the public. However, while they may be tolerated by their regional administrations, the Spanish federal government has been and is clearly opposed, stating that they are forms of trafficking by organised criminals, and has (repeatedly) prosecuted several club owners. In 2015, three Supreme Court judgements – enough to produce a binding precedent – stated that 'organised, institutionalised and persistent cultivation and distribution of cannabis among an association open to new members is considered drug trafficking'. Neither of these two examples are at the level of the Netherlands where a national prosecutors' guideline effectively allows the coffee shops to exist.

It is a misconception that cannabis is legal in the Netherlands. Personal possession or sale of any cannabis in the Netherlands is a crime punishable by prison; but arresting and criminalising sellers who adhere to certain guidelines, and users possessing small quantities for personal use of any drug, is not considered to be a priority. For 20 years, the number of shops has been steadily falling while the restrictions have been increasing; only at the end of 2017 do we see a halt in this trend with the cultivation trials.

Portugal

The Perception

Portugal 'decriminalised' or 'legalised' all drug use in 2001, the first country in the world to do so. This has been a 'resounding success' or a 'disastrous failure', according to the commentator's political position. While the change took effect in 2001, criticised by many at an international level, the wider world did not really notice until 2009 when a report was published by the Cato Institute which appeared to paint the Portuguese system as the panacea to all drug problems.

The Background

In Portugal, the main drug control law was first passed in 1993. Under this law, drug use itself, as well as possession for personal use, was a criminal offence punishable with imprisonment of up to three months, or up to one year if the quantity of illicit drugs found in possession exceeded three daily doses. It did, however, already state that in minor cases punishment could be waived.

By the end of the 1990s, Portugal witnessed a serious drug problem affecting all sectors of society; widespread addiction among users, marginalisation, high rates of HIV/AIDS infections, drugs-related deaths, public nuisance and insecurity. This triggered a wide debate among both professionals and politicians that led to the adoption in 1999 of one of the first, and probably more comprehensive, national drugs strategies in Europe. This strategy was already recognising the decriminalisation of drugs use as a way to reach out to the more marginalised population of users and bring them into contact with care services. Users were now to be considered as individuals in need of health care more than criminals to be punished.

The Current Policy

The year after the 1999 strategy was approved, the Portuguese parliament adopted law 30/2000, which came into force on 1 July 2001, officially decriminalising the use and personal possession of drugs.

The key word here is 'decriminalisation', as distinct from 'legalisation'. The new law maintained the status of illegality for using or possessing any drug for personal use without authorisation. However, the offence changed from a criminal one, with prison a possible punishment, to an administrative one. The procedure and mechanism for dealing with such offences also changed and is now dealt with under an administrative procedure. When a person is caught in possession of no more than 10 daily doses of drugs (their corresponding gram limits had already been established in a regulation), and the police have no suspicions or evidence that supply offences are involved, the drug will be seized. The case will then be transmitted to the system of Commissions for the Dissuasion of Drug Addiction (CDT) managed by the Ministry of Health. From now on a drug user answers for his/her drug law offence to a panel of health and legal experts, not to police and magistrates. Here is the fundamental change of Portugal, and the striking difference with all other systems around the world, including the American drug courts or alternatives to punishments in other EU member states. The objective has changed from punishment for breaking the law, to assistance to overcome a potential health, social or existential problem.

The formation of these 'civil tribunals' is key. The CDTs, spread across the national territory, are composed of three members: a legal expert, appointed by the Ministry of Justice, a health professional and a social worker, appointed by the Ministry of Health. The CDTs are supported by a small team of health professionals who meet the person charged with illegal drug use/possession, in order to evaluate his/her situation with the aim of treating eventual addictions and rehabilitating the person. Sanctioning by fine (though not for dependent users), even if possible, is not the main objective in this phase. The ground-breaking change, often not perceived nor discussed within sensational media reports, that is at the basis of the Portuguese system is the inclusion of the principle of 'humanity' in the 1999 strategy, manifesting itself in the absence of paternalism and moral judgement between the judging State and the drug consumer.

The effects of the law – or at least, the changes in various relevant indicators – have been monitored and argued over. Press coverage is rarely nuanced and tends to paint the Portuguese model as the world's answer to drug problems without commenting how similar changes in indicators, for instance HIV infection among injecting drug users, opioid substitution treatment access, and drug-related deaths, have been seen in many countries in Europe without such a legal change.

The 2017 study on the Effects of Dissuasion Intervention (SICAD, 2017) found that important changes in illicit psychoactive substances use were identified among the drug using offenders interviewed by the Commissions (CDT), (but not in alcohol use). Offenders reported stopping use (cannabis and cocaine) or reducing frequency of use (cannabis), and also some changes in the circumstances (less use alone) and contexts of illicit substances use (less consumption at music festivals, for instance), including fewer bad experiences related to consumption. The study also found an increase in risk perceptions on the probability of occurring problems in case of illicit substance use (also related to alcohol drinking but at an inferior level), as well as on the risk assessment of the health consequences of using cannabis (for instance, in comparison with alcohol or tobacco), of sporadic cocaine use, and of NPS use in comparison with other drugs. Three quarters of the participants attributed some responsibility for these changes to the CDTs, mainly in the reduction and cessation of consumption.

The change in the law has changed also the work of police and magistrates in their daily practice. Police forces finding a person in possession of a quantity of drugs (under the limit of the daily use) will now seize the substance and instruct the user to appear in the next 72 hours in front of the CDT for his/her hearing. The Prosecutor will now deal only with cases of drug trafficking. If the prosecutor receives a 'file' on a drug user (drug use/possession within the established daily doses or if the quantities are above the limit but there is no evidence of trafficking), he/she would not open a case but would send the file to the CDT.

The 2001 law might have contributed to reinforcing the conviction, also among non-health professionals, that drug dependence is a treatable health condition and that the person caught in possession of drugs has his/her owns needs and rights to care. Portuguese legislation supports this underlying philosophy including, besides the decriminalisation law, a comprehensive legal system in support of drug dependent users to contribute to reducing the risks and minimising the damage caused by drug use. So together with the removal of criminal sanctions and consequent stigma towards drug users, in 2001, Portugal approved another law embodying the concept of harm reduction: the Decree-law 183/2001, on 21 June 2001 (SICAD, 2001). This comprehensive law regulates harm reduction interventions overall, as well as drop-in centres for dependent users, refuges and shelters, mobile centres for the prevention of infectious diseases, low-threshold substitution programmes (methadone and buprenorphine), syringe exchange schemes, contact and information units and street workers. The law introduced the possibility for setting up 'programmes for supervised drug use', meaning drug consumption facilities, but as of today (June 2018) these programmes have not been implemented in the territory.

Portugal's drugs policy is clearly different to other national drug policies worldwide, which are heavily based on the threat of punishment as dissuasion from the use of drugs. The 'radicalism' in Portugal is to have reduced the emphasis on punishment, relying on medical and social professionals to deal with a health and social problem. On the international scene, while Portugal supports the EU approach for a more balanced, comprehensive, evidence based policy on drugs, it is not lobbying other countries to follow in its footsteps and does not profess this change as an exportable best practice. Nonetheless today, Portugal is praised as a model of best practices, fully committed to the principles of the Drug Control Conventions, putting health and welfare at its centre and applying a balanced, comprehensive and integrated approach, based on the principle of proportionality and the respect for human rights (INCB President, 2016).

The Broader Context

Spain and Italy have never committed to criminal punishment for drug use offences, and we will see how the Czech Republic also had 'non-criminal' punishments in the period 1990–1998, before the Portuguese law was passed. Indeed, drug use itself is not an offence at all in Italy, and several other European countries, so Portugal's 'non-criminal' offence of use might yet be considered rather punitive by some. Even now in Europe we see comparable yet different approaches. Austria has increasingly changed its system to divert as many users as possible to health systems rather than punishment, but has maintained the possibility of criminal prosecution in the law; while Croatia clearly decriminalised minor drug possession offences but did not make major changes to its responses, so the emphasis remains on (non-criminal) punishment even if some diversion to treatment is available. While there have been many discussions of moving to the Portuguese model, particularly in Norway since 2011 and Ireland since 2015, the only comparable change was made in Malta in 2015, with its law on treatment instead of imprisonment.

In summary, other countries had 'decriminalised' drug possession offences before. Several European countries, such as Spain and Italy, had never criminalised such offences, and the key point about the Portuguese system is not the decriminalisation but the nationwide and consistent focus on health-related responses rather than penalties for users.

The Czech Republic

The Perception

The Czech Republic is among those countries whose drug policy is regarded as pragmatic or even too liberal, depending on the viewpoint. This is probably because of a decriminalisation in 2010 and the subsequent political discourse in recent years.

The Background

Possession of a drug for personal use was a criminal activity during soviet times. It ceased to be a criminal offence in 1990 due to an amendment of the criminal code, but in 1998, the law was again changed to criminalise personal possession of a quantity 'greater than small' (Mravcik, 2015). Quantities found under that amount would receive a punishment under the Act on Misdemeanours, usually a small fine from the police or other local administrative entity. As in several European countries, the Act did not define the term 'quantity greater than small'; but an instruction of the Supreme Public Prosecutor did set out certain quantities of drugs and that guidance was used by the police and the prosecutors on a common basis, though it was not obligatory for the judges. In 2001, the government decided to differentiate drugs in the criminal code according to their health and social risks, initially in three, and finally in two groups: cannabis and other drugs (Zabransky, 2004). The re-criminalisation of drug possession from 1999 was evaluated by a study in 2001, the Impact Analysis Project of New Drugs Legislation (PAD), and findings suggested that the tougher law did not deliver the desired deterrent effect but that was more costly for the country in economic and health terms (Zabransky, Miovsky, Gajdosıkova, Mravcık, in Mravcik, 2015). The recommended differentiation between drug types took until 2009 to implement, and the new criminal code came into force on January 2010. For the first time, a Government Regulation clearly specified what quantities would be considered 'greater than small', rather than leaving them to non-binding prosecutor guidelines. This is often referred as a 'decriminalization of cannabis possession' (see Červený, Chomynová, Mravčik, & Van Ours Jan, 2015). The perception may stem from an article in the English-language newspaper the Prague Post, reporting on the new law at the end of 2009 and declaring it a decriminalisation; there was no reference to the fact that the system of misdemeanour fines had existed previously, would continue, and it was only the threshold quantities which had been clarified. While EMCDDA was aware of this misinterpretation and published a clarification article in its DrugNet newsletter (2010) that seemed to receive little coverage and so the perception has continued.

In 2013, the Government Regulation establishing the quantity thresholds was declared unconstitutional (only Parliament, not Government, should define a criminal offence) but the thresholds were re-established with little variation in a Supreme Court standpoint issued in 2014.

The Current Policy

Drug use 'per se' is not regarded as an offence. Possession of a drug for personal use is a criminal offence for 'quantity greater than small' according to the expression used in the Czech law (Mravcik, 2015). Possession of less than 10 g of herbal cannabis and 5 g of hashish, 40 pieces of magic mushrooms, five blotters (small paper pieces) of LSD, four tablets of Ecstasy, 1.5 g of methamphetamine, 1.5 g of heroin, 1 g of cocaine was not considered a criminal offence. Since 1998, if anyone is caught with a small quantity of drugs on him/her without intention to supply, the police/prosecutors would deliver the case to the local Police units, or from 2009 the municipal authorities, that are competent to impose a non-criminal sanction to the offender, such as a fine or warning; but from 2010 the distinction is more clear. Possession of 'greater than small' quantities of cannabis could result in a jail sentence of up to one year. For other illicit drugs, the sentence was two years. Here, we see the distinction between penalties for cannabis and other drug possession that had been recommended several years previously.

It can be seen from the various changes that this system provoked a large debate in the Czech society and among professionals and was often under review. The evaluation of the 2010 law reducing penalties for cannabis possession was also evaluated by Cerveny et al. (2015), suggesting that the lower penalties applied by the policy change did not seem to affect the age of onset of cannabis use, the supply of cannabis in the country, nor the perceived risks related to cannabis use, nor persuade abstainers to start cannabis use. In this way, it suggested that there were no major negative effects of the law on the main social and epidemiological indicators, which is a common concern for any policy change that reduces penalties (Cerveny, 2015).

The prosecutor or court can also conditionally suspend the prosecution when the offender who abuses addictive substance(s) committed the crime under the influence of or in connection with the above-mentioned abuse. Protective treatment can be imposed together with the penalty or with its suspension. Nevertheless, the protective treatment is not imposed when it is obvious that its purpose will not be achieved.

Judicial practice demonstrates a 'soft' approach against offenders who possessed a drug for personal use. A range of discretionary alternatives of criminal sanction are available to the judge who may decide to apply them instead of imprisonment for the offenders whose offences are not too serious. These are often a suspended sentence (of imprisonment, with or without probation) if the offence would entail a sentence of imprisonment shorter than three years. A community service involving 50–300 hours of unpaid work designed to be of benefit to the local community can also be imposed, or a community service with probation involving up to one year of supervision.

Both in the EU and on the international scene the Czech Republic has consistently, in recent years, promoted a balanced, comprehensive and evidence-based approach to drug policy, supporting decision making based on evidence, monitoring and evaluation. The Czech Republic is also very vocal about a rebalancing of international policies towards a social and health centred approach, which focusses on demand and harm reduction without neglecting the need to counter illicit drug production and trafficking (United Nations General Assembly Special Session (UNGASS), 2016).

Overall, the Czech Republic has consistently expressed and assessed its drug policy in line with these best practices since its first strategy document in 1993, and it was one of the first countries to evaluate its strategy in 2004.

The Czech Republic has implemented a range of drug demand responses and is among the growing group of countries (13 in 2017) that now addresses substance use problems (illicit drugs, alcohol, tobacco) and addictions (gambling) in a broadly focussed strategy (since 2014, when the 2010 Czech strategy was updated). Moreover, the health-centred approach (three out of four objectives of the national strategy: (1) primary prevention; (2) treatment and social reintegration; (3) harm reduction and (4) drug supply reduction and regulation), links very much with the new health and human-right-centred approach defined in April 2016 by the UN general assembly in the UNGASS outcome document.

It cannot be excluded that the recent policy on medical cannabis has added to the perception of the Czech Republic as being liberal in its drugs policy. In 2013, the Czech Republic became only the second country in Europe, after the Netherlands (2003), to develop a fully legal system of production and prescription of cannabis herb for medical use.

The Broader Context

The Czech Republic is one of 10 countries in the EU28 that has a minor offence of possession of any drug, where no incarceration is possible, and this has been the case for 20 years already; only the quantities have changed. Various European countries have experimented over this time with the clarity of threshold quantities, either establishing them for prosecution clarity or abolishing them as overly rigid. The EMCDDA has developed a working definition of the act of 'decriminalisation'[2] as opposed to 'depenalisation' or 'legalisation', but there remains no objective test for it, and it seems to be applied or rejected according to the values

[2]What is decriminalisation of drugs? https://www.youtube.com/watch?v=9NKhpujqOXc

of the commenter more than to objective reference to criminal codes or criminal records. Certainly in Europe, countries have various ways in which a user will not be convicted, but these may be due to the laws, police or prosecutor guidelines, or the powers of discretion of the judiciary.

The integration in one common strategy of the issues of alcohol, tobacco, illicit drugs and gambling makes The Czech Republic drugs policy among the most comprehensive in the EU and elsewhere.

With regard to prescription of cannabis for medical purposes, systems have been developed in Italy, Croatia (both 2015), Germany, Poland (both 2017) and Denmark in 2018, while Ireland and Luxembourg are advancing in their national developments. Like many medicines in the EU, prescription rules and practices vary between countries.

Discussion

Dutch, Portuguese and Czech drug policy approaches, seen through the lenses of their drug legislations, are similar but different, not least as they are operating in different social contexts and facing different phenomena in the field of drugs. One thing found in common in these three systems is the institutional questioning of the belief that criminal punishment should be the default response to a drug user.

In all three countries, possession of a small amount of cannabis for personal use does not attract criminal charges or penalties. However, in many other European countries possession of cannabis for personal use is also considered to be a minor offence and no incarceration is possible. Portugal goes further in extending this principle to all drugs, but here again it is not alone in the EU; another eight countries exclude imprisonment for minor possession of any drug for personal use. As this is more common than might be thought at first, it is far from being an indicator of a radical approach to drugs. It may be adopted for a number of different reasons: avoid gaining a criminal record, avoid overloading the justice system and reduce costs, attract users to treatment, etc. Internationally it is in line with the most recent interpretations of the INCB on conformity with the UN drugs conventions, and it is supported by the EU drug strategy.

The policies analysed follow established European best practices in developing drug policies and strategies, in that they monitor the drug situation, draw on available research evidence and respond to evaluation. In all analysed cases expert commissions (in the Netherlands and Portugal) and scientific evaluations (in the Czech Republic) are at the origin of breakthrough changes, suggesting a link between evaluation, expert consultation and policy making processes.

In the international scene, these three countries are fully integrated in the EU approach as enshrined in the variety of EU drugs strategies and plans adopted since the year 2000.[3]

If a distinction should be noted, this might be found in the public discourse around the goals and the objectives of the international drug control system.

---

[3]http://www.emcdda.europa.eu/publications/topic-overviews/policy-evaluation_en

In national statements at UN level, the Czech Republic has denounced the failures of the current systems (Commission on Narcotic Drugs (CND),2016), and of the war on drugs, which is in the words of the Czech Minister of Health Svatopluk Němeček at the UNGASS 2016, 'fuelling HIV', 'deaths' and 'a de facto prohibition on controlled medicines' (UNGASS, 2016). The Czech Republic adopted the UNGASS Outcome Document, even though regretting 'the denial of evidence in several parts', in order to continue the discussion and the coordination on international drug policy, feeling that UNGASS 2016 was not the end of the debate but its beginning (UNGASS, 2016). The fact that Czech officials have denounced international drug policy as not evidence-based, and defended principles of a rational and effective drug policy oriented towards human rights and public health and based on scientific evidence and best practice, might have supported the perception of a liberal position in drug policy.

The Dutch public discourse has often stressed that its national policy is strongly rooted in the principles of the 'balanced approach' and of 'evidence base'. At the High Level Segment of the CND in 2014, the Netherlands robustly defended its harm reduction and coffee shop policy, insisting the latter was based in the principles of state sovereignty and discretion and thus in line with interpretation of international treaties. It presented both as having given clear and successful results in the improvement of public health (CND, 2014).

Portugal has always presented its drug policy internationally with a relatively low-key policy discourse. It has never claimed to have found the silver bullet of drug policy, only a solution that was needed and that worked in the Portuguese context and realities of the end of the twentieth century. The key difference has been a consistent and coherent policy approach, enshrined in law, rather than having a punitive legislation with guidelines for soft enforcement; and by addressing the drug user through entities based in the Ministry of Health, not Interior or Justice. In 2015, at the 58th CND in Vienna, the then President of the INCB Mr Sipp delivered a strong encouragement to Portugal for its drug policy. He recognised that the Portuguese system is not unique, as non-criminal responses to the possession of small quantities for personal use can be found in many other countries. However, he stated that, in the lead up to the General Assembly Special Session on the World Drug Problem, the Portuguese approach could be considered as a model of best practice (INCB President, 2016).

All three countries' legal approaches are presented as sitting comfortably in and not outside the EU drug policy approach, as consolidated in the variety of EU common positions presented in the last years including at UNGASS 2016, and clearly established in the EU Drugs Strategy 2013–2020 (European Union Consilium, 2013). Their differences are to be found in the tone and the nuances of the expressions used, but in all three systems analysed, we can see the pursuit of a balanced, evidence based drug policy that supports the delivery of effective responses to established and emerging drug problems. If a common approach were to be expected after UNGASS, a conservative prediction may be that their policy models that offer differing alternatives to the criminalisation of the user are taken as examples of what policy variation is possible still within the Conventions. Nevertheless, there have been major changes in national politics and cannabis policy since 2012 around the globe, and so a more radical scenario might also be envisaged. Following the influential changes in the United States, there has been the Czech legalisation of medicinal cannabis in 2013 and an attempt by the Portuguese Left Bloc to legalise cannabis for recreational purposes in 2015; the Left Bloc then entered government and succeeded to legalise cannabis for medicinal purposes in June 2018. From late 2017, the Dutch government has agreed to establish trials to solve the 'back-door problem' of supplying the coffee shops, which earlier governments had refused for years. So, while unlikely when considered today, it would not be beyond the realms of possibility to see one or more of these countries supporting a position to regulate some means of supplying cannabis for non-medical purposes in the coming years.

We will continue to observe.

References

Červený, J., Chomynová, P., Mravčik, V., & Van Ours Jan, C. (2015). *Cannabis decriminalisations and the age of onset of cannabis use, No. 2015-007*. Tilburg, The Netherlands: Department of Economics, CentER, Tilburg University.

Cohen, P. (1994). The case of the two Dutch drug policy commissions. An exercise in harm reduction 1968–1976. Paper presented at the 5th international conference on the reduction of drug-related harm, 7–11 March 1994, Addiction Research Foundation, Toronto. Revised in 1996.

Commission on Narcotic Drugs (CND). (2014). Statement of the Netherlands at the high-level segment of the 57th session of the commission on narcotic drugs, Vienna, 14 March 2014. Retrieved from http://www.unodc.org/documents/commissions/CND/CND_Sessions/CND_57/HLS/Statements/Fri_14th_PM/02_Netherlands_140314_pm.pdf

Commission on Narcotic Drugs (CND). (2016). Statement of Czech Republic at the special segment on the preparation for the special session of the General Assembly on the World Drug Problem to be held in 2016. Retrieved from http://www.unodc.org/documents/commissions/CND/CND_Sessions/CND_59/Statements/10_Czech_Republic.pdf

European Monitoring Centre for Drugs and Drug Addiction. (2010). Drugnet newsletter. Retrieved from http://www.emcdda.europa.eu/system/files/publications/525/176513_DrugnetEurope_EN_web_200895.pdf

European Monitoring Centre for Drugs and Drug Addiction (EMCDDA). (2011, June). *Drug policy profiles — Portugal*. Lisbon, Portugal: EMCDDA.

European Monitoring Centre for Drugs and Drug Addiction. (2017a). *The Netherlands, country drug report 2017*. Luxembourg: Publications Office of the European Union.

European Monitoring Centre for Drugs and Drug Addiction. (2017b). *Portugal, country drug report 2017*. Luxembourg: Publications Office of the European Union.

European Monitoring Centre for Drugs and Drug Addiction. (2017c). *Czech Republic, country drug report 2017*. Luxembourg: Publications Office of the European Union.

European Monitoring Centre for Drugs and Drug Addiction. (2017d, June). *European legal database on drugs*. Lisbon, Portugal: EMCDDA.

European Monitoring Centre for Drugs and Drug Addiction. (2017e). EU drug strategy 2013–2020. Retrieved from http://www.emcdda.europa.eu/document-library/eu-drugs-strategy-2013-20

European Union Consilium. (2013). European Union drugs strategy 2013–2020. Brussels: European Union. Retrieved from http://www.consilium.europa.eu/en/documents-publications/publications/european-union-drugs-strategy-2013-2020/

Filipková, T. (2015). Cannabis policy in the Czech Republic, TNI (Sept. 25, 2015), Retrieved from https://www.tni.org/en/article/cannabis-policy-in-the-Czech-republic. Retrieved from https://perma.cc/3LXC-NG8Y

Greenwald, G. (2009). *Drug decriminalization in Portugal: Lessons for creating fair and successful Drug Policies*. Cato Institute. Retrieved from https://www.cato.org/publications/white-paper/drug-decriminalization-portugal-lessons-creating-fair-successful-drug-policies

Laar, M. V., & Ooyen-Houben, M. (Eds.). (2009). *Evaluation of the Dutch national drug policy*. WODC, Trimbo Instituute. Retrieved from https://english.wodc.nl/onderzoeksdatabase/evaluatie-drugsbeleid.aspx

Mravcık, V. (2015). (De)criminalisation of possession of drugs for personal use: A view from the Czech Republic. *International Journal of Drug Policy*, 26(2015), 705–707.

Reconvened fifty-eighth session of the CND. (2015). Statement of the President of the International Narcotics Control Board (INCB), Mr. Werner Sipp, Special event: A public health approach as a base for drugs policy: The Portuguese case, Vienna, 9 December 2015.

Report of the International Narcotics Control Board. (INCB). (2001). pp. 167–169 E/INCB/2001/1.

SICAD – General-Directorate for Intervention on Addictive Behaviours and Dependencies Ministry of Health, Estratégia nacional de luta contra a droga, PRESIDÊNCIA DO CONSELHO DE MINISTROS, Resolução do Conselho de Ministros no 46/99.

SICAD. (2001). General-Directorate for Intervention on Addictive Behaviours and Dependencies Ministry of Health, Decree-law no. 183/2001, of 21st June.

SICAD. (2017). General-Directorate for Intervention on Addictive Behaviours and Dependencies Ministry of Health – Portugal. Executive summary effects of dissuasion intervention, based on the Commissions for the Dissuasion of Drug Addiction Activity. Retrieved from http://www.sicad.pt/BK/EstatisticaInvestigacao/EstudosConcluidos/Lists/SICAD_ESTUDOS/Attachments/180/Executive%20Summary%20Dissuasion.en.pdf

Statement of the President of the International Narcotics Control Board (INCB). Mr. Werner Sipp, at a Special event on the Portuguese case, at the Reconvened fifty-eighth session of the CND, on 9 December 2015.

The Guardian. (2017). The long read, Portugal's radical drugs policy is working. Why hasn't the world copied it? Retrieved from https://www.theguardian.com/news/2017/dec/05/portugals-radical-drugs-policy-is-working-why-hasnt-the-world-copied-it

UN General Assembly Special Session (UNGASS) on drugs. (2016). Statement of Czech Republic Ministry of Health Mr. Svatopluk Němeček. Retrieved from https://www.youtube.com/watch?v=x7s5_7W6-sQ

Zabransky, T. (2004). Czech drug laws as an arena of drug policy battle. *Journal of Drug Issues*. *34*(3), 661–686.

Chapter 11

The European Union in Panglossian Stagnation

Caroline Chatwin

Abstract

This chapter provides a critical exploration of the European Union's impact on the 2016 United Nations General Assembly Special Session (UNGASS) proceedings and Outcome document. It demonstrates that the ability to produce a European 'common position' ahead of the UNGASS debates represents a significant step forward in the ability to 'speak with one voice' in the global illicit drug policy arena, and has played an important role in ensuring key issues such as human rights and public health remain on the agenda. In highlights, however, a European failure to engage with issues such as the continuing suitability of the international drug conventions to preside over the current climate of drug policy innovation and experimentation, and the unintended consequences of a 'war on drugs' approach. Ultimately, therefore, it argues that these failures will hamper the development of a more progressive and effective global drug policy.

Keywords: European union; drug policy reform; UNGASS 2016; global drug policy; United Nations

Introduction

The European Union (EU) with regard to the United Nations General Assembly Special Session (UNGASS) 2016 Outcome Document as a significant success, as evidenced by this extract from a recent speech made at the sixtieth session of the Commission on Narcotic Drugs (CND) held in Vienna from

Collapse of the Global Order on Drugs: From UNGASS 2016 to Review 2019, 233–249

doi:10.1108/978-1-78756-487-920181011

13 to 17 March, 2017: 'The EU and its Member States would like to emphasise that the outcome of the General Assembly on the world drug problem held in 2016 is a major step forward in our ability to tackle together the world drug problem' (EU, 2017a, p. 1). Furthermore, it is keen to emphasise the role that it played in the development of that Outcome document: 'We appreciate the inclusion of several of our proposals in the Outcome document' (EU, 2016, p.1). Finally, recent internal (European Commission, 2017a; European Parliament, 2016) and external (RAND, 2017) evaluations of European drug policy, undertaken since the UNGASS 2016 meeting, have been quick to emphasise the significant internal success for the EU represented by the ability to reach a 'common position' (EU, 2015) on UNGASS 2016; no mean feat in the contentious area of illegal drug policy on which the EU has often been described as divided (Boekhaut van Solinge, 1999; Chatwin, 2003; Tops, 2001).

This chapter critically explores the common position put forward by the EU in preparation for UNGASS 2016. It acknowledges the significance of the EU's ability to speak 'with one strong voice'(Council of the European Union, 2012, p. 7) in this area and suggests that the call for drug policies that are 'built upon a sound public health approach, based on scientific evidence and supported by reliable and objective monitoring systems and evaluation, in compliance with human rights' (EU, 2015, p. 2) represents an important step forward in terms of what Member States have previously been able to agree on. An engagement with recent EU contributions to ongoing drug policy debates and preparations for the next UN High Level Ministerial drugs meeting in 2019 further suggests that the EU remains firmly committed to championing change in drug policy in line with the principles outlined above.

While undeniably playing a role in ensuring key issues have made it onto the global drug policy agenda, the EU has, however, also played a significant role in defending the status quo by confirming their ongoing and unwavering support of the current system of international drug control encapsulated by the international drug and psychotropic substance conventions: 'Finally, I would like to underline the position of the EU and its Member States that the three UN Drug Control Conventions and the Universal Declaration on Human Rights are the framework of the global response to the world drug problem' (EU, 2016, p. 1). This chapter, therefore, also explores the limitations of an approach that refuses to acknowledge the failures of existing drug policy or the lack of progress towards global targets to eradicate or significantly reduce drug use. It concludes that the EU is beginning to take the stage as an important global voice on drug policy related matters, but that its capacity to advocate for change is somewhat hampered by its lack of engagement with the continuing suitability of existing systems of international drug control.

The Drive to 'Speak with One Voice'

Drug policy is, inherently, an international issue and the EU has been active in this area since the late 1980s. Seeking to build on the United Nations' success in gaining near global agreement to the prohibition of drugs, illicit drug policy was quickly earmarked as an area for 'ever closer union' within Europe. In the late 1980s and early 1990s when European social policy was in its infancy, the European Parliament organised two commissions charged with investigating the possibility of determining the most effective existing strands of European drug policy, with a view to engendering their implementation across Europe (Blom & van Mastrigt, 1994). When both commissions failed to reach consensus on the most effective style of drug policy and, furthermore, noted that drug policy was an area entrenched in national culture, the principle of subsidiarity (Duff, 1993) was applied and policies designed to control illicit drugs were left in the hands of national governments.

European-level involvement in the control of illicit drugs, however, has remained strong. This is partly evidenced by the significant number of groups and bodies created within the EU in this area including, for example, the Horizontal Drugs Group, which monitors and discusses all cross-pillar activities in the fields of drugs and the European Monitoring Centre for Drugs and Drug Addiction (EMCDDA), which collates and disseminates information on all aspects of the European drug situation In addition, the EU has at regular intervals since 1990, published clear guiding principles in the development of drug policy within Europe via its European Drug Strategy and Action Plans. Finally, more significant inroads into harmonisation of European drug policy have been made in several areas. Framework Decisions have been ratified in two areas of drug policy making – the creation of minimum maximum penalties in serious drug trafficking offences (Council of the European Union, 2004a) and the sharing of information and control of New Psychoactive Substances (NPS) (Council of the European Union, 2005). The other observable trend within European drug policy has been towards the principle of harm reduction with every European Member State now offering a minimum level of needle exchange and substitution treatment programmes (Rhodes & Hedrich, 2010).

Recent drug policy documents produced by the EU have increasingly emphasised the benefits of international cooperation and coordination. The 2009–2012 European Drug Action Plan (Council of the European Union, 2008) included specific aims in this area: to adopt EU common positions on drugs in international fora; and to promote an EU approach to the illegal drug problem. Further, the 2005–2012 European Drug Strategy declared coordination 'key to the establishment and conduct of a successful strategy against drugs (Council of the European Union, 2004b, p. 8). Continuing in this trend, the last European Drug Strategy (Council of the European Union, 2012, p. 7) aims to 'ensure that the EU speaks with one strong voice in international forums'.

This ability to 'speak with a single voice' has proven difficult to achieve in practice. 'Drugs are a sensitive and highly political issue. The debate is often polarised between a more enforcement-oriented approach focussing on measures to combat trafficking and a more tolerant approach that focusses on prevention and reduction of drugs-induced health disorders. The dichotomy is visible both within all the Member States and also between them' (Commission of the European Communities, 2003, p. 4). Within Europe there are a variety of approaches to drugs – consider for example the contrast between the Netherlands where separation of the markets, normalisation of drug users and the application of harm reduction are highly evident policy strategies, and Sweden which operates a zero tolerance approach based on the aim of a drug-free society and which employs criminal sanctions against drug use and coercive treatment (Chatwin, 2011). In attempting to speak for Europe on this issue, the EU must navigate a delicate line, which takes care to be inclusive of all the national policies that fall within its borders.

The creation of a European 'common position' on UNGASS 2016 thus represents somewhat of a success for the development of European drug policy. Its contribution to global debates on the future of drug policy control prove that Europe can 'speak with one voice' and, within the EU, it has been lauded as a major step forward towards increased coordination in this area. A recent mid-term evaluation of the current Drug Strategy and Action Plan (European Commission, 2017a, p. 10) reported that 'one key area in which the Strategy and Action Plan add value is enabling the EU to speak with one voice in international fora, as demonstrated in the run up to UNGASS 2016'. An adjunct document further emphasises the success of the 'common position' as 'the 2016 outcome document was largely coherent with the EU UNGASS position and the EU Strategy and Action Plan' (European Commission, 2017b, p. 1). The preparation and presentation of a 'common position' on the future of global drug policy, thus represents an internal success for the EU in this area. This chapter will now go on to explore the 'added value' that the 'common position' has had on the UNGASS 2016 procedures and, by extension, on global drug policy debates in general.

The Common Position: Champions of Change?

On the 11th November, 2015, the EU's common position (EU, 2015) on UNGASS 2016 was agreed as a summary of their contribution to discussions. Broadly speaking, its central arguments surround the support of balanced and evidence-based drug policies, the importance of a public health and harm reduction approach and the importance of respect for human rights and shared responsibility. It also emphasised the need to involve civil society in drug policy debates, the importance of a commitment to alternative development, the value of the international drug control system in governing the scientific and medical use of drugs, the need to work towards sustainable development targets and the need to address new facets of the illicit drug problem, such as clear/darknet markets and NPS (EU, 2015). In many ways, based on the content outlined above, this can be viewed as a progressive (or at least 'politically correct' (Bewley-Taylor & Jelsma, 2016, p. 5)) document attesting to a balanced European approach and an appreciation of the major issues facing drug policy makers active on the global stage. It also represents a significant step forward in terms of what European Member States have been able to agree on previously.

As a first detailed example of internal progress, Europe has long been seen as an advocate of the principle of harm reduction within drug policy: the desire to reduce the harm that results from both drugs *and drug policy* rather than solely to focus on reducing the overall number of drug users (Lenton & Single, 1998). The provision of substitution treatment to people who are dependent on heroin and services which offer clean needles to people who inject drugs are the most established and enduring harm reduction initiatives and several European countries were early adopters of these measures. The Netherlands, for example, adopted methadone maintenance in Amsterdam and a needle exchange programme in Rotterdam in the early 1980s (Marlatt, 1996). Similar measures were adopted in the United Kingdom under Margaret Thatcher in an effort to reduce the sharing of needles, attract new people into service provision and increase the overall health of dependent drug users (O'Hare, 2007). Spurred on by the AIDS/HIV crisis of the 1980s, these measures were quickly adopted throughout much of Europe and beyond. Today, every European Member State has some level of needle exchange and substitution treatment provision within its borders (Rhodes & Hedrich, 2010). To place this in a global context, 90 countries and territories (out of 158 reporting injecting drug use) now offer some form of needle exchange programme and 80 offer some form of opioid substitution treatment (Harm Reduction International, 2016).

Many European countries have experimented with further, less well established, harm reduction measures: for example, the provision of heroin on prescription has been implemented in Germany, the Netherlands and Switzerland; drug-checking services are present in the Netherlands, Portugal and Austria; and drug consumption rooms are operating in the Netherlands, Germany, Denmark, Spain, France, Luxembourg and Switzerland. Yet, despite this long history of the early adoption of harm reduction measures and the fact that many European countries continue to be at the forefront of latest harm reduction developments, the EU has faced an uphill struggle to advocate for harm reduction, even within its own borders. This is partly because some European countries have been slow to fully adopt harm reduction practices into their national strategies. Sweden, for example, only tolerated substitution treatment and needle exchange on a very minimal experimental basis for many years and Eastern European countries continue to offer very limited versions of these baseline harm reduction initiatives: in 2010, the 12 countries that joined the EU since 2004 only accounted for 2% of the substitution treatment available within Europe (EMCDDA, 2010).

The EU's relative impotence in this area can be demonstrated by referencing the 2004 Catania Report (ENCOD, 2004), which proposed a radical change in European drug policy based on a comprehensive failure to meet its principal aims (developed, of course, in line with UN aims and objectives) of eradicating or significantly reducing the use of drugs and attendant problems within its borders. Instead, a drug policy based around harm reduction, the application of scientific evidence and a balanced approach encompassing public health as well as law enforcement and criminalisation was advocated (ENCOD, 2007). The report was ostensibly approved by the European Parliament in 2004, but was immediately followed by a new European Drug Strategy and Action Plan in 2005 that made only minimal references to harm reduction due to a lack of consensus in this area and adhered to the familiar aims of eradicating or significantly reducing drug use.

In more recent EU drug policy-related documents, the principle of harm reduction has gained a stronger foothold. There is still minimal reference to this principle in the overall Drug Strategy, but it achieves an increased presence in the detailed objectives of the Action Plans (Rhodes & Hedrich, 2010). Given some member states' (e.g. Sweden and, more recently, the United Kingdom) resistance to encouraging and supporting harm reduction measures, the strong promotion of harm reduction initiatives on the global stage, via the agreed European common position document, therefore represents a considerable step forward in EU positioning on drugs. Within this document, harm reduction is mentioned both generally, as a guiding principle of global drug policy, and specifically in the call to increase the provision of substitution treatment throughout the world 'as such measures have proved effective in reducing the number of direct and indirect drug related deaths and notably blood borne infectious diseases associated with drug use' (EU, 2015, p. 5). Given the generally accepted effectiveness of substitution treatment, this can be viewed as a providing a potentially positive impact on the global stage.

The promotion of a human rights agenda in relation to drug policy provides another example of an area where the EU can provide a positive global influence in the control of illicit substances. This is an issue that has received increased global attention, particularly surrounding the unfairness of a global drug policy which concentrates all its efforts on reducing supply while neglecting to address demand, thus disadvantaging producer countries (Youngers & Roisin, 2005). Pryce (2012, p. 93) summarises the argument: 'The unintended consequence of the belief that drugs are evil has been a less than scrupulous global attitude to human rights and liberties, an erosion of the values of the societies which prohibition is designed to protect'. In this area, the application of the death penalty and the occurrence of extra-judicial killings have become focal points for global debate.

Amnesty International (2011) has reported on the routine shooting of child cannabis farmers in Iran, Hope (2015) documents the 682 civilians who have been killed as a result of counter narcotics operations in Mexico since December 2012, and according to an investigation by the *Philippines Daily Inquirer* (2016) there were 1,278 drug-related killings in the first 100 days of President Duterte's government of the Philippines. A report on the use of the death penalty for drug-related offences found that there are at least 33 countries that prescribe the death penalty for drug-related offences, and at least 10 of these have the death penalty as a mandatory sanction (Gallahue & Lines, 2015). The strongest message in the EU common position document thus, perhaps unsurprisingly, addresses this issue on which European agreement is not unexpected and designates the abolition of the death penalty, for all crimes including drug-related offences, as 'an absolute priority' (EU, 2015, p. 3).

It is important to remember that many argue, however, that human rights abuses are also prevalent within the control of illicit substances in consumer countries. For example, a report produced for the Beckley Foundation Drug Policy Programme (Barrett et al., 2008) highlights: the arrest and ill treatment of drug users to meet drug reduction targets in Russia, Kazakhstan and the United Kingdom; detention and coercive treatment, sometimes including forced labour and moral education as in China; the denial of services to those who are imprisoned or to other vulnerable populations as in the United Kingdom and Europe; and the discriminatory application of drug control as seen in the United States where African-American men are sent to prison at 13.4 times the rate of white men. The EU common position document also makes an attempt to address some of these areas.

For example, the common position document recommends 'proportionality' (EU, 2015, p. 4) in the punishment of those found guilty of drug offences, recognises that drug interventions and treatment in prisons need to be 'substantially improved' (EU, 2015, p. 5), and draws attention to the 'right of the drug user to give an informed consent to treatment' (EU, 2015, p. 3). The language used here, however, is less strong with the introduction of phrases such as 'as appropriate' and 'except in exceptional circumstances' attesting to the fact that agreement here, even among European Member States, is harder to secure. In Sweden, for example, it has been possible to detain by force both youth and adult drug users who were not willing to take part in drug treatment voluntarily since the 1980s (Tops, 2001). It could also be argued that Sweden's practice of not separating, for example, cannabis from other drugs in terms of range and severity of punishments, and pursuing the users of drugs as well as the suppliers, as lacking in proportionality. Again, significant progress can be seen in this area – the ability to agree a 'common position' has provided the EU with a strong vehicle for pushing human rights issues, like the death penalty, which are agreed upon throughout Europe. An interesting contrast is provided by the weaker positioning on human rights abuses more likely to affect European countries.

It is difficult to evaluate the precise nature of the impact that the EU common position on UNGASS 2016 played in developing the final UNGASS Outcome Document. Fordham and Jelsma (2016, p. 1) suggest the Outcome document has been 'critical in shifting drug policy narrative towards public health, harm reduction and human rights', and Nougier and Fernandez Ochoa (2017, p. 1) similarly propose that it represents an unprecedented shift 'towards ensuring public health, development and human rights concerns are not peripheral, but central to drug policy'. The UNGASS positioning papers of many other global regions/bodies also mentioned these factors, but the ability of Europe to 'speak with one strong voice' and champion these issues has undoubtedly played a part in ensuring their prominence in future global debates.

The Common Position: Defenders of the Status Quo?

Thus far, the evidence suggests significant gains for Europe in the field of international drug policy influence, in terms of being able to speak with one voice and use that position to push forward some of the more liberal global drug policy ideas, in particular around public health, harm reduction and human rights. This, however, is far from the whole story. In the run up to UNGASS 2016, many commentators and experts imagined an 'open and honest' (Ban Ki Moon, 2013, p. 1) debate emerging on the failures of drug policy to date. Furthermore, one area of particular focus promised to be the continuing suitability of existing international drug control conventions in light of recent systems of cannabis regulation in Uruguay and American States such as Colorado and Washington, which can be viewed as being in direct contravention of the terms of these treaties.

The EU common position document is unequivocal in its support for the international conventions in their current form and entirely dismissive of any need for change in this central area of global drug control: 'The three UN Drug Control Conventions, which provide the international legal framework for addressing the drugs phenomenon, and the Universal Declaration on Human Rights are the cornerstones of the global response to the world drug problem … the EU and its Member States reiterate that the drug control treaties must be acknowledged and respected in developing and implementing national drug policies and laws' (EU, 2015, p. 2). To further clarify the position, the common position goes on to say: 'There is sufficient scope and flexibility within the provisions of the UN Conventions to accommodate a wide range of approaches to drug policy in accordance with national and regional specificities' (EU, 2015, p. 2). This section will critically explore the consequences of maintaining this line.

It is perhaps unsurprising that this is the European view of the international conventions. After all, this is a continent that has arguably long exploited the flexibility of the conventions. Take, for example, the coffee shop system facilitating the small-scale sale of cannabis in the Netherlands; the trend towards the decriminalisation of cannabis or all drugs for personal consumption epitomised by Portugal's change in policy in 2001; the cannabis growing cooperatives that exploited a legal loophole in Spanish drug laws and have since spread throughout Europe. As these examples attest, Europe has indeed found considerable 'room for manoeuvre' (Dorn & Jamieson, 2000) within the international conventions. To be clear, the European position, correctly (Bewley-Taylor & Jelsma, 2016), maintains that while these practices may push the boundaries of the treaties, they do not break them.

There are two main problems with this approach. First, while the European 'soft defections' (Bewley-Taylor, 2012) may fall within the possible flexibility of the international conventions, the regulated markets practised in Uruguay and some American States clearly do not. In particular, the fully commercialised markets of, for example, Colorado or Washington State, fly in the face of international demands to treat illicit drugs as 'a serious evil for the individual … fraught with social and economic danger' (United Nations, 1961, p. 1). By ignoring this problem, Europe (and indeed the UNGASS 2016 Outcome Document) sidesteps this issue and allows a situation to continue whereby the international conventions are clearly being contravened. Jelsma (2015) cautions that international agreements in other areas (e.g., human rights) will ultimately be weakened if there are no consequences to contravening the international drug conventions. In this vein, it is interesting to note that countries such as the Russian Federation and China that practise strict national drug policies and that have faced accusations of drug-related human rights abuses, are also staunch supporters of the ability to interpret the existing conventions flexibly (Bewley-Taylor & Jelsma, 2016), as this allows them to retain practices such as forced treatment or the death penalty.

Furthermore, the issue may become significantly more pertinent to Europe in the near future. Public opinion surveys in the Netherlands have cited increasing levels of support for the full legalisation of cannabis. In 2013, 65 per cent of those surveyed reported that they would be in favour of introducing to the

Netherlands the Uruguayan system whereby the production, sale and consumption of cannabis were all legalised (Rolles, 2014). Forty-one municipalities within the Netherlands have endorsed a manifesto proposing the regulation of cannabis production, and 25 of the 38 largest municipalities have applied to the Ministry of Justice for permission to experiment with various forms of authorised cannabis production and wholesale supply (Rolles, 2014). Similarly, city officials in Copenhagen have made four applications to national government to implement a trial system of regulated cannabis sales administrated by the public authorities (Mortimer, 2016).

In fact, the EU provides a good example of the limitations of drug-policy developments that take place within a flexible interpretation of the international conventions. One example of these limitations is provided by the coffee shop system in the Netherlands which represents a pragmatic attempt to separate the markets for cannabis and other drugs, while working within the UN conventions. To this end, the use, purchase and small-scale sale of cannabis is generally tolerated, and is primarily facilitated through the coffee shop system. A significant grey area inherent in this policy, however, is what Korf (2008) has termed the 'back door' issue. While use, purchase and small-scale sale of cannabis may be tolerated, there exists no legal way for coffee shops themselves to attain larger amounts of cannabis, because the production and commercial supply of cannabis is not tolerated. This places coffee shops in a precarious semi-legal position whereby the front door sales of cannabis are regulated, but the backdoor supply of coffee shops remains in the hands of criminals. A recent review of the Netherlands' separation of the markets policy concludes that: 'If there is one lesson to take away from the Dutch experiences, it is that when taking steps towards regulating cannabis … these should include the entire chain of supply, from production to consumption' (Grund & Breeksema, 2013, p. 12). The current coffee shop 'backdoor' problem has been created largely because the Dutch tried to effect their relaxation of cannabis policy in accordance with the terms of the international conventions: Room and Mackay (2012, p. 7) therefore recognise that the international treaties have 'blocked experimentation with regulated domestic drug markets'.

Further limitations can be observed by a more general examination of decriminalisation. Many countries in Europe now operate some form of decriminalisation (removal of or reduction in criminal penalties) of the possession of drugs for personal use. However, in an effort to stay within the parameters of the UN conventions, they often retain some form of civil or minor criminal penalties against those behaviours (Room, 2012). Room and Reuter (2012) report that, despite widespread decriminalisation efforts towards cannabis, the number of cannabis users coming into contact with the criminal justice system has actually increased, and attributes that finding to the fact that civil or more minor criminal penalties are actually easier to enforce. As penalties are reduced they become more likely to be operationalised and, counter-intuitively, the result is a widening of the net (Room, et al., 2010) of those caught up in efforts to control the use of drugs – crucially, *because* countries are trying to work within UN conventions (Room & Reuter, 2012). Bewley-Taylor (2013, p. 61) therefore suggests that 'working inside the confines of the UN treaty system and generating changes in rather than changes of regime actually sustains larger structures of harm'.

These examples demonstrate that a flexible interpretation of international treaties does not address more radical instances of drug policy reform and limits the impact of softer drug-policy relaxation. It is disappointing that the EU has not been able to push forward the debate on international treaty reform in this area, instead defending the status quo, despite the fact that drug policy innovation will continue to be restricted and some global national policies will continue to operate outside the terms of the conventions. One way in which the EU could have engendered improvement in this area would have been to support calls for an expert group to examine the options for reform of the global drug policy regime (Jelsma, 2015). Such a move would have been in line with broad EU support for the development of evidence-based policy and would have provided a first step towards bringing the conventions in line with global practice. Neither the EU 'common position' document nor the UNGASS 2016 Outcome Document, however, contain any reference to the creation of an 'expert group' charged with the further exploration of this issue.

Another area on which the EU has been conspicuously silent is the failure of the war on drugs. In some ways, the pressure for UNGASS 2016 can be seen as an indirect consequence of a rising global appreciation of the failure of 'war on drugs' strategies of drug control. In the United States, Obama's administration moved away from war on drugs' terminology and the Global Commission on Drug Policy, comprised of influential representatives from around the globe, was created in 2011 to call for a paradigm shift in drug policy towards drug policies that are both more effective and less harmful (Global Commission on Drug Policy, 2011). Pryce (2012) documents the many failures of the war on drugs to end or significantly reduce the production, consumption and trade of illegal drugs, while at the same time noting the considerable negative 'unintended consequences' such policies have had on both producer and consumer countries. A public recognition of these unintended consequences and their particular impact on drug producer countries by three Latin-American leaders (Fordham & Jelsma, 2016) contributed to the impetus for UNGASS 2016. It is therefore a significant and important omission that the EU 'common position' does not make any mention of the failure of war on drugs and the need to move away from policies associated with it in favour of more progressive forms of prevention that focus on public health and human rights.

Of course, even if the EU had acknowledged the failure of the war on drugs, it is unlikely this would have been adopted in the final UNGASS Outcome document as there are still plenty of global supporters of war on drugs style policies: Russia for example has promised to renew the commitment to fighting the war on drugs as part of UNGASS 2016 discussion (Fordham, 2016). This omission, however, together with continuing support for unrealistic and over-zealous aims of 'a world free of drug abuse' and the adoption of cautious language such as 'as appropriate' and 'in accordance with national legislation' around more progressive points, has considerably weakened the EU's position as advocates for the development of a more effective global drug policy. In combination with unwavering support for the treaties as they stand, it provides evidence that the EU is unable to think outside the existing drug policy control toolbox (Seddon, 2014) and advocate for meaningful change at a global level.

Conclusion: An Evaluation of EU Contributions to Global Drug Policy Debates

The UNGASS 2016 Outcome Document has met with mixed approval with some lauding it as a progressive move towards public health, harm reduction and development (Fernandez Ochoa & Nougier, 2017), while others feel it has proved a missed opportunity to overhaul and modernise the global drug control system (Global Commission on Drug Policy, 2016). From an EU viewpoint, the result of UNGASS 2016 has been largely positive. EU contributions to CND meetings since UNGASS 2016 confirm strong support for the outcome document which they describe as 'the greatest milestone in the international drugs policy development' (EU, 2017a, p. 1) and which, as previously mentioned, they feel is a good reflection of European drug policy in general (European Commission, 2017b, p. 27). External evaluations of EU drug policy have also suggested that the EU should now seek to 'build on the momentum from the successful negotiation at UNGASS … in order to exert greater European influence on shared concerns in the area of the drug phenomenon' (RAND, 2017, p. 16).

To some extent this has been the case. As preparations get underway for the next High Level Ministerial meeting on international drug control in 2019 there have been several opportunities. At the 60th Session of the CND in March 2017, the EU continued to push for the abolition of the death penalty and the greater contribution of civil society to ongoing debates (EU, 2017a); at the intercessional meeting in November 2017 it sought to 'further strengthen the link between the UNGASS recommendations and drug-related Sustainable Development Goals' (EU, 2017b, p. 2); and in October 2016 it committed to considerable funding to aid the Community of Latin America and Caribbean States achieve sustainability development targets (European Commission, 2016) . The European Commission (2017a) evaluation of EU drug policy also attests to the intention to make internal changes to EU drug policy based on the UNGASS 2016 Outcome Document. For example, it recommends that the three pillars underlying the EU drug strategy, based around demand reduction, supply reduction and international cooperation, should be aligned instead to the seven-pillar approach raised at UNGASS which, for example, divides demand reduction into prevention and treatment, and availability and access for medical and scientific purposes.

The successful negotiation of a common European position that pursues a public health, sustainable development, evidence based and human rights oriented approach, under a flexible interpretation of the current treaties, is a significant achievement for the membership of the EU. It aligns with their goals to increase coordination and cooperation between Member States and to 'speak with one voice' on the global stage. A flexible interpretation of existing conventions allows them to justify the varied innovative policy strategies within their borders without becoming embroiled in contentious debates about the need for treaty reform (Bewley-Taylor, 2013). It fits with their experience of the 'added value' of multi-levels of governance in which international, national and local governing bodies all have an important part to play in the implementation of effective policy. The Outcome document generally aligns with the EU position (although not in some key areas such as the elimination of the death penalty) reflecting the potential impact of its contribution. Its adoption will require little change within the borders of the EU other than some minor tweaks to the structure of drugs policy.

The exact purpose of the UN High Level Ministerial meeting in 2019, following so close on the heels of UNGASS 2016, remains to be precisely determined. Another international drug control meeting is needed because the current Political Declaration and Plan of Action were not reviewed at UNGASS 2016 and are due to expire. Part of the mandate of recent CND meetings has been to decide the aims of this meeting – should it, for example, be an honest evaluation of the effectiveness of global drug control in general and the 2016 Outcome document in particular, a lively debate after a period of reflection on the outcomes of 2016, an opportunity to negotiate a new outcome document, or a chance to focus on providing a practical roadmap to implementing the Outcome document (International Drug Policy Consortium, 2016)? At the most recent CND meeting, the EU has been clear on its own position on this matter: 'Efforts should be focussed on implementing commitments made during the UNGASS in 2016. We should not negotiate a new political document' (EU, 2017b, p. 3). It seems clear that the result of UNGASS 2016 was a resounding success in terms of European drug policy. While the EU can continue to push single issues, such as the death penalty, at international fora, they are ultimately happy with the status quo of an international drug policy that continues to strive for a drug-free world, that views the last 40 years of international drug policy as a tangible success and which continues to be framed by existing international drug conventions.

For many, Europe is a continent already associated with drug policy experimentation and innovation giving rise to interventions such as Dutch coffee shops, Spanish cannabis clubs and Portuguese decriminalisation. We should not, however, be surprised at this failure to 'champion change' in international drug policy discussions. For a start, 'European countries have not experienced to the same extent, the high human cost in terms of violence, insecurity and mass incarceration experienced in Latin America' (Fordham & Jelsma, 2016, p. 1). Furthermore, illegal drugs can be viewed as a complex policy problem existing in a state of flux (Mulgan, 2004), bound up with moral values and susceptible to emotional responses (Ritter, 2009). Available evidence thus remains open to interpretation, particularly given that there are no commonly agreed upon indicators of success in drug policy. Pryce (2012) lists many disincentives to advocating for significant policy change in a complex field such as that of drugs – ideological beliefs that drugs are morally reprehensible, fear of the unknowns of alternative systems, the political difficulties of challenging the global status quo, bureaucratic inertia inspired by the enormity of changing international agreements, and the vested interests of whole industries that have sprung up around drug treatment and enforcement agencies.

For the EU, perhaps the greatest of these obstacles relates to the political difficulties of challenging the status quo. In an exploration of the continuation of a 'war on drugs' approach under the Obama regime, despite official indications that it was to be abandoned as a term, Youngers (2011, p. 341), concludes that a 'tough on drugs' approach is popular with constituents and encourages leaders to play 'on public fears, turning a public health issue into an all-out war on addictive substances and those who supply them'. Telling people what really needs to be done in terms of the alleviation of poverty, the treatment of addicts, and the nurturing of global regions that are susceptible to drug trade related corruption, is a strategy much less likely to win support and would require courageous leadership indeed (Isacson, 2005). Furthermore, given the fear associated with the unknown outcomes of any relaxation of the global drug policy regime, to take even the first step towards such a position could be politically problematic (Reuter, 2011). Finally, with 30 years of international drug policy making under its belt, the EU is well placed to understand the difficulties in engendering international agreement in this area.

While we continue to cling to the illusion that we are making progress towards an ultimate aim of a drug free world, without acknowledging the manifold and significant unintended consequences of the existing system of global drug control, which often impact disproportionately on vulnerable regions of the world, we cannot see real progress in global drug policy, and we will continue to suffer from its unintended effects. If the EU really wants to see a more progressive global drug policy, first steps must be to acknowledge existing failures and associated harms, and to lobby to ensure that existing legislation does not stand in the way of the development of innovative and experimental policies, such as cannabis regulation. It is difficult to imagine how we could move forward in terms of drug policy, towards more effective context appropriate strategies, if we do not or cannot innovate. Ultimately, the EU's performance on the global stage of drug policy thus remains hampered by its failure to engage with the continuing suitability of the existing systems of international drug control.

References

Amnesty International. (2011). *Addicted to death: Executions for drug offenses in Iran.* Amnesty International Ltd: London.

Ban Ki-moon, (2013). *Statement: Secretary-General's remarks at special event on the international day against drug abuse and illicit trafficking.* Retrieved from http://www.un.org

Barratt, D., Lines, R., Schleifer, R., Elliott, R., & Bewley-Taylor, D., (2008). *Recalibrating the regime. The need for a human-rights based approach to international drug policy*, The Beckley Foundation Drug Policy Programme. Retrieved from https://www.internationaldrugpolicy.net

Bewley-Taylor, D. (2013). Towards revision of the UN drug conventions: Harnessing like-mindedness, *International Journal of Drug Policy*, *24*(1), 60–68. doi:10.1016/j.drugpo.2012.09.001

Bewley-Taylor, D. (2012). *International drug control: Consensus fractured.* Cambridge: Cambridge University Press.

Bewley-Taylor, D., & Jelsma, M. (2016, June). *UNGASS 2016: A Broken or B-r-o-a-d Consensus? UN summit cannot hide growing divergence in the global drug policy landscape*. Transnational Institute (TNI), Drug Policy Briefing 45.

Blom, T., & van Mastright, H. (1994). The future of the Dutch model in the context of the war on drugs. In Leuw E. & Haen Marshall I. (Eds.), *Between prohibition and legalisation: The Dutch experiment* (pp. 255–281). Amsterdam and New York: Kugler Publications.

Boekhout van Solinge, T. (1999). Dutch drug policy in a European context. *Journal of Drug Issues*, *29*, 511–528.

Chatwin, C. (2003). Drug policy developments within the European Union: The destabilizing effects of Dutch and Swedish drug policies. *British Journal of Criminology*, *43*, 567–582.

Chatwin, C. (2011). *Drug Policy Harmonization and the European Union*. Basingstoke: Palgrave Macmillan.

Commission of the European Communities. (2003). *Communication from the Commission to the European Parliament and the Council on Coordination on Drugs in the European Union*. Retrieved from http://www.eur-lex.europa.eu

Council of the European Union. (2004a). *Framework Decision 2004/757/JHA of 25 October 2004, laying down minimum provision on the constituent elements of criminal acts and penalties in the field of illicit drug trafficking*. Brussels: OJ L355.

Council of the European Union, (2004b) *EU Drugs Strategy 2005-2012*. Retrieved from http://www.emcdda.europa.org

Council of the European Union. (2005). *Framework decision 2005/387/JHA of 10 May 2005 on the information exchange, risk assessment and control of new psychoactive substances*. Brussels: OJ L127.

Council of the European Union. (2008). EU Drugs Action Plan for 2009–2012. *Official Journal of the European Union*. Retrieved from http://www.emcdda.europa.org

Council of the European Union. (2012). EU drugs strategy (2013–2020). *Official Journal of the European Union*, 2012/C 402/01.

Dorn, N., & Jamieson, A. (2000). *Room for Manoeuvre: overview of comparative legal research into national drug laws of France, Germany, Italy, Spain, the Netherlands and Sweden and their relation to three international drugs conventions: A study by drug scope for the Independent Inquiry on the Misuse of Drugs Act, 1971*. Drugscope: London.

Duff, A. (1993). *Subsidiarity within the European community*. London: Federal Trust for Education and Research.

EMCDDA. (2010). *Annual Report 2010: the state of the drugs problem in Europe*. Retrieved from http://www.emcdda.europa.eu

ENCOD. (2004). *Catania Report: European Parliament Recommendation to the Commission and the European Council on the Drugs Strategy 2004-2012*. Retrieved from http://www.action.encod.org

ENCOD. (2007). *Common press release of Giusto Catania MP and ENCOD*. Retrieved from http://www.encod.org

European Commission. (2017a). *Evaluation of the implementation of the EU drugs strategy 2013–2020 and of the EU Action Plan on drugs 2013–2016: A continuous need for an EU Action Plan on Drugs*. Brussels: 15.3.2017 COM (2017) 195 final.

European Commission. (2017b). *Commission staff working document: Evaluation of the implementation of the EU Drugs Strategy 2013–2020 and the EU Action Plan on Drugs 2013–2016*. Brussels: 15.3.2017 SWD (2017) 95 final.

European Commission. (2016, October 26). *EU support to the COMMUNITY of Latin America and Caribbean States (CELAC)* Press Release. Brussels.

European Parliament. (2016). *A review and assessment of EU drug policy*. Directorate General for Internal Policies: PE 571.400.

European Union (EU), (2015), *Common Position on UNGASS 2016*. Retrieved from https://www.unodc.org

European Union (EU). (2016). *European Union statement on UNGASS 2016 at 59th Session of the Commission on Narcotic Drugs*, Vienna, 14th March, 2016.

European Union. (EU). (2017a). *Statement on the occasion of the Commission on Narcotic Drugs 60th anniversary session*, Vienna, 13th–17th March, 2017.

European Union (EU). (2017b). *European Union statement on the occasion of the Intersessional Meeting 16–17 November 2017*, Vienna, 17 November 2017.

Fernandez Ochoa, J., & Nougier, M. (2017). *How to capitalise on progress made in the UNGASS outcome document*. International Drug Policy Consortium: Briefing paper, February 2017.

Fordham, A. (2016, May 3). The drugs consensus is not pretty: It's been ripped apart at the seams. *Huffington Post*. Retrieved from http://www.huffingtonpost.co.uk

Fordham, A., & Jelsma, M. (2016), *Will UNGASS 2016 be the beginning of the end for the 'war on drugs'?* Transnational Institute. Retrieved from http://www.tni.org

Gallahue, P., & Lines, R. (2015), *The death penalty for drug offences: Global overview 2015*. London: Harm Reduction International.

Global Commission on Drug Policy. (2016). *Public statement by the Global Commission on Drug Policy on UNGASS 2016*. Global Commission on Drug Policy, New York: April 21 2016.

Global Commission on Drug Policy. (2011). *War on Drugs: Report of the Global Commission on Drug Policy*. Retrieved from http://www.globalcommissionondrugs.org

Grund, J. P., & Breeksema, J. (2013). *Coffee shops and compromise: Separated illicit drug markets in the Netherlands*. Open Society Foundations. Retrieved from http://www.opensocietyfoundations.org

Harm Reduction International. (2016). *The global state of harm reduction 2016*. Retrieved from https://www.hri.global

Hope, A. (2015). *Plus Ca Change: Structural continuities in Mexican counternarcotics policy*. Retrieved from https://www.brookings.edu

International Drug Policy Consortium. (2016, November 29). *What comes next? Post-UNGASS options for 2019–20*. Transnational Institute. Retrieved from: https://www.tni.org

Isacson, A. (2005). The U.S. military in the war on drugs. In Youngers C. A. & Rosin's E. (Eds.), *Drugs and democracy in Latin America. The impact of U.S. policy*. London: Lynne Reinner Publishers.

Jelsma, M. (2015). *UNGASS 2016: Prospects for treaty reform and UN system-wide coherence on drug policy*. Brookings Institute. Retrieved from http://www.globalinitiative.net

Korf, D. J. (2008). An open front door: The coffee shop phenomenon in the Netherlands. In Rodner, S. Sznitman, B. Olsson, B. & Room R. (Eds.), *A cannabis reader: Global issues and local experiences – Perspectives on cannabis controversies, treatment and regulation in Europe*. Luxembourg: Office for Official Publications of the European Communities. EMCDDA monograph no. 8.

Lenton, S., & Single, E. (1998). The definition of harm reduction. *Drug and Alcohol Review*, 17, 213–220.

Marlatt, G. A. (1996). Harm reduction: Come as you are. *Addictive Behaviours*, *21*(6), 779–788.

Mortimer, C. (2016). Copenhagen makes fourth bid to legalise cannabis to help reduce gang warfare. *The Independent*, Monday 19 December, 2016.

Mulgan, G. (2004). Government, knowledge and the business of policy making: The potential and limits of evidence-based policy. *Evidence and Policy*, *1*(2), 215–226.

Nougier, M., & Fernandez Ochoa, J. (2017). *How to capitalise on progress made in the UNGASS Outcome Document: A guide for advocacy* IDPC. Retrieved from http://www.idpc.net

O'Hare, P. (2007). Merseyside, the first harm reduction conferences, and the early history of harm reduction. *International Journal of Drug Policy*, *18*, 141–144.

Philippines Daily Inquirer. (2016, October 16). *Story in numbers war on drugs*. Retrieved from https://www.newsinfo.inquirer.net

Pryce, S. (2012). *Fixing Drugs: the politics of drug prohibition*. Basingstoke: Palgrave Macmillan.

RAND. (2017). *Mid-term assessment of the EU drug strategy 2013–2020 and final evaluation of the Action Plan on Drugs 2013–2016*. Retrieved from https://www.rand.org

Reuter, P. (2011). *Options for regulating new psychoactive drugs: A review of recent experiences* UK Drug Policy Commission: London.

Rhodes, T., & Hedrich, D. (Eds.). (2010). *EMCDDA monographs. Harm reduction: Evidence, impacts and challenges*. Retrieved from http://www.emcdda.europa.eu

Ritter, A. (2009). How do drug policy makers access research evidence? *International Journal of Drug Policy*, *20*, 70–75.

Rolles, S. (2014). *Cannabis policy in the Netherlands: Moving forwards not backwards*. Retrieved from https://www.tdpf.org.uk

Room, R. (2012). Reform by subtraction: The path of denunciation of international drug treaties and reaccession with reservations. *International Journal of Drug Policy*, *23*, 401–406. doi:10.1016/j.drugpo.2012.04.001

Room, R., Fischer, B., Hall, W., Lenton, S., & Reuter, P. (2010). *Cannabis Policy: Moving beyond stalemate*. Oxford: Oxford University Press/The Beckley Foundation.

Room, R., & MacKay, S. (2012). *Roadmaps to reforming the UN drug conventions*. A Beckley Foundation Report. Retrieved from http://www.beckleyfoundation.org

Room, R., & Reuter, P. (2012). How well do international drug conventions protect public health? *The Lancet*, *379*, 84–91. doi:10.1016/S0140-6736(11)61423-2

Seddon, T. (2014) Drug policy and global regulatory capitalism: The case of new psychoactive substances (NPS). *International Journal of Drug Policy*. doi:10.1016/j.drugpo.2014.03.009

Tops, D. (2001). *A Society with or without drugs? Continuity and change in drug policies in Sweden and the Netherlands*. Lunds Dissertations in Social Work 5, Lund University, Lund..

United Nations. (1961). *Single convention on narcotic drugs*, 1961. Retrieved from http://www.druglibrary.org/schaffer/legal

Youngers, C. A. (2011). *The Obama administration's drug control policy on auto-pilot*. IDPC briefing paper, April 2011. Retrieved from http://www.idpc.net

Youngers, C. A., & Rosin, E. (Eds.). (2005). *Drugs and democracy in Latin America*. London: Lynne Reiner Publishers.

Chapter 12

United States Drug Policy: Flexible Prohibition and Regulation

Zara Snapp and Jorge Herrera Valderrábano

Abstract

This chapter explores the historical context of drug control in the United States, the ongoing regulation of the cannabis market at the State level and the role of the United States in the international negotiations related to the United Nations General Assembly Special Sessions (UNGASS) on drugs in 1998 and 2016. We continue by analysing the position, allies and activities of the United States before and during UNGASS 2016 to provide an understanding of possible scenarios related to the 2009 Political Declaration and Plan of Action review to take place via a High-level Ministerial Segment within the 2019 Commission on Narcotic Drugs meeting. While US drug policy is not expected to positively shift in the next few years, State-level regulation of cannabis is expected to continue and create pressure from below.

Keywords: UNGASS 2016; regulation; social justice; cannabis; US drug control; drug policy

Introduction

The United States has been a leading and forceful voice in drug control policy for more than 100 years, evangelising a zero-tolerance approach, which seeks to eradicate, interdict and incarcerate psychoactive plants and the people who grow, distribute or use them; and that in some cases has been used as a means of social control. However, the jig is up, as numerous US States begin to regulate the cannabis market for medical and adult use. Although the country has maintained a Federal prohibition on regulation, States have thus far been permitted to continue these innovations, with primarily positive impacts on social justice indicators such as reduction in arrests and detentions, increased tax revenue that has

Collapse of the Global Order on Drugs: From UNGASS 2016 to Review 2019, 251–268

doi:10.1108/978-1-78756-487-920181012

been channelled towards school construction, educational and health initiatives and treatment programs.

In 2008, the United Nations (UN) Office on Drugs and Crime identified five negative and unintended consequences of global drug control: the first being the creation of a criminal, violent and lucrative market with a value of around 320 billion dollars a year (UNODC, 2005, p. 128); the second the focus on law enforcement and punitive measures and not on health; the third the geographic displacement or the so-called 'balloon effect', where repressive policies cause issues to shift elsewhere, but the problem does not change; the fourth is the displacement of substances or pressure in the market in which the lack of access to a substance means an increase in the consumption of another substance (which could be more risky); and finally, the stigmatisation of users that reduces the tendency to seek treatment or health services when a person requires them (UNODC, 2008, p. 21).

The amount spent annually on the war on drugs in the United States adds up to more than $50 billion dollars. This law-enforcement based strategy has delivered disastrous outcomes, most visibly as a mass incarceration issue with clear racial disparities. The United States has the highest incarceration rate in the world, with 2,157,000 persons imprisoned in 2016 in federal, state and local prisons and jails (Drug Policy Alliance (DPA), 2016. p. 6). Nearly 80% of people in Federal prisons and almost 60% of people in State prisons for drug offences are African-American or Latino; and more than 250,000 people have been deported from the United States for drug law violations every year since 2007 (DPA, 2015a, 2015b, p. 8). The racist war on drugs is delivering negative outcomes that are costing the government millions of dollars, and the countries that follow this path are not having any better results. At the international level, 18% of people in prison are there for a crime related with drugs (UNODC, 2016, p. 101), and 33 countries still apply the death penalty for drug offenses (Global Commission on Drug Policy, 2016, p. 19).

United States Drug Policy: Historical Overview

Currently, illegal psychoactive substances have been consumed by humans for thousands of years for a diverse range of purposes. During the nineteenth century, heroin was used to treat respiratory illness, cocaine was popularly used in health drinks and remedies and morphine was regularly prescribed by doctors as a pain reliever (Diniejko, 2002, p. 3). However, the turn of the century was accompanied by a heightened awareness – and fear – that psychoactive substances had the potential for causing physical and emotional dependency. As a result, local jurisdictions began to impose restrictions on the use of cocaine and opium. In 1914, the United States issued its first Federal drug policy, commonly known as the Harrison Narcotics Act, which restricted the manufacture and sale of marijuana, cocaine, heroin and morphine (Sharp, 1994, p. 19).

Following the implementation of the bill, in 1939, the Treasury Department created the Federal Bureau of Narcotics (FBN), led by Harry J. Anslinger. Under his tenure, psychoactive substances were harshly criminalised, increasing penalties particularly for crimes related to cannabis (Cantor, 1961, p. 12); and the agency pushed the issuing of the Narcotics Control Act of 1956, which created 'the most punitive and repressive anti-narcotics legislation ever adopted by Congress. All discretion to suspend sentences or permit probation was eliminated (...) and the death penalty could be invoked for anyone who sold heroin to a minor' (McWiliams, 1990, p. 116). This discourse is again gaining prominence under the current Trump administration with the opioid plan including the death penalty for people who sell drugs (Anapol, 2018, p. 2).

In the years following the creation of the FBN, the agencies entrusted with enforcing the punitive law continued to reinforce the fear of drugs and to propagate myths regarding their relationship with crime. The FBN used this propaganda as a supposedly preventative measure that linked the use of drugs with insanity, murder and sex crimes (McWilliams, 1990, p. 70); and even though some efforts, such as the enactment of the Narcotic Addict Rehabilitation Act of 1966 that catalogued 'narcotic addiction' as a mental illness (Friedman et al., 1982, p. 119), were made to see the problem from a public health perspective, drug use was still considered a crime. Indeed, the Act paved the road for increased Federal expenditures on drug abuse treatment, but the criminalisation of people who use drugs was more present than ever.

In June 1971, President Nixon declared a 'war on drugs' by dramatically increasing the size and reach of Federal agencies to enforce drug control measures. The policy was justified by stigma, rather than on scientific evidence, and falsely correlated the use of drugs with violent crime. The policy primarily targeted the same vulnerable populations that, because of a lack of opportunities created and fostered by the state and society, committed crimes. This situation has even been admitted by John Ehrlichman, counsel and Assistant to the President of Domestic Affairs under Nixon, during an interview for *Harper's Magazine*:

> The Nixon campaign in 1968, and the Nixon White House after that, had two enemies: the antiwar left and black people. You understand what I'm saying? We knew we couldn't make it illegal to be either against the war or black, but by getting the public to associate the hippies with marijuana and blacks with heroin, and then criminalising both heavily, we could disrupt those communities. We could arrest their leaders, raid their homes, break up their meetings, and vilify them night after night on the evening news. Did we know we were lying about the drugs? Of course, we did. (Baum, 2016, p. 6)

The United States' ideological expansion that characterised those and the following years, shaped the international regime on drugs. The Single Convention on Narcotic Drugs, ratified by UN member states in 1961, aimed to replace the various multilateral treaties that existed in this field and merge them into a single document. The Convention arose in response to the concern for the 'physical and moral health of humanity', through the principle of limiting the use of narcotic drugs for medical and scientific purposes on the premise that 'addiction to narcotic drugs constitutes a serious evil for the individual and is fraught with social and economic danger to mankind', asserting that signing parties should be 'conscious of their duty to prevent and combat this evil' (Wagner et al., 2001, p. 62).

The 1961 Convention focussed on the eradication of the supply of substances derived from plants, such as cannabis, cocaine and heroin. The primary responsibility for the significant reduction in cultivation was placed on producing countries, rather than focussing on reducing demand in high consuming countries. Seventy-three member states, among them Germany, the United States, France, Mexico and the United Kingdom, committed themselves to expand existing control measures to eradicate the cultivation of plants from which narcotic substances are derived.

With the emergence of new substances during the anti-war movement in the United States, the UN proposed to issue a new convention on this matter. In 1971, the Convention on Psychotropic Substances was approved, responding to the diversification and expansion of the spectrum of drugs in the world, including new psychotropic substances such as amphetamines and psychedelics (UN, 1971). The purpose of these two treaties was the introduction of an international control system for psychotropic substances to limit possession, use, trafficking, distribution, import, export, manufacture and production, to exclusively medical and scientific purposes.

The negotiations regarding the contents and objectives of the 1971 Convention fractured into two groups based on national interests and industries. On one side, the more developed countries with strong pharmaceutical industries and a growing demand for psychotropic drugs; and on the other, the less developed countries without a substantial internal demand, or a pharmaceutical lobby (Armenta & Jelsma, 2015, p. 17). As a result, unlike the Single Convention, the 1971 Convention focussed on chemical substances and permits exemptions for plants having long-standing cultural and traditional uses. 'The 1971 Convention [concentrated] in a newly invested category of "psychotropic" substances, and did not list any plants as such in the relevant schedules. This has caused endless confusion as the conventions were translated into national laws, since governments had to decide' which to prohibit (Henman & Metaal, 2014, p. 3).

After several years, the United Nations Convention against Illicit Traffic in Narcotic Drugs and Psychotropic Substances of 1988 was adopted. This included criminal sanctions in order to combat the production, possession and illicit trafficking of drugs; following the path that the United States had defined and promoted for many years, even though producer countries such as Mexico pushed for possession to be criminalised in order to balance the burden of responsibility. The Convention exhorted international cooperation through, for example, the extradition of drug traffickers, controlled delivery (rationing) and referral to treatment (UN, 1988). Despite noting that previous efforts to combat the use, trafficking and production of narcotic drugs had not had the expected result and even threatened legitimate economies, stability, security and sovereignty of states; the treaty did not address the issue directly. Previous conventions focussed on the criminalisation of producers and traffickers, but the 1988 Convention also included the possibility of criminalising users, calling on states to adopt measures that considered the possession of illegal substances as a criminal offense.

It is worth noting that the 1988 Convention against Illicit Traffic in Narcotic Drugs and Psychotropic Substances was planned and promoted at a strategic timeframe by the United States. The Vienna Convention on the Law of Treaties, signed in 1969 but entering into force in 1980, is a UN treaty concerning the international law on treaties between states. This is the authoritative guide on the formation and effects of treaties and obligates its parties to adapt domestic legislations when a State ratifies a treaty (Aust, 2006, p. 2). This could allow for drug policy changes via the inter se option, modifying the treaties between specific parties (Transnational Institute (TNI), 2016b, p. 5). Inter se agreements would allow member states to make bilateral (or trilateral) agreements across like-minded governments that maintain the original commitment of the treaties to promote the health and welfare of humankind, but who want an alternative framework through which to innovate their policies, in this case, drug policies. An inter se modification would mean that the provisions in the treaties that are not part of the modification continue to be in force TNI (2016a, p. 11).

The law is certainly a tool for harmonising specific rights and policies. However, in the hands of the United States, and in the 1980s, it was the perfect medium through which to spread its ideological expansion. Through the Convention on the Law of the Treaties, the United States has been able to permeate its values at a domestic level in countries party to the Convention against Illicit Traffic in Narcotic Drugs and Psychotropic Substance; and in the name of this and other goals, funded programs in other countries (such as the Colombia Plan and Merida Initiative) to implement a punitive policy (Delgado-Ramos y Romano, 2011, p. 7).

More than 50 years of a punitive policy towards psychoactive substances in the United States that have laid the foundation of the current international drug control regime have not delivered the expected outcomes of reducing either the supply or the demand of psychoactive substances. Given the increase in drug consumption and production worldwide, in 1998 the UN General Assembly held a special session to address the global issue on drugs (United Nations General Assembly Special Session or UNGASS). Under the slogan 'A world without drugs: Yes, we can!' the member states committed themselves to eliminating the production, transit and use of illegal drugs, especially cannabis, opium and coca, within 10 years.

This focus on a deadline, rather than truly evaluating advances or regressions in drug control, was pushed by the United Nations Drug Control Program's Executive Director, who developed a plan to eradicate cultivation titled Strategy for Coca and Opium Poppy Elimination (SCOPE). This plan was strongly supported by the Clinton Administration, and State Department officials pushed the goal of 'a vigorous fight against international production, trafficking and abuse of illicit drugs' (TNI, 2013, p. 4) among the G8 countries as a means of assuring international backing and funding for the ambitious plans of the UNDCP.

Other countries doubted the capacity of the SCOPE program to reach its goals and it was therefore never presented at the 1998 UNGASS. Instead, the focus turned towards the Action Plan on International Cooperation on the Eradication of Illicit Drug Crops and on Alternative Development which was adopted at the meeting. During the preparations for the UNGASS, there was also a proposal to install an independent expert committee to evaluate the progress of drug control, but it was removed in the negotiations process (TNI, 2013, p. 6). The United States, along with allies such as the United Kingdom, had objected to the idea of an independent review. As a compromise position, the UN Secretary General Kofi Annan (now an active member of the Global Commission on Drug Policy) appointed 13 'high-level experts' to 'undertake a comprehensive review of how the efforts against illicit drugs have evolved within the United Nations System' (TNI, 2013, p. 6).

The outcome of the UNGASS 1998 became known as the UN decade against drug abuse (Verma, 2017, p. 3), which was a period characterised by the establishment of a prohibitionist regime at the international level that focussed predominantly on law enforcement, and paid little regard to the promotion of health and human rights, by almost entirely ignoring the good practices of protecting the rights of people who use drugs, as well as the many risk and harm reduction strategies and programs recently implemented in Europe during the previous ten years (Malinowska, 2013, p. 3).[1].

Following a decade of the strategy, the international community came together in Vienna, Austria, in 2009 to evaluate progress. The UN member states acknowledged that they had not reached the targets set forth, and that the measures undertaken had had additional serious consequences in terms of negative impacts on human rights with a focus on punitive measures, rather than health, the enlargement of a criminal market, displacement of both production and consumption trends commonly known as the 'balloon effect', and increased stigma towards people who use drugs (UNODC, 2009a, 2009b, p. 163). However, Member States chose to adopt a new Political Declaration and 10-year Plan of Action (UNODC, 2009a, 2009b) that reaffirmed the previous (some might say unachievable) targets with the objective of convening the next UNGASS on drugs in 2019, to evaluate and measure the progress made over that decade. Meanwhile, the United States advanced its agenda of foreign intervention across Latin America and other regions, under the guise of fighting the supply side of the drug war (Buxton, 2011).

The date for the international review of the 2009 Plan of Action was moved forward to 2016, following a request by the governments of Mexico, Guatemala and Colombia to review the current policies and to discuss the political alternatives of drugs as a means of addressing the ongoing problem of violence in the region. In anticipation of UNGASS 2016, human rights bodies, academics, activists and civil society organisations created an 'inside' and 'outside' strategy to influence the dialogue and debate towards a focus on human rights, public health, development and harm and risk reduction policies (Snapp, 2017, p. 111). At UNGASS 2016, the United States was faced with the dilemma of continuing to promote a discourse focussed on eradicating production and combatting drug trafficking, while States were actively moving towards regulating cannabis for adult purposes.

Reform Policies in the United States

The use, possession, sale, cultivation, manufacturing and transportation of cannabis are illegal in the United States under Federal law. In 2013, the so-called Cole Memo from the Federal government under the Obama administration articulated that if

[1]Switzerland was and continues to be an important reference point when it comes to best practices to address the health harms caused by the use of drugs. For more information, see Malinowska (2013).

a state approves a law to decriminalise cannabis for recreational or medical use, it can do so, under the condition that there is a regulatory system with specific rules and conditions. This was later rescinded by the Trump administration's Attorney General, Jeff Sessions, on 4 January 2018. While concrete actions have not yet been taken against cannabis businesses under the Trump administration, a recent memo was sent from Sessions titled: Guidance Regarding Use of Capital Punishment in Drug-Related Prosecutions. Although directly related to the opioid epidemic, a federal law exists, making possible to apply the death penalty against people who cultivate or possess more than 60,000 marijuana plants or 60,000 k (Ingold 2018). It is unlikely that it would be used in this manner, but it certainly could include some of the large-sale growers in states where legal regulation has been implemented.

At the international level, cannabis is classified under Schedule I of the Controlled Substances Act of 1970, the highest classification under the legislation (World Health Organization, 2017, p. 2). Part of the reason why cannabis is still illegal at the US Federal level is because it is classified on this list. A substance, drug or medication within Schedule I, as defined by the Office of Drug Administration (DEA), is a substance that has a high potential to be abused by its users and does not have acceptable medical uses (DEA, 2017, p. 2). But individual State laws do not always conform to the Federal norm. The proposals at the State level for a shift towards cannabis have been quite successful.

In 2012, Colorado and Washington became the first States to legalise the sale and possession of cannabis for recreational purposes when they passed the Colorado 64th Amendment and the Washington 502 Initiative, which are frameworks similar to those aimed at regulating alcohol, allowing possession up to one ounce for adults over 21 years old. Unlike the 502 Initiative, the 64th Amendment of Colorado allowed the personal cultivation of up to six plants, and both consider commercial cultivation and sale, subject to regulation and taxes (Smith, 2012, p. 3). This process undoubtedly sparked an avalanche of regulations of the plant for its various recreational, therapeutic and medicinal uses, throughout the United States.

By November 2014, 25 states had enacted cannabis laws, removing incarceration for small amounts of marijuana and/or legalising the possession, distribution and sale of marijuana. In 2014, the states of Alaska and Oregon, together with Washington, D.C., legalised the recreational use of marijuana, with laws similar to those of Colorado and Washington (Toor, 2014, p. 1). However, the 'Cromnibus' bill prevented Washington, D.C. from making additional changes to their laws, allowing domestic cultivation and use, but not commercial sale (Matthews, 2014, p. 2), putting in place a decriminalisation model that may reduce the problem of mass incarceration, but is not tackling criminal organisations' revenues. In the following two years, Delaware and Illinois also went down the decriminalisation path; and Louisiana, Pennsylvania, Virginia, Georgia, Oklahoma, Wyoming and Ohio have enacted medical cannabis laws.

November 8, 2016, was a historic date not only because of the election of Donald Trump but also because a total of nine States in the United States voted to regulate, to varying degrees, the use of cannabis. Voters in California, Arizona, Nevada, Massachusetts and Maine expressed their opinion on state legislation initiative to regulate the adult use of marijuana; while in Arkansas, Florida, North Dakota and

Montana, citizens decided whether to approve the use of marijuana for medicinal purposes. Voters in the States decided to take a step forward towards the regulation of cannabis. Eight out of the nine states facilitated access to the plant. Only Arizona, a state where cannabis for medicinal purposes was already legal, and that was trying to regulate the use for adult purposes, rejected the new legislation.

California, the most populous State in the United States, became the next State to regulate, with 39 million people approving cannabis for adult use, and became the first border State with Mexico to do so (Lopez, 2018, p. 4). With a margin of 56% in favour and 44% of voters against, voters passed Proposition 64, making California the fifth State to legalise the adult use of cannabis. With the approval of the measure, it will be legal for adults over the age of 21 to use, cultivate and sell marijuana. These commercial activities will be regulated by the authorities with a tax of 15% and an additional charge of $9.25 USD per ounce (Steinmetz, 2016, p. 8).

Additionally, voters in Nevada decided to legalise the use, possession, cultivation and sale of marijuana for recreational purposes, meaning that residents 21 years old or older can own up to one ounce of the plant, and that medical marijuana dispensaries can apply for licenses in order to sell for recreational purposes (Gilbert, 2016, p. 5). Moreover, 53.5% of residents of the State of Massachusetts also said yes to marijuana for recreational purposes, allowing the use and possession of up to one ounce of marijuana in the streets, up to 10 ounces and growing six plants in their homes, for those over 21 years old. The laws implemented include taxes of 3.75% for the sale of the plant in Massachusetts and 15% in the case of Nevada (Ballotpedia, 2016).

Maine was the next State to legalise the recreational use of cannabis on election day. Fifty per cent of voters said yes, and now people over 21 can possess up to two and a half ounces of marijuana. The plant can be grown, distributed and sold, opening the doors to the plant's retail stores and social clubs around the state. It should be noted that a 10% tax on the sale of cannabis was established, and this is subject to various regulations and local restrictions (AP, 2015, p. 2).

On the medical side, voters in the States of Florida, North Dakota, Montana and Arkansas approved existing initiatives on medicinal cannabis. Votes in Florida and North Dakota were decisively approving of these initiatives.

The Florida Amendment 2, which has even been claimed as having 'the potential to be one of the most permissive regimes on this issue in the nation' (Ingraham, 2016) passed with the support of 71% of the electorate. In addition to including the possibility of prescribing cannabis for diseases such as HIV, cancer and post-traumatic stress disorder, the measure now allows doctors to prescribe the use of the plant for 'other debilitating medical conditions of the same class or classes comparable or similar to those listed, and for which a doctor believes that the use of marijuana would be likely to outweigh the potential risks to a patient's health' (N.a., 2015). On the other hand, 64% of the voters in North Dakota agreed with the new positive policies regarding medical marijuana on the ballot. The North Dakota measure approved allows doctors to recommend the use of the plant for another series of severe medical conditions (Morgan et al., 2015, p. 5).

Montana had already legalised medical marijuana in 2004, but seven years later, State lawmakers severely restricted the program, causing a dramatic decrease in providers for patients registered by the state (Hernández, 2016, p. 3). In 2016, 57% of the residents in the state decided to reactivate the program (Wallace, 2016, p. 10), which removed the restrictions that limited the suppliers, allow research on the plant and ensure the access of cannabis for patients suffering from chronic pain diseases. Although the vote was narrower than expected in Arkansas, 53% of voters decided that doctors should be allowed to prescribe medical marijuana to their patients (Marijuana Policy Project (MPP), 2016, p. 3).

In 2017, West Virginia legalised medical cannabis through a ballot measure (MPP, 2017a, 2017b, 2017c, p. 5), and Indiana legalised low-THC, High-CBD cannabis oil (MPP, 2017, p. 5). Moreover, in that same year, New Hampshire decriminalised cannabis through State legislature. The law signed in New Hampshire intends to reduce fines for possession of up to three-quarters of an ounce of marijuana from $2,000 USD to $100 USD for a first or second offence and a $300 USD fine for a third offence (MPP, 2017, p. 6). Even though the model is still restrictive, the State took the 22nd position on the list of States that have eliminated the possibility of jail time for those convicted of simple possession.

In July 2018, Vermont became the first State to legalise recreational cannabis by way of the State legislature, allowing residents who are 21 years old and older to cultivate, possess and consume marijuana. The law did not create a retail market for the sale of recreational marijuana. Instead, 'the law decriminalises the possession of one ounce or less of marijuana and allows adults to grow up to two mature and four immature plants' (Griffaton, 2018, p. 2). This legal change created precedent in being the first State to have the legislature regulate, rather than relying on ballot initiatives promoted by citizens.

The regulation of cannabis has boosted the economy in the states. In 2017, the Colorado Department of Revenue raised $247,368,473 dollars from fees, licenses and taxes. (CRD, 2004, 1). Moreover, the cannabis regulation has also openned up the possibility to implement social justice principles and policies. Colorado started building schools from taxes collected through the cannabis regulation. The Building Excellent Schools Today program (BEST) receives $40 million dollars from cannabis taxes (CDE, 2017, 4). On the other hand, the Marijuana Tax Cash Fund will fund housing, health and mental aid projects, with $ 28.7 billion dollars (CSGJH, 2017, 3).

It is evident that States in the United States have managed to position themselves successfully against the Federal legislation on cannabis throughout the country. Most States have legislation that permit the use of medical marijuana, and as of February 2018, a total of nine States have regulated the use, possession, cultivation and distribution of the plant for adult use. Despite all of these events, cannabis remains an illegal drug at the Federal level. The discourse of the United States in the international arena has remained as the main promoter of the current war on drugs and supporter of the drug control treaties in international law. The most likely outcome for the country appears to be one where States continue to regulate for adult use, with no change in policy at the Federal level. This will mean that the United States will continue to be aligned with the international conventions, but also concede legislation at a State level which will continue to generate tensions between State and Federal law.

The United States and UNGASS 2016

During the UNGASS on drugs (2016), many member states, including Canada, Colombia, Ecuador, Mexico, New Zealand, The Netherlands and Switzerland among others, raised their voices regarding the importance of a new approach to psychoactive substances. United States national and international drug control measures were at a crossroads, with Michael Botticelli, the first drug czar to come from the 'recovery' community, advocating for a move towards a health-based approach at a national level and Ambassador Brownfield taking a nuanced perspective with the so-called 'Brownfield Doctrine', which allowed the US government to maintain the flexibility of the conventions for regulating on a local or State level, while maintaining Federal prohibitions.

The United States took advantage of the lack of transparency in the preparatory process for UNGASS and benefitted from the decision to hold the discussions in Vienna, instead of New York. This might have eased the participation of Latin American and Caribbean countries and others in the Global South. The process was dominated by the conservative forces of the UN drug control agencies based in Vienna. The United States took advantage of this opaque UNGASS process to play a moderated role, never advocating or promoting what was happening on a State level and protecting their international interests of eradication and interdiction throughout Latin America.

To organise the Special Session, the Commission on Narcotic Drugs (CND) created a Preparatory Board of UNGASS, which was in charge of organising the participation activities to address all substantive and organisational issues in an open manner, for and during the special segments of the preparatory sessions. The Preparatory Board was elected on the basis of a regional distribution of officials of the 57th Session of the CND. It was chaired by the Ambassador of Egypt and included representatives of other countries, including Hungary, Portugal, Iran, Colombia and El Salvador.

Many UN member states of the Global South, such as the Caribbean and African regions, have no permanent representation in Vienna and therefore were not able to fully participate in the negotiations on the outcome document. The General Assembly encouraged the participation of all member states in the preparations for UNGASS and requested the 'provision of assistance for the least developed countries' (TNI, 2016b) for that purpose; but did not seem to have included extra resources to comply with the request.

While a select group of countries was holding informal meetings to draft an underrepresented outcome document (TNI, 2016b, p. 1), the United States invested efforts throughout the UNGASS process to put pressure on some member states – particularly Latin American countries – not to express themselves in favour of international reform. In the preparatory process, the United States showed its complicated and flexible commitment to the international status quo, even when an increasing number of states inside were demonstrating the opposite.

As noted above, some states raised their voices to demand a new strategy against drugs. Several countries had already made legislative changes to allow cannabis for medicinal and personal use, supporting a paradigm shift. Mexican President Enrique Peña Nieto spoke of the need to move from prohibition towards effective regulation; the president of Colombia, Juan Manuel Santos, highlighted the injustice of the cultivators and young people in his country, declaring that the war on drugs had failed overwhelmingly; and President Evo Morales of Bolivia was clear in his rejection of the intervention from the United States in Latin American affairs (CINU, 2016a, 2016b, 2016c). However, the United States stood in the same conservative position, advocating flexibility of the conventions, but pushing foreign interventions.

Michael Botticelli, director of the White House Office of National Drug Control Policy in the Obama administration, declared during the meeting that 'law enforcement efforts should focus on criminal organisations – not on people with substance use disorders who need treatment and recovery support services' (Botticelli, 2016, p. 2), proposing a clear need to fully decriminalise drugs. However, by stating that '… the United States strongly supports drug policy reform under the framework of the three UN Conventions. Critical reforms, such as providing better access to treatment and less punitive approaches in our justice systems, are explicitly allowed by the Conventions' (Botticelli, 2016, p. 2), the country managed to establish a moderate position as a spectator, given the domestic legislative changes on the subject, but not as an agent for change in the international realm.

Using the same passive argument on the flexibility of the international drug control treaties, the United States tried to dodge questions by the international community over the regulation models already in place in several States within the country. However, despite these statements, the Federal policy on the matter remained punitive, and the government has not been open to a national regulation of the cannabis market. Early indications are that a punitive, federal policy will continue to be the norm under the Trump Administration.

Despite the illusion of reform of the current drug policy at the international level, the outcome document was plagued with similar irregularities to those of the preparatory process. Although the inputs presented for the zero draft of results included some proposals, the Board succeeded in censoring the document resulting from the negotiations in Vienna, filtering the changes proposed by member states and civil society organisations. In addition, it adopted the outcome document on the first day of UNGASS, instead of the third and last day of the session, as was scheduled in the provisional program. While this did not allow for the creation of an 'open and wide-ranging debate, considering all the available options' (Ki-Moon, 2013. p. 2), as proposed by the Secretary General of the UN, Ban Ki-moon, there was clear progress made within the document to include issues that had not previously emerged within drug control documents.

The outcome document did not address the critical shortcomings of international drug policy; nor did it address key cultural rights such as indigenous use of plants; and it did not recognise human rights violations in the name of drug control, such as the death penalty. However, in the months following the adoption of the document, it became clear that the reform-oriented countries had won a great battle against the 'status-quo' bloc. And although a true evaluation did not take place on the global level, countries used their statements to bring the lack of consensus to the General

Assembly and demonstrate that reform can happen at a national level, through evidence-based programs that have a clear impact on the lives of communities.

The UNGASS process showed that, despite the inertia within the UNODC, there was a chorus of countries that used 'their time at the podium to call for progressive changes, including Canada, Jamaica, Uruguay, Colombia, Mexico, Czech Republic and New Zealand' (Hetzer, 2016, p. 6). Additionally, UN agencies such as the United Nations Development Program, the United Nations High Commissioner on Human Rights and the United Nations University came out strongly in favour of recognising the impacts of drug control on development, full respect for human rights in drug control and improved drug control indicators (Doward, 2016). The country statements in particular demonstrate that the 'Vienna Consensus' has shattered, with some member states ignoring key issues such as the death penalty, decriminalisation, regulated markets and development (TNI, 2016b, p. 14), while others such as Uruguay, Colombia, the Netherlands, Canada and Switzerland highlighted the developments in their countries. The UNGASS served to identify that there is a group of like-minded countries, academics, and civil society organisations seeking more humane ways to address issues around drugs. There is a roadmap that can be traced and used for developing less punitive strategies on the legal side; and provide more benefits to those seeking new opportunities on the regulatory side.

Ignoring Reality in 2019: The Elephants in the Room

Following UNGASS 2016, the preparations for the 2019 review of the Plan of Action on International Cooperation towards an Integrated and Balanced Strategy to Counter the World Drug Problem began. Members of the CND have shown little to no appetite to undertake another long negotiation process such as that which happened during the UNGASS, so it was decided that the 2019 meeting would take place under the auspices of a High-Level Ministerial Segment. CND Resolution 60/1 from 2017 determines that the Ministerial Segment will 'take stock of the implementation of the commitments made to jointly address and counter the world drug problem, in particular in light of the 2019 target date'. The so-called 'modalities' resolution that was passed at the 2018 CND does not have any new preambular language but rather simply reaffirms the resolution passed in 2017 in its entirety.

Polarisation has now become the norm at the annual CND meeting, with one side pushing for more progressive language that includes references to harm reduction, recognises the rights of people who use drugs and condemns the death penalty for drug offences; and the other side, which advocates for continuing to have 'aspirational' goals of eradicating psychoactive plants and substances from the globe and seeks to consolidate the conventions as the cornerstone of drug control policy, ignoring the advances made in the UNGASS document and refusing the inclusion of the seven thematic chapters. Two consecutive years of this polarisation has instead demonstrated beyond doubt that the 'Vienna consensus' has been broken. Member States from the progressive wing are ready to defend the UNGASS document as the most recent consensus and are unwilling to give up an inch of what they gained during those negotiations. The status-quo oriented countries seek to weaken language and ensure that the 2009 targets are those that guide the 2019 debate.

The review in 2019 will mark another inflection point, where an increased number of Member States will break the taboo in their country declarations and articulate their support for harm reduction, human rights, indigenous rights and development. Success will be defined by these pioneers coming forward to say that the 'world free of drug (or drug abuse)' language is dangerous because it justifies mass incarceration, forced treatment and the violation of human rights. The elephant in the room will be both the positive shifts underway (harm reduction programs, cannabis regulation and development opportunities), but also the negative consequences of drug control measure (such as the extrajudicial killings in the Philippines, the use of the death penalty and forced treatment). Policy reform advocates are now pushing Member States to highlight the advances and name the violations.

Under a Trump Administration, the United States is unlikely to undertake dramatic reforms at Federal level, but what happens at the local and State level will have repercussions on drug policies over the long term. The focus on Trump must be directed to the positive results of a lucrative market undergoing for the states and the need to implement programs and take decisions at a national level.

The social justice impacts of the legal regulation of the cannabis markets will need to be monitored, evaluated and shared with other jurisdictions. Governments, such as Canada, and citizens in the United States will surely vote to regulate their cannabis markets in the coming years. The innovative mechanisms to address the overdose crisis related to opioids will also need to be shared, for example, heroin-assisted therapy programs and supervised consumption facilities in Canada, Switzerland and other countries. Localities will work to find solutions to the crises in their communities.

2019 will not change the global state of drug control. The international drug control regime is entrenched in a slow process of wordsmithing. Instead, we will witness continued cracks in the consensus. This consensus has resulted in wide-scale human rights violations, has justified numerous military interventions and continues to greatly harm both people who use drugs and communities around the globe. Rather than focus on what has not worked, as the consensus is dismantled, we will need to demonstrate what does work. Local, evidence-based programmes with results will need to be elevated to the international level, so that governments can begin to implement policies that put human rights, full-spectrum harm reduction and development at the centre.

References

Anapol, A. (2018). *Trump opioid plan will include death penalty for some drug dealers: report*. Retrieved from http://thehill.com/homenews/administration/378618-trump-opioid-plan-will-include-death-penalty-for-drug-dealers-report

AP. (2015). *Maine becomes fourth state to legalize recreational marijuana this year*. Portland, ME: CBS News.. Retrieved from http://www.cbsnews.com/news/maine-becomes-fourth-state-to-legalize-marijuana-for-recreational-use/. Accessed on February 28, 2018.

Armenta, A., & Jelsma, M. (2015). *The UN Drug Control Conventions*. Transnational Institute. Retrieved from https://www.tni.org/es/publicacion/las-convenciones-de-drogas-de-la-onu?content_language=en. Accessed on February 26, 2018.

Aust, A. (2006). *Vienna convention on the law of treaties*. Oxford Public International Law. Retrieved from http://opil.ouplaw.com/view/10.1093/law:epil/9780199231690/law-9780199231690-e1498. Accessed on February 27, 2018

Ballotpedia. (2016). *Nevada Marijuana Legalization, Question 2. Ballotpedia: The encyclopedia of American politics*. Retrieved from https://ballotpedia.org/Nevada_Marijuana_Legalization,_Question_2_(2016)

Baum, D. (2016). Legalize it all. *Harper's Magazine*. Retrieved from https://harpers.org/archive/2016/04/legalize-it-all/. Accessed on February 27, 2018.

Borchardt, D. (2017). *$1 Billion in marijuana taxes is addictive to State Governors. Forbes*. Retrieved from https://www.forbes.com/sites/debraborchardt/2017/04/11/1-billion-in-marijuana-taxes-is-addicting-to-state-governors/#6ee7c07a2c3b. Accessed on February 27, 2018.

Botticelli, M. (2016). *Remarks to the Special Session of the UN General Assembly on the world drug problem*. ONDCP. Retrieved from http://statements.unmeetings.org/media2/7657455/usa.pdf. Accessed on March 2, 2018.

Buxton, J. (2011). Forward into history: Understanding Obama's Latin American policy. *Latin American Perspectives*, *38*, 4.

Cantor, D. (1961). The criminal law and the narcotics problem. *Journal of Criminal Law and Criminology*, *51*(5), 2. Retrieved from https://scholarlycommons.law.northwestern.edu/cgi/viewcontent.cgi?article=4977&context=jclc. Accessed on February 2018.

CDE. (2017). Marijuana tax revenue and education, state government of Colorado. Retrieved from http://www.denverpost.com/2017/07/09/colorado-schools-get-300-million-boost-from-pot-sales/. Accessed on March 2, 2018.

CINU. (2016a). *Disolver la DEA: Pide el presidente de Bolivia en la Asamblea General*. United Nations System. Retrieved from http://www.un.org/spanish/News/story.asp?NewsID=34913#.WgIcTLaZP-Z. Accessed on March 2018.

CINU. (2016b). *Colombia: No hemos ganado la guerra contra las drogas, debemos replantear el enfoque*. United Nations System. Retrieved from http://www.un.org/spanish/News/story.asp?NewsID=34915#.WgIcPbaZP-Z. Accessed on March 2, 2018.

CINU. (2016c). *Speech by Presidente enrique Peña Nieto at UNGASS 2016*. United Nations System. Retrieved, from http://www.cinu.mx/comunicados/2016/04/el-problema-mundial-de-las-dro/. Accessed on March 2, 2018.

Cole, J. (2013). *Memorandum for all United States Attorneys*. Retrieved from https://www.mpp.org/federal/cole-memo/. Accessed on March 17, 2018.

Colorado site of Governor John Hickenlooper (CSGJH). (2017). Gov. *Hickenlooper signs long bill for 2017–18*. CSGJH. Retrieved from https://www.colorado.gov/governor/news/gov-hickenlooper-signs-long-bill-2017-18. Accessed on March 2, 2018.

CRD. (2014). *Marijuana tax data*. Colorado Department of Revenue. State Government of Colorado. Retrieved from https://www.colorado.gov/pacific/revenue/colorado-marijuana-tax-data. Accessed on March 2, 2018.

Delgado-Ramos, G., & Romano, S. (2011). *Plan Colombia e Iniciativa Mérida: Negocio y seguridad interna. El Cotidiano*. Retrieved from http://www.elcotidianoenlinea.com.mx/pdf/17010.pdf. Accessed on February 28, 2018.

Diniejko, A., & Litt, D. (2002). *Victorian drug use*. The Victorian Web. Retrieved from http://www.victorianweb.org/victorian/science/addiction/addiction2.html. Accessed on February 26 2018.

Doward, J. (2016). *The UN's war on drugs is a failure. Is it time for a different approach?* Retrieved from https://www.theguardian.com/world/2016/apr/02/un-war-on-drugs-failure-prohibition-united-nations. Accessed on March 2, 2018.

Drug Enforcement Administration (DEA). (2017). *Drug scheduling*. DEA. Retrieved from https://www.dea.gov/druginfo/ds.shtml. Accessed on February 27, 2018.

Drug Policy Alliance (DPA). (2015a). *Race and the drug war*. DPA. Retrieved from http://www.drugpolicy.org/issues/race-and-drug-war. Accessed on March 16, 2018.

Drug Policy Alliance. (2015b). *Marijuana legalization in Washington after 1 year of retail sales and 2.5 years of legal possession*. DPA. Retrieved from https://www.drugpolicy.org/sites/default/files/Drug_Policy_Alliance_Status_Report_Marijuana_Legalization_in_Washington_July2015.pdf. Accessed on July 2015.

Drug Policy Alliance (DPA). (2016). *Drug war statistics*. DPA. Retrieved from http://www.drugpolicy.org/issues/drug-war-statistics. Accessed on February 25, 2018.

Fernandez Ochoa, J., & Nougier, M. (2017) *How to capitalize on progress made in the UNGASS outcome document*. Retrieved from http://idpc.net/publications/2017/03/how-to-capitalise-on-progress-made-in-the-ungass-outcome-document. Accessed on March 2, 2018.

Forman, J. (2018). *From prohibition to progress: A status report on marijuana legalization*. Drug Policy Alliance. Retrieved from https://www.drugpolicy.org/press-release/2018/01/prohibition-progress-what-we-know-about-marijuana-legalization-eight-states. Accessed on March 2, 2018.

Friedman, S., Horvat, G., & Levinson, R. (1982). Narcotic Addict Rehabilitation Act :Its impact on Federal Prisons. *Contemporary Drug Problems Journal*, *11*, 1

Global Commission on Drug Policy. (2016). *Avanzando la reforma de la política de drogas*. Global Commission on Drug Policy. Retrieved from http://www.globalcommissionondrugs.org/wp-content/uploads/2016/11/GCDP-Report-2016_ES.pdf. Accessed on October 2017.

Gilbert, B. (2016). 4 states just voted to make marijuana completely legal. Business Inside. Retrieved from http://www.businessinsider.com/marijuana-states-legalized-weed-2016-11/#1-massachusetts-1. Accessed on February 28, 2018.

Griffaton, M. (2018). Vermont legalizes recreational marijuana. *Lexology*. Retrieved from https://www.lexology.com/library/detail.aspx?g=34fdfad9-208e-4b82-b21e-08d5b549a4cd. Accessed on March 2, 2018.

Henman, A., & Metaal, P. (2014). Time for a wake-up call: Aan historical and ethnographic approach to the regulation of plant-based stimulants. Transnational Institute. Retrieved from https://www.tni.org/files/download/dlr_27_eng-web.pdf. Accepted 27 February 2018.

Hernández, M. (2016). California, Nevada y Massachusetts legalizan la mariguana. *The Huffington Post*. Retrieved from http://www.huffingtonpost.com.mx/2016/11/09/california-nevada-y-massachusetts-legalizan-la-mariguana-con-fi/. Accessed on March 1, 2018.

Hetzer, H. (2016). *UNGASS outcome: Missed opportunity for UN, but global reform movement grows and continues to push for better drug policies*. Drug Policy Alliance. Retrieved from http://www.drugpolicy.org/blog/ungass-outcome-missed-opportunity-un-global-reform-movement-grows-continues-push-better-drug-po. Accessed on March 2, 2018.

Ingold, J. (2018). *Jess Sessions' latest memo pushes prosecutors to seek the death penalty against big drug dealers. That could include legal marijuana business owners.* Retrieved from https://www.denverpost.com/2018/03/22/jeff-sessions-death-penalty-memo-drug-dealers-marijuana/. Accessed on March 20, 2018.

Ingraham, C. (2016). Marijuana wins big on election night. *The Washington Post.* Retrieved from https://www.washingtonpost.com/news/wonk/wp/2016/11/08/medical-marijuana-sails-to-victory-in-florida/?utm_term=.7bd2aa848dc2. Accessed on February 28, 2018.

Ki-Moon, B. (2013). *Remarks at special event on the International day against drug abuse and illicit trafficking.* United Nations Secretary General Office. Retrieved from https://www.un.org/sg/en/content/sg/speeches/2013-06-26/remarks-special-event-international-day-against-drug-abuse-and. Accessed on March 2, 2018.

Landreth, S. (2017). *Medical cannabis permit applications, City of Oakland California.* Retrieved from http://www2.oaklandnet.com/government/o/CityAdministration/OAK064043. Accessed on March 2, 2018.

Lopez, G. (2018). California's new legal marijuana market marks the beginning of the end of prohibition. *Vox.* Retrieved from https://www.vox.com/policy-and-politics/2018/1/2/16840600/california-marijuana-legalization. Accessed on March 1, 2018.

Malinowska, K. (2013). *For safe and effective drug policy, look to the Dutch.* Open Society Foundations. Retrieved from https://www.opensocietyfoundations.org/voices/safe-and-effective-drug-policy-look-dutch. Accessed on February 27, 2018.

Mariani, S. (2017). *Lessons learned from marijuana legalization in Washington State.* Washington State Department of Social and Health Services. Retrieved from http://www.theathenaforum.org/sites/default/files/Keynote_PA%20Lessons%20Learned%20in%20marijuana%20legalization%20Final%2006%2020%2017.pdf. Accessed on March 2, 2018.

Marijuana Policy Project (MPP). (2017a). *New Hampshire's marijuana Decriminalization Bill takes effect tomorrow.* MPP. Retrieved from https://www.mpp.org/news/press/new-hampshires-marijuana-decriminalization-bill-takes-effect-tomorrow/. Accesses 1 March 2018.

Marijuana Policy Project (MPP). (2017b). *Summary of Indiana's low-THC cannabis oil program.* MPP. Retrieved from https://www.mpp.org/states/indiana/summary-indianas-low-thc-cannabis-oil-program/. Accessed on March 1, 2018.

Marijuana Policy Project (MPP). (2017c). *The West Virginia Medical Cannabis Act.* Retrieved, from https://www.mpp.org/states/west-virginia/west-virginia-medical-cannabis-act/. Accessed on March 1, 2018.

Matthews, D. (2014). The biggest loser in the Cromnibus: The rights of DC residents. *Vox.* Retrieved from http://www.vox.com/2014/12/13/7384639/cromnibus-marijuana-dc-veto. Accessed on March 1, 2018.

McGuinness, C. (2017). California's legal pot law is helping give felons their lives back. *VICE.* Retrieved from https://www.vice.com/en_us/article/59z5qz/californias-legal-pot-law-is-helping-give-felons-their-lives-back. Accessed on March 2, 2018.

McWilliams, J. (1990). *The protectors: Harry J. Anslinger and the Federal Bureau of Narcotics.* Newark, NE: University of Delaware Press.

Morgan, R., (2015). Initiative petition. (2015). State of North Dakota. Retrieved from https://vip.sos.nd.gov/pdfs/measures%20Info/Petitions%20Being%20Reviewed/Compassionate%20Care%20Act/11.30.2015.NDCCA.Final.wPetitionTitle&Changes.pdf. Accessed on March 1, 2018.

Marijuana Policy Project (MPP). (2016). *Overview of Arkansas' Medical Marijuana Amendment*. MPP. Retrieved from: https://www.mpp.org/states/arkansas/overview-arkansass-medical-marijuana-amendment/. Accessed on March 2, 2018.

N.a. (2015). Use of marijuana for debilitating medical conditions. *My Florida*. Retrieved from http://dos.elections.myflorida.com/initiatives/fulltext/pdf/50438-3.pdf. Accessed on March 1, 2018.

Reed, J. (2016). *Marijuana legalization in Colorado. Early findings*. Colorado Department of Public Safety. Retrieved from https://cdn0.vox-cdn.com/uploads/chorus_asset/file/6470551/Colorado_arrest_report.0.pdf. Accessed on March 2, 2018.

Sessions, J. (2018). *Memorandum for all United States Attorneys*. Retrieved from https://www.justice.gov/opa/press-release/file/1022196/download. Accessed on March 17, 2018; https://www.justice.gov/file/1045036/download. Accessed on March 20, 2018.

Sharp, E. (1994). *The dilemma of drug policy in the United States*. New York, NY: HarperCollins College Publishers.

Smith, A. (2012). Marijuana legalization passes in Colorado and Washington. *CNN*. Retrieved from http://money.cnn.com/2012/11/07/news/economy/marijuana-legalization-washington-colorado/. Accessed on March 1 2018.

Snapp, Z. (2017). *Un pie adentro y el otro afuera: las OSC y la agenda multilateral de drogas. Participación de las Organizaciones de la Sociedad Civil en la Agenda Multilateral de México*. Secretaría de Relaciones Exteriores de México. Retrieved from https://www.gob.mx/cms/uploads/attachment/file/285212/Participaci_n_de_las_OSC_en_la_Agenda_Multilateral_de_M_xico.pdf. Accessed on February 26, 2018.

Steinmetz, K. (2016). What to know about marijuana legalization in California. *TIME*. Retrieved from http://time.com/4565438/california-marijuana-faq-rules-prop-64/. Accessed on February 28, 2018.

Todd, T., & Smith, J. (2016). The Crime in Washington 2016 Annual Report. WASPC. Retrieved from http://www.waspc.org/assets/CJIS/2016%20crime%20in%20washington.small.pdf. Accessed on March 2, 2018.

Toor, A. (2014). New highs: Marijuana now legal in Alaska, Oregon, and Washington D.C. *The Verge*. Retrieved fromhttp://www.theverge.com/2014/11/5/7157993/marijuana-legalization-vote-oregon-washington-dc-alaska-florida. Accessed on March 1, 2018.

Transnational Institute (TNI). (2013). *Background on UNGASS 1998*. Retrieved from https://www.tni.org/en/article/background-of-ungass-1998. Accessed on March 17, 2018.

Transnational Institute (TNI). (2016a). *Cannabis regulation and the UN drug treaties: Strategies for reform*. Retrieved from https://www.tni.org/files/publication-downloads/cannabis_regulation_and_the_un_drug_treaties_june_2016_web_0.pdf. Accessed on March 15, 2018.

Transnational Institute (TNI). (2016b). *The UNGASS outcome document: Diplomacy or Denialism?* TNI. Retrieved from https://www.tni.org/es/node/22895. Accessed on March 2, 2018.

United Nations (UN). (1971). *Convention on psychotropic substances, 1971*. UNODC. Retrieved from https://www.unodc.org/pdf/convention_1971_en.pdf. Accessed on February 2018.

United Nations (UN). (1988). *Convención de las Naciones Unidas contra el tráfico ilícito de estupefacientes y sustancias Psicotropicas*. UNODC. Retrieved from https://www.unodc.org/pdf/convention_1988_es.pdf. Accessed on February 28, 2018.

United Nations Office on Drugs and Crime (UNODC). (1999). Global illicit drug trends. ODCCP studies on drugs and crime. Retrieved from https://www.unodc.org/pdf/report_1999-06-01_1.pdf. Accessed on February 2018.

United Nations Office on Drugs and Crime (UNODC). (2005). *World Drug Report 2005* (p. 128). United Nations. Retrieved from https://www.unodc.org/pdf/WDR_2005/volume_1_chap2.pdf. Accessed on October 10, 2017

United Nations Office on Drugs and Crime (UNODC). (2008). *World drug report 2008, Executive summary* (p. 21). United Nations System. Retrieved from https://www.unodc.org/documents/wdr/WDR_2008/WDR_2008_eng_web.pdf. Accessed on October 10, 2017.

United Nations Office on Drugs and Crime (UNODC). (2009a). *Political declaration and plan of action on the world drug problem*. United Nations System. Retrieved from https://www.unodc.org/documents/ungass2016/V0984963-English.pdf. Accessed on February 26, 2018.

United Nations Office on Drugs and Crime (UNODC). (2009b). *World drug report 2009*. United Nations System. Retrieved from https://www.unodc.org/documents/wdr/WDR_2009/WDR2009_eng_web.pdf. Accessed on February 27, 2018.

United Nations Office on Drugs and Crime (UNODC). (2016). *World drug report 2016* (p. 101). United Nations System.

United Nations Office on Drugs and Crime (UNODC). (2018). *Draft decision I*. United Nations System. Retrieved from https://www.unodc.org/documents/commissions/CND/CND_Sessions/CND_60/ECOSOC_2017/Draft_dec_I_ECOSOC_60CND.pdf. Accessed on March 2, 2018.

Verma, K. (2017) UNGASS: The world is failing to learn the right lessons from its 'war' on drugs. *The Wire*. Retrieved from https://thewire.in/33302/the-world-is-failing-to-learn-the-right-lessons-from-its-war-on-drugs/. Accessed on February 28, 2018.

Wagner, T., & Carbone, L. (2001). *Fifty years after the declaration: The United Nations' record on human rights*. New York, NY: University Press of America.

Wallace, A. (2016, November). A greener America: Marijuana's big statement in Election 2016. *The Cannabist*. Retrieved from http://www.thecannabist.co/2016/11/08/election-2016-marijuana-results-states-recreational-medical/66994/

Way, A. (2013). *Colorado one year later: Thousands not arrested for marijuana, millions of dollars saved*. Drug Policy Alliance. Retrieved from http://www.drugpolicy.org/blog/colorado-one-year-later-thousands-not-arrested-marijuana-millions-dollars-saved. Accessed on March 2, 2018.

World Health Organization. (2017). *Substances under international control*. World Health Organization. Retrieved from http://www.who.int/medicines/areas/quality_safety/sub_Int_control/en/. Accessed on February 27, 2018.

Chapter 13

West Africa

Leandre Banon and Maria-Goretti Ane

Abstract

As in other parts of the world, the 'war on drugs' in West Africa has led to significant focus on criminal justice, compromising public health and human rights without reducing the scale of drug trafficking, production and use. West Africa is not only a transit zone, local production and consumption continue to rise unabated. The Economic Community of West African States has described drug issues as the enemy of the state and the rule of law, and has called on members States to fight the 'scourge'.

The failure of the current policies has been vividly documented by the West Africa Commission on Drugs through its 2014 report titled "Not Just in Transit: Drugs, the State and Society in West Africa".

In response, civil society organisations and activists have contributed to raising awareness of the harm being caused by the current repressive drug policies in West Africa and engaged their respective national governments in evidence-based drug policy reform.

These engagements culminated in regional consultations that gave birth to the West African Common Position for the 2016 United Nations General Assembly Special Session (UNGASS) with a call for harm reduction and an evidence based drug policy for the region. Unfortunately, the UNGASS outcome was not as revolutionary as expected by the West African progressive voices, who have therefore continued to engage their governments to make the 2019 High Level Ministerial segment a turning point in the global drug debate.

Keywords: Ghana; ECOWAS drug policy; transit countries; West Africa; Civil Society; Narcotics Commission Bill

Collapse of the Global Order on Drugs: From UNGASS 2016 to Review 2019, 269–276

doi:10.1108/978-1-78756-487-920181013

Drug States in West Africa

Until recently, the West Africa region has been perceived as only a transit zone of drugs from Latin America to European Countries Markets. This general perception started changing in June 2014 with the release of the West Africa Commission on Drugs (WACD) flagship report titled, "*Not Just in Transit: Drugs, the State and Society in West Africa*" (WACD, 2014).

In early 2013, former UN General Secretary Kofi Annan convened the WACD, chaired by the former President of Nigeria, Olusegun Obasanjo.[1] The Commission was made up of commissioners from diverse backgrounds in West Africa such as politics, civil society, health, security and the judiciary. After 18 months of research, looking at the evidence, consulting experts from the region and visiting some of the most affected countries and communities in the region, WACD released its flagship report, including a series of evidence-based recommendations for drug policies across the region, in June 2014.

The report shed light on the impact of the drug market in West Africa. According to the report, drug trafficking is a new threat to the development of West Africa. The reports states that West Africa is not only a transit zone for drugs from Latin America to Europe but also that local production and consumption are on the rise. Organised crime syndicates exist at all levels of society in West Africa and pose a threat to good governance, peace and stability, economic growth and public health in a region that has only recently emerged from decades of violent conflict. For example, the yearly value of cocaine transited through West Africa in 2013 was estimated by the UN to be $1.25 billion, which is higher than the national budgets of many West African countries including Liberia, Cape Verde, Sierra Leone, The Gambia and Guinea-Bissau (United Nations Office on Drugs and Crime (UNODC), 2013).

This massive amount has a deadly effect on governance and sustainable development. There has been an exponential increase in corruption and impunity, which benefits the barons but adversely affects citizens who possess or consume very small quantities of drugs (Banon, 2016a). The region is seeing an increase in drug trafficking, production and consumption, a situation that continues to ruin many lives. The harm created by the increase in drug consumption in the region is worrying, but even more disturbing are the consequences of the application of the prohibitionist approach to dealing with the problem. West African governments' responses to the phenomenon have focused on stringent punitive measures with national drug laws and approaches across the region rooted in the prohibitionist interpretations of the international drug conventions.

The majority of the national laws were drafted and adopted around the time of the global adoption of the 1988 Convention Against Illicit Traffic in Narcotic Drugs and Psychotropic Substances, and the subsequent push from the United States and the UNODC to promote punitive drug policies around the world (Bridge & Loglo, 2017, p. 1).

[1]Former President Olusegun Obasanjo is also a Commissioner with the Global Commission on Drug Policy

Drug possession or use is treated as a criminal offence across West Africa with up 25 years imprisonment in Nigeria, 20 years in Togo and at least five years in Ghana and Sierra Leone among others. This approach has led to a significant focus on criminal justice, compromising public health and human rights, and has undermined citizens' well-being and become an obstacle to good governance, democratic consolidation and development efforts in the region. Further, this punitive approach has only resulted in increasing societal stigmatisation of drug use; driving the use of it underground; promoting the choking of prisons with drug users who should rather be supported to deal with their problematic drug use and facilitated corruption and discrimination as rich or wealthy drug users 'buy or pay' their way out of criminal sanctions, while the poor get thrown behind bars.

To that end, the WACD report recommends that removing criminal sanctions for drug use is one of the most effective ways to reduce drug-related harms, to facilitate access to treatment, and to free up resources for law enforcement to focus on more selective deterrence and targeting of high-value traffickers.

Civil Society Engagement in West Africa

The alarming state of drug policy in West Africa has led to a civil society movement advocating for drug policy reform across the region. A group of civil society actors/organisations, known as the West Africa Drug Policy Network (WADPN), came together to contribute to the improvement of drug policy in the region through evidence-based advocacy, raising awareness, public campaigns and engagement with West African governments. The Network has grown into a formidable group with a strong presence in sixteen West African countries. The various country chapters have contributed to raising awareness of the harm being caused by the current repressive drug policies in the region and engaged their respective national governments in evidence-based drug policy reform.

Civil society organisations have been on the frontline of the call for drug policy reform in West Africa. For example, since 2014, on the 26 June of every year, as part of the global campaign *Support Don't Punish*, civic activists take to the streets in West African countries to raise awareness of the harm being caused by the current harsh drug policies in the region (Banon, 2016b). They call for change in laws and policies that impede access to harm reduction interventions and other evidence-based services and to end the criminalisation of people who use drugs.

National and Regional Dialogues Leading to UNGASS 2016 and the West Africa UNGASS Position

With the opportunity given by the 2016 United Nations General Assembly Special Session (UNGASS) on the world drug problem to evaluate and adjust current drug policies to ensure that they respond to national and regional realities, actions were taken at national and regional levels by government bodies and civil society organisations in West African countries, which ensured full participation in the discussions as well as identifying necessary drug policy reforms at national levels.

Civil society led a series of discussions among key stakeholders from the various sectors involved in drug policy formulation, implementation and compliance.

From October 2015 to January 2016, the WADPN, in collaboration with the West Africa Civil Society Institute (WACSI), facilitated national multi-sectoral meetings on drug policy reform in three target countries, Benin, Senegal and Ghana, to shape discourse among key stakeholders in these countries from relevant public sector institutions that engage in drug policy formulation and implementation. The overall objective of the national, multi-stakeholder meetings was to raise key national issues pertaining to drug policy in the targeted countries as well as to shape a West Africa UNGASS position. A significant number of cross-cutting recommendations emanated from the three meetings. The recommendations included the need to reform drug policy within West Africa to focus on public health in relations to drug users instead of a criminal justice approach. The meetings recommended that more resources needed to be allocated to facilitate treatment, interventions and facilities for drug users. Key officials also emphasised the need to approach the drug problem from a national 'security and safety' and public health standpoint.

The issue of harm reduction was discussed at length and a recommendation made that it should be integrated into national drug policy in addition to demand and supply reduction. There was also a proposal to strengthen the collaboration between civil society and government in the fight against drug trafficking, consumption and production. The three national meetings culminated in a region-wide consultation for governments' officials and national law enforcement agencies from 12 selected West African States and regional institution bodies such as the Economic Community of West African States (ECOWAS) and UNODC. The consultation interrogated measures put in place at regional and national levels to deal with drug production, consumption, trafficking and organised crime.

The West Africa Common Position was signed and endorsed by 41 government officials and other stakeholders (from 12 West African countries who attended the regional consultation) and was submitted to the UNGASS for consideration and discussion (WAPDN, 2016).

The key recommendations outlined in the West Africa Common Position included:

- Tackle drugs from a public health perspective, not only as a national security and safety issue.
- Allocate more resources to facilitate treatment, interventions and facilities for people who use drugs.
- Integrate harm reduction in national drug policies to complement demand and supply reduction.
- Make substitution treatments and risk management available and accessible to people who use drugs.
- Ensure balance and proportionality in both drug demand and drug supply policies, and focus the punitive criminal sanction component of the policies on drug traffickers and suppliers.

- Allocate adequate resources for institutions to undertake research and support evidence-based drug policies.
- Harmonise drug legislation within the West African region to deny drug traffickers a haven in any West African country.
- Promote and operationalise alternative measures to incarceration or non-custodial sentencing mechanisms for minor non-violent drug-related offences in accordance with the international drug conventions.
- Ensure the provision of opiates and other essential uncontrolled medicine for palliative care and pain relief as enshrined in WHO convention.
- Strengthen collaboration between civil society and government in the effort to address the risk associated with drug trafficking, consumption and production.

With respect to government-led initiatives, the governments of Ghana and Sierra Leone established a national multipartite committee (including civil society) in developing their respective country position papers for the UNGASS 2016.

In Ghana, the then President constituted a steering committee chaired by the Minister of Foreign Affairs to deliberate on Ghana's position. The inter-ministerial committee was comprised representatives from the ministries of Foreign Affairs, Interior, Health, Gender, Food and Agriculture, with other members from civil society and the Narcotics Control Board.

Propositions made by the committee for consideration for inclusion in the final paper included the issues of decriminalisation, public health, human rights, alternative livelihood for cannabis farmers, harm reduction strategies, alternative to incarceration, alternative use of cannabis for pain relief and medicinal use, as well as health facilities for problematic drug use treatment.

As a result of all of these inclusive consultations, some West African countries clearly and openly took a progressive stand at UNGASS 2016. According to Ghana's former Minister of Foreign Affairs, Hannah Tetteh, "the Government of Ghana vowed to step up efforts to improve the quality and the depth of the dialogue that has been generated ahead of UNGASS to ensure that in rebalancing international policy on drugs, policy emphasis is placed on human rights and public health by including treatment, care, harm and risk reduction" (UNGASS, 2016).

Ghana has a serious shortage of morphine for cancer patients. It is estimated that nearly 90% of cancer and AIDS patients in Ghana cannot be treated adequately with the current level of morphine supply. The Government of Ghana expressed its dismay at UNGASS about the inadequate opioid access for palliative care and called for the establishment of a high-level, independent, expert commission supported by the World Health Organisation to analyse the state of global access to controlled medicines and advise on measures to improve it.

Regional Reponses to West Africa Drug Issue – ECOWAS Action Plan on Drug Use in West Africa

The ECOWAS seeks to contribute to the reduction of drug abuse, illicit drug trafficking and related organised crime in West Africa through the implementation of the ECOWAS Regional Action Plan 2016–2020 (ECOWAS, 2016). The new Action Plan was launched at the 71st General Assembly of the United Nations held in September 2016 (UNODC, 2016). Implemented largely by UNODC and ECOWAS with funding from the EU, the plan supports drug prevention activities and drug dependence treatment, legislative development and drug law enforcement across member states. Inter alia, the plan highlights the necessity of targeting high- and middle-level drug offenders, while offering alternatives to incarceration for people who use drugs – including treatment, rehabilitation and reintegration services where needed.

The Action Plan also calls for harm reduction services to be made available, including evidence-based treatment options and opioid substitution, across West Africa. In line with its Drug Action Plan (2016–2020), the ECOWAS set up the West African Epidemiology Network on Drug Use (WENDU) to provide a sustainable system of relevant, valid and reliable data on drug use and illicit drug trafficking (ECOWAS, 2017). In addition, the network strategises on the collection, analysis and dissemination of drug-related information at the national and regional levels (ECOWAS, 2017b). Furthermore, ECOWAS organised a three-day capacity building workshop in early 2018 in Abuja, Nigeria, to equip CSOs with the necessary skills and knowledge to develop and carry out effective evidence-based prevention interventions as well as familiarise them with regional drug policies and prevention initiatives.

However, in the view of civil society activists, much more can be done by ECOWAS, as stated by Maria Ane, Member of the WADPN – Ghana Chapter, "as much as ECOWAS is to be commended for these efforts and positive steps taken, there is still the need to address key issues like the need for decriminalisation (which is distinct from legalisation), proportionality in our sentencing, and government support for proven harm reduction services. These need to be strong calls made by ECOWAS, as people continue to be punished, marginalised and tormented through inhumane criminal justice responses, with lives being ruined just for the possession of small amounts of a drug" (Loglo, 2016).

Building up to 2019 High Level Ministerial Segment

The positive outcomes of the multipartite and inclusive consultation that took place prior to the 2016 UNGASS have paved the way for multi-sectoral meetings and discussion on the drafting of the new Ghana Narcotics Bill. During the last quarter of 2015, the Parliament of Ghana Selected Committee from Defence and Interior had a three-day stakeholder consultation to discuss with civil society, religious leaders and experts, proposals contained in the new drug bill. The bill emphasised the importance of drug law that supports people who use drug and harm reduction programmes (Banon, 2017).

As a result of the December 2016 presidential and legislative elections, even though the bill went through the second reading in parliament, the bill could not be passed. However, giving the momentum and the extent of the discussion on the bill and the bipartisan support for the new legislation, the new government is committed to ensure that the bill is passed by the end of the four-year term of the current legislature.[2]

Under the prospective legislation, people will not face criminal sanctions for possessing drugs for personal use. The current law does not make a distinction between possession for use and trafficking, a situation that the bill sought to resolve. If the law passes, Ghana will become the first Sub-Saharan country to decriminalise personal drug use and possession.

At the international level and as part of the preparation towards the 2019 High Level Ministerial segment Ghana expressed its commitment to support the creation of an appropriate forum to encourage member states, international organisations, academia and civil society to share robust scientific evidence about the wide range of drug control and criminal justice response policy intervention and their outcomes (Ghana Government, 2019). It is therefore likely that Ghana will retain its progressive stance during the discussion leading to the 2019 High Level Ministerial segment especially if the new bill is passed before the international gathering.

West Africa's contribution to the 2019 High Level Ministerial segment would be definitely aligned to the African Union and West Africa common positions for the UNGASS 2016.

Another key player in the discussion is Senegal, the only West African country that runs a government led harm reduction centre even though the laws are still punitive. Senegal's harm reduction centre was set up in response to the UDSEN study on the high prevalence rate of HIV among people who inject drug.

For the study, 1,324 heroin and/or cocaine users in Dakar were surveyed. Among this group, the prevalence of HIV was 5.2%, while nearly a quarter were living with hepatitis C. For those who injected drugs, the prevalence was even higher: 9.4% for HIV and 38.9% for HCV. Women were also found to be at greater risk of contracting HIV. Senegal's harm reduction centre can prescribe methadone and has facilities for social activities. The centre also provides needle and syringes to drug users in the various ghettos of Dakar.

Ghana and Senegal would be the lead countries of West African reform movement ahead of and during the various discussion leading up to the 2019 High Level Ministerial segment.

[2]The bill has undergone stakeholders meeting in July 2017 led by the current administration, and further inputs have been made by civil society organisations. The next step is to lay it before Cabinet and once cabinet approves it, it will be sent to parliament for consideration and the necessary procedures will flow from there.

References

Banon, L. (2016a). *Sustainable development under threat from drug trafficking in West Africa*. Retrieved from https://www.dailymaverick.co.za/article/2016-06-01-op-ed-sustainable-development-under-threat-from-drug-trafficking-in-west-africa/#.WhOrykpl-M9

Banon, L. (2016b). *Drug policy reform gets a foothold in West Africa*. Retrieved from https://www.dailymaverick.co.za/article/2016-10-06-op-ed-drug-policy-reform-gets-a-foothold-in-west-africa/#.WhOrxkpl-M9

Banon, L. (2017). *West Africa reform agenda looks to decriminalise drug use*. Retrieved from https://www.dailymaverick.co.za/article/2017-08-09-west-africa-reform-agenda-looks-to-decriminalise-drug-use/#.WhOrx0pl-M9

Bridge, J., & Loglo, M., (2017). *Drug laws in West Africa: A review and summary*. London: International Drug Policy Consortium

ECOWAS. (2016). *ECOWAS Ministers adopt Action Plan to Address Illicit Drug Trafficking, Organized Crimes and Drug Abuse in West Africa*. Retrieved from http://www.ecowas.int/ecowas-ministers-adopt-action-plan-to-address-illicit-drug-trafficking-organized-crimes-and-drug-abuse-in-west-africa/

ECOWAS. (2017a). *CSOs in West Africa recommend Network for Drug Prevention and Treatment*. Retrieved from http://www.ecowas.int/csos-in-west-africa-recommend-network-for-drug-prevention-and-treatment/

ECOWAS. (2017b). *ECOWAS established the West African Epidemiology Network on Drug Use (WENDU) in the Republic of Benin, 5th–6th April 2017*. Retrieved from http://www.edup.ecowas.int/the-launch-of-the-west-african-epidemiology-network-on-drug-use-wendu-in-the-republic-of-benin/

Leprêtre, A., Ba, I., Lacombe, K., Maynart, M., Toufik, A., Ndiaye, O., Kane, C. T., Gozlan, J., Tine, J., Ndoye, I., Raguin, G., & Girard, P. M. (2015). Prevalence and behavioural risks for HIV and HCV infections in a population of drug users of Dakar, Senegal: the ANRS 12243 UDSEN study. *Journal of the International AIDS Society* 18, 19888. Retrieved from http://www.jiasociety.org/index.php/jias/article/view/19888 | http://dx.doi.org/10.7448/IAS.18.1.19888

Loglo, M. (2016). *The new ECOWAS action plan on the drug problem in West Africa*. Retrieved from http://idpc.net/blog/2016/10/the-new-ecowas-action-plan-on-the-drug-problem-in-west-africa

United Nations Office on Drugs and Crime (UNODC). (2013). *Transnational organized crime in West Africa: A threat assessment*. Dakar, Senegal: UNODC.

United Nations Office on Drugs and Crime (UNODC). (2016). *UNODC/ECOWAS jointly launch efforts to support West Africa against drugs and crime*. Retrieved from https://www.unodc.org/westandcentralafrica/en/2016-09-20-unodc-launches-new-rp-west-africa.html

United Nations General Assembly Special Session on Drugs (UNGASS). (2016). *Statement by Honourable Hanna Serwaah Tetteh, Minister for Foreign Affairs and Regional Integration, Ghana*. New York, NY: UNGASS.

West Africa Commission on Drugs (WACD). (2014, June). *Not just in transit drugs, the State and Society in West Africa*. WACD,. Retrieved from http://www.wacommissionondrugs.org/report/

West Africa Drug Policy Network (WADPN). (2016). *West Africa common position towards the UNGASS*. Retrieved from http://www.unodc.org/documents/ungass2016//Contributions/Civil/WADPN/West_Africa_Common_Position_toward_the_UNGASS_Final.pdf

Chapter 14

Switzerland: Moving Towards Public Health and Harm Reduction

Frank Zobel and Larissa J. Maier

Abstract

The Swiss drug policy once was very progressive in the 1990s when the harm related to drug use was most visible to the public. Failure of repression opened the room for more innovative harm reduction approaches. In 2008, the four-pillar model including the legal basis for substitution and heroin-assisted treatment of opioid use disorders as well as for other harm reduction facilities was approved by the population that had learned about the success of these measures. Less violence, better health outcomes among people who use drugs and less stigma supported the change of attitudes in the population towards a public health-based approach when dealing with drug use. Switzerland first received heavy criticism for the autonomous policy change at the international level while it is nowadays often cited as best practice example for dealing with people with an opioid use disorder. Otherwise, the country has usually been quiet in drug policy discussions at the UN level. Nevertheless, Switzerland's reappointment to the Commission on Narcotic Drugs, the central drug policy-making body within the United Nations for a period of four years starting in 2018 is promising, given their unblemished recommendation for human rights-based drug policies including the abolition of the death penalty for drug offences, among other things. Alongside cannabis policy changes at the international level, Switzerland witnessed an unexpected development in cannabis availability and sales. However, the country is still rather conservative with regard to current cannabis policies, although cannabis with less than 1% of THC can be sold legally and the possession of up to 10 g will be followed by a fine only, if at all. Switzerland is open to experiment with new regulations but only if the law allows for that. To conclude, the strong sense of connectedness with the international community may support Switzerland's next steps towards public health and evidence-based harm reduction.

Collapse of the Global Order on Drugs: From UNGASS 2016 to Review 2019, 277–288

doi:10.1108/978-1-78756-487-920181014

Keywords: Swiss; harm reduction; drug policy; human rights; cannabis; regulation

A Brief History of Switzerland's Drug Policy

Switzerland's drug policy is often used as a best practice example given its progressive and innovative approach during the 1990s. However, the relatively liberal view and inclusion of harm reduction in the policy were not the result of a rational decision-making process at the time but rather an experimental response to a major drug crisis. It received some heavy criticism at international level, notably by UN bodies who reminded the government that harm reduction programmes are not substitutes for demand reduction programmes (INCB, 1993). Nevertheless, similar reforms occurred in many other European countries some years later. Importantly, the position on safe drug consumption facilities has evolved positively over the years. The INCB Annual Report for 2016 mentioned for the first time a clear recommendation in favour of this approach (INCB, 2017).

The first Swiss narcotics law was adopted in 1924 and created a national drug control system mainly focussing on opium and cocaine (Hänni, 1998). After the Second World War, controls were extended to many other substances, including cannabis, and a national authority was established. The range of drug-related offences was also extended and the sanctions increased (Hänni, 1998). The use of drugs other than alcohol spread more widely in the 1960s. In 1969, the highest court criminalised personal possession of the controlled substances with no reference to 'drugs' per se (Hansjakob & Killias, 2012). That year, about 500 drug-law offences were registered and 60 kg of hashish were seized (Heller, 1992). A few years later, heroin seizures and a first drug-related death were recorded. In 1975, a revision of the narcotics law came into force. During the debates in parliament, two different visions of drug policy had clashed: one was in favour of criminalising drug use in order to combat drug trafficking, promote public order and reinforce prevention. The other pointed to the contradictions of a policy seeking both to punish and to help people who use drugs (Boggio et al., 1997). The result was a compromise: drug use and possession were to be systematically prosecuted but with relatively low sanctions (a fine and no criminal record). The prosecutor could also refrain from applying any sanction under certain circumstances. The new law pledged local authorities to develop prevention programmes and provide treatment for people with a substance use disorder. Treatment was, however, abstinence-oriented, and opioid substitution was only allowed under strict regulations and surveillance (Csete & Grob, 2012; Hänni, 1998; Klingemann, 1998).

In 1975, when the revised law was implemented, about 5,000 drug law offences and 35 drug-related deaths were registered. Two years later, around 4,000 people were estimated to have developed a substance use disorder (Heller, 1992). Rising drug consumption accompanied an increasingly rebellious youth movement that sparked off street fights with police in several cities in 1980 (Boggio et al., 1997; Grob, 2009). One aim of the youth movement was the creation of autonomous youth centres in the larger cities, and in 1982 the Zurich youth centre opened the first drug consumption room (Uchtenhagen, 2009). By the mid-1980s, Switzerland was facing a growing drug crisis. More than one hundred drug-related deaths were recorded while the estimate of the number of people with a opioid use disorder was now at 10,000 (Grob, 2009). Moreover, around 15,000 drug-law offences were recorded every year (Heller, 1992) with no sign that law enforcement had an impact on the supply and use of illegal drugs. Drug-related acquisitive crime, such as pharmacy burglaries and housebreaking, was rapidly increasing (Kraushaar & Lieberherr, 1996) notably because of the high price of heroin. Early data also showed that a significant number of people who injected drugs in Switzerland were HIV+ (Uchtenhagen, 2009) and people feared the disease could spread in the general population. The link between the spread of HIV/AIDS and injecting drug use was key for the future of Switzerland's drug policy (Kubler, 2000). People who used drugs were progressively not only considered as criminals but also as vulnerable people in need of urgent help.

In late 1986, people who used drugs in Zurich, mainly heroin, settled in a park – the Platzspitz – located near the main train station as local authorities decided to stop chasing them around the city because it neither reduced public nuisances nor crime (Kraushaar & Lieberherr, 1996). The park became Zurich's infamous Needle-Park, and it contributed to an overhaul of the country's drug policy. Low-threshold harm reduction interventions, such as the distribution of clean needles and syringes, were introduced during the early 1980s, to help prevent the spread of hepatitis and, later, of HIV/AIDS. In 1985, the medical officer of the canton of Zurich threatened to revoke the licence of doctors and pharmacists who provided sterile injection material to people who used drugs and 300 doctors submitted a petition with support from the medical association (Uchtenhagen, 2009). The cantonal parliament then authorised these harm reduction measures and in 1987, the ZIPP-AIDS project began operation at Platzspitz, handing out thousands of sterile syringes every day (Grob, 2009). In Berne, an NGO created a low-threshold facility with a small drug consumption room in 1986 (Wietlisbach, 2014) which later received the support of the city's authorities. Both Berne and Zurich, as well as a few other Swiss-German cities, adopted harm reduction as a component of their dug policy (Kraushaar & Lieberherr, 1996).

A New National Drug Policy

In Switzerland, illegal drugs were considered a major concern in the first half of the 1990s (Longchamp et al., 1998) with an estimated 30,000 people with a opioid use disorder and 700 people annually dying from overdoses or AIDS. As a consequence, the Swiss Federal Office of Public Health (SFOPH) published its first ever National Drug Strategy which introduced the Swiss 'four pillars' policy (prevention, treatment, harm reduction and law enforcement). It retained prohibition as the policy framework but allowed for new approaches, mainly harm reduction measures. The value conflicts within drug policy were managed through wide financial and technical support by the federal authorities and the cantons, and by allowing players to meet and discuss at national conferences and within coordinating bodies. Syringe-exchange programmes and supervised drug consumption rooms were increasingly implemented, and other controversial measures, such as heroin-assisted treatment or syringe exchange in prisons, were developed as scientific trials to respect the international law. Attempts were made to close the country's needle parks. The drug scene in Zurich moved, however, to an abandoned train station (Letten) which became the city's next needle park (Kraushaar & Lieberherr, 1996). Letten was closed in 1995, involving both the federal government and the cantons. Acquisitive crime and public nuisance declined dramatically at that time.

By the mid-1990s, over 20,000 needles and syringes were being distributed daily in Switzerland, 15,000 people were accessing treatment, mostly methadone maintenance following changes to the conditions determining eligibility, and several cities opened facilities with a supervised drug consumption room (Zobel & Dubois-Arber, 2004). In response to these developments, two coalitions formed around very different ballot initiatives. One, 'Youth Without Drugs', launched by politically conservative circles, proposed to end harm reduction measures, including most opioid maintenance treatment. The other, 'Droleg', called for the legalisation of drugs and regulated drug markets. The new policy appeared as a pragmatic middle ground, supported by a growing coalition of professionals and policy makers and the first drop in the incidence of drug related problems for over a quarter of a century. Both ballot initiatives were rejected by more than 70 percent of voters in 1997–1998. A referendum against heroin-assisted treatment was also defeated in 1999 (Savary, Hallam, & Bewley-Taylor, 2009). The country's drug policy had undergone a major change, supported by the Swiss voters, but so far without significant changes to the narcotics law.

Shifting Cannabis Policy

As in many other countries, cannabis use among young people increased during the 1990s. The Swiss cannabis market changed from an imported resin to a mostly locally grown herbal market. At the policy level, cannabis remained first and foremost an issue of prevention and law enforcement, as treatment demand was low and harm reduction was not developed in this area. The decriminalisation of cannabis use or its legalisation appeared as the main options for cannabis policy reform. These options were supported by the national advisory board on drugs and by an expert Commission tasked to make propositions for a revision of the narcotics law. Both recommended abandoning the prosecution of drug use. The national advisory board went further in a dedicated cannabis report of 1999 (EKDF, 1999) proposing two models: (1) to stop prosecuting cannabis use and reduce the obligation to prosecute its production and sales and (2) to allow a state regulated cannabis market. In 2001, after a public consultation, the Swiss government submitted a revision proposal of the narcotics law to parliament, institutionalising harm reduction, legalising cannabis use and allowing a regulated cannabis market. The proposal remained on hold for three years during which many cantons reduced their law enforcement efforts against the cannabis market. As a result, about 400 illegal cannabis shops operated in 2002 (Leimlehner, 2004). This unregulated market contributed to the lower house's refusal, in 2004, to discuss the revision proposal by a vote of 102 to 92.

This rejection led to the closure of the existing cannabis shops. The shop owners and other cannabis activists immediately started to collect signatures for another federal ballot initiative requiring the legalisation and market regulation of cannabis. They were joined by harm reduction advocates. In parallel, the Swiss parliament partially revised the narcotics law to finally provide a legal basis for heroin-assisted treatment of opioid use disorders. The revision was similar to the one proposed in 2001, but without the section on cannabis. This was still too much for conservative groups, who organised a referendum against that revision. This resulted in Swiss citizens being called to vote, in November 2008, on both an initiative for cannabis legalisation and market regulation; and a referendum against a revision of the law institutionalising harm reduction and heroin-assisted treatment. The cannabis initiative was rejected by 63% of voters, but the revision of the narcotics law was accepted by 68% (Savary, Hallam, & Bewley-Taylor, 2009). Harm reduction was now fully institutionalised, but cannabis legalisation had been rejected by both the parliament and citizens.

An Unsatisfactory Cannabis Reform

It took the parliament a few years to return to the cannabis issue. The rise in the number of recorded offences had no noticeable impact on demand or supply but on the workloads of cantonal justice departments. An old parliamentary initiative was therefore revived and used for a partial revision of the narcotics law in order to decriminalis cannabis use. Adults caught using and/or carrying no more than 10 g of cannabis were then administered a fine of 100 Swiss Francs (about 85 euros). The law came into force in October 2013, and a recent study showed big differences in cantons applying cannabis use decriminalisation (Zobel et al., 2017). The Swiss narcotics law with its successive revisions provides sufficient contradictions and ambiguities to allow for very diverse interpretations by law enforcement at the cantonal level. Recent court decisions stating that cannabis possession of less than 10 g was not to be punished anymore confirmed and added to the growing confusion about the way cannabis use is to be sanctioned or not. In parallel with developments at the national level, some Swiss-German cities started exploring the possibility of cannabis regulation at the local level and thereby continuing experimenting drug policy alternatives at the local level as had successfully been done during the 1980s and 1990s. They were joined in 2014 by the French-speaking canton of Geneva, where a group of political representatives called for a local trial with cannabis social clubs following the models in Spain and Belgium.

This group of cities and cantons continued to grow[1] and started to work together on different cannabis production and distribution schemes (Zobel & Marthaler, 2016). A legal opinion suggested that the only possible way to develop cannabis regulation at the local level was through scientific trials falling under

[1]Zürich (city), Bern (city), Geneva (canton), Basel-Stadt (canton), Thun (city), Winterthur (city), Biel/Bienne (city), Luzern (city), Lausanne (city)

article 8 of the narcotics law. Two cities (Berne and Zurich) and two cantons (Basel and Geneva)[2] decided to be the first to propose such trials. Four target populations for cannabis distribution/sales were defined (1) adults who currently use cannabis, (2) underaged adolescents with problematic cannabis use patterns, (3) adults with problematic cannabis use patterns and (4) adults who were prescribed medical cannabis and self-medicate. During the summer of 2017, the city of Bern submitted the first proposal for a special authorisation under the narcotics law. The project was to permit the sales of cannabis through existing pharmacies to about 1,000 adult residents who were already using cannabis and who would receive a prevention/harm reduction intervention through their smartphone. The proposal had been successfully submitted to the ethics committee, and the funding for the research was secured through the Swiss National Science Foundation. The city of Zurich and two other cities (Lucerne and Biel/Bienne) aimed to implement the same project if it was accepted.

The authorisation was however rejected by the Swiss Federal Office of Public Health (SFOPH) on the ground that recreational cannabis use does not fall under the exemption for medical experiments foreseen by the law. The SFOPH agreed that such experiments would be useful and that a small change in the law – an aricle allowing for non-medical public health research trials – could provide the means for a positive response. In December 2017, more than half of the members of the Swiss parliament signed a petition in favour of such a new article in the narcotics law. In addition, the pressure of cantons had impact on the federal parliament. In 2017, the green party introduced a parliamentary initiative[3] for the legalisation of cannabis and the regulation of its market. While the initiative has in theory little chance to succeed, it could provide the parliament with an alternative if the current cannabis policy continues to be challenged from all sides. Changes in cannabis policy at the international level have also triggered the first steps of a new ballot initiative for the legalisation of cannabis. The association *Legalise it* has already provided a short text inviting the government to legalise and regulate cannabis and started to collect money for such an initiative. In 2018, a committee was set up to collect the necessary 100,000 signatures to enable a vote on the initiative in three to four years.

Alongside cannabis policy changes at the international level, Switzerland witnessed an unexpected development in cannabis availability and sales. In 2011, the country increased the level of THC legally separating industrial hemp from illegal cannabis from 0.2% to 1%. One of the goals was to reduce the number of false positive cases of industrial hemp that had naturally occurring THC levels above

---

[2]Both Basel-Stadt and Geneva are so called city-cantons made out of a main city (Basel and Geneva) and its immediate surrounding. Other cantons, such as Berne and Zurich, have much larger territories and dozens or hundreds of municipalities of different size.

[3]A parliamentary initiative is a proposal submitted to the parliament by one of its members. It needs first to be examined by the relevant commission which decides if it is worth taking up. If the response is positive, it becomes a law proposal and needs to go through the ordinary legislative process.

the old limit. The threshold of 1% was adopted because other Swiss legislations used this figure and because nobody thought that cannabis with less than 1% of THC would be of any interest in a market where cannabis had usually levels of more than 10%. This proved however to be wrong as the new burgeoning legal US market introduced new low THC and high CBD cannabis varieties which, particularly in the medical sector, found a customer base.

In 2016, two entrepreneurs asked the Swiss authorities if their product – cannabis flowers with less than 1% of THC and high levels of CBD – could be sold legally as a tobacco substitute with the same warnings and taxation as cigarettes. After getting a positive answer, they sold their product and branded it as 'legal cannabis'. It was rapidly sold out and triggered the development of a new cannabis industry with, in early 2018, already more than 500 registrations to sell low THC products as tobacco substitute. Two of the country's largest supermarket chains as well as one of its largest newspaper shop chains have started selling 'legal cannabis', making it available even in small towns.

The situation brought uncertainty for law enforcement bodies as legal and illegal cannabis couldn't be distinguished without expensive laboratory tests. Nonetheless some cantons decided to test all cannabis samples but it proved to be very complicated and costly. New guidelines for street police officers, including some that are barely legal, were also introduced. In late 2017, a rapid test was made available and could help reduce the uncertainty for police officers and perhaps also the inappropriate application of the law. New health-oriented shops selling CBD tinctures, oils, lotions and other products also appeared. A chain called 'Cannabis counters' (Hanftheke) opened a first shop in November 2016 and had 29 shops eight months later. The branding of the products includes a strong reference to their Swiss origin and quality and the customers notably include older people. So far, it remains unclear what will happen with the type of products they are more likely to buy. These cannot be advertised as therapeutic products as this would bring them under the law on medical products and make them illegal without proof of efficacy. And, even if they are sold as usual or alimentary products, they might not be legal because of the way they are produced. A crackdown on non-smokable products is therefore a true possibility but this might differ from canton to canton. Switzerland has allowed medical cannabis since 2014. People with multiple sclerosis can be prescribed the medication Sativex®[4] directly by their doctor to help reduce spasms. For all other diagnoses and symptoms, the physician needs to submit a special request to the SFOPH and renew it every six months. The medication, which can be very expensive, is only sometimes reimbursed by the health insurances, and on a case by case basis. Despite the high administrative burden for the physicians, the high costs, the limited number of medications as well as limited evidence regarding the effectiveness, the number of requests for medical cannabis is constantly increasing. A request for the

[4]The available cannabis medicines include mainly Sativex® (CBD/THC 1/1), Dronabinol® (THC) as well as two preparations of a cannabis oil (Sativaoil; CBD/THC 0.3/1) and a cannabis tincture (CBD/THC 1/2) prepared and sold by only two pharmacies in the country.

simplification of the system has already been made within the parliament in order to provide better treatment options for people with an indication who currently often decide to self-medicate.

Switzerland and the UNODC

Switzerland fights organised crime, the drugs trade and human trafficking as well as corruption and money laundering through its active participation in various international organisations and conventions. At the same time, it is committed to promoting human security and the rule of law. In 2017, Switzerland has been reappointed to the Commission on Narcotic Drugs, the central drug policy-making body within the United Nations for a period of four years, starting in January 2018. Switzerland has been appointed to the commission several times in the past (1961–1975, 1988–1995, 1997–2001 and 2004–2011), but the current term could become one of the most interesting ones in regard of the review and renewal of the existing Political Declaration and Plan of Action in 2019. In general, Switzerland shares a common voice with other European countries in the Commission without having submitted specific proposals themselves. Importantly, the only clear repeated recommendation is to abolish the death penalty for drug-related offences. At the 61st meeting of the Commission on Narcotic Drugs in Vienna in March 2018, Switzerland sponsored three side events on the topics of abolishing the death penalty, the world drug *perception* problem and measuring of the impact of drug policies. Switzerland is clear about the aim to align drug policies with the 2030 Agenda.

Therefore, the Swiss government advocates for better and different data to support the UNODC Annual Report Questionnaire (ARQ) that is based on the self-report of governments of the Member States and thus, often inaccurate and biased. Switzerland is interested in developing a framework for policy coherence while noticing the difficulties of measuring the outcome. Creating an external advisory committee to monitor the progress and to support governments in the data collection is seen as key. Also, indicators related to the Sustainable Development Goals (SDGs) should be included, first and foremost on SGDs 1, 3, 5 and 16. Data on the effects of drug policies are greatly lacking and should be collected additionally. For this, the SDG indicators could be a model to improve drug policy indicators. Finally, outcome-oriented metrics should be prioritised when it comes to data collection efforts. This includes that key components of the UNGASS outcome document are implemented in the ARQs as well as the incorporation of gender policy. Drug demand reduction indicators might be more relevant than supply. Yet, the 2009 declaration focusses on supply reduction only and may no longer fit for purpose when following the UNGASS 2016. In any case, Switzerland promotes evidence-based research to inform drug policies and emphasises the importance of integer non-biased research to move forward.

Only recently, an INCB mission visited Switzerland to discuss the implementation of the three international drug control conventions and to review drug control developments in the country. The focus lied on trafficking and abuse of narcotic drugs, psychotropic substances and control precursor chemicals and measures taken to address them, as well as challenges regarding access and availability of substances under international control for medical purposes. This was the first mission since 2000, coordinated by the SFOPH. Consultations were held with the directors and senior officials of the SFOPH, Swissmedic, Foreign Affairs, Federal Police and Cantonal Police Berne. Meetings with members of the Federal Commission on Addiction and NGO representatives were also held. The mission also visited a company manufacturing internationally controlled substances and the safe drug consumption facility provided by the NGO 'Contact Foundation' in Berne. The results will be published in the INCB Annual Report 2018 to be expected early 2019.

Conclusions

Switzerland underwent an important drug policy change in the late 1980s and early 1990s, becoming one of the most innovative countries in this area. Still today, almost half of all the patients who have access to heroin-assisted treatment in the world live in Switzerland, while the prevalence of heroin use is much higher in other countries with no or insufficient medical treatment options. Another example of the depth of change are the various established drug checking services in Switzerland who operate on-site at parties and festivals since 1998 and fixed-site in Zurich (since 2006) and Berne (since 2014) on a weekly basis (Barratt, Kowalski, Maier, & Ritter, 2018). Offers like these are generally the first contact with the treatment system for otherwise hidden populations with potentially risky drug use patterns.

As Switzerland is otherwise known for being rather conservative, one might legitimately wonder why and how this was, and still is, possible. The size of the drug problem certainly provided a window of opportunity for policy change. Youthful experimentation with drugs, at a time when heroin became largely available, and the inappropriate response of a very conservative state contributed to the nurturing of a large drug problem. The country's wealth might also have made it particularly interesting for criminal groups to engage in drug supply. The speed with which the HIV/AIDS epidemic was identified and the visible harm also added to the understanding of the size of the problem. Switzerland was aware of the HIV epidemic among people who injected drugs early, possibly earlier than many other countries. The country also did not have just one drug problem but many different ones, with some disproportionally large ones in cities such as Bern and Zurich. The country's federal structure and dispersion of powers played an important role in drug policy change. Within the comparatively small cities and cantons of Switzerland, drug policy players had to meet and discuss to find practical and pragmatic solutions to everyday problems of coexistence. Differences in the size of drug problems, but also in cultural and administrative traditions, led to multiple policies and interventions, including innovative ones. These came mostly from the German-speaking part of the country, where the role of the State tends to be less important and the one of private institutions, including NGOs, more important than in French- and Italian-speaking regions. This policy diversity among cities and cantons later provided an opportunity for the federal state to develop a common framework. Direct democracy also provided a learning opportunity both for policy makers and citizens. The period 1997–1999, with its three national votes on drug policy, was an extraordinary period of societal debate on drug policy and the diffusion of knowledge on drugs issues. It also favoured the development of coalitions of like-minded people and showed that the 'harm reduction' coalition was now stronger than the 'abstinence' coalition. Before that, local initiatives and referendums had provided knowledge on how to handle the drug issue publicly in order to secure a majority of votes.

All these elements contributed to a significant move in the boundaries of the prohibition paradigm, with the implementation of ideas and measures considered unacceptable until then by many drug policy players nationally and internationally. Switzerland could also have been the first country to legalise cannabis and fully regulate its market, almost a decade before Uruguay and some US States decided to do it. This did not happen, however, notably because there was no public health or security crisis with cannabis which would have provided an opportunity for trying alternative models. Neither was there a strong lobbying group as nowadays exists in the United States. All there was, and still is, is a societal debate on the coherence of drugs and alcohol policies and on the moderate impact and possibly high costs of law enforcement. This debate is still ongoing and one might reasonably foresee that, if cannabis policy change comes to Europe, Switzerland may be among those who implement it. Notably, the international law will be respected but alternative public health-based approaches of regulating currently illegal drugs are likely to follow. Given that illegal drugs have always been and are now more easily available than ever, monitoring changing drug markets is of utmost importance to understand and react on trends in drug use. This includes new strategies with regard to current regulations that are necessarily to protect people who use drugs from the potential harms related to the illegal status of the drugs. Switzerland therefore encourages honest conversations about potential risks related to drug use to increase knowledge about effects and side effects. Harm reduction has proven to be best practice in many scenarios where problems with drugs were experienced. The international community also seems to move more and more to this direction aiming to improve public health by increasing (drug) education, which is positive to see.

References

Barratt, M., Kowalski, M., Maier, L., & Ritter, A. (2018). *Global review of drug checking services operating in 2017*. Drug Policy Modelling Program Bulletin No. 24. Sydney, Australia: National Drug and Alcohol Research Centre, UNSW Sydney.

Boggio, Y., Cattacin, S., Luca, B. & Cesoni, M.L.. (1997). *Apprendre à gérer: La politique suisse en matière de drogues*. Genève: Georg.

Csete, J. (2010). *From the Mountaintops: What the world can learn from drug policy change in Switzerland*. Budapest: Open Society Institutes.

Csete, J., & Grob, P. J. (2012). Switzerland, HIV and the power of pragmatism: Lessons for drug policy development. *International Journal of Drug Policy, 23*, 82–86.

Eidgenössische Betäubungsmittelkommission. (1983). *Drogenbericht*. Bern: Eidgenössische Betäubungsmittelkommission.

Eidgenössische Kommission fur Drogenfragen – (EKDF). (2008). *Cannabis 2008: Update zum Cannabisbericht 1999*. Bern: EKDF.

Eisner, M. (1999). Déterminants de la politique suisse en matière de drogue: l'exemple du programme de prescription d'héroïne. *Déviance et Société*. *23*(2), 189–204.

EKDF. (1999). *Cannabis report of the Swiss Federal Commission for drug issues (EKDF)*. Retrieved from http://www.ukcia.org/research/ekdf.pdf

Grob, P. J. (2009). *Zurcher "Needle-Park": Ein Stuck Drogengeschichte und-politik 1968–2008*. Zurich: Chronos Verlag.

Hänni, C. (1998). *Im Spannungsfeld zwischen Arzneimittel und Rauschgift: Zur Geschichte der Betaubungsmittelgesetzgebung in der Schweiz*. Bern: SGGP/SSHP.

Hansjakob, T., & Killias, M. (2012). Repression in der Drogenpolitik. In Eidgenössische Kommission fur Drogenfragen (Ed.) *Drogenpolitik als Geselschaftspolitik: Ein Ruckblick auf dreissig Jahre Schweizer Drogenpolitik*. Zurich: Seismo, 59–72.

Heller, A. (1992, April). Am Ziel? Chronik eines verlorenen Kampfes. *NZZ Folio*. Retrived from http://folio.nzz.ch/1992/april/am-ziel. Accessed on November 5, 2015.

INCB. (1993). *Report of the International Narcotics Control Board for 1993*. New York, NY: UNODC.

INCB. (2017). *Report of the International Narcotics Control Board for 2016*. New York, NY: UNODC.

Klingemann, H. (1998). Harm reduction and abstinence: Swiss drug policy at a time of transition. In Klingemann H. & Hunt G. (Eds.), *Drug treatment systems in an international perspective: Drugs, demons and delinquents*. Thousand Oaks: SAGE, 94–111.

Kraushaar, B., & Lieberherr, E. (1996). *Drogenland im Mafialand: Entwicklung, kommentar und materialen zur drogensituation in der Schweiz*. Zurich: Werd Verlag.

Kubler, D. (2000). *Politique de la drogue dans les villes suisses entre ordre et santé: Analyse des conflits de mise en oeuvre*. Paris: L'Harmattan.

Kubler, D. (2001). Understanding policy change with the advocacy coalition framework: An application to Swiss drug policy. *Journal of European Public Policy, 8*(4), 623–641.

Leimlehner, E. (2004). Der cannabismarkt in der Schweiz. Strukturen, Veränderungen und Risiken. *Abhängigkeiten, 2/2004*, pp. 1–8.

Longchamp, C. (1998). *Pragmatismus statt Polarisierung: Die Entwicklung von Einstellungen und Verhaltensweisen zur Drogenpolitik der Schweiz in den 90er Jahren*. Muri: SGGP.

Savary, J.-F., Hallam, C., & Bewley-Taylor, D. (2009). *The Swiss Four Pillars Policy: An evolution from local experimentation to federal law*. London: Beckley Foundation.

Uchtenhagen, A. (2009). Heroin-assisted treatment in Switzerland: A case study of policy change. *Addiction,105*, 29–37.

Uchtenhagen, A. (2011). The role of coalitions in drug policy: Some theoretical and observational considerations. *Addiciones, 23*(3), 183–187.

Wietlisbach, J. (2014). *Die Geschichte des Berner Fixerstubli: Entwicklungstendenzen von Ende der 1970er Jahre bis 1994*. Bern: Universität Bern (Masterarbeit).

Zobel, F. & Dubois-Arber, F. (2004). *Evaluation of the confederation's measures to reduce drug-related problems: Fourth Synthesis Report 1999–2002*. Lausanne: University Institute of Social and Preventive Medicine.

Zobel., F., Homberg, C., & Marthaler, M. (2017). *Les amendes d'ordre pour consommation de cannabis: Analyse de la mise en œuvre*. Lausanne: Addiction Suisse.

Zobel, F., & Marthaler, M. (2016). *Nouveaux développements concernant la régulation du marché du cannabis (3ème édition): de A (Anchorage) à Z (Zürich)*. Lausanne: Addiction Suisse.

Zobel, F., & So-Barazetti, B. (avec la collaboration de Arnaud, S.). (2004). *La gestion de l'innovation dans le cadre du ProMeDro*. Lausanne: Institut universitaire de médecine sociale et préventive.

Chapter 15

Epilogue

Mike Trace

The chapters in this book have given detailed analysis of the processes towards, and outcomes from, the 2016 United Nations Special Session on the World Drug Problem. They also contain a range of perspectives on the prospects for the next point of review of global drug policies, scheduled to be held at the Commission on Narcotic Drugs in Vienna in March 2019.

Beyond the many semantic, symbolic and substantive debates recorded here, the most significant outcome of the 2016 United Nations General Assembly Special Session (UNGASS), in my opinion, is that it represented the end of an era. A 50-year era during which member states had worked hard to maintain unity behind a single global strategy for controlling the consumption of psychoactive drugs – a strategy characterised by disapproval and denunciation of all forms of recreational consumption, widespread punishment of consumers and suppliers and concerted law enforcement action to physically restrict the movement of drugs and precursors, and therefore their availability to potential consumers.

This unity had for 50 years been much cherished by governments and their diplomatic representatives. The agreement of an (almost) universally ratified set of UN conventions on what was primarily a social policy issue was seen in its time as a major diplomatic achievement, and governments have for decades felt constrained in moving away from the orthodoxy they created, fearing criticism from other member states or the International Narcotics Control Board.

But the period preceding and since the 2016 UNGASS has been notable for a clear fragmentation of language, priorities and policy directions of national governments. While many governments have remained broadly loyal to the orthodox language of harsh condemnation and punishment, and a belief that continued implementation of these strategies will lead to 'a world free of drug abuse', others have moved their focus away from repression and law enforcement, and towards treatment of dependence and protection of public health and human rights. Most notably, the contributions of the various United Nations agencies themselves acknowledged the limited progress made in reducing supply and demand over the

Collapse of the Global Order on Drugs: From UNGASS 2016 to Review 2019, 289–291

doi:10.1108/978-1-78756-487-920181015

previous 50 years and emphasised the positive benefits of policies that emphasised health, treatment and social integration.

This breaking of a 50 years orthodoxy obviously creates diplomatic difficulties, but has to be seen as a positive development, as it has given national and local governments more freedom to pursue policies that reduce needless and disproportionate punishments, and that improve health and social support for people who use drugs. Many such innovations are being implemented around the world now, the evaluations of which will form an important backdrop to the United Nations review in 2019.

But those hoping for a new consensus to emerge from the upcoming review are likely to be disappointed – the strategies and negotiating positions of the key member states are likely to be even more divergent than they were in 2016. As a generalisation, it is authoritarian governments that are attracted by harsh drug policies that accord with their wider approach to social problems, and that can be used as a justification for expanded law enforcement or military budgets, and the constriction of civil freedoms. None of the loudest voices in support of authoritarian drug policies at the 2016 UNGASS – Russia, the ASEAN bloc, Pakistan, Egypt – are likely to change their views on drug control in the intervening three years.

Similarly, those countries that are pursuing new approaches – some EU members, Canada, New Zealand and many central and South American countries – are unlikely to return to the economically and socially wasteful 'war on drugs' strategies pursued previously. Most legislative, health and social innovations in this field are proving to be broadly successful, and will only become more attractive and widespread among genuinely social democratic governments in the coming years. Of course, the crucial role played in 2019 by the United States will depend entirely on who is in the White House at that time and the nature of that government's relationship with the United Nations itself.

So, we should prepare ourselves for a very difficult round of diplomatic negotiations, and a political declaration that, while approved by consensus, will be an awkward amalgamation of diametrically opposing views. We can, however, hope (and work) for some positive and constructive outcomes from 2019 – focusing less on the consensus process and more on the production of clear statements from the UN agencies and groups of like-minded member states:

- *A meaningful assessment of progress.* While acknowledging the political and diplomatic necessity of recognising achievements, the UN agencies should produce a clear and realistic analysis of the extent to which the objectives of the system (which were the eradication, or at least significant reduction, of the scale of illicit production, distribution and consumption) have been achieved.
- *Acknowledgment of the need for modernisation.* Member states that truly believe in learning from evidence should now acknowledge that this evidence shows that two key elements of the previous orthodoxy – the attempt to deter consumers through punishment, and strong enforcement to stifle the illicit distribution of drugs around the world – have failed, and alternative uses found for the resources previously expended in these areas.

- *Objective evaluation of new approaches.* Member states who have pursued, or who are interested in pursuing, alternative approaches should create formal mechanisms for reviewing and sharing the evidence and lessons learned from these initiatives and present their findings to the Commission on Narcotic Drugs.
- *An honest approach to future reviews.* The United Nations Office on Drugs and Crime should bring forward a clear set of high level objectives (explicitly linked to the Sustainable Development Goals) for the next period of international drug control that can be used as the basis for assessment of member states' progress in the next 10 years.

One of the positive developments of recent years has been the growth of a professional and articulate civil society voice in the United Nations drug policy debates. This diverse group of organisations has been instrumental in framing debates, advising governments and proposing resolutions to difficult issues. These organisations have also played an important role in reporting on and scrutinising government exchanges that all too often have taken place behind closed doors. Looking forward to 2019, the civil society groups can contribute to a high-quality outcome by themselves producing analytical material that articulates the true current position with international drug control – what objectives were set out in 1961 and 2009; the extent to which they have been achieved; and what evidence has been accumulated on what works. There is also good work being done on understanding and articulating a clearer and more relevant set of drug policy objectives that are explicitly linked to the 2030 Sustainable Development Goals.

Civil society, and academic institutions, should also be looking beyond 2019 to help governments out of the drug policy dilemma that is now facing them. Given the clear and growing trend for local and national implementation of policies and programmes that breach the spirit and letter of the established treaties, how can the international community find a 'new equilibrium' for drug control that allows for a much wider range of approaches to facilitating medical and scientific use of an ever-growing list of psychoactive substances, while regulating and controlling their distribution for personal use? There are important processes already beginning through the World Health Organisation (on cannabis scheduling), and among some governments (on treaty law) that are beginning to confront the need to modernise the system – but these face formidable diplomatic and political obstacles that can only be overcome through careful analysis and negotiation.

We are now undoubtedly entering the era of increasingly fragmented approaches to drug control. This is not necessarily a bad thing – certainly preferable to the continuation of ineffective policies that waste resources and work against social justice and public health and welfare. But it is important that the international community manages this process in a positive, transparent and evidence-based way – avoiding the kind of polarised and unproductive debates we witnessed in the period running up to the 2016 UNGASS. At the time of writing, however, there seems little sign of such willingness to find new balances and compromises in time for 2019.

Index

Note: Page numbers followed by "*n*" with numbers indicate footnotes.